Introduction to
COMPUTER
SCIENCE
A Structured Approach

Second Edition

Introduction to
COMPUTER
SCIENCE

A Structured Approach

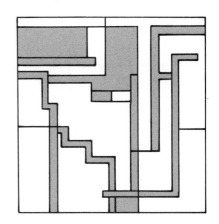

Second Edition

Neill Graham

West Publishing Company
St. Paul   New York   San Francisco   Los Angeles

Library of Congress Cataloging in Publication Data

Graham, Neill, 1941-
  Introduction to computer science.

  Bibliography: p.
  Includes index.
  1. Structured programming. I. Title.
QA76.6.G68 1982   001.64'2   81-21969
ISBN 0-314-63243-3   AACR2   INTL. ISBN 0-314-69794-2
  2nd Reprint—1982   2nd Reprint—1982

Contents

v

PART TWO
ALGORITHMS AND PROGRAMS

Preface

This book is intended as a text for either a one-semester or a two-semester introductory computer science course. There is more than enough material for a one-semester course, leaving instructors free to choose the topics most suitable for their particular classes. If a programming language such as Pascal is taught as well, then there is ample material for a two-semester course.

Most of this book requires no mathematical preparation beyond the usual elementary and high school courses. No previous acquaintance with variables or expressions is assumed, so students who have forgotten (or never had) high school algebra aren't at a disadvantage.

(The last two chapters of the book, on numerical methods, require somewhat more mathematical preparation—about equivalent to the introductory college algebra and trigonometry courses. Although some ideas from calculus are introduced, no previous knowledge of the subject is assumed.)

Every computer science text needs some language or notation in which to present algorithms. Some books use flowcharts for this purpose. But following the recommendations of the advocates of structured programming, this book uses an informal *algorithmic language* or *pseudocode* instead. However, flowcharts *are* introduced in the chapters on algorithm construction in order to acquaint students with them and to help illustrate the basic control structures. Later, the flowcharts are dropped, and students are led to rely on the algorithmic language alone.

The algorithmic language is intended to be an *informal* notation rather than a rigidly specified programming language. Although beginners will do well to use the language as it is described in the text, the instructor and advanced students shouldn't hesitate to modify features or add new ones as might be required by a particular problem.

Variable declarations are optional in the algorithmic language and are usually omitted. Information about data types can be easily presented in informal comments, either in the algorithm or in the surrounding text. There seems to be little need to burden the student with additional formal machinery for this purpose.

Algorithms are printed in uppercase letters only. Students who have previously encountered a programming language such as BASIC or FOR-TRAN will find this format more familiar (and perhaps less threatening) than the alternative boldface-and-italics format. But there certainly isn't any need for students to print their own algortihms in uppercase only. Ordinary handwritting can be used, as suggested in Figure 14-1. It may help to underline keywords in handwritten algorithms.

The book contains a supplement showing how to translate algorithms from the algorithmic language into the Pascal programming language.

The book begins with an introductory chapter that presents an overview of computers, information processing, algorithms, programs, and flowcharts.

Part 1 surveys computer hardware, information representation, and software. The chapter on software goes somewhat more deeply into the subject than do many introductory texts, introducing such important ideas as multilevel machines and processes.

Part 1 can be omitted or delayed by instructors who prefer to get their students writing programs as soon as possible.

Part 2, on algorithm construction, is the heart of the book. Variables, values, and expressions are introduced, as are the basic control structures of sequence, selection, and repetition. A chapter on functions and procedures is included as is one on algorithm design and testing.

Part 3 shifts the emphasis from control structures to data structures. Arrays were introduced in Part 2 to demonstrate an important application of repetition. Now strings, stacks, records, linked lists, trees, and graphs are taken up. The chapter on trees develops further the idea of recursion, which was introduced in Part 2.

Part 4, on files, is an introduction to the ideas of data processing and information retrieval. For sequential files, a file update algorithm is presented, as are several methods of external sorting. For random files, the emphasis is on retrieving designated records. Methods discussed include hashing and indexed sequential access methods for primary key retrieval as well as multilists and inverted files for secondary key retrieval.

Part 5, on numerical methods, takes up the half-interval method for solving nonlinear equations as well as the Gauss-Jordan and Gauss-Seidel methods for systems of linear equations. Graphs are used to illustrate the conversion problems for the Gauss-Seidel method.

The final chapter of the book is devoted to numerical integration. To make this material accessible to students who haven't studied calculus, the notation and terminology of calculus are avoided. Instead, we concentrate on the physically intuitive idea of a moving object whose velocity is specified as a function of position and time or whose acceleration is specified as a function of velocity, position, and time.

In this edition, some minor changes suggested by users have been made in the algorithmic language. Subroutines are now referred to as procedures; the RETURN statement has been eliminated; and the repetition constructions have been modified to resemble more closely those found in Pascal and other modern programming languages.

Chapters 1, 2, 3, 9, and part of 17 have been extensively rewritten. For the example computer in Chapter 2, a simple hypothetical computer replaces the PDP-11, whose many addressing modes caused confusion. In Chapter 9, the discussion of call by name has been eliminated, since modern programming languages do not use this method of parameter passing. In Chapter 17, the file update algorithm in the first edition has been replaced with a far superior one due to W. H. J. Feijen.

Perhaps the most important change was to replace the FORTRAN supplement with one on Pascal, which is rapidly becoming the most popular language for teaching computer science. The supplement uses the popular UCSD version of Pascal, which, because of the presence of a string data type, fits the algorithmic language a lot more closely than do some other versions. Students are warned of the few nonstandard features of UCSD Pascal. UCSD Pascal is sufficiently similar to most other versions of Pascal that users of other versions should have to make at most minor adjustments to the programs in the supplement.

I would like to thank the following persons for their valuable comments, criticisms, and suggestions: Edward Bowdon, Randy Byers, Nell Dale, Robert Dourson, Paul Emerick, Olin Johnson, William Moldrup, Rex Page, Robert Paul, Michael Stimson, and J. Stanely Warford.

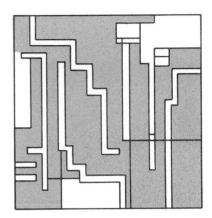

Chapter 1

Introduction: Computers, Information, and Algorithms

There was a time when the word "computer" invariably referred to the mammoth data processing installations used by large organizations. These days, however, we can find computers almost anywhere: in automobiles, in cameras, in games, in household appliances. There are computers that fit in your pocket, computers that sit on your desk, and computers that fill a room. There are computers that cost hundreds of dollars, computers that cost thousands, and computers that cost millions.

Yet no matter how much computers differ in size, cost, and internal construction, they all have two characteristics in common:

- A computer is a machine for processing information. It does this by manipulating symbols (such as letters, digits, and punctuation marks) that represent information.

- Whatever processing a computer does is controlled by a set of detailed, step-by-step instructions called a *program*.

These two characteristics of computers determine the subject matter of computer science. Since a computer is an information-processing machine, computer science is the science of information processing. (Computer science is sometimes called *information science*, and in some languages it is known by a term that translates literally into English as "informatics.") Since a computer must be controlled by a detailed set of instructions, computer science studies *algorithms*, sets of instructions for carrying out particular information-processing tasks.

1

1.1 The Information-Processing Machine

Information. The word *information* means facts and ideas. These facts and ideas are independent of the form in which they are expressed. If you inform me that I am invited to your house at eight o'clock next Thursday, then this information will be the same regardless of whether you tell me in person, send me a note, call on the phone, or send a telegram.

Symbols. Information is an abstraction. Yet we do not use abstractions to communicate with one another! We use facial expressions; bodily movements; inarticulate grunts, groans, cries, and laughter; spoken English (and other languages); notes; memos; letters; telegrams; telephone calls; pictures; and many other concrete, physical things.

Before we can manipulate information, or even pass it from one person to another, we must represent it in some concrete, physical form. The physical things we use to represent information are called *symbols*. The letters of the alphabet, the sounds we make when speaking, the electrical currents that travel over telephone wires, the electromagnetic waves that our TV sets pick up—these are all examples of symbols. Figure 1-1 gives some additional examples.

Anything we do with information must actually be done with the concrete symbols that represent the information. To write a love letter, for

FIGURE 1-1. Some frequently used symbols.

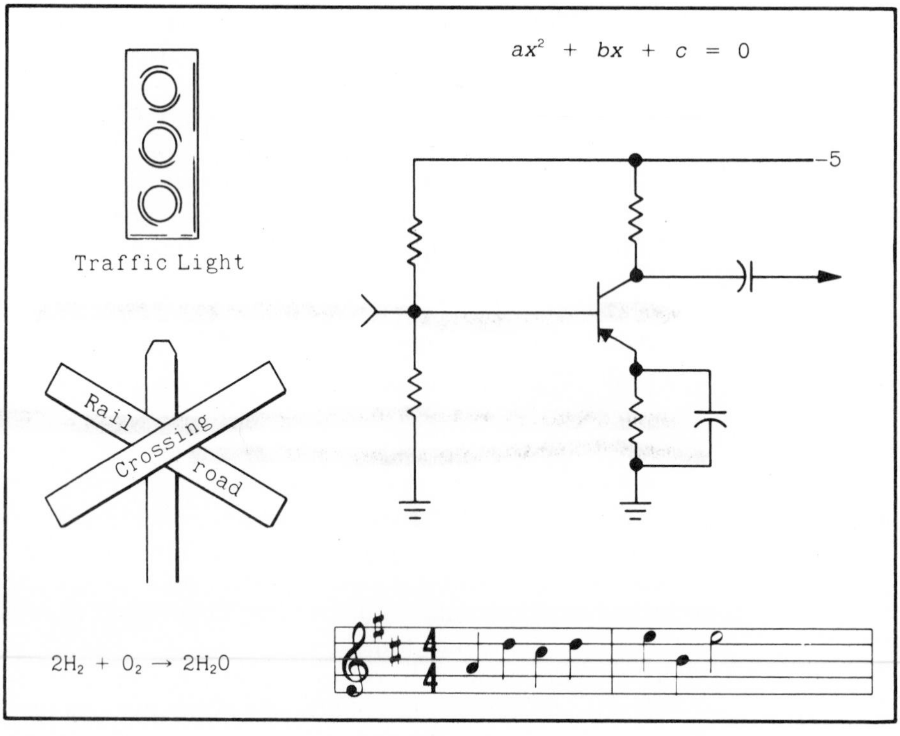

instance, you need to make a large number of marks on a piece of paper with pen or pencil. Whatever the emotional content of the letter, the only way you can express that content is by arranging marks on paper in the proper order.

Data. We use the word *data* to mean information represented by concrete symbols a computer can manipulate. Computer people often use the words *data* and *information* almost interchangeably. But to be precise, we should use *data* when we want to emphasize the symbols themselves, and we should use *information* when we want to emphasize the facts and ideas that the symbols represent.

By the way, the word *data*, by derivation, should be plural, the word *datum* being the singular form. But in computing, it usually makes more sense to use *data* as a mass noun, like *grass* or *sand*. We say "the data has been processed" just as we say "the grass has been cut" or "the sand has been shoveled."

Data processing and *symbol manipulation* are two other terms we can use to describe what a computer does. *Information processing* describes what we are out to accomplish. *Data processing* and *symbol manipulation* refer more specifically to the manipulations a computer must carry out to process information.

A computer can manipulate any kinds of symbols that can be translated into electrical signals. With modern electronics technology, most kinds of symbols can be so translated. In addition to the usual letters, digits, and punctuation marks, computers can process pictures, drawings, speech, music, and electrical sensing and control signals for other machines.

A computer will manipulate meaningless combinations of symbols just as readily as meaningful ones. Computer people refer to meaningless data as *garbage*; they use the phrase "garbage in, garbage out" to describe what happens when garbage is fed into a computer.

Examples of Information Processing. The kinds of information-processing tasks a computer can perform are so varied that it's impossible to summarize them in a few words. But the following examples will give you some feeling for the computer's versatility.

Arithmetical Calculations. The digits 0 through 9 are symbols, and the familiar operations of arithmetic are manipulations that can be carried out on those symbols. Until the twentieth century, arithmetic was the only kind of symbol manipulation that was mechanized to any degree.

Computers can indeed do arithmetic very fast and very accurately. This has consequences of which most people are unaware.

For instance, one reason you can now purchase relatively inexpensive cameras with high-quality lenses is that those lenses were designed with the aid of a computer. For each trial design, the computer calculates the paths of thousands of light rays through the lens. If the calculated paths are unsatisfactory, the computer makes changes in the trial design and calculates a new set of paths. The process continues until it arrives at a satisfactory design or until the computer gives up because a predetermined number of attempts have failed to find an acceptable design.

Perhaps because "compute" originally meant "to do arithmetic," when people think of computers they seem to think of arithmetic first. Computers were invented to solve mathematical problems, and this remains one of their important applications. But they can do other jobs, too. Many computer applications involve little or no arithmetic.

Word Processing. You enter the first draft of a letter, term paper, article, or book into the computer. Then you revise it by directing the computer to insert, delete, and rearrange specific pieces of material. When the results meet your expectations, you can order the computer to type out a perfect copy.

Game Playing. A computer, particularly one equipped with a television-like display, makes a fantastic "gameboard." Computers are now widely used in home electronic and video games as well as those found in arcades. Even the traditional pinball machine now has a computer inside. Many people who own their own personal computers use them, in part, for game playing.

Nor are computers limited to the popular "space battle" games. There are computer programs that play checkers and backgammon at the championship levels. Chess-playing programs that run on large computers can challenge expert- and master-level players. Chess-playing programs that run on small computers, including the special-purpose chess-playing machines, are good enough to challenge the average chess player.

Controlling Machines. Computers can control other machines. For instance, some late-model cars use a computer to "tune" the engine continuously while the car is running. The computer monitors such things as engine speed, power demand, and power output. It adjusts such things as fuel-feed rate, fuel-air mixture, and spark timing for best performance. This constant tuning improves the performance of the engine, reduces the amount of fuel it uses, and reduces the amount of pollution it produces.

A general-purpose manipulating machine controlled by a computer is known as a *robot.* Currently, robots do many repetitive tasks in factories, such as welding automobile bodies. In the future, robots may be sent to work in places that are dangerous for human beings, such as in deep mines, at the bottom of the ocean, and in outer space.

Computer-Assisted Instruction. The computer presents a student with a small segment of a lesson and one or more questions on that segment. If the student answers the questions correctly, the computer moves on to the next segment. Otherwise, it provides additional review of the material the student didn't know. Thus a student is "led by the hand" through a subject, exposed only to the material needed to achieve understanding. Although this isn't as good as a personal tutor, it may be the next best thing.

Data-File Management and Information Retrieval. A computer can maintain large data files and retrieve individual items from those files on request. A researcher, for instance, can enter a list of keywords describing his or her interests into the computer, and the computer returns a list of all the papers in the researcher's field of interest that contain one of the keywords in their titles or abstracts. Or a doctor can type in a list of symptoms and get back the latest information on diseases having those symptoms.

1.2 The Instruction-Following Machine

An All-Purpose Machine. A computer carries out a particular information-processing task by following a set of detailed instructions. To change the task, all we have to do is change the instructions.

The catch is that the computer won't perform any task until we have provided it with the necessary instructions. This doesn't mean, however, that the person who uses the computer will have to provide the instructions. Instructions for doing many tasks may be available from the computer manufacturer or from companies that specialize in publishing computer programs. Some computers, called *special-purpose computers*, come with the instructions for doing a particular task permanently installed, so the computer always does that task and no other. The computers built into consumer products are of this type.

You sometimes hear people say, "a computer can only do what it's told to," as if this were some limitation on the machine. Quite the contrary! To be sure, a dishwasher doesn't have to be told how to wash dishes and a lawnmower doesn't have to be told how to mow lawns. But then, a dishwasher can only wash dishes and a lawnmower can only mow lawns. On the other hand, a single computer can compute the orbit of a spaceship, play a game of chess, print your "computer portrait," or make out your paycheck, provided only that it is given the proper instructions for each job.

One of the founders of computer science, the Hungarian-American mathematician John von Neumann, once said that a computer is an "all-purpose machine." We might qualify this to "all-purpose information-processing machine," since after all it won't mow the lawn. That a computer can "do what it's told to" is precisely what makes it all-purpose.

Algorithms. An algorithm, you recall, is a set of instructions for carrying out a particular task. When an algorithm is expressed in such a way that the instructions can be carried out by a computer, we call it a *program*. Our use of the words *algorithm* and *program* is analogous to our use of *information* and *data*. The algorithm is the abstract idea; the program is its concrete realization in a form suitable for use with a computer. Like *information* and *data*, the words *algorithm* and *program* are often used almost interchangeably.

Every correct algorithm comes with a guarantee that, if we faithfully follow its instructions, we will solve a particular problem or accomplish a particular task. For this guarantee to hold, every algorithm must have the following three characteristics:

1. *An algorithm is precise*. Each step of an algorithm must specify exactly what action is to be taken. There's no room for vagueness. What's more, each step has to be given explicitly. None can be "understood" or "assumed."

Since it's almost impossible to achieve the necessary precision in English, people have devised a variety of *algorithmic languages* and *programming languages*. These are analogous to the notations used in music, mathematics, dance, chemistry, knitting, and crocheting to express technical ideas more concisely and precisely than is possible in English.

2. *An algorithm is effective*. No instruction may be impossible to carry out for the person or machine executing the algorithm.

Suppose, for instance, that an algorithm demands that we take the square root of 2 with perfect precision. The square root of 2 is given by

$$\sqrt{2} = 1.4142135623 \ldots$$

where the dots indicate an infinite sequence of additional digits. This unending sequence of digits could never be worked out in a finite amount of time, could never be written out on a blackboard or a piece of paper, could never be stored inside any computer. An algorithm that demands we take the square root of two with perfect precision, then, is not effective.

Another example: we might give an algorithm for solving our energy problems that calls for a machine that produces more energy than it consumes. But physicists have proved that such a machine, called a perpetual-motion machine, cannot exist. Therefore, an algorithm that calls for the use of a perpetual-motion machine cannot be effective.

3. *An algorithm must terminate*. When a person or machine executes an algorithm, he, she, or it must eventually reach a point where the task is complete and no more instructions remain to be executed. The execution of an algorithm must not go on indefinitely.

You may find it hard to see how an algorithm, which only contains a finite number of instructions, can ever fail to terminate. Surely after we have carried out each instruction, there will be nothing else left to do but stop.

The catch is that an algorithm may specify that some instructions are to be carried out repeatedly until a given condition occurs. A recipe, for instance, might say "stir the pudding over low heat *until* it comes to a boil." If the terminating condition never occurs, the repetition will continue indefinitely. Suppose the recipe had just said, "stir the pudding gently until it comes to a boil," without saying that it should be heated. Someone who took the recipe literally—and computers always take algorithms literally—would have a lot of stirring to do.

Note that while the three characteristics just given are necessary for an algorithm to live up to its guarantee, they are not sufficient. An incorrect algorithm might possess all three characteristics, yet still contain erroneous instructions that prevent it from accomplishing the task for which it was designed.

The Euclidean Algorithm. Let's take as an example one of the oldest recorded algorithms, Euclid's algorithm for finding the greatest common divisor of two numbers. To see just what this algorithm is supposed to accomplish, let's recall a few elementary properties of numbers.

To begin with, we will be working with the nonnegative integers, 0, 1, 2, 3, 4, and so on. For short, however, we will usually say *number* instead of *nonnegative integer*.

We say that one number *divides* another when the first number goes into the second evenly, leaving no remainder. We also say that the second number is *divisible* by the first. Thus 3 divides 6 and 6 is divisible by 3, since 3 goes into 6 exactly two times with no remainder. In the same way, 4 divides 12, 7 divides 21, and 8 divides 32.

On the other hand, 3 does not divide 10, 4 does not divide 18, and 5 does not divide 13. In each case, when we carry out the division, we are left with a remainder.

For any number we can make a list of its *divisors*—all of the other numbers that divide it. The divisors of 6, for instance, are 1, 2, 3, and 6. The divisors of 10 are 1, 2, 5, and 10. The divisors of 7 are 1 and 7. And so on. Note that the divisors of a number always include 1 and the number itself.

Now let's consider two numbers, say 6 and 8. The divisors of 6 are 1, 2, 3, and 6. The divisors of 8 are 1, 2, 4, and 8. The two numbers have the divisors 1 and 2 in common. We say that 1 and 2 are the *common divisors* of 6 and 8. Another example: The divisors of 18 are 1, 2, 3, 6, and 9. The divisors of 24 are 1, 2, 3, 4, 6, 8, and 12. The common divisors of 18 and 24 are 1, 2, 3, and 6.

Notice that any pair of numbers has at least one common divisor, since 1 is a divisor of every number.

Given the common divisors of two numbers, one common divisor is greater than all the others. This is the *greatest common divisor* of the two numbers. Since the common divisors of 6 and 8 are 1 and 2, the greatest common divisor of 6 and 8 is 2. Since the common divisors of 18 and 24 are 1, 2, 3, and 6, the greatest common divisor of 18 and 24 is 6. Since 1 is the only common divisor of 5 and 7, the greatest common divisor of 5 and 7 is 1.

What we want to construct is an algorithm for finding the greatest common divisor of two numbers without going to the trouble of finding all the divisors of each number.

Before we go any further, you might well want to ask to what use we can put the greatest common divisor once we have found it. There are many such uses, but one of the most familiar ones is reducing fractions. To reduce a fraction to its lowest terms, we divide both the numerator and the denominator by the greatest common divisor of the two. Thus, to reduce 18/24 to lowest terms, we divide both the numerator and denominator by 6, which is the greatest common divisor of 18 and 24. The result is 3/4, which is indeed 18/24 reduced to lowest terms. Any computer program that manipulates fractions as fractions (instead of changing them to decimals) must be able to find greatest common divisors, so it can reduce the results of its calculations to their lowest terms.

Planning the Algorithm. Euclid's algorithm is based on two properties of numbers. Mathematics students can easily prove these properties; however, we will be content here with illustrating them by means of examples.

Property 1. When we divide a larger number by a smaller number, the greatest common divisor of the remainder and the smaller number is the same as the greatest common divisor of the original two numbers.

For example, the greatest common divisor of 24 and 10 is 2. Now divide 24 by 10

$$
\begin{array}{r}
2 \\
10 \overline{)\ 24} \\
20 \\
\hline
4
\end{array}
$$

The remainder is 4. The greatest common divisor of 10 and 4 is also 2.

Another example: The greatest common divisor of 35 and 25 is 5. Now divide 35 by 25:

$$
\begin{array}{r}
1 \\
25 \overline{)\ 35} \\
25 \\
\hline
10
\end{array}
$$

The remainder is 10. The greatest common divisor of 25 and 10 is 5, the same as the greatest common divisor of 35 and 25.

Property 2. The greatest common divisor of a number and 0 is that number. The greatest common divisor of 15 and 0 is 15, the greatest common divisor of 10 and 0 is 10, the greatest common divisor of 7 and 0 is 7, and so on.

Now here's our plan. We will start with the two numbers whose greatest common divisor we are to find and divide the larger by the smaller. Property 1 tells us that the smaller number and the remainder of the division have the same greatest common divisor as the original two numbers. Let's, then, replace the original two numbers with the smaller number and the remainder of the division.

Let's repeat this process. On each repetition we divide the larger of the two numbers by the smaller. We then replace the larger number by the smaller and the smaller by the remainder of the division. No matter how many times we repeat this, the greatest common divisor of the current two numbers will be the same as that of the two numbers we started out with.

What do we accomplish by all this? When we divide a larger number by a smaller one, the remainder is less than either the divisor or the dividend. After each repetition, then, the smaller of the two numbers will be less than the smaller of the two numbers on the previous repetition. If we carry out enough repetitions, the smaller number getting less and less with each repetition, then eventually the smaller number will become 0.

But now we can bring in Property 2. When one of two numbers is 0, the other number is the greatest common divisor of the two. So when the smaller of the two numbers we are working with is 0, the larger is the greatest common divisor of the two. But by Property 1, this is also the greatest common divisor of the two numbers we started with and so is the answer we are seeking.

Figure 1-2 illustrates how to calculate the greatest common divisor of 99 and 55 using the Euclidean algorithm. The first step is to divide 99 by 55 and get the remainder, which is 44. By Property 1, the greatest common divisor of 55 and 44 is the same as the greatest common divisor of 99 and 55.

Therefore, we turn our attention to 55 and 44. We divide 55 by 44 and get the remainder, which is 11. By Property 1, the greatest common divisor of 44 and 11 is the same as the greatest common divisor of 55 and 44 and so is the greatest common divisor of 99 and 55.

So we turn our attention to 44 and 11. We divide 44 by 11 and get the remainder, which is 0. By Property 2, the greatest common divisor of 11

FIGURE 1-2. Using the greatest common divisor algorithm to show that the greatest common divisor of 99 and 55 is 11.

```
Step 1:
                   Larger number is 99          55 )99
                                                     1
                   Smaller number is 55             55
                   Remainder is 44                  44

Step 2:
                                                     1
                   Larger number is 55          44 )55
                   Smaller number is 44             44
                   Remainder is 11                  11

Step 3:
                                                     4
                   Larger number is 44          11 )44
                   Smaller number is 11             44
                   Remainder is 0                    0

Step 4:
                   Larger number is 11
                   Smaller number is 0

                   (Since the smaller number is 0, the value of
                   the larger number, 11, is the greatest common
                   divisor of 99 and 55.)
```

and 0 is 11. By Property 1, 11 is also the greatest common divisor of 44 and 11, 55 and 44, and 99 and 55. Therefore 11 is the answer we are seeking, the greatest common divisor of 99 and 55.

We can outline the algorithm we have arrived at as follows:

```
WHILE (the smaller number is not 0) DO
     (Divide the larger number by the smaller and get
     the remainder. Replace the larger number by the
     smaller and the smaller by the remainder.)
END WHILE
```

"WHILE . . . DO" and "END WHILE" are part of an *algorithmic language* that will be developed more fully in later chapters. All the instructions between WHILE . . . DO and END WHILE are to be carried out repeatedly as long as the condition between WHILE and DO is true.

Stepwise Refinement. Now let's refine our algorithm by translating the English language description just given into a more precise notation. The technique of refining an algorithm by replacing English language descriptions by more precise ones is called *stepwise refinement*.

To state our algorithm more precisely, we must be able to refer to any of the numbers involved in the calculation. To do this, we will assign the numbers names. Let's imagine boxes drawn on the blackboard, with the names beside them, as shown in Figure 1-3. As the execution of the algo-

FIGURE 1-3. The named boxes hold the values that will be manipulated by the greatest common divisor algorithm. The values in the boxes will change as the execution of the algorithm proceeds.

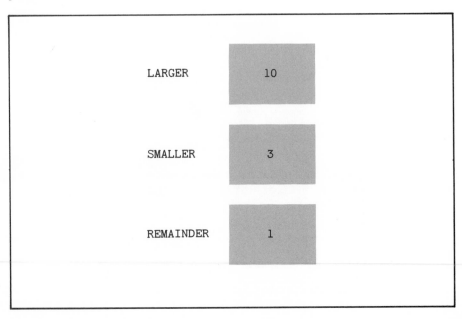

rithm proceeds, we will erase the numbers in the boxes and replace them
with new, updated values. We will need to keep track of three numbers in
this way: the larger number (LARGER), the smaller number (SMALLER),
and the remainder we get when we divide the larger number by the smaller
(REMAINDER).

We will also need two special signs. MOD is the mathematician's sign
for the remainder of a division. Thus 6 MOD 4 = 2, 20 MOD 7 = 6, 99
MOD 55 = 44, and so on.

The arrow sign ← means that the value on the right is to be copied
into the box named on the left. Thus LARGER ← 5 means that 5 is to be
written in the box labeled LARGER, replacing whatever number was previously there. LARGER ← SMALLER means that the number in SMALLER
is copied into LARGER, replacing whatever number was previously in
LARGER. And

```
REMAINDER ← LARGER MOD SMALLER
```

means that we are to divide the number in LARGER by the number in
SMALLER and place the remainder in REMAINDER. We can read the sign
← as "becomes." Figure 1-4 illustrates MOD and ←.

Instructions such as LARGER ← 5 constitute *imperative statements*;
they command us to take some action, in this case to write the number 5
in the box labeled LARGER. Usually we refer to these imperative statements as just *statements*, for short.

These preliminaries aside, here is our refined algorithm:

```
WHILE SMALLER ≠ 0 DO
    REMAINDER ← LARGER MOD SMALLER
    LARGER ← SMALLER
    SMALLER ← REMAINDER
END WHILE
```

The statements between WHILE SMALLER ≠ 0 DO and END WHILE
are to be executed repeatedly as long as the number written in SMALLER
is not 0. The first of the repeated statements says to divide the number in
LARGER by the number in SMALLER and put the remainder of the division in REMAINDER. The second repeated statement says to copy the number in SMALLER into LARGER. The third repeated statement says to copy
the number in REMAINDER into SMALLER.

We can illustrate the execution of an algorithm with a *trace*, such as
the one shown in Figure 1-5. Figure 1-5 illustrates the computation of the
greatest common divisor of 133 and 49.

The statements on the left side of Figure 1-5 are the statements of the
algorithm, listed in the order in which they are executed. Because of repetition, each statement is executed more than once and so appears in the
trace more than once.

Each row of numbers on the right gives the contents of LARGER,
SMALLER, and REMAINDER. The row of numbers preceding each statement gives the contents of LARGER, SMALLER, and REMAINDER before

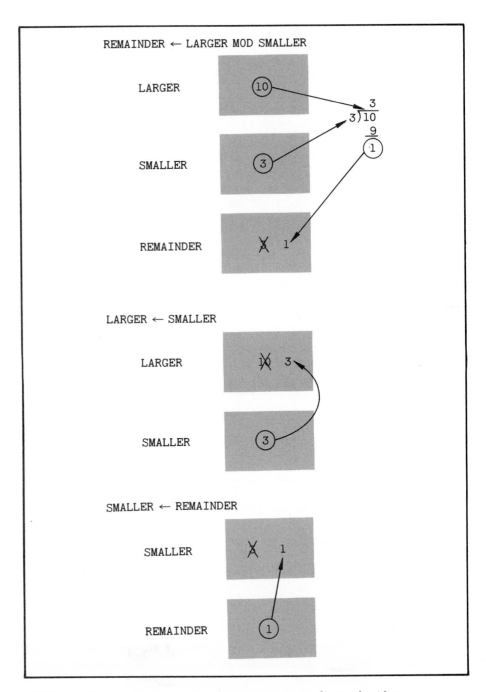

FIGURE 1-4. The special signs used in the greatest common divisor algorithm.

the statement is executed. The row of numbers following the statement gives the contents of these three locations after the statement is executed. Comparing the two rows reveals the effect of the statement.

The initial contents of LARGER and SMALLER are 133 and 49, re-

	LARGER	SMALLER	REMAINDER
	133	49	
REMAINDER ← LARGER MOD SMALLER			
	133	49	35
LARGER ← SMALLER			
	49	49	35
SMALLER ← REMAINDER			
	49	35	35
REMAINDER ← LARGER MOD SMALLER			
	49	35	14
LARGER ← SMALLER			
	35	35	14
SMALLER ← REMAINDER			
	35	14	14
REMAINDER ← LARGER MOD SMALLER			
	35	14	7
LARGER ← SMALLER			
	14	14	7
SMALLER ← REMAINDER			
	14	7	7
REMAINDER ← LARGER MOD SMALLER			
	14	7	0
LARGER ← SMALLER			
	7	7	0
SMALLER ← REMAINDER			
	7	0	0

FIGURE 1-5. A trace of the execution of the greatest common divisor algorithm. The row of numbers preceding each statement shows the contents of LARGER, SMALLER, and REMAINDER before the statement is executed. The row of numbers following the statement shows the contents of the same locations after the statement has been executed. Comparing the two rows reveals the effect of the statement.

spectively, the numbers whose greatest common divisor is to be calculated. REMAINDER is empty until a number is placed in it by the statement

REMAINDER ← LARGER MOD SMALLER

We can do a few things to dress up our algorithm. Let's use the statement

INPUT LARGER, SMALLER

to indicate that the input data for the problem—the numbers whose greatest common divisor we are to find—are to be placed in LARGER and SMALLER. Also let

```
OUTPUT LARGER
```

indicate that LARGER contains the result of the calculation, the answer to be displayed to the person who wanted the calculation done. Finally, let's give the algorithm a name: GREATEST__COMMON__DIVISOR. (In names, we use underlines instead of hyphens since hyphens are too easy to confuse with minus signs.) Figure 1-6 shows the dressed-up version of the algorithm.

1.3 Flowcharts

Another way to display an algorithm is with a *flowchart*. A flowchart consists of boxes containing instructions and connected together by lines. We follow the lines from box to box, executing the instructions inside each box as it is encountered. Special symbols mark the starting point and possible stopping points. A decision symbol directs us to one of two possible paths; which path we follow depends on whether the condition inside the decision symbol is true or false.

The Flowchart Symbols. Figure 1-7 shows the various flowchart symbols:

■ Terminal Symbol. This oval, which contains either the word START or the word STOP, indicates the starting and stopping points in the flowchart. A flowchart can only have one starting point, but it may have many possible stopping points.

■ Process Symbol. This rectangle is used for any data-processing operations for which no other symbol is reserved. Most of the instructions of an algorithm will appear in process symbols.

FIGURE 1-6. The algorithm GREATEST__COMMON__DIVISOR.

```
ALGORITHM GREATEST_COMMON_DIVISOR
    INPUT LARGER, SMALLER
    WHILE SMALLER ≠ 0 DO
        REMAINDER ← LARGER MOD SMALLER
        LARGER ← SMALLER
        SMALLER ← REMAINDER
    END WHILE
    OUTPUT LARGER
END GREATEST_COMMON_DIVISOR
```

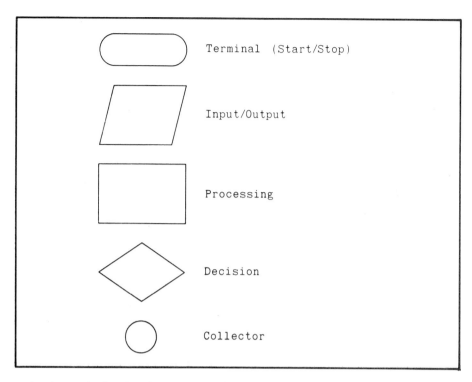

FIGURE 1-7. The five flowchart symbols. The use of each symbol is described in the text.

■ *Input/Output Symbol.* This parallelogram is used for INPUT and OUT-PUT instructions.

■ *Decision Symbol.* This diamond-shaped symbol contains a condition. If the condition is true, the path marked TRUE is to be followed. If the condition is false, the path marked FALSE is to be followed.

■ *Collector Circle.* Collector circles are points at which different paths join together.

The Flowchart for GREATEST_COMMON_DIVISOR. Figure 1-8 shows the flowchart for the greatest-common-divisor algorithm.

The most interesting thing about this flowchart is the way repetition is represented. Notice the loop that starts at the collector circle, passes through the decision symbol, then passes through the process symbol containing the instructions to be repeated, and ends up back at the collector circle.

Let's work our way around this loop. We start at the collector circle and go to the decision symbol. There we look in the box SMALLER and see if the number there is 0. If SMALLER ≠ 0, we follow the path marked TRUE, execute the repeated instructions, go back to the collector circle, and then arrive at the decision symbol once again. There we check the

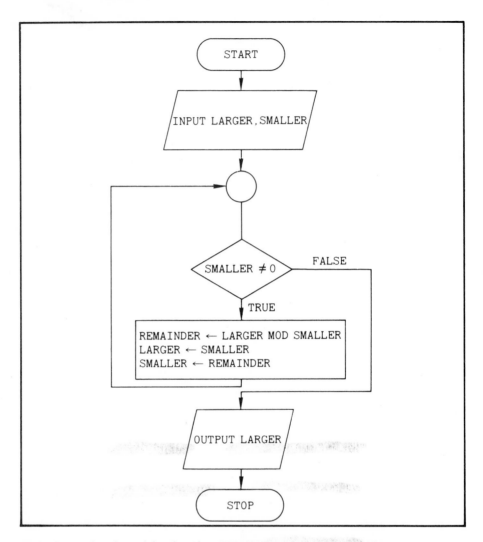

FIGURE 1-8. Flowchart of the algorithm GREATEST__COMMON__DIVISOR.

condition SMALLER ≠ 0 once again. If it still holds true, we go around the loop again. This keeps up as long as we find SMALLER ≠ 0 when we come to the decision symbol.

Eventually a time will come when we reach the decision symbol and find that SMALLER ≠ 0 is no longer true. Then we take the path marked FALSE, which leads us to the output symbol and from there to the stopping point.

A flowchart describing a repetition always contains a loop. In fact, programmers often use the word *loop* as a synonym for *repetition*, even when the repetition in question is not depicted by a flowchart.

For simple algorithms, a flowchart allows us to see the structure of the algorithm at a glance. For more complex algorithms, however, the flowchart becomes an intricate maze in which it's all too easy to get lost. For more complex algorithms, we will find our algorithmic language to be a better method of presentation than flowcharts.

Review Questions

1. What are the two defining characteristics of a computer?

2. What do we mean by *information?*

3. Information is an abstract concept. What are the concrete things that we actually use to record information and to pass it from one person to another.

4. Give ten examples of symbols. Avoid obvious ones like the letters of the alphabet.

5. Give some examples of professions that are largely devoted to information processing. What kinds of symbols does each manipulate?

6. Distinguish between *information* and *data.*

7. Give two other terms that can be used in place of *information processing* to describe what a computer does.

8. What do computer people mean when they refer to *garbage?*

9. Give an example of where the ability of computers to do complex arithmetical calculations has led to improved consumer products.

10. Explain *word processing.*

11. How can computers be used for game playing? Describe a computer game you have encountered in an arcade or in someone's home.

12. How can a computer be used to improve automobile performance?

13. What do we mean by *computer-assisted instruction?*

14. Give two examples of *information retrieval.*

15. It has been said that (a) "a computer can only do what it's told to," and (b) "a computer is an all-purpose machine." To what characteristic of computers do both of these statements refer?

16. Distinguish between an *algorithm* and a *program.*

17. Why do we usually use some formal notation instead of English for stating algorithms?

18. Give an example of an instruction that couldn't be carried out by any person or machine and so would prevent an algorithm containing it from being effective.

19. Give several examples of everyday algorithms (directions, recipes, and so on) that might fail to terminate if the person following them didn't exercise common sense.

20. Define the greatest common divisor of two numbers. What is one common application of the greatest common divisor?

21. Describe Euclid's algorithm for finding the greatest common divisor of two numbers.

22. Explain those features of our algorithmic language that we made use of in presenting Euclid's algorithm.

23. What is a *trace*? For what purpose is it used?

24. Draw the five types of flowchart symbols and give the purpose of each.

25. What do computer people mean by a *loop*? How does the term relate to flowcharts?

Exercises

1. Execute the greatest-common-divisor algorithm using 84 and 63 as the initial values of LARGER and SMALLER. Show the values of LARGER, SMALLER, and REMAINDER after the execution of each statement.

2. In the greatest-common-divisor algorithm, suppose that the larger number is initially placed in SMALLER and the smaller number in LARGER. Show that the algorithm will still give the correct answer. (*Hint:* What will have happened after the first execution of the repeated statements?)

3. Show that the greatest-common-divisor algorithm will still work when the initial values of LARGER and SMALLER are the same.

4. Give what you consider to be convincing arguments that:
(a) The greatest-common-divisor algorithm always terminates.
(b) When it terminates, the value of LARGER is the greatest common divisor of the initial values of LARGER and SMALLER.

Note: To do the following four exercises, you will need to be able to express some additional arithmetical operations in the algorithmic language. The algorithmic language uses +, −, *, and / for addition, subtraction, multiplication, and division, respectively. Computer languages usually use * and /, which can be found on the keyboards of most computer input devices, in place of × and ÷, which cannot.

5. Write an algorithm to input the numerator and denominator of a fraction and output the numerator and denominator of the same fraction reduced to lowest terms. Thus if the fraction in question is 12/16, the input to the algorithm will be 12 and 16, and the output will be 3 and 4.

6. Write an algorithm to input the numerator and denominator of each of two fractions and output the numerator and denominator of the sum of the two fractions. The sum is to be reduced to lowest terms. For instance, if the fractions to be added are 3/4 and 1/12, then the input is 3 and 4 (first fraction) and 1 and 12 (second fraction). The output is 5 and 6, representing 5/6.

7. Write an algorithm to input the numerator and denominator of each of two fractions and output the numerator and denominator of their product, reduced to lowest terms.

8. Write an algorithm to input the numerator and denominator of each of two fractions and output the numerator and denominator of their quotient, reduced to lowest terms.

PART ONE

COMPUTER HARDWARE AND SOFTWARE

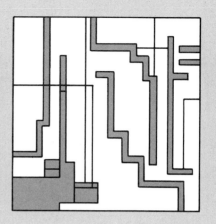

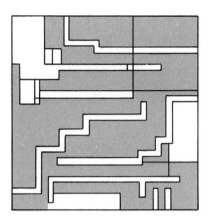

Chapter 2

Computer Hardware and Information Representation

A *computer system* is a collection of machines and programs designed to carry out information-processing tasks. The machines are the *hardware* of the computer system. The programs that direct the machines are the *software*.

In this chapter, we will look at computer hardware and at methods for representing information inside the hardware. In the following chapter, we will turn our attention to computer software.

2.1 The Hardware

Figure 2-1 shows the hardware components of a typical computer system: the *central processing unit, main memory, input and output devices,* and *auxiliary memory*. The different components communicate with one another over a group of wires known as a *bus*.

We apply the word *memory* to any component used for storing data. Some people prefer the word *storage* to *memory*, so in other books you will see references to *main storage* and *auxiliary storage*. Auxiliary storage is also often called *mass storage*.

The *input, output, and auxiliary memory devices are known as peripherals* because they often occupy different cabinets than do the central processing unit and main memory. This isn't always the case, however, so there are computer systems for which some or all of the "peripherals" occupy the same enclosure as the central processing unit and main memory.

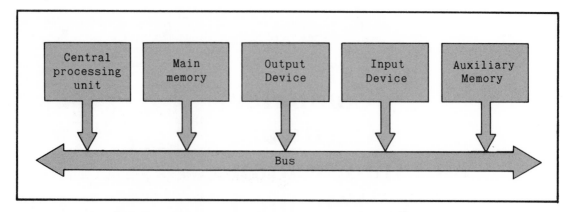

FIGURE 2-1. The hardware components of a typical computer system. There can be any number of auxiliary memory, input, and output devices.

Main Memory. Main memory is used to store two things: the program that the computer is currently executing and the data that it is currently manipulating. We can think of main memory as a kind of scratchpad or blackboard that holds not only the data the computer is working with but the instructions it's following as well.

Main memory is divided up into a large number of separate *memory cells* or *memory locations*. Each memory location holds a fixed amount of data and has an *address* by which it can be referred to for the purpose of storing data in it or retrieving data from it. We can picture main memory as a collection of post office boxes. The boxes correspond to memory locations and the box numbers correspond to addresses.

The Central Processing Unit. The central processing unit (often abbreviated to *central processor* or to CPU) carries out the calculations called for by the program and controls the other components of the system as well.

The central processor operates in a *fetch-execute cycle*. During the fetch part of the cycle, the central processor fetches the next instruction of the program from main memory. During the execute part of the cycle, the central processor carries out the operation called for by the instruction.

If the requested operation requires the use of other hardware components, such as input or output devices, then the central processor sends these devices the necessary control signals so that each device does its part.

No matter what job the computer system may be doing, the central processor is just fetching and executing instructions, one after another. Clearly, the ability of the system to do any complex job, such as playing chess, lies with the program and not with the central processor, which is just following orders. For this reason, we usually give the program credit for the job rather than the computer. We speak of a program that plays chess or a program that makes out payrolls rather than a computer that plays chess or a computer that makes out payrolls.

In recent years, engineers have learned how to construct an entire central processing unit on a tiny chip of silicon that can be mass produced at low cost. A central processing unit constructed on a single silicon chip (or on a small number of chips) is called a *microprocessor*. Some other computer components, most notably main memory, can also be constructed on silicon chips.

The availability of microprocessors and other low-cost computer components makes it possible to use computers in many places where they would have once been out of the question, such as in games, automobiles, and household appliances. The resulting changes in the ways people use computers are known as the *microprocessor revolution*.

Input and Output Devices. Input and output devices allow the computer system to communicate with the outside world. Looked at another way, input and output devices translate between symbols convenient for human beings (such as the letters of the alphabet) and the codes that the computer hardware needs.

There are many different kinds of input and output devices, corresponding to the many different kinds of data that we want to be able to process with computers. There are speech synthesizers that let a computer talk, music synthesizers that let it play music, plotters that let it draw pictures, and special devices that convert sounds from a microphone or pictures from a television camera into a form suitable for computer processing.

Instead of trying to survey all of these exotic devices, however, we will confine our attention to the input and output devices you are most likely to encounter as a student. These are *computer terminals, keypunches, card readers,* and *high-speed printers*.

A *computer terminal* consists of a typewriterlike keyboard and (depending on the kind of terminal) either a televisionlike display screen or a typewriterlike printer. The terminal is connected to the rest of the computer system by wires, which may be and often are ordinary telephone lines.

Data typed on the keyboard is transmitted over the connecting wires to the computer. Data received over the wires from the computer is (depending on the kind of terminal) either displayed on the screen or typed out by the printer.

Instead of data being transmitted directly to the computer as soon as it is typed, as with a computer terminal, sometimes it is punched on cards first. The most popular kind of punched card is divided into 80 columns, each of which can hold the punched holes representing one character. Thus, a standard punched card can hold one typed line, which may be up to 80 characters long.

We prepare punched cards with a device known as a *keypunch*, which is equipped with a typewriterlike keyboard. Data typed on the keyboard is punched on the cards. The keypunch will also print the typed characters along the top edge of the card. The printed line is for a human reader; the punched holes represent the same information for the computer.

To make data punched on cards available to the computer system, we feed the cards into an input device known as a *card reader*, which obtains the data from the cards by sensing the punched holes. The computer system can punch its own cards using an output device known as a *card punch*. Often a card reader and a card punch are combined in the same unit.

Often computer systems must produce large amounts of printed output, such as bills for all of a company's customers or checks for all of its employees. For this purpose, a *high-speed printer* is used. One widely used type of high-speed printer is called a *line printer*, since it prints an entire line in a single operation. Some high-speed printers can print thousands or even tens of thousands of lines per minute. They may use exotic technologies such as laser beams.

Auxiliary Memory. The outstanding property of main memory is that it allows very fast access to memory locations. Data can be stored in or retrieved from a particular memory location in a time measured in billionths of a second. Rapid access to data and instructions allows the entire computer system to do its work faster.

On the other hand, main memory isn't suitable for long-term storage of large data files and program libraries. Its storage capacity is limited. Even worse, some kinds of main memory are volatile—their contents are erased when the power is turned off.

We use auxiliary memory for long-term storage of large amounts of data. If we think of main memory as the computer system's scratchpad, then we can think of auxiliary memory as its filing cabinet. Access to data items stored in auxiliary memory, however, is much slower than for data stored in main memory. For this reason, data in auxiliary memory is usually moved in blocks to main memory for processing, then returned to auxiliary memory when processing is complete.

There are two kinds of auxiliary memory in widespread use: *magnetic tape* and *magnetic disks*.

The magnetic tape that computers use is similar to that used by home tape recorders, although its width may be different, and it may move past the record and playback heads at a different speed.

The main drawback of magnetic tape is familiar to anyone who has ever used a tape recorder. Suppose you have a number of musical selections recorded on a tape. If you want to play the selections in the same order in which they are recorded on the tape, you have no problem. You just put on the tape and let it play. But if you want to play a selection near the middle of the tape first, then one near the beginning, then one near the end, and so on, you will waste a lot of time winding and rewinding the tape for the next selection.

In short, tape is a *sequential-access medium*—items recorded on tape can be retrieved most rapidly when they are played back in the same order in which they were recorded. If we want to play them back in some other order, we must waste time winding and rewinding the tape.

Magnetic disks (usually just called *disks*) look something like phonograph records but work on the same principle as magnetic tape—the data is recorded as magnetic patterns rather than in grooves.

To understand how a disk works, imagine a phonograph-record-like disk attached to a spindle—a spinning rod. An *access arm* coming in from the side points toward the center of the spinning disk. The access arm looks like a two-pronged fork, with one prong going above the disk and the other below it. At the end of each prong is a *read-write head* that records and plays back data. The head on the top prong records and plays back from the top surface; the head on the bottom prong does the same from the bottom surface.

The access arms can move the read-write heads either in toward the center of the disk or out toward its edge. When a read-write head is in a particular position, the portion of the disk that moves under it as the disk spins is called a *track*. Unlike the grooves of a phonograph record, the tracks on a disk can't be seen by looking at the disk—they are just the invisible paths along which data is recorded.

In operation, the access arm positions the read-write head over the track on which data is to be written or from which data is to be read. The actual reading or writing takes place when the rotation of the disk carries the desired part of the track beneath the read-write head.

In contrast to tape, disks require no winding or rewinding to access a particular data item. Instead the access arm positions the read-write head over the track containing the desired item. Shortly thereafter, the spin of the disk carries the item beneath the read-write head. Data items stored on disk can be accessed in any order desired; for this reason, disks are called *random-access media*.

Magnetic tapes and most types of disks are *removable media*—they can be removed from the computer system's tape and disk drives and stored separately in libraries. The number of tapes and disks stored in the libraries may far exceed the number that can be mounted on the system's tape and disk drives at any one time. If we consider the tapes and disks stored in libraries as part of the computer system's auxiliary memory, then the capacity of auxiliary memory is virtually unlimited.

2.2 Information Representation

The parts that a machine is made of determine the most natural way to represent information inside the machine. For instance, mechanical desk calculators—largely museum pieces now!—are made of gears and other mechanical components. Each digit stored in the machine is represented by a gear with ten teeth and ten possible positions. One possible position represents a 0, the next position represents a 1, the next a 2, and so on through 9.

Computers, on the other hand, are made of electrical circuits, each of which can be switched on or off. Whereas a gear in the desk calculator could have ten different positions, or states, a circuit in a computer can only have two. Either current is flowing in the circuit, in which case it is on, or else no current is flowing, in which case it is off.

Yet we can represent information with these two-state circuits just as well as we can with gears or indeed with any other mechanism. Let's look at some examples.

Suppose we have only one circuit. We can represent two alternatives, one corresponding to the circuit being off, and the other corresponding to it being on.

For instance, we could use the circuit to represent the answer to a yes-or-no question by letting "yes" correspond to the circuit being on and letting "no" correspond to the circuit being off. We can present our method of representing, or coding, the answer with a table like the following:

no   off
yes   on

Now suppose we have two circuits instead of one. With two circuits we have four combinations:

off-off   on-off
off-on   on-on

With two circuits we can represent four alternatives. For instance, we could represent the four seasons of the year as follows:

fall   off-off
winter   off-on
spring   on-off
summer   on-on

Obviously, the particular correspondence we chose—off-off for fall, off-on for winter, and so on—is completely arbitrary. There are, in fact, 24 different ways of representing the four seasons using two circuits, and all of them are equally satisfactory.

Now suppose we have three circuits. We can represent eight alternatives, as follows:

off-off-off   on-off-off
off-off-on   on-off-on
off-on-off   on-on-off
off-on-on   on-on-on

We could use these to represent the seven days of the week, for instance, and still have one alternative left over:

Sunday   off-off-off
Monday   off-off-on
Tuesday   off-on-off
Wednesday   off-on-on
Thursday   on-off-off
Friday   on-off-on
Saturday   on-on-off

The combination on-on-on isn't used.

You should be able to see that whenever we add another circuit, we double the number of alternatives we can represent. This is because now we can use all the combinations we had before in two different ways—once with the newly added circuit off and once again with the newly added circuit on.

So we don't have to actually work out all the combinations to be able to say that four circuits will give us 16 alternatives, five circuits will give us 32 alternatives, six circuits will give us 64 alternatives, and so on.

Binary Codes. We use the term *binary code* for any method of representing information with two-state circuits. The word *binary*, you may recall from your other studies, refers to two—in this case the two possible states of each circuit.

When we talk about binary codes, we don't want to be worried about writing the words *off* and *on* in complicated combinations such as:

off-on-off-off-on-on-off-on

To avoid this, we use the symbols 0 and 1 to stand for *off* and *on*.

What's more, we can use 0s and 1s in ways that have nothing to do with circuits or currents. For instance, we can represent a 1 by a hole punched in a particular position of a card and a 0 by the absence of a hole in that position. Or we can represent a 0 by a certain piece of magnetic tape being magnetized in one direction and a 1 by that piece of tape being magnetized in the opposite direction.

When 0 and 1 are used in this way, we call them *binary digits* or *bits*. A binary code is a method of representing information using combinations of bits.

All our previous examples could be rewritten using 0 and 1 instead of *off* and *on*. Thus we could represent the four seasons with two bits:

fall	00
winter	01
spring	10
summer	11

and the seven days of the week with three bits:

Sunday	000
Monday	001
Tuesday	010
Wednesday	011
Thursday	100
Friday	101
Saturday	110

The combination 111 is not used.

The number of bits we need to represent a given number of alternatives is the same as the number of two-state circuits. So we aren't surprised to find that with one bit we can represent 2 alternatives, with two bits we can represent 2 × 2 or four alternatives, with three bits we can represent 2 × 2 × 2 or eight alternatives, and so on.

Repeated products of a number with itself are called the *powers* of that number. Mathematicians have a special shorthand notation for powers called *exponential notation*. In exponential notation, 2 × 2 is written 2^2, 2 × 2 × 2 is written 2^3, 2 × 2 × 2 × 2 is written 2^4, and so on. By convention, 2^0 represents 1 and 2^1 represents 2. The raised number representing the number of 2s to be multiplied together is called an *exponent*, from which exponential notation gets its name.

Thus, with one bit we can represent 2^1 alternatives, with two bits we can represent 2^2, with three bits we can represent 2^3, and so on.

Character Codes. The most common way to communicate information to a computer is to represent it first using the letters, digits, and punctuation marks with which we are all familiar. An input device then converts these characters into binary codes that the computer can manipulate. For output, an output device converts the computer's binary codes into symbols meaningful to humans.

For this approach to work, we need a *character code*—a standard scheme for representing characters by combinations of bits. There is more than one such code in use. But the most widely used one is the *American Standard Code for Information Interchange*, usually abbreviated to ASCII, which is pronounced *as' key*.

The ASCII code uses seven bits to represent each character. Seven bits gives us 2^7 or 128 alternatives, so ASCII can represent 128 characters. This is enough to represent the upper- and lower-case letters, the digits, the punctuation marks, and a small number of special signs. In addition, ASCII has 32 nonprinting *control characters* that are used to control printing equipment and to make it easier for different pieces of equipment to exchange messages with one another.

Figure 2-2 illustrates the ASCII code. To find the code for any character, note which column and row of the table contain the character in question. The three bits at the head of the column containing the character are the leftmost three bits of the code. The four bits to the left of the row containing the character are the rightmost four bits of the code. Thus, the code for A is 1000001, the code for B is 1000010, and so on.

The two- and three-letter abbreviations represent control characters. We won't go through all of them since many are used for specialized technical purposes. The following three are commonly used: CR, *carriage return*, returns the typing mechanism to the left margin; LF, *line feed*, advances the paper by one line; BEL, *bell*, causes a bell or other alarm device to sound.

Binary Notation. The system for representing numbers that we all learned about in school makes use of the ten digits 0 through 9. We call this system the *base-10* or *decimal system*, and we say that a number represented this way is in *decimal notation*.

In a computer we have only two symbols at our disposal: 0 and 1. The

		Leftmost Three Bits							
		000	001	010	011	100	101	110	111
	0000	NUL	DLE	Space	0	@	P	`	p
	0001	SOH	DC1	!	1	A	Q	a	q
	0010	STX	DC2	"	2	B	R	b	r
	0011	ETX	DC3	#	3	C	S	c	s
	0100	EOT	DC4	$	4	D	T	d	t
	0101	ENQ	NAK	%	5	E	U	e	u
	0110	ACK	SYN	&	6	F	V	f	v
Rightmost	0111	BEL	ETB	'	7	G	W	g	w
Four	1000	BS	CAN	(	8	H	X	h	x
Bits	1001	HT	EM	)	9	I	Y	i	y
	1010	LF	SUB	*	:	J	Z	j	z
	1011	VT	ESC	+	;	K	[	k	{
	1100	FF	FS	,	<	L	\	l	|
	1101	CR	GS	–	=	M	]	m	}
	1110	SO	RS	.	>	N	^	n	~
	1111	SI	US	/	?	O	_	o	DEL

FIGURE 2-2. The ASCII code. The two- and three-letter abbreviations represent control characters. Examples are CR (carriage return), LF (line feed), and BEL (bell).

most natural way to represent numbers, then, is to take 0 and 1 as our digits and use the *base-2* or *binary number system*. Numbers represented in the binary system are said to be in *binary notation*.

The easiest way to understand the binary system is by comparing it with the decimal system. It will help, then, to begin by reviewing some properties of decimal notation.

The number 10 enters the base-10 system in two ways:

1. Every number is represented by a combination of the ten digits 0, 1, 2, 3, 4, 5, 6, 7, 8, and 9.

2. The digits of a decimal number, taken from right to left, represent units, tens, hundreds, thousands, and so on. The numbers 1, 10, 100, 1000, and so on are just the powers of 10, the values we get by starting with 1 and multiplying repeatedly by 10.

Thus, the decimal number 8,274 can be analyzed as:

Thousands	*Hundreds*	*Tens*	*Units*
8	2	7	4

That is, 8,274 represents eight thousands, two hundreds, seven tens, and four units. Arithmetically, we can express this as:

$$8274 = 8 \times 1000 + 2 \times 100 + 7 \times 10 + 4 \times 1$$

The number 2 plays exactly the same role in the binary system that 10 does in the decimal system. Thus 2 enters the binary system in the following two ways:

1. Every number is represented using some combination of the two digits 0 and 1.

2. The digits of a binary number, taken from right to left, represent units, twos, fours, eights, and so on. The numbers 1, 2, 4, 8, and so on are the powers of 2, the numbers we get by starting with 1 and multiplying by 2 repeatedly.

Thus, the binary number 1101 can be analyzed as:

Eights	Fours	Twos	Units
1	1	0	1

That is, 1101 represents one eight, one four, zero twos, and one unit. Arithmetically, we can express this as:

$$1101 = 1 \times 8 + 1 \times 4 + 0 \times 2 + 1 \times 1 = 13$$

We see that 1101 represents the same value in binary notation that 13 does in decimal notation.

The equation in the previous paragraph could be confusing, since we might not realize that 1101 is in the binary system and wonder how one thousand, one hundred and one can equal thirteen. When the possibility of confusion exists, we use a subscript to indicate the base in which a particular number is written. Thus we write thirteen in the binary system as 1101_2, and we can write the equation in the last paragraph more clearly as:

$$1101_2 = 1 \times 8 + 1 \times 4 + 0 \times 2 + 1 \times 1 = 13$$

We can see how to count in binary notation by imagining a counter, such as the mileage indicator on a car. Suppose, however, that each dial of the counter has only two digits, 0 and 1, instead of the usual 0 through 9. What's more, whenever a dial turns from 1 back to 0, it causes the dial to the left to advance one place, just as happens with an ordinary counter when a dial turns from 9 back to 0.

Suppose the counter has four dials. Its initial reading is 0000. The first count causes it to advance to 0001. The next count causes the rightmost dial to turn from 1 back to 0. This, in turn, causes the next dial to the left to advance one position. So after two counts the counter reads 0010. After three counts it reads 0011; after four counts it reads 0100 (Why?); after five counts it reads 0101; and so on.

Numbers with fractional parts can be represented in binary notation using the same approach that we use in decimal notation. The integer and fractional parts of the number are separated by a "decimal point," hereafter called a *radix point*, since its function is independent of any particular number system.

In the decimal system, the digits to the left of the radix (decimal) point, taken from left to right, represent tenths, hundredths, thousandths, and so on. We can analyze 27.45 as:

Tens	Units	Tenths	Hundredths
2	7	4	5

Thus, 27.45 represents two tens, seven units, four tenths, and five hundredths. Arithmetically, we can express this as:

$$27.45 = 2 \times 10 + 7 \times 1 + 4 \times \frac{1}{10} + 5 \times \frac{1}{100}$$

In binary notation the digits to the right of the radix point, taken from left to right, represent halves, quarters, eighths, and so on. We can analyze 11.101_2 as:

Twos	Units	Halves	Quarters	Eights
1	1	1	0	1

Thus, 11.101_2 represents one two, one unit, one half, zero quarters, and one eighth. Arithmetically, we can express this as:

$$11.101_2 = 1 \times 2 + 1 \times 1 + 1 \times \frac{1}{2} + 0 \times \frac{1}{4} + 1 \times \frac{1}{8}$$
$$= 2 + 1 + .5 + .125$$
$$= 3.625$$

2.3 Operations On Binary Values

The Arithmetic Operations. Let's start with addition. The addition table for binary numbers is as follows:

```
0 + 0 = 0
0 + 1 = 1
1 + 0 = 1
1 + 1 = 10 (that is, 0 and 1 to carry)
```

Notice how simple this is compared to the addition table for the decimal system that we all had to learn as schoolchildren. The simplicity of the addition table leads to a corresponding simplicity in the electrical circuits in the computer that do the additions.

With the help of the addition table, we can easily work out a binary addition. Throughout this section we will use four-bit binary numbers as examples. To help you follow the examples, the decimal value of each binary number will be written in parentheses besides the binary value:

```
  1001   (9)
+ 0101   (5)
  1110   (14)
```

Notice that the addition in the rightmost column produces a carry.

As in decimal notation, the addition table also provides us with the information we need to do subtractions:

```
  1001   (9)
− 0101   (5)
  0100   (4)
```

Notice that the subtraction in the next-to-leftmost column requires a borrow.

The multiplication table for the binary system is as follows:

$0 \times 0 = 0$
$0 \times 1 = 0$
$1 \times 0 = 0$
$1 \times 1 = 1$

This is even simpler than the addition table, since no carries are involved.

For multiplication, we can arrange our work in the same way that we do in the decimal system:

```
       1010     (10)
×      1101     (13)
       1010
      0000
     1010
    1010
   10000010     (130)
```

Of course, we normally don't bother to write out a row of zeros when doing a multiplication. The row of zeros is written out here, however, to help make clear the overall pattern of the multiplication.

Like multiplication, division is done much as in the decimal system, but using the binary addition and multiplication tables.

```
            1101      (13)
1011 ) 10010110      (150)
       1011
       1111
       1011
        1001
        0000
        10010
         1011
          111      (7)
```

The Logical and Shift Operations. The arithmetic operations all assume that the binary values being operated on represent numbers. Sometimes, however, we need to engage in what programmers call "bit twiddling"— manipulating the individual bits of arbitrary binary codes. The logical and shift operations provide us with the means for doing this.

The logical operator OR gives a result of 1 if either or both of its operands are 1. We can define the OR operator by means of a table similar to the ones we used for addition and multiplication:

```
0 OR 0 = 0
0 OR 1 = 1
1 OR 0 = 1
1 OR 1 = 1
```

One application of OR is to set any particular bits of a binary value to 1. For instance, by ORing a four-bit binary value with 0010, we can set the second bit from the right to 1 while leaving the remaining three bits unchanged:

```
      1001              0111
OR  0010          OR  0010
    ----              ----
      1011              0111
```

In each case the second bit from the right is set to 1, regardless of whether it was 0 or 1 initially.

The exclusive or operation XOR is similar to OR except it gives 0 when both its operands are 1:

```
0 XOR 0 = 0
0 XOR 1 = 1
1 XOR 0 = 1
1 XOR 1 = 0
```

We can use the XOR operation to flip particular bits from 0 to 1 or 1 to 0. For instance, XORing with 0010 will change the second bit from the right to 1 if it was 0 and to 0 if it was 1. The other three bits remain unchanged:

```
       1001               0111
XOR  0010          XOR  0010
     ----               ----
       1011               0101
```

If we XOR a four-bit value with 1111, we flip all four bits:

```
       1010
XOR  1111
     ----
       0101
```

This bit-flipping operation is so important that we define a separate operator, NOT, for it:

NOT 0 = 1
NOT 1 = 0

Then we can use NOT to change 1010 into 0101:

NOT <u>1010</u>
    0101

The operator AND yields 1 only if both of its operands are 1:

0 AND 0 = 0
0 AND 1 = 0
1 AND 0 = 0
1 AND 1 = 1

We can use AND to set any particular bits to 0. For instance, ANDing a four-bit value with 1001 will set the two middle bits to 0 while leaving the two outer bits unchanged:

      1101   0111
AND <u>1001</u>   AND <u>1001</u>
      1001   0001

The logical operations allow us to change particular bits, but they don't provide any means for changing the positions of bits. The shift operations remedy this by allowing us to shift all of the bits to the left or right.

The *shift left* operation, SHL, shifts all of the bits one place to the left. A 0 is shifted into the rightmost position:

SHL <u>1101</u>
    1010

The *shift right* operation, SHR, shifts all of the bits one place to the right. A 0 is shifted into the leftmost position:

SHR <u>1011</u>
    0101

Here is a typical application of shifting. Suppose we have 2 four-bit values, 1011 and 0110. We want to isolate the rightmost two bits of each and put them together to form a single four-bit value, 1110.

To do this, we start with the first value 1011 and shift it one place to the left:

SHL <u>1011</u>
    0110

Now shift to the left again:

SHL <u>0110</u>
      1100

Next, we take the second value, 0110, and set its two leftmost bits to 0 to make room for the two bits we obtained from the first value:

        0110
AND <u>0011</u> ·
        0010

Finally, we use the OR operation to combine our two intermediate results, 1100 and 0010, to get the desired final result, 1110:

     1100
OR <u>0010</u>
     1110

The logical operations allow us to change the values of bits without changing their positions; the shift operations allow us to change the positions of bits without changing their values. We can always find some combination of logical and shift operations to carry out any bit manipulations that we wish.

2.4 Octal and Hexadecimal Notation

As suitable as binary numbers are for use inside a computer, they give people trouble. For instance, consider the following 24-bit binary number:

110000100011101001001011

Can you copy this number down without making a mistake? Can you look at it and then copy it down from memory? Can you call it out for someone else to copy down? Try comparing it with:

110000100011101001011011

Are the two numbers the same? If not, where do they differ?

Chances are that you found the tasks set in the last paragraph difficult or impossible to carry out. Human beings find long strings of 0s and 1s tedious or impossible to work with. Some people, impressed with the extreme simplicity of the binary addition and multiplication tables, have suggested that human beings should switch to the binary system. No way! Who wants to make out a check for $1000001101 instead of $525 or for $1111101000 instead of $1000?

To avoid the problems of working with binary numbers, programmers usually use one of two alternative notations, *octal* and *hexadecimal*. Each is so closely related to binary notation that we can convert between octal and binary or between hexadecimal and binary at a glance. Yet each is enormously easier than binary notation for human beings to work with.

Octal Notation. One way to make long binary numbers easier to deal with is to mark off the digits in groups of three, the way we do with decimal numbers. Let's try this with the first 24-bit binary number that we looked at earlier:

110,000,100,011,101,001,001,011

This helps some, but we can go even further. Let's replace each group of three bits by the single digit that has the same numerical value. Thus, we replace 000 by 0, 001 by 1, 010 by 2, and so on. The digits that replace the three-bit groups are called octal digits. Figure 2-3 shows the correspondence between octal digits and three-bit groups.

Replacing each three-bit group in the example by the corresponding octal digit, we get:

60435113

This is certainly easier to deal with than the original binary number. You should have no trouble copying it down, either while looking at it or from memory, or in calling it out to someone else. You were asked to compare the first binary number with a second one. If we transcribe the second binary number into octal, we get:

60435133

Now you should have no difficulty in seeing not only that the two numbers are different but exactly where the difference lies.

We can work the process just described in reverse, of course. That is, given an octal number, we can convert it to binary by substituting the

FIGURE 2-3. The correspondence between octal digits and three-bit groups.

Octal Digit	Three-Bit Group
0	000
1	001
2	010
3	011
4	100
5	101
6	110
7	111

proper three-bit group for each octal digit. For example, to convert the octal number 5743 to binary, we substitute 101 for 5, 111 for 7, and so on. This gives us:

101,111,100,011

or, after removing the commas:

101111100011

The octal number system represents numbers using the eight digits 0, 1, 2, 3, 4, 5, 6, and 7. Octal notation is a *base-8* number system for the same reasons that binary notation is a base-2 system and decimal notation is a base-10 system.

Where confusion might result, we can use the subscript 8 to indicate that a number is in octal notation:

$$5743_8 = 101111100011_2$$

Hexadecimal Notation. Instead of marking off binary digits in groups of three, we could mark them off in groups of four instead. Let's try this with the first of the 24-bit binary numbers we have been using as examples:

1100,0010,0011,1010,0100,1011

Following the same path that we did for octal, we would like to replace each four-bit group by a single digit.

This idea runs into trouble at once. There are 16 possible four-bit binary numbers. But we only have the 10 digits 0–9 at our disposal. To put our plan into effect, we have to come up with six more digits from somewhere.

What we do is this: we use the digits 0–9 for the four-bit groups 0000 through 1001. For the 6 four-bit groups 1010 through 1111, we use the letters A through F. Using letters for digits may seem strange at first, but the practice has a long history. The ancient Greeks, Romans, and Hebrews all used the letters of their alphabets to represent numbers.

Figure 2-4 shows the correspondence between the four-bit groups and the hexadecimal digits 0–9 and A–F. For each of the digits A–F we have to bear in mind two things—the bit pattern it represents and the numerical value it represents. Thus, we should think of A as representing 1010 and ten; of B as representing 1011 and eleven; and so on. The need to learn both the bit patterns and the numerical values for A–F makes hexadecimal slightly harder than octal for beginners to master.

Replacing the four-bit groups in our example by hexadecimal digits, we get:

C23A4B

Again, you should have no trouble copying or remembering this number.

```
      Hexadecimal Digit      Four-Bit Group
            0                    0000
            1                    0001
            2                    0010
            3                    0011
            4                    0100
            5                    0101
            6                    0110
            7                    0111
            8                    1000
            9                    1001
            A                    1010
            B                    1011
            C                    1100
            D                    1101
            E                    1110
            F                    1111
```

FIGURE 2-4. The correspondence between hexadecimal digits and four-bit groups.

If we write our second example 24-bit binary number in hexadecimal, we get:

C23A5B

You should again have no trouble seeing both that the two numbers differ and exactly where they differ.

By using Figure 2-4 in reverse, we can easily convert from hexadecimal to binary. To convert AC9F to binary, for instance, we first replace each hexadecimal digit by the corresponding four-bit group:

1010,1100,1001,1111

Omitting the commas gives us the corresponding binary value:

1010110010011111

The hexadecimal system represents numbers using the 16 digits 0–9 and A–F. Thus, hexadecimal is a *base-16* number system. Where confusion might otherwise result, we can use a subscript of 16 to indicate that a number is written in hexadecimal notation:

$$AC9F_{16} = 1010110010011111_2$$

The word *hexadecimal* is often abbreviated to *hex*.

2.5 A Simple Computer

In this section we will look at a very simple computer. The computer will be a hypothetical one since we can make a hypothetical computer much

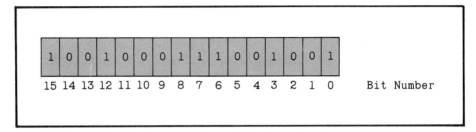

FIGURE 2-5. A 16-bit word.

simpler and easier to understand than any real computer. In spite of this computer's simplicity, however, its overall structure is similar to that of real computers, and it will serve as a good introduction to real machines.

Words. A computer normally works not with individual bits but with groups of bits called *words*. The number of bits in a word varies from one computer to another. Typical word sizes are 8 bits, 12 bits, 16 bits, 32 bits, 36 bits, and 60 bits. Some computers allow words of several different sizes; others have only one word size.

Our computer will use only one word size, 16 bits. All the data and instructions that it works with must fit into 16-bit words. Figure 2-5 illustrates the 16-bit word of our computer.

We can represent a 16-bit word conveniently by means of four hexadecimal digits. Figure 2-6 shows several words of data with their hexadecimal representations. Note that if the number of bits in our computer's words had been a multiple of three instead of four, we would have probably used octal notation instead of hexadecimal notation. Why?

Data and Instruction Formats. To keep our computer simple, we will allow it to manipulate only one kind of data—signed whole numbers in the

FIGURE 2-6. Three examples of how we can represent the contents of a 16-bit word by four hexadecimal digits.

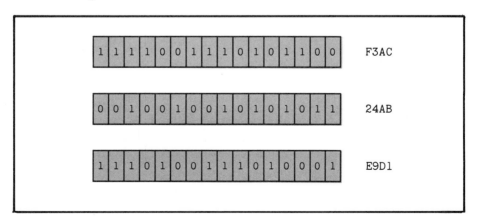

range $-32,767$ through $+32,767$. In addition to the data the computer is going to manipulate, the computer's instructions must also be stored in main memory. Each data item and instruction must fit into exactly one word. We need to see, then, how to code both data items and instructions in 16-bit words.

We already know now to represent whole numbers using binary notation. So far, however, we haven't said anything about representing *signed numbers*—numbers that can be positive or negative. The simplest method of doing this is the *sign-magnitude representation*, illustrated in Figure 2-7. One bit of the word represents the sign of the number; the other 15 bits represent the magnitude.

A's Figure 2-7 shows, the leftmost bit of the word is the *sign bit*. When this bit is 0, the number contained in the word is positive; when the sign bit is 1, the number contained in the word is negative.

The rightmost 15 bits of the word represent the *magnitude* of the number in ordinary binary notation. Note that 15 bits gives us 2^{15} or 32,768 alternatives—sufficient to represent magnitudes in the range 0 through 32,767.

For example, consider the word:

0000000000000011

This has a sign bit of 0 and a magnitude of 000000000000011. In binary notation, as in decimal notation, we can ignore leading zeros, so the magnitude of the number represented is just 11_2, which equals three. The word 0000000000000011, then, represents $+3$.

Now consider the word:

1000000000000011

The magnitude is the same as before, but the sign bit is now 1 instead of 0. Therefore, this word represents -3 instead of $+3$.

We can write these words more compactly using hexadecimal notation instead of binary. Thus, 0003 hexadecimal represents $+3$, and 8003 hexadecimal represents -3. (Remember that the bit pattern corresponding to 8 is 1000.)

FIGURE 2-7. Our computer stores numbers in the sign-magnitude representation. The leftmost bit of a word represents the sign of the number. The remaining fifteen bits represent the magnitude of the number.

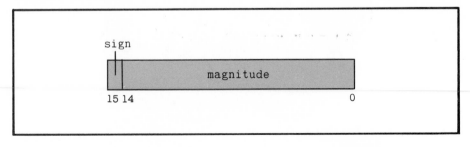

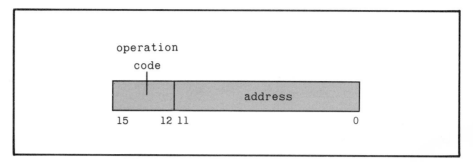

FIGURE 2-8. The format for the instructions of our computer. The leftmost four bits of a word hold the operation code, which tells the computer what operation to carry out. The rightmost twelve bits usually hold the address of a memory location that the computer will have to refer to in order to carry out the requested operation.

Not only do we have to represent the data the computer is going to manipulate, we have to represent its instructions as well. Each instruction consists of an *operation code* and an *address*. The operation code specifies the operation that the computer will carry out. The address part allows the instruction to refer to a location in main memory. If a particular instruction doesn't need to refer to any main memory location, its address part isn't used.

Figure 2-8 shows the format for instructions. As with data items, each instruction fits into one word. The leftmost four bits of the word give the operation code; the rightmost 12 bits give the address.

This subdivision works nicely with the hexadecimal notation. When an instruction is written in hexadecimal, the leftmost hex digit gives the operation code. The remaining three digits give the main-memory address. Thus for the instruction 2C0E, 2 is the operation code and C0E is the main-memory address.

Main Memory Organization. As Figure 2-9 shows, the main memory of our computer is made up of individual memory locations, each of which holds one word, 16 bits. Each memory location has an address, which consists of 12 bits or three hexadecimal digits. (Remember that the address part of each instruction occupies 12 bits or three hex digits.) With 12 bits we can represent 2^{12} or 4,096 alternatives. Therefore, our computer's memory can consist of, at most, 4,096 words. The address of the first word is 000 (hex); the address of the last word is FFF.

The Central Processing Unit. The central processor of a computer contains a small number of memory locations called registers. Some of these hold the data that the central processor is currently manipulating. Others help the central processor keep track of such crucial information as its place in the program and the results of tests it has carried out.

Figure 2-10 shows the registers of our hypothetical computer that the programmer can manipulate directly. A description of these registers is sometimes called the *programming model* of the computer. The central

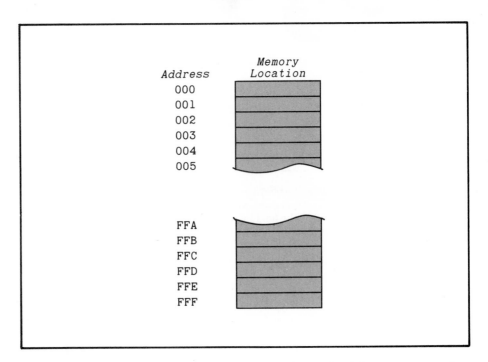

FIGURE 2-9. The main memory of our computer. The address of each location consists of 12 bits and can be represented by three hexadecimal digits. The addresses, expressed in hexadecimal, run from 000 through FFF.

processor has other registers for its own internal use, but since these are not accessible to the programmer, they are not part of the programming model.

As we see from Figure 2-10, the central processor of our computer contains exactly three registers accessible to the programmer: the *accumulator*, the *condition-code register*, and the *instruction-address register*.

The *accumulator* is analogous to the display register of a calculator. It holds one of the *operands* for each arithmetic operation, one of the values on which the operation will be performed. The other operand is in main memory at the address given in the instruction for the arithmetic operation. After the operation has been carried out, the result is stored in the accumulator. Since the accumulator must be able to hold any data item the computer can manipulate, it holds one word or 16 bits. We say that it is "16 bits wide."

Most modern computers have a number of accumulators, usually 8 or 16. This means that some of the intermediate results in a calculation can be stored in the central processor instead of in main memory. When these results are needed later in the calculation, the central processor doesn't have to take the time to fetch them from main memory.

The computer contains a *compare* instruction that compares the contents of the accumulator with the contents of a designated main-memory location. The comparison can have three possible outcomes: (1) the contents of the accumulator are less than those of the main-memory location,

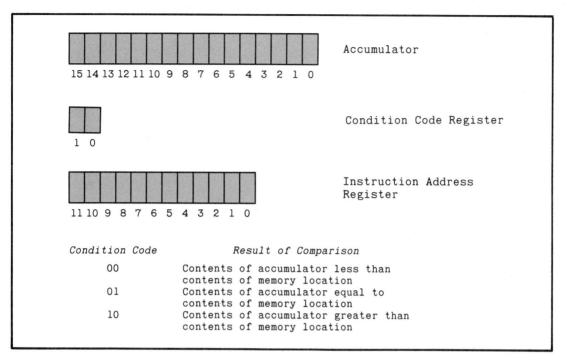

FIGURE 2-10. The central processing unit of our computer contains three registers that the programmer can manipulate directly. The accumulator holds the data that is currently being manipulated, serving somewhat the same purpose as the display on a calculator. The condition code register records the result of comparing the contents of the accumulator with that of a particular main memory location. The table at the bottom of the figure shows the meaning of the contents of the condition code register. The instruction address register contains the address of the next instruction to be executed.

(2) the contents of the two locations are equal, and (3) the contents of the accumulator are greater than those of the main-memory location.

The *condition-code register* is a two-bit register that stores the outcome of a comparison. The outcomes are coded as follows: 00 if the contents of the accumulator are less than those of the main memory location, 01 if the contents of the two are the same, and 10 if the contents of the accumulator are greater. The combination 11 isn't used. The condition codes are summarized in Figure 2-10.

The *instruction-address register* contains the address of the next instruction the computer is to execute. During the fetch part of its fetch-execute cycle, the central processor fetches the next instruction from the address contained in the instruction address register.

As soon as the instruction is fetched, the central processor adds 1 to the contents of the instruction address register. Therefore, normally, successive instructions will come from successive memory locations. However, certain instructions called *jump* instructions change the contents of the instruction address register to a value specified in the instruction, thus causing the computer to jump to some other part of its program and continue execution from there.

Since the instruction address register holds an address, and an address occupies 12 bits, the instruction address register is 12 bits wide.

The instruction-address register is also often called the *program counter*.

The Instructions. The most important part of the description of any computer is the description of its instruction set. Figure 2-11 shows the instruction set for our hypothetical computer. For each instruction the figure gives its operation code, which consists of a single hex digit. Also given is a three-letter abbreviation, called a *mnemonic**, which is easier to remember than the operation code.

The Load-and-Store Instructions. These are the instructions that load values from main memory into the accumulator and store values from the accumulator into main memory.

In our examples we will write each instruction in two ways: once as it is actually stored in the computer, with a hexadecimal operation code and address; and once in an easier-to-read form with the mnemonic in place of the hexadecimal operation code.

The *load-accumulator* instruction, LDA, copies the contents of the addressed location into the accumulator. The contents of the addressed location does not change. Thus,

1074   LDA 074

loads the contents of location 074 into the accumulator. The contents of location 074 remain unchanged.

FIGURE 2-11. The instructions for our hypothetical computer. We will usually refer to the instructions by their mnemonics, which are easier to remember than the operation codes.

Operation Code	Mnemonic	Instruction
1	LDA	load accumulator
2	STA	store accumulator
3	ADD	add
4	SUB	subtract
5	MUL	multiply
6	DIV	divide yielding integer quotient
7	MOD	divide yielding remainder
8	CMP	compare
9	JMP	unconditional jump
A	JLT	jump if less than
B	JEQ	jump if equal to
C	JGT	jump if greater than
D	IN	input
E	OUT	output
F	HALT	halt

*A *mnemonic* is anything that serves as a memory aid.

The *store-accumulator* instruction, STA, copies the contents of the accumulator into the addressed location. The contents of the accumulator remain unchanged. Thus,

213F   STA 13F

stores the contents of the accumulator into location 13F.

The Arithmetic Instructions. The arithmetic instructions are ADD, SUB, MUL, DIV, and MOD. There are two division instructions, DIV and MOD. DIV yields the integer quotient; MOD yields the remainder.

For each instruction, one of the numbers on which the operation is to be carried out is in the accumulator; the other is in the memory location specified in the instruction. The result of the operation is always stored in the accumulator; the contents of the memory location always remain unchanged.

For subtraction, the contents of the memory location are subtracted from the contents of the accumulator. For division, the contents of the memory location are divided into the contents of the accumulator.

For example, the instruction

3402   ADD 402

adds the contents of location 402 to the contents of the accumulator. The result goes into the accumulator; the contents of location 402 remain unchanged.

The instruction

43CD   SUB 3CD

subtracts the contents of location 3CD from the contents of the accumulator. The result goes into the accumulator; the contents of location 3CD are unchanged.

The instruction

613F   DIV 13F

divides the contents of location 13F into the contents of the accumulator. The result goes into the accumulator; the contents of location 13F remain unchanged.

Real computers often have a single instruction that yields both the quotient and the remainder of a division. Because one instruction produces two results, however, there must be two data registers in the CPU for storing the two results. Since our computer only has one data register in the CPU—the accumulator—each instruction can produce only one result. Hence we need two division instructions, one for the quotient and one for the remainder.

Real computers can carry out many data-manipulating operations besides the arithmetic operations. At a minimum, they can do the logical and shift operations described earlier in this chapter. For simplicity, however, the data manipulations our hypothetical computer can carry out were restricted to the arithmetical operations.

The Compare Instruction. The *compare* instruction and the *jump* instructions are crucial for allowing the computer to make decisions—to choose one set of instructions or another to execute depending on the conditions that exist at the time the program is executed. The *compare* instruction, CMP, compares the contents of the accumulator with that of the designated memory location; it records in the condition-code register whether the contents of the accumulator were less than, equal to, or greater than the contents of the main-memory location.

Thus, the instruction

8134   CMP 134

compares the contents of the accumulator with the contents of location 134; it records in the condition-code register whether the contents of the accumulator are less than, equal to, or greater than those of location 134.

The Jump Instructions. The *unconditional jump* instruction, JMP, loads its address part into the instruction-address register. This causes the computer to take its next instruction from the specified address. The computer jumps to the point in its program specified in the *jump* instruction and continues execution from that point. Thus,

9431   JMP 431

causes the computer to jump to location 431 and continue execution of the program from there.

JLT, JEQ, and JGT are the *conditional jump* instructions. For each one, the jump takes place only if the contents of the condition-code register have a particular value. If the contents of the condition-code register do not have the required value, the jump does not take place, and the computer continues execution with the instruction in the memory location following the one that contains the jump instruction.

JLT jumps only if the contents of the condition-code register are 00 (less than); JEQ jumps only if the contents are 01 (equal to); and JGT jumps only if the contents are 10 (greater than).

Thus,

A305   JLT 305

causes the computer to jump to location 305 in the program only if the contents of the condition-code register are 00 (less than). Otherwise, the computer continues with the instruction in the memory location following the one that contained the *jump* instruction A305.

The Input and Output Instructions. The *input* instruction, IN, transfers data from the computer's single input device to main memory; the *output* instruction, OUT, transfers data from main memory to the computer's single output device.

Thus,

D205   IN 205

reads one number from the input device and stores it in location 205. The instruction

E157   OUT 157

sends the number in location 157 to the computer's output device. The contents of location 157 remain unchanged.

The *halt* instruction, HALT, causes the CPU to stop fetching and executing instructions and go into a standby mode. The address part of the HALT instruction is ignored. Thus,

F000   HALT

causes the central processing unit to stop fetching and executing instructions.

A Sample Program. Figure 2-12 shows an example of a program for our computer. The program computes the greatest common divisor of two positive integers using the algorithm given in Chapter 1.

The program uses four locations to hold data:

Location	*Address*
LARGER	00F
SMALLER	010
REMAINDER	011
ZERO	012

The locations LARGER, SMALLER, and REMAINDER correspond to the three "boxes" for holding data that were introduced in connection with the algorithm (and we now realize that those boxes are nothing other than memory locations). The memory location 012 holds the constant 0, which is needed for a comparison. We name this location ZERO.

The first two instructions of the program input values for LARGER and SMALLER and store them in main memory:

D00F   IN LARGER
D010   IN SMALLER

The next step is to see if the contents of SMALLER are 0; if they are, the computer will jump to location 00D, which contains instructions for

Address	Instruction or Data	Mnemonic	Explanation
000	D00F	IN LARGER	Input value for LARGER
001	D010	IN SMALLER	Input value for SMALLER
002	1010	LDA SMALLER	Compare SMALLER ...
003	8012	CMP ZERO	... with ZERO ...
004	B00D	JEQ 00D	... and exit loop if equal
005	100F	LDA LARGER	Divide LARGER ...
006	7010	MOD SMALLER	... by SMALLER ...
007	2011	STA REMAINDER	... and save remainder
008	1010	LDA SMALLER	Copy value of SMALLER ...
009	200F	STA LARGER	... into LARGER
00A	1011	LDA REMAINDER	Copy value of REMAINDER ...
00B	2010	STA SMALLER	... into SMALLER
00C	9002	JMP 002	Jump to start of loop
00D	E00F	OUT LARGER	Output value of LARGER
00E	F000	HALT	Terminate execution
00F	0000	LARGER	Storage for LARGER
010	0000	SMALLER	Storage for SMALLER
011	0000	REMAINDER	Storage for REMAINDER
012	0000	ZERO	Storage for constant 0

FIGURE 2-12. A program for computing the greatest common divisor of two nonnegative integers. The first column gives the addresses of the memory locations holding the program. The second column gives the contents of those locations. The third column gives the mnemonics for the instructions (locations 000-00E) and for the memory locations used to store data (locations 00F-012).

outputting the value of LARGER and halting the computer. If the value of SMALLER is not 0, the computer does not jump but continues with the following instructions:

1010	LDA SMALLER
8012	CMP ZERO
B00D	JEQ 00D

Now come the repeated instructions from the algorithm. We divide the contents of LARGER by the contents of SMALLER and store the remainder in REMAINDER. Then we store the contents of SMALLER in LARGER and the contents of REMAINDER in SMALLER:

100F	LDA LARGER
7010	MOD SMALLER
2011	STA REMAINDER
1010	LDA SMALLER
200F	STA LARGER
1011	LDA REMAINDER
2010	STA SMALLER

Now we must arrange for the seven instructions just given to be repeated as long as the contents of SMALLER are not 0. We do this by having the computer jump back to location 002, the part of the program that tests whether or not the contents of SMALLER are 0:

9002   JMP 002

As we have seen, the instructions beginning at location 002 compare the contents of SMALLER with 0; if the two are equal, then the computer jumps to location 00D. Beginning at 00D are instructions for outputting the value of LARGER—the answer—and halting the computer

E00F   OUT LARGER
F000   HALT

In this program, note particularly how the unconditional *jump* instruction is used to jump back to a previous instruction, thus creating a loop. Also note how the *compare* and conditional *jump* instructions are used to exit from the loop when a given condition is satisfied. These are common programming techniques.

Review Questions

1. What is a *computer system?*

2. Distinguish between *hardware* and *software.*

3. Name the hardware components common to most computers, and give a brief description of each.

4. What is a *microprocessor?* What is the *microprocessor revolution?*

5. Contrast the characteristics and uses of main and auxiliary memory. What are the two most widely used kinds of auxiliary memory?

6. Give two examples showing how the parts out of which a machine is made influence the way it represents information.

7. What is a *bit?*

8. What is a *binary code?* Give two examples of binary codes.

9. What is the *ASCII code?* How are the characters $\times$, 5, $, and + coded in ASCII? How is a blank space coded in ASCII?

10. Give two statements that characterize the decimal number system. Give the corresponding statements for the binary number system.

11. How can we make it clear whether 101 is the binary representation of five or the decimal representation of one hundred and one?

12. Describe how numbers with fractional parts can be represented in binary notation?

13. Contrast the addition and multiplication tables for the binary system with those for the decimal system.

14. Describe four logical operations and give one application of each.

15. Describe the two shift operations discussed in this chapter.

16. Why do programmers use octal and hexadecimal notation?

17. Describe the octal and hexadecimal systems.

18. What is a *word*?

19. Describe one way of representing signed numbers in a computer?

20. For the computer described in this chapter, what is the purpose of the *accumulator?* The *condition-code register?* The *instruction-address register?*

21. Describe the instructions that allow a computer to make decisions.

Exercises

1. Using the table for the ASCII code given in this chapter, show how a short message would be coded in ASCII. Don't forget to code punctuation marks and blank spaces as well as letters and numbers.

2. Find the decimal value corresponding to each of the following binary numbers:

(a) 110   (b) 1101
(c) 110011   (d) 10101101

3. Work each of the following problems in binary arithmetic:

(a) 0101 + 1010   (b) 0111 + 0110
(c) 0111 − 0101   (d) 1000 − 0011
(e) 1010 × 0110   (f) 1111 × 1111
(g) 11001000 ÷ 1101   (h) 10001100 ÷ 1111

4. Carry out each of the following logical and shift operations:

(a) 1001 OR 0101   (b) 1110 AND 0100
(c) 1010 XOR 0110   (d) NOT 1001
(e) SHL 1111   (f) SHR 0010

5. Convert each of the following binary values to octal:

(a) 110101   (b) 010111010
(c) 110111110   (d) 101010100001

6. Convert each of the following octal values to binary:

(a) 57   (b) 615
(c) 274   (d) 7136

7. Convert each of the following binary values to hexadecimal:

(a) 10011110   (b) 100111000001
(c) 001100011101   (d) 1110100111011100

8. Convert each of the following hexadecimal values to binary:

(a) AB

(b) F3D

(c) 2EB

(d) 5A3C

9. Write a program for the computer described in this chapter that will input five numbers and output their sum.

10. Write a program for the computer described in this chapter that will input the numerator and denominator of a fraction and output the numerator and denominator of that fraction reduced to its lowest terms.

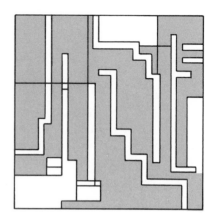

Chapter 3

Computer Software

The software of a computer system, you recall, consists of the programs that direct the hardware.

There are two kinds of software: *systems software* and *applications software*. Systems software consists of programs that help people write and execute other programs. Applications software consists of programs for doing all the other jobs unrelated to computer programming, such as making out payrolls, playing games, or tracking spacecraft.

This chapter is devoted to systems software. In the following chapters we will be looking at many of the techniques used to write applications software.

3.1 Programming Languages and Language Processors

To get a computer system to execute our programs, we must phrase those programs in a language the system can understand. Languages intended for this purpose are known as *programming languages*. Most programming languages are not directly intelligible to the computer hardware. The computer system can process programs written in these languages only with the aid of systems programs called *language processors*.

Machine Language. The central processing unit of a computer system can only execute instructions expressed in a binary-coded form known as *machine code* or *machine language*. Programmers usually express machine codes in either octal or hexadecimal notation, depending on which is more convenient for the machine in question.

We are already familiar with one machine language; in the previous chapter we looked at the machine language for a simple, hypothetical computer. In fact, we wrote a program in machine language for that computer—a program to compute the greatest common divisor of two numbers. Let's recall the first few instructions of that program, expressed in hexadecimal:

D00F
D010
1010
8012

We notice at once the worst problem of machine language: obscurity. Only by looking at the table of instruction codes given in the previous chapter can we see that the operation code D instructs the computer to input data, that 1 instructs it to transfer a value from main memory to its accumulator, or that 8 causes it to compare the contents of its accumulator with a value in main memory.

And what about the address parts of these instructions? What is the significance of the data stored in location 00F or location 010 or location 012? The machine code gives us no clue, and we would be unlikely to figure out the answer ourselves without turning back to the discussion in Chapter 2. It's extremely difficult for one machine-language programmer to figure out, just from looking at the program, what the machine-language programmer who wrote the program had in mind.

Another problem: Almost every instruction in a machine-language program contains an address referring to a location in main memory. If a program has to be revised—and it's common to have to revise programs to meet changing needs—then the locations in which the various instructions and data items are stored will likely change as well. This means that even a small revision may make it necessary to change the address part of almost every instruction in the program.

Finally, machine-language programs are phrased in computer-oriented terms. They refer to such features of the internal construction and operation of a computer as the accumulator, the condition-code register, operation codes, and main-memory addresses. We would prefer to state our instructions in the same terms we would ordinarily use to tell another person how to solve the problem that the computer is to solve.

Assembly Language. We can make machine language a bit easier to work with by using meaningful mnemonics in place of the octal or hexadecimal codes for operations and memory locations. The result is known as *assembly language*, since the mnemonics specify component parts that can be assembled into machine-language instructions.

We are already somewhat familiar with assembly language, since in the previous chapter we used mnemonics such as LDA, ADD, LARGER, and SMALLER to help us understand the machine language of our simple computer. Assembly language is just a systematic use of such mnemonics.

Figure 3–1 shows an assembly-language program for computing greatest common divisors. This program corresponds to the machine-language program given in Chapter 2. The caption to the figure explains some of the details of assembly language. You aren't expected to learn these details, however, but merely to note that the assembly language program is easier to understand than a list of octal or hexadecimal machine codes.

The central processor of a computer cannot execute assembly language. It can only execute machine codes. Before an assembly-language program can be executed by a computer, it must be translated into machine language.

Fortunately, the computer itself can do the translation. After all, a computer is a general-purpose, information-processing machine, and translating from one programming language to another is a valid information-processing task. As with any other task, the computer must be controlled by an appropriate program in order to carry out the translation.

A program that translates from assembly language to machine language is called an *assembler*. An assembler is an example of a *translator*. It is

FIGURE 3-1. The listing of an assembly-language program for computing greatest common divisors. The first two columns give the machine-language program: the first column gives the address of the memory locations holding the instructions and the second column gives their contents. These columns are produced by the assembler, not the human programmer. Mnemonics, called labels, are defined in the third column. Each label represents the address of the instruction or data item next to which it appears. Thus LOOP represents the address 002, FINISH the address 00D, and so on. DW (define word) instructs the assembler to reserve the indicated number of words of memory. DC (define constant) instructs the assembler to reserve a word containing the specified constant (zero in this case).

```
000 D00F                   IN   LARGER      INPUT VALUE FOR LARGER
001 D010                   IN   SMALLER     INPUT VALUE FOR SMALLER
002 1010    LOOP           LDA  SMALLER     COMPARE SMALLER ...
003 8012                   CMP  ZERO        ... WITH ZERO ...
004 B00D                   JEQ  FINISH      ... AND EXIT LOOP IF EQUAL
005 100F                   LDA  LARGER      DIVIDE LARGER ...
006 7010                   MOD  SMALLER     ... BY SMALLER ...
007 2011                   STA  REMAINDER   ... AND SAVE THE REMAINDER
008 1010                   LDA  SMALLER     COPY VALUE OF SMALLER ...
009 200F                   STA  LARGER      ... INTO LARGER
00A 1011                   LDA  REMAINDER   COPY VALUE OF REMAINDER ...
00B 2010                   STA  SMALLER     ... INTO SMALLER
00C 9002                   JMP  LOOP        JUMP TO START OF LOOP
00D E00F    FINISH         OUT  LARGER      OUTPUT VALUE OF LARGER
00E F000                   HALT             TERMINATE EXECUTION
00F         LARGER         DW   1           STORAGE FOR LARGER
010         SMALLER        DW   1           STORAGE FOR SMALLER
011         REMAINDER      DW   1           STORAGE FOR REMAINDER
012 0000    ZERO           DC   0           STORAGE FOR CONSTANT 0
                           END
```

also an example of a language processor. And finally, it is our first example of a systems program.

Assembly language is not the last word in programming languages, however. It's nothing more than sugar-coated machine language, and it retains many of the problems of the latter. In assembly language, we must still phrase our programs in terms of machine-oriented concepts such as central processor registers and main-memory locations, rather than in terms of the ideas most natural to the problem or to the user. Also, each instruction that we want to give the computer still has to be broken down into very small steps, such as individual loads, stores, additions, and subtractions.

Higher Level Languages. To avoid the problems of assembly language and machine language, people have devised a number of *higher-level* or *user-oriented* languages. These languages allow programmers to instruct the computer in the terms most natural for a particular problem, user, or field of endeavor.

Because there are so many problems, users, and fields of endeavor, there are a large number of higher level languages, around 170, in fact. Fortunately for students of programming, only a few of these, around 10, are in really widespread use.

Among the most popular programming languages are BASIC, COBOL, FORTRAN, and Pascal.

BASIC—Beginner's All-purpose Symbolic Instruction Code—was originally designed as an extremely simple language for teaching programming to beginners. Now BASIC is the most widely used programming language in education. Because of its simplicity, it is easy to implement on small computers, so many of the small computers now used by individuals, professionals, and small businesses are programmed in BASIC.

COBOL—Common Business Oriented Language—is the most widely used programming language in business data processing. COBOL is oriented toward the processing of the large files of data that occur in business applications. The language caters to business users by allowing instructions to be stated in the English-like words and phrases business people prefer rather than as mathematical formulas.

FORTRAN—Formula Translator—is one of the oldest and most well-known programming languages. As its name suggests, FORTRAN caters to scientists, mathematicians, engineers, and others who must work with formulas. For many years FORTRAN was the only higher level language available on many computer systems, so just about every imaginable computer application has at one time or another probably been programmed in FORTRAN.

Pascal. This general-purpose language, which is named after the French philosopher and mathematician Blaise Pascal, has recently become extremely popular for teaching computer science, edging out old standbys like FORTRAN and BASIC. Consequently, the programming language appendix of this book, which in the first edition covered FORTRAN, now covers Pascal.

Compilers and Interpreters. Of course, a computer's central processor can no more directly execute a program written in a higher level language than it can execute an assembly-language program. As with assembly language, a program in a higher level language can be executed only through a language processor.

We can translate a program in a higher level language into machine language, just as we did for assembly language. A translator for a higher level language is known as a *compiler.* The program to be translated (or compiled) is called the *source program;* the translated machine-language program is called the *object program*.

Another approach to getting a program in a higher level language executed is to use an *interpreter* program. Like a compiler, an interpreter accepts a source program as input. But instead of translating the source program into machine language, the interpreter carries out the instructions in the source program. The interpreter executes the source program in exactly the same way that the central processing unit executes a machine-language program.

The following analogy may help make clear the difference between compilers and interpreters. Suppose we wish to talk to a person who doesn't speak our language. We have three choices: (1) we can learn the other person's language, (2) we can get someone to translate what we say into the other person's language, or (3) we can teach the other person our language.

Choice 1, learning the other person's language, corresponds to programming in machine language. Choice 2, having our remarks translated, corresponds to using a compiler. And choice 3, teaching the other person our language, corresponds to using an interpreter.

Figure 3–2 contrasts compilers and interpreters. A compiler takes a source program in a higher level language as input and produces a machine-language object program as output. An interpreter takes as input the source program and the data the source program is to process. The output from the interpreter is the output produced when the source program is executed.

(Both compilers and interpreters may produce additional helpful information to the programmer, such as a printout, or listing, of the source program and messages advising the programmer of errors detected in the source program.)

Interpreters are often more convenient to use than compilers, if only because with an interpreter the program is executed in one step, whereas with compilation we need two steps—translation and execution. Also, compilation requires the computer system to store both the source program and the object program, while for interpretation there is no object program; only the source program has to be stored. This last feature often makes interpreters preferable to compilers for very small computers.

On the other hand, an interpreted program may execute 10 to 100

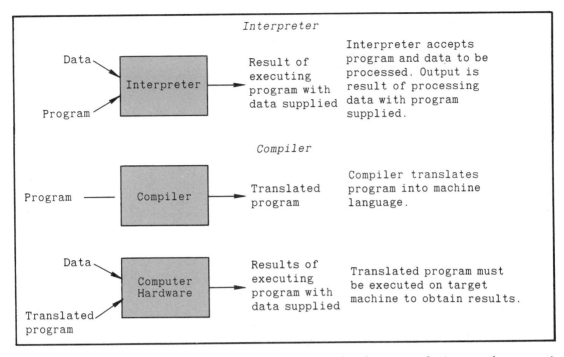

FIGURE 3-2. An interpreter produces the results of executing the interpreted program. A compiler produces a machine-language program, which must then be executed by the computer hardware to obtain the desired results.

times slower than a translated one. The reason is that most programs call for some statements to be executed repeatedly, perhaps thousands of times. A compiler translates each statement only once, regardless of how many times the translated statement will eventually be executed. An interpreter, however, must analyze a statement every time it is executed. An interpreter may analyze the same statement many thousands of times.

Both compilers and interpreters are examples of language processors.

3.2 The Operating System

The operating system is a systems program that oversees the flow of programs and data through the computer system. Other names for the operating system are *supervisor*, *monitor*, and *master control program*.

In older computer systems, the computer operator controlled the computer system directly using the computer's front panel controls. In modern computer systems, the operator controls the system indirectly by making requests of the operating system. As a result, the elaborate control panels of early computers are rapidly disappearing. The controls of a modern computer often consist of no more than a switch for turning the computer on, a button that causes the operating system to be loaded into memory and executed, and a computer terminal through which the operator can communicate with the operating system.

A computer user can also give commands to the operating system. Commands to the operating system are known as *system commands*. Punched cards containing system commands are called *control cards*.

A machine-language program (which could have been compiled from a higher level language) can also contain commands for the operating system.

The exact mechanism by which the program transmits commands to the operating system varies from one computer to another. One commonly used method depends on the fact that for many machines there are values of the operation code that do not correspond to any machine-language commands. These otherwise unused operation codes can represent commands for the operating system.

When the central processor encounters an operation code that does not represent a machine-language command, it transfers control to the operating system. The operating system analyzes the operation code, carries out the command that it represents, then returns control to the user's program.

One advantage of this technique is that commands for the operating system are represented in exactly the same way as machine-language commands; the programmer doesn't have to distinguish between the two. Commands that are included in the machine language of a more expensive model of a computer may be interpreted by the operations system on a less expensive model.

Operating systems can support two methods of interacting with computers: *batch processing* and *interactive processing*.

In *batch processing*, you submit to the computer system a *job*, which consists of a series of system commands together with programs to be executed and data to be processed. (The system commands can also refer programs and data already stored in the computer system's auxiliary memory.) The operating system accepts your job when you submit it and stores it in auxiliary memory along with the jobs of other users. Your job is executed when the operating system gets around to it; you must return later to pick up the output produced when your job was executed.

Batch jobs can be submitted from computer terminals or they can be punched on cards. In the latter case, each user punches a job deck consisting of all the control cards, program cards, and data cards the system will need. The user leaves the job deck at the computer center for execution. Periodically, computer center personnel collect the job decks that have been submitted and feed them into a card reader. The printed output produced when a job is executed, together with the job deck, is placed where it can be picked up by the user when he or she returns to the computer center.

In *interactive processing*, each user communicates with the computer system via a computer terminal. Each user engages in a conversation with the operating system or whatever program the user is running. When the user gives a command or enters data, the program responds. When the user gives another command or enters more data, the program responds to that, and so on. The program's response to a particular data item or command may determine what data item or command the user will want to enter next.

Batch processing is like leaving your dirty clothes at a laundry and coming back to pick them up after they have been washed. Interactive processing is like using a do-it-yourself laundry, where you are personally involved in every aspect of washing and drying.

In contrast to the situation with laundries, interactive processing is ordinarily far more convenient than batch processing. The user can see the results of each command to a program before going on to the next command. If the user makes a mistake, it can be detected and corrected at once. Computer applications in which interactive processing is essential include word processing, computer-assisted instruction, and game playing. It is most desirable for writing and testing programs, even if the program in question, once developed, will be used for batch processing.

The following is a list of the responsibilities of a modern operating system:

- At the request of a user, the system loads a machine-language program from auxiliary memory and executes it. The operating system must see that the program has access to the input data specified by the user and that its output is sent to the destination (say, a particular printer) requested by the user.

- The system arranges for source programs to be interpreted or to be translated and executed. The degree of support that an operating system provides for translators and interpreters has an enormous impact on the convenience of using higher level languages on that system. In the ideal case, the computer system should simply seem to understand the higher level languages, and the user should have to give as little thought as possible to the details of interpretation or translation.

- The system maintains program libraries in auxiliary memory. Programs stored in the libraries can be called forth and executed by system commands or control cards.

- The system creates and maintains named data files in auxiliary memory. The operating system keeps a directory showing where each file is stored in auxiliary memory, so users can refer to files by their names and leave it up to the operating system to find them.

- The system manages the flow of data from input devices and to output devices. The operating system can handle input and output devices in the same way that it does files in auxiliary memory. Thus, a program can be written without regard to whether its input, say, will come from and input device such as a card reader or from a file stored on tape or disk.

- The system maintains security by making sure that programs and data files are used only by those who are authorized to do so. Computer security becomes more important all the time as more and more personal and financial data is stored in computer systems.

- The system keeps an account of the computer system resources that each person uses, such as how long that person's jobs occupy the central processor or how much data that person has stored in auxiliary memory. Each user can then be billed for those resources.

■ The system allocates computer system resources based on priorities. Users with high priorities get the first chance at scarce resources.

■ The system arranges for more than one program to execute at the same time and for these programs to share the system's resources. We will discuss this function in more detail later in the chapter.

Of course, not all of these functions are appropriate for every computer system. Such functions as accounting and security are essential for a computer system having many users but would be out of place on a small system used by a single person.

3.3 Virtual and Multilevel Machines

Virtual Machines. When we write a program in a higher level language and the computer system follows the instructions in our program, as far as we are concerned the computer system understood the higher level language. It's of no concern to us whether the central processor can execute commands in the higher level language (not likely!), whether our program was first translated into machine language, or whether our program was executed under the control of an interpreter program.

To all appearances, we are faced with a machine that can understand the higher level language we are using. People sometimes name such a machine after the language it understands. We can speak of a BASIC machine, which understands BASIC; a FORTRAN machine, which understands FORTRAN; a Pascal machine, which understands Pascal; and so on.

Each of these "programming-language machines" consists, of course, not of hardware alone, but hardware in combination with a translator or interpreter for the language in question. And the translator or interpreter will require a substantial assist from the operating system in order to perform its duties, so we should consider the operating system to be part of the programming-language machine as well.

We use the adjective *virtual* for any part of a computer system that could conceivably be a hardware component but is actually realized through a combination of hardware and software. A machine realized through hardware alone is called a *physical machine*. Our BASIC machine, FORTRAN machine, and so on are *virtual machines*, since they are realized by the computer hardware in combination with a translator or interpreter and the operating system.

The operating system itself implements a virtual machine, since it provides operators, users, and programmers with commands that are not available from the unassisted hardware. We can summarize the reasons for using an operating system by saying that an operating system implements a virtual machine that is far more convenient to use than the underlying physical machine.

In fact, to come right down to it, we can think of any program as implementing a virtual machine. For example, we can think of the program we wrote in the last chapter for computing greatest common divisors as implementing a "greatest-common-divisor machine." And why not? There's nothing in the hardware of our computer that has anything to do with computing greatest common divisors. Yet once we place our greatest-common-divisor program in the computer's memory and set the computer to executing it, we have a machine that will compute the greatest common divisor of any two numbers we provide—a greatest-common-divisor machine.

To summarize: Every program defines a virtual machine, whose behavior is the behavior that the computer displays when it is executing the program. We will refer to the hardware machine on which the virtual machine executes as the *underlying physical machine*.

The programs that implement a virtual machine are sometimes stored in *read-only memory*, or *ROM*. The contents of read-only memory are permanent and cannot be changed by the user. Software that is permanently installed in read-only memory is called *firmware*. For instance, the computers used in consumer products such as cameras and television sets have their programs in firmware. Small computers sometimes have a BASIC interpreter in firmware.

When the programs are in firmware, it may be difficult for a user to decide whether a particular machine is physical or virtual. Here are two examples of machines you have used without suspecting them of being virtual:

Pocket Calculators. Pressing a key on a pocket calculator causes a built-in microprocessor to execute part of a firmware program. Each key causes a different part of the program to be executed. The underlying physical machine can only carry out relatively simple operations, such as adding two single digits, like 5 and 4, or shifting all the digits of a number one place to the right or left. Complicated operations such as multiplications, divisions, and square roots require long sequences of the simple operations that the microprocessor can carry out. The firmware program determines what sequence of operations will be carried out for each key that is pressed.

Microprogrammed Computers. Sometimes the instruction set of a computer is implemented by means of a firmware program executing on a simpler physical machine. Programs used for this purpose are called *microprograms*; the technique of implementing a computer's instruction set in this way is called *microprogramming*. Without consulting the manufacturer's technical manuals, it's impossible for a computer user to tell whether or not a particular computer is microprogrammed.

Multilevel Machines. So far, we have assumed that every virtual machine is realized through a program executing on an underlying physical machine. But the underlying machine need not be physical. It can be a virtual machine, implemented by a program executing on some other machine. And the "other machine" can itself be a virtual machine, implemented by a program executing on still another (physical or virtual) machine, and so on.

In short, we can think of a complicated machine as structured into levels, as shown in Figure 3–3. The lowest level is a physical machine. Each of the higher levels corresponds to a virtual machine, implemented by a program executed by the next lower level.

Users view such a multilevel machine from the top down. That is, the top level is the one most visible to users, and for some machines it is the

FIGURE 3-3. A machine structured into levels. The bottom level is the physical machine. Every other level is a virtual machine realized by means of a program that is executed by the machine on the next lower level.

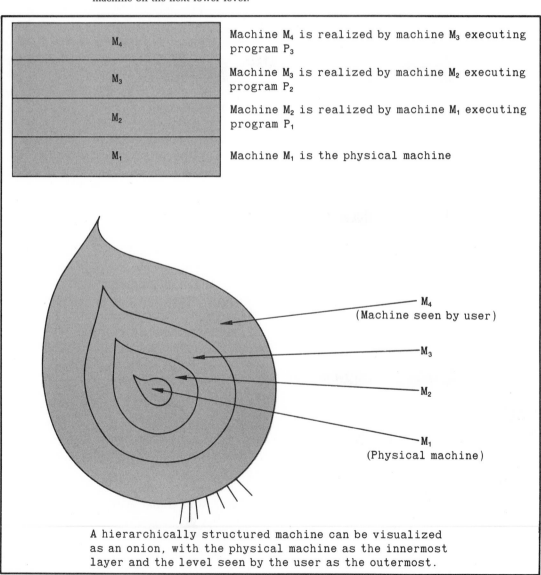

M$_4$	Machine M$_4$ is realized by machine M$_3$ executing program P$_3$
M$_3$	Machine M$_3$ is realized by machine M$_2$ executing program P$_2$
M$_2$	Machine M$_2$ is realized by machine M$_1$ executing program P$_1$
M$_1$	Machine M$_1$ is the physical machine

M$_4$
(Machine seen by user)

M$_3$

M$_2$

M$_1$
(Physical machine)

A hierarchically structured machine can be visualized as an onion, with the physical machine as the innermost layer and the level seen by the user as the outermost.

only level visible to users. For this reason, we can picture a multilevel machine as an onion, as shown in Figure 3–3. The top-level machine is on the outside for all to see. The bottom-level physical machine is hidden away deep down in the center of the onion.

Figure 3–4 shows the level structure of a modern computer system. The machine-language level is the one we discussed in Chapter 2. Each of the other levels has been discussed, or at least mentioned, in this chapter.

For most computers these levels aren't impassable barriers. That is users can write their own programs, even in machine language if desired. Some computers even allow users to write microprograms for the bottom-level physical machine, thus redefining the computer's instruction set. A level that allows access to the levels below it is said to be *transparent*.

3.4 Processes

For a small computer, it is perfectly reasonable for only one person at a time to use the machine, just as only one person at a time can use a typewriter, a calculator, or an office copier.

A large, expensive computer system must serve many people, however, and it is far more convenient for all concerned if a number of people can work with the computer at the same time, instead of everyone having to wait in line for sole possession of the machine. We want to arrange matters so that many different activities can proceed simultaneously on a single computer system, all of them sharing the resources of the system, such as the central processor and main memory.

To realize this kind of sharing, we must be able to stop a program at any point in its execution to give another program its turn at some system resource. We can best understand the problems of stopping and starting an executing program by developing the idea of a *process*.

Let's begin by considering a program being executed by the central

FIGURE 3-4. The level structure of a modern computer system.

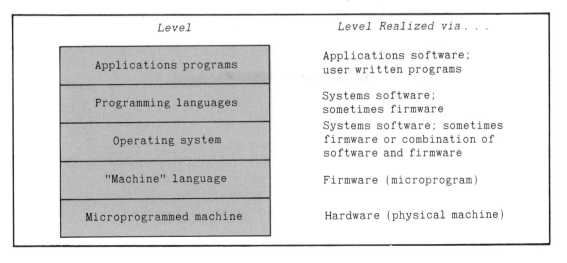

Level	Level Realized via . . .
Applications programs	Applications software; user written programs
Programming languages	Systems software; sometimes firmware
Operating system	Systems software; sometimes firmware or combination of software and firmware
"Machine" language	Firmware (microprogram)
Microprogrammed machine	Hardware (physical machine)

processor of a computer system. Suppose we stop the central processor after it has finished executing one instruction and before it starts to execute the next one. What will we find in main memory and the central processor's registers? Or, to put it another way, what *must* be in main memory and in the central processor's registers so that, when we start the central processor up again, execution of the program will continue from where it left off, exactly as if no stop had taken place?

For the central processor to be able to pick up where it left off, we need three things:

- *The program*, of course.

- *The data the program is processing.* This data may be in the central processor's registers, in main memory, or in auxiliary memory. If this data were lost, it would be as if you were in the middle of working a problem out on the blackboard, and while you were out of the room for a moment, somebody erased the board.

- *The address of the next instruction to be executed.* This is what keeps the central processor's place in the program being executed. Since this address "points out" the next instruction to be executed, it is often referred to as the *pointer* to the next instruction. When a program is actually being executed, the pointer to the next instruction resides in the central processor's instruction-address register.

These three components—program, data, and pointer to the next instruction—make up a process. Figure 3–5 illustrates the three components of a process.

The most important property of a process is that its execution may be stopped at any time and, when restarted later, will proceed exactly as if nothing had happened. The components of a process that occupy main memory and the central processor's registers do not have to remain there while execution is halted. They could be moved to auxiliary memory, for instance. As long as all three components are restored before execution resumes, execution will proceed exactly as if it had not been interrupted.

We say that a process is *active* when it is actually being executed and *inactive* otherwise. The components of an active process reside in the central processor's registers, in main memory, and perhaps partially in auxiliary memory. An inactive process may reside anywhere, but it will usually be found in either main or auxiliary memory.

A process consists of a program being executed by a machine, and we already know that this combination defines a new virtual machine. Indeed, a process has many features reminiscent of a machine or even a living organism. A process leads an independent existence, interacting with users through input and output devices or exchanging messages with other processes. A process can even create offspring, which will carry out their assigned tasks and report back to the parent process. With tongue only slightly in cheek, people have referred to a process as "an organism that lives in a computer system."

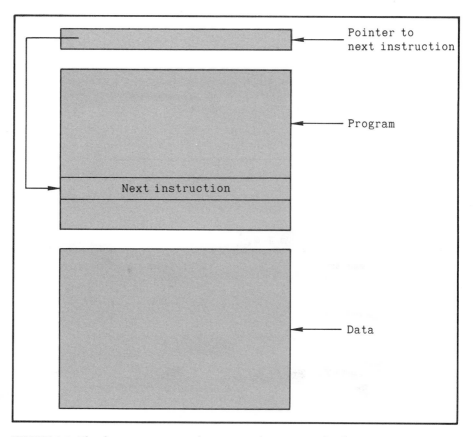

FIGURE 3-5. The three components of a process: the program, the data it is processing, and a pointer to the next instruction to be executed.

The machine that executes a process is called a *processor*. Often this is the central processing unit of a computer system. It could be a virtual machine, however, implemented by means of an interpreter. Also, a computer system may have a number of hardware processors, in which case we just speak of *processors*, since we cannot single out any one of them as being central.

If a computer system does have a single central processor, then only one process can be active at a time. But there may be many inactive processes present in main and auxiliary memory. We can arrange for the central processor to switch from one process to another in round-robin fashion, executing a few hundred instructions of one process, then a few hundred instructions of the next, and so on until each process has had its turn at the central processor. Almost all large computer systems, and many small ones, use this principle in one form or another.

If we don't look too closely at what is going on, it will seem that all the processes are being executed simultaneously. Only when we investigate the fine details do we notice that the central processor is actually being switched from one process to the next. Usually, we find it more informative to concentrate on the processes and think of them as being executed simultaneously, instead of trying to follow the central processor as it jumps from one unrelated process to another.

We already know that we can think of a computer system as a multi-level machine. The idea of a process provides us with another point of view: We can also think of a computer system as a collection of simultaneously executing processes. Of course, somewhere a physical machine is necessary to execute the processes. But the way the system appears to its users is determined by the features of the virtual machines defined by the simultaneously executing processes, not by the underlying hardware.

3.5 Applications to Computer Systems

Interrupts. An interrupt takes place when the central processor receives a special signal, called an *interrupt request*, indicating some event has occurred that needs immediate attention. In response to the interrupt request, the central processor deactivates the process it is currently executing and activates another one designed to handle the situation that caused the interrupt.

For instance, an input device that has data for the system can request an interrupt. The interrupt causes the central processor to switch from the process it is executing to a "device handler" process that obtains the data from the input device and transfers it to main memory. This accomplished, the process that was active when the interrupt occurred can be resumed.

Interrupts allow the computer system to respond to events that occur at unpredictable times without having to stand idle waiting for them to occur. A secretary, who must answer the phone as well as do other work is in a similar situation. The secretary does other work until the phone rings. When it does, he or she takes the call and then resumes the work at hand.

Ordinarily, it is the operating system that responds to interrupts. After the operating system has done whatever is necessary to handle the condition that caused the interrupt, it determines whether to reactivate the process that was suspended by the interrupt or whether to activate some other process.

Multiprogramming. Suppose we want to execute a number of programs at the same time on a computer system having a single central processing unit. The operating system can create a separate process for each program, then switch the central processor from one process to another as has already been described. This technique is known as *multiprogramming*.

The operating system supervises the sharing of the central processor among the processes. Before giving control of the central processor to a particular process, the operating system sets a hardware timer, a kind of alarm clock, to interrupt after a certain *time slice* or *time quantum* has elapsed. When time runs out, the interrupt returns control to the operating system, which then gives another process its turn at the central processor. Typical time quanta would be in the range of .01 to 100 seconds, the value chosen depending very much on the nature of the system and the uses for which it is intended.

Since peripheral devices are mechanical rather than electronic, they operate much more slowly than the central processor. It would be very wasteful to have the central processor stand idle while a process was waiting for a peripheral device to complete its work. Instead, while one process is waiting on a peripheral, the central processor should be working on another process.

For this reason, users' processes aren't allowed to control peripheral devices directly. Requests for input, output, and access to auxiliary memory must be channeled through the operating system.

When the operating system receives a request for a peripheral device, it directs the device to initiate the requested operation. At the same time, it removes the process making the request from those waiting in line for their turns at the central processor. As long as the process is waiting on the peripheral device, it loses its turns at the central processor.

When the peripheral device has completed the requested operation, it notifies the operating system via an interrupt. The operating system puts the process that made the request back in line so it can resume taking its turns at the central processor.

Time Sharing. Time sharing is a form of interactive processing in which many terminals—hundreds, perhaps—are connected to the same computer. The computer system serves all the users at the same time, so that each user seems to have the undivided attention of the computer system.

Time sharing is a form of multiprogramming. Each terminal communicates with one or more processes, and these processes share the central processor as already described. But time sharing is distinctive in two ways:

- A user should get rapid response to any input. This means that the time quanta must be short, so that each process will be activated frequently enough to be able to respond to user input without excessive delay.

- There are usually far more processes present than can be accommodated in main memory. Combined with the requirement for frequent activation, this means that processes, or parts of them, are constantly being moved back and forth between main and auxiliary memory.

Multiprocessing, Distributed Processing, and Ultracomputers. In the past most computers had a single central processing unit. If there were other processors, they played subordinate roles, such as controlling peripheral devices. But now that the microprocessor revolution has made processors relatively inexpensive, we are seeing more and more systems built around a number of identical processors, none of which is subordinate to the others. These processors can be organized in several different ways.

In *multiprocessing*, all the processors share a single main memory. This sharing presents some problems. All of the processors compete for use of the bus connecting them with main memory and for access to main memory itself. Using more than one bus and dividing main memory into parts that can be accessed separately by different processors helps alleviate these problems but doesn't eliminate them.

In *distributed processing*, each processor has its own main memory. When necessary, the processors send messages to one another over interconnecting wires, which can be telephone lines or other standard communication links. The processors, with their main memories, need not be in the same location; they can be spread throughout a building, a country, or even the entire world. Each processor can be part of an independent computer system, with the separate systems connected together to form a *computer network*.

On the drawing boards for the future are *ultracomputers*, each having hundreds or thousands of processors. Each processor would have its own main memory, and the processors would be in a network that would allow any processor to communicate with any other.

These hardware advances challenge the ability of software developers to keep up with them. At present, we know very little about writing programs to make effective use of more than one processor. To give just one example of the problems that arise, should we assign each process to a separate processor? Should we use time-sharing techniques to let each processor handle more than one process? Or should we divide up one process among several processors, so that different parts of its program can be executed simultaneously? For that matter, how can we decompose a program into parts that can be executed simultaneously?

At present we do not know. We have arrived at the frontiers of computer science, where there are far more questions than answers.

Review Questions

1. Compare *machine language*, *assembly language*, and *higher level languages* with respect to their ease of use.

2. What is a *translator*?

3. What is an *interpreter*?

4. What is the disadvantage of an interpreter as compared with a translator? What are some of its advantages?

5. What is the *operating system*? What are some other names for the operating system?

6. Give three sources from which the operating system can accept commands.

7. Compare *batch* and *interactive* processing.

8. Describe eight functions performed by an operating system.

9. What do we mean by a *physical machine*? A *virtual machine*?

10. What is *read-only memory*? Distinguish between software and *firmware*.

11. Give two examples of virtual machines.

12. What is a *multilevel machine*? In what way is a multilevel machine analogous to an onion?

13. What are the three components of a *process*?

14. Distinguish between *active* and *inactive* processes.

15. How can we characterize a computer system in terms of processes?

16. What is an *interrupt*? Describe its effect in terms of processes.

17. What is a *time slice* or *time quantum*?

18. What happens in a multiprogramming system when a process requests an operation to be performed by a peripheral device?

19. What is *time sharing*? What special features of time sharing distinguish it from other forms of multiprogramming?

20. What kinds of challenges do recent hardware advances and likely future ones pose for computer science?

PART TWO

ALGORITHMS/
AND
PROGRAMS

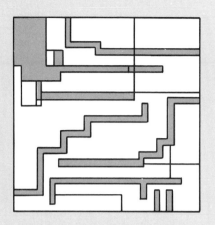

Chapter 4

Values and Expressions

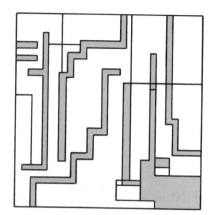

We now turn to the main object of this book, learning how to construct algorithms and write computer programs.

An algorithm or program must be written in some language. The question of what languages we shall use for this purpose is of first importance.

Languages. What language should we use for our algorithms? From the discussion in Chapter 3, it might seem that one of the higher level programming languages would be most suitable. But practical higher level languages suffer from several drawbacks:

■ To allow the implementation of a reasonable efficient translator or interpreter, severe restrictions may be placed on the constructions allowed in the language. For instance, user-defined names may be limited to two or six or eight characters, leading to drastic, almost unreadable abbreviations.

■ Overspecification: Programming languages require the user to specify many details, such as the kind of data to be stored in each memory location, the maximum size of lists and tables, and the exact position of output on the printed page. Translators and interpreters require these details to do their work efficiently. But the details only get in the way when one is trying *to think up a solution to a problem.*

■ A programming language is rigidly defined, either by standard specifications or by the translator or interpreter available on a particular computer system. The user is not allowed to invent new language features, no matter how desirable they might be for expressing the solution to a particular problem.

Programming languages that avoid one or more of these problems have been devised, but they are not the most widely used or readily available languages. Some, for instance, will execute only on very large computers.

Because of these drawbacks, we will create our algorithms not in a computer programming language but in an *informal algorithmic language*. The name *algorithmic notation*, reminiscent of mathematical or chemical notation, might be more suggestive of its informality and its human orientation. The algorithmic language is for *thinking about algorithms*. It is for scribbling on the backs of envelopes, not for typing in at computer terminals or punching on computer cards.

Once we have created an algorithm we will find it straightforward to translate the algorithm into whatever programming language happens to be available.

Traditionally, flowcharts have been used as an informal notation for algorithms. For complicated algorithms, however, flowcharts become intricate and mazelike, hard to draw and hard to follow. For this reason flowcharts are not emphasized as much now as they once were.

Provided they do not become too complex, however, flowcharts can give an overview of an algorithm at a single glance. Also, since flowcharts are still widely used in the data processing industry, the student should be familiar with them. For these reasons, many of the algorithms in this book are illustrated with flowcharts. Your instructor may wish you to draw a flowchart or two to become familiar with them. But in general you are not expected to draw flowcharts for the algorithms you create, or to think in terms of flowcharts when you create an algorithm.

To get our algorithms executed by a computer we must first convert them from the algorithmic language to one of the standard programming languages. This book contains a supplement showing how to translate algorithms into the Pascal programming language. The supplement gives Pascal translations for a number of the algorithms we will study in the main text.

4.1 Data Types and Values

Before we can start writing algorithms to manipulate data, we must say something about the kind of data we are going to manipulate.

It is customary to classify data into different *types*, depending on the operations we might wish to carry out on it. For instance, numbers are one type of data, and strings of alphabetic characters—say, people's names—are another. For numbers we probably want to carry out the usual operations of arithmetic—addition, subtraction, multiplication, and division. We are more likely to be interested in putting people's names in alphabetical order, however, or joining together first, middle, and last names to form full names. Since these operations are drastically different, we consider numbers and character strings to be different *data types*.

We will encounter new data types as we progress through the book, and eventually means will be provided for you to create your own new data types. For the moment, however, we will work with two data types: *real numbers* and *character strings*.

Real Numbers. Numbers are certainly one thing we want to be able to process with our algorithms, so we will need a data type consisting of numbers. More specifically, the data type will consist of the kind of numbers mathematicians call *real numbers*.

For any data type, the data items that belong to it are said to be *values* of that type. Thus, 100 and 3.1416 are values of type real number. We will define a data type informally by illustrating its possible values. We now do this with the real numbers—that is, the values of type real number.

The real numbers include the *nonnegative integers* 0, 1, 2, 3, and so on. Thus,

25   540   87   1000000   0

are real numbers.

A real number may be positive or negative, and this may be indicated with a + or − sign. If no sign is present, the number is assumed to be positive:

−25   +540   87   −1000000   0

A real number can contain a decimal point:

3.1416   −2.54   +6.63   345.29   0.05

When a number has a large number of leading or trailing zeros, *exponential notation* may be used to write it compactly. Consider the following example:

3.5E4

The number following the E is called the *exponent*. If the exponent is positive, it indicates the number of places the decimal point should be moved to the *right*. When moving the decimal point, we supply extra zeros as necessary. Thus, 3.5E4 is equivalent to

35000.

or simply,

35000

Here are some more examples:

Exponential Notation	Ordinary Notation
7.25E+3	7250
6.435E9	6435000000
5.425E2	542.5

If the exponent is negative, it indicates that the decimal point should be moved that many places to the *left*, as in the following examples:

Exponential Notation	Ordinary Notation
7.25E–3	.00725
6.435E–9	.000000006435
5.425E–2	.05425

We do not place any limits on the size of a real number nor on the number of significant digits it can contain. But such limits do exist for all computers and programming languages. These limits must be kept in mind when converting an algorithm to a computer program.

Character Strings. A character string is simply a sequence of characters. The permissible characters are:

The letters of the alphabet:

A B C D E F G H I J K L M N O P Q R S T U V W X Y Z

The digits:

0 1 2 3 4 5 6 7 8 9

Punctuation marks and special signs:

! @ # $ % ¢ & * ( ) _ – + = : ; , . ? / " and others

The blank space:

When we write a character string in the algorithmic language, we will enclose it in single quotation marks, to prevent it from being confused with the various words, signs, and numbers that also occur in the language. The following are character strings:

```
'GOOD MORNING'
'3.1416'
'$%#&@!¢'
' '            (one blank space)
''             (the null string, which contains no
                  characters at all)
```

Blank spaces always count as characters. Remember from Chapter 2 that the blank space has its own code—0100000—and in computer memory is treated just like any other coded character. Thus, all of the following strings are different:

```
''          null string
' '         one blank space
'  '        two blank spaces
'   '       three blank spaces
```

We must never confuse strings with other items in the language, even though they may consist of the same characters. Thus, 315 is the real number "three hundred fifteen," whereas '315' is the string consisting of a 3, a 1 and a 5. The number 315 can enter into an arithmetical calculation, but the string '315', never. In the same way, OUTPUT is a word having a specific meaning in the language, but 'OUTPUT' is just another string.

4.2 The Output Statement

We will express an algorithm as a series of imperative *statements*. (The term *instruction* or *command* would be better than *statement*, but *statement* is traditional.) Most statements begin with a *keyword* that describes the function of the statement. The keyword is followed by any data or other items necessary to the purpose of the statement.

The OUTPUT statement consists of the keyword OUTPUT followed by one or more data items, separated by commas. The statement instructs the computer to print or display the data items on some output device, such as a printer or a video display screen. Thus,

```
OUTPUT 3.1416
```

will cause the computer to print

```
3.1416
```

and

```
OUTPUT 'HAVE A NICE DAY.'
```

will cause it to print

```
HAVE A NICE DAY.
```

When an OUTPUT statement contains more than one data item, the items are printed one after another on the same line. Thus,

```
OUTPUT 1,2,3,4,5
```

prints

```
1 2 3 4 5
```

and

```
OUTPUT 'THE VALUE OF PI IS APPROXIMATELY', 3.1416
```

prints

```
THE VALUE OF PI IS APPROXIMATELY 3.1416
```

We will *not* worry about the technicalities of exactly how items are positioned, or spaced out, on the line. This is one of the petty details that is best postponed until the algorithm is translated into a computer program.

Each new OUTPUT statement starts a new line of printout. Thus, the statements

```
OUTPUT 'HELLO.'
OUTPUT 'HOW ARE YOU?'
OUTPUT 'CAN I HELP YOU?'
```

would print

```
HELLO.
HOW ARE YOU?
CAN I HELP YOU?
```

4.3 Simple Arithmetic Expressions

The operations of arithmetic are specified by the following five *arithmetic operators:*

```
+       addition
-       subtraction
*       multiplication
/       division
**      exponentiation
```

The operators for addition and subtraction are the same as in ordinary arithmetic. Multiplication is represented by the asterisk, which is the closest thing to a multiplication sign that can be found on most computer printers. A slash, /, stands for division; the other division sign, ÷, is also notoriously absent from most computer printers.

Exponentiation is what is more commonly referred to as "raising to a power." The number to the left of the ** is multiplied by itself the number of times specified by the number to the right of the **. Thus,

```
5**3 = 5 times 5 times 5 = 125
```

```
3**2 = 3 times 3 = 9
2**3 = 2 times 2 times 2 = 8
```

Fractional exponents may also be used. Thus, 2**0.5 equals the square root of 2.

An *arithmetic expression* is formed by placing an arithemetic operator between two numbers, called *operands*. The following are arithmetic expressions:

```
3+4    6-5    3*7    3/2    4**3
```

The *value* of an arithmetic expression is the result of applying the operator to the two operands:

```
Expression     Value
   3+4           7
   6-5           1
   3*7          21
   3/2           1.5
   4**3         64
```

Arithmetic expressions can appear in OUTPUT statements. The computer evaluates each expression and prints the value. Thus,

```
OUTPUT 3+4, 6-5, 3*7, 3/2, 4**3
```

would print

```
7 1 21 1.5 64
```

Note that

```
OUTPUT '3**4 =', 3**4
```

would print

```
3**4 = 81
```

since '3**4 =' is not an expression, but just a character string. It is not evaluated but just printed as is.

4.4 More Complex Arithmetic Expressions

Often the calculations we wish to instruct the computer to carry out are far more complex than a single addition, subtraction, multiplication, division, or exponentiation. We would like whenever possible to specify these more complicated calculations by single expressions.

To do this, we can write down several operands separated by operators, such as

```
2+3*4
3-4/7**3*5+2
```

But this brings up an interesting question. In what order shall we carry out the operations? The result we get will certainly depend on the order we choose. In

```
2+3*4
```

for instance, if we do the addition first and then the multiplication, we get

```
2+3*4 =
   5*4 =
    20
```

On the other hand, if we do the multiplication first, we get

```
2+3*4 =
2+12 =
14
```

Not the same at all!

The matter is resolved by assigning the different operators *priorities*. Operators with higher priority are applied before those with lower priority. Operators with the same priority are applied in left-to-right order as they occur in the expression.

The following table gives the priorities of the arithmetic operators:

```
**              highest priority
* and /
+ and -         lowest priority
```

Operators on the same line (such as + and −) have the same priority.

Here are some examples of evaluation using priorities:

Example 1:

```
2+3*4 =
2+12 =          Multiplication first ...
14              ... then addition.
```

Example 2:

```
2*3**4 =
2*81 =          Exponentiation first ...
162             ... then multiplication.
```

Example 3:

```
4+3**2  =
4+9  =          Exponentiation first ...
13              ... then addition.
```

Example 4:

```
2+3*5**2  =
2+3*25  =       Exponentiation first ...
2+75  =         ... then multiplication ...
77              ... and then addition.
```

Operators with the same priority are evaluated in left-to-right order:

Example 5:

```
3+4-2  =
  7-2  =        Addition first ...
    5           ... then subtraction.
```

Example 6:

```
12/4*3  =
   3*3  =       Division first ...
     9          ... then multiplication.
```

Warning: Because of the occurrence of built-up fractions like

$$\frac{12}{4*3} = \frac{12}{12} = 1$$

in ordinary arithmetic, people sometimes expect the multiplication in Example 6 to be done before the division. But this is incorrect; multiplication and division have the same priority and are evaluated in left-to-right order as they occur in the expression.

Sometimes we want the operators in an expression to be applied in a different order than that dictated by the priorities. We can enforce the order we want by enclosing part of the expression in parentheses. The part of the expression in parentheses is evaluated first, regardless of the priorities:

Example 7:

```
(2+3)*4  =
   5*4  =       Parentheses first ...
    20          ... then rest of expression.
```

Example 8:

```
(4+3)**2  =
   7**2  =      Parentheses first ...
     49         ... then rest of expression.
```

Example 9:

```
((2+3)*4)**2 =
      (5*4)**2 =      Inner parentheses first ...
         20**2 =      ... then next outer ones ...
            400       ... and then rest of expression.
```

4.5 Functions

Not all operations are represented by signs, at least by signs that are available on computer printers and display devices.

Consider the *absolute value* operation, which leaves a positive number unchanged but changes a negative number into the corresponding positive one. We can indicate this operation as follows:

```
ABS(5)  = 5
ABS(-5)  = 5
ABS(3.1416)  = 3.1416
ABS(-3.1416)  = 3.1416
```

ABS is called a *function*. The number following the function in parentheses is its *argument*. The function, together with its argument, forms an expression whose value is the result of applying the function to its argument.

The argument of the function may itself be an expression. Since the argument is in parentheses, it is evaluated before applying the function:

Example 10:

```
ABS(5-6*3) =
ABS(5-18) =
ABS(-13) =
    13
```

A function with its argument can be used as part of another expression:

Example 11:

```
3+2*ABS(7-50) =
3+2*ABS(-43) =
3+2*43 =
3+86 =
    89
```

An expression containing a function can be used anywhere any other expression can. For example, the statement

```
OUTPUT ABS(5), ABS(-5), ABS(5-6*3), 3+2*ABS(7-50)
```

would print

5 5 13 89

Here are two other useful functions:

INT. The INT function discards the fractional part of a number—the part to the right of the decimal point—and retains only the *integer* part:

```
INT(3.1416) = 3
INT(25) = 25
INT(4.75) = 4
INT(-3.1416) = -3
INT(-4.75) = -4
```

SQRT. The SQRT function yields the square root of its argument:

```
SQRT(25) = 5
SQRT(9) = 3
SQRT(2.25) = 1.5
```

The square root of a negative number, such as SQRT(-25) is undefined, since the result is not a real number. An attempt to take such a square root on a computer would probably result in an error message and the termination of your program.

4.6 Writing Algorithms

An algorithm is a sequence of statements in the algorithmic language. The statements are executed—the instructions in them are obeyed—one after another in the order in which they are written. (We will later encounter statements that can modify the order of execution.) We can "frame" an algorithm for display as follows:

```
ALGORITHM algorithm-name
    statements of algorithm
END algorithm-name
```

For example,

```
ALGORITHM EXPRESSIONS
    OUTPUT '3+5 =', 3+5
    OUTPUT '3-5 =', 3-5
    OUTPUT '3*5 =', 3*5
    OUTPUT '3/5 =', 3/5
    OUTPUT 'SQRT(1.69) =', SQRT(1.69)
END EXPRESSIONS
```

Executing EXPRESSIONS causes the following printout to be produced:

```
3+5  =  8
3-5  =  -2
3*5  =  15
3/5  =  0.6
SQRT(1.69)  =  1.3
```

In this book, algorithms are printed using all capital letters for easy readability and to make them stand out from the surrounding text. This is not necessarily the best way to write out algorithms by hand. A good form for handwritten algorithms is to use lowercase letters and underline keywords such as ALGORITHM, END, and OUTPUT, to make them stand out. Figure 4-1 shows the greatest-common-divisor algorithm from Chapter 1 handwritten in this form.

FIGURE 4-1. A convenient handwritten form for the algorithmic language. Underlining the keywords is optional.

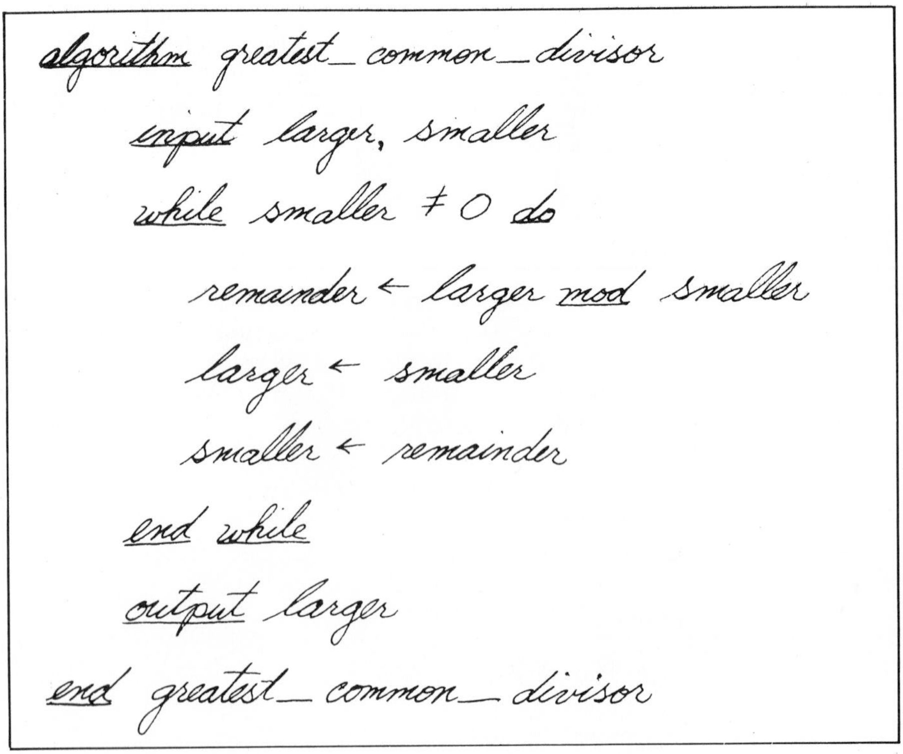

```
algorithm greatest_common_divisor
    input larger, smaller
    while smaller ≠ 0 do
        remainder ← larger mod smaller
        larger ← smaller
        smaller ← remainder
    end while
    output larger
end greatest_common_divisor
```

Review Questions

1. Give three reasons why the commonly used programming languages are not the ideal languages for expressing algorithms.

2. Compare the uses of an algorithmic language, such as the one used in this book, and a computer programming language.

3. Once upon a time it was recommended that a programmer always draw a flowchart before writing a program. Is this still recommended? Why or why not?

4. What is the basis for classifying data into different types?

5. What is a *value*?

6. What two data types are taken up in this chapter?

7. Give examples of five real numbers.

8. In writing algorithms, we do not place any limit on the size or precision of real numbers. Do we have the same freedom when translating an algorithm into a computer program?

9. Give five different character strings, each consisting entirely of blank spaces.

10. Any character that indicates the beginning or end of a particular construction is called a *delimiter*. What is the delimiter for character strings?

11. Distinguish between 3.1416 and '3.1416'.

12. Name two data types whose values can be printed by an OUTPUT statement.

13. Name the five arithmetic operators introduced in this chapter, and give the sign for each.

14. What does the simplest possible arithmetic expression consist of?

15. Explain the use of priorities to determine the order in which operators are applied in arithmetic expressions.

16. Why are parentheses needed in arithmetic expressions?

17. Name four functions defined in this chapter.

18. What is the *argument* of a function?

19. When a function occurs in an expression, which is evaluated first, the argument of the function or the rest of the expression?

20. Give an example showing how algorithms will be presented in this book. Give both the printed and the handwritten forms.

Exercises

1. Write each of the following in exponential notation:

(a) 1000   (b) 254000
(c) 345600000   (d) 1000000000
(e) .01   (f) .00015
(g) .00235   (h) .0000054

2. Write each of the following in ordinary notation:

(a) 1E5   (b)1.25E + 4
(c) 6.02E23   (d) 7.549E + 2
(e) 3.5E − 1   (f) 6.43E − 2
(g) 7.05E − 5   (h) 1E − 1

3. Evaluate:

(a) 3 + 12 − 4   (b) 3 + 4*12
(c) 4 + 12/4   (d) 12/4 − 3
(e) 24/6*4   (f) 3*3**3
(g) 3 + 2*5 + 7   (h) 2*5 − 3*4 + 6/2
(i) 3*4**2 − 3*4   (j) 3**2 + 5**2 + 7**2
(k) 4**3/8   (l) 12/4/3

4. Compare the results of evaluating the parenthesized and unparenthesized expressions.

(a) 10/5*2   10/(5*2)
(b) 12 − 4*3   (12 − 4)*3
(c) 3*4**2   (3*4)**2
(d) 3 − 4 + 12   3 − (4 + 12)
(e) 7 − 4 − 3   7 − (4 − 3)
(f) 16/4/2   16/(4/2)

5. What will each of the following sets of OUTPUT statements print?

(a) OUTPUT 'PI =', 3.1416

(b) OUTPUT 'PI ='
    OUTPUT 3.1416

(c) OUTPUT 'ONE TWO THREE'
    OUTPUT 'FOUR FIVE SIX'
    OUTPUT 'SEVEN EIGHT NINE'

6. Evaluate:

(a) ABS(− 25)   (b) INT(24.17)
(c) ABS(100)   (d) SQRT(3**2 + 4**2)
(e) SQRT(100)   (f) SQRT(81)
(g) INT(− 4.7)   (h) ABS(− 24.9)
(i) ABS(3 − 10)   (j) ABS(10 − 3)
(k) 3 + 5*INT(3/2)   (l) INT(.5)

7. Write an algorithm to print the following picture of a tree.

8. Write an algorithm to print some picture or design of your own devising. (This kind of art is a favorite pastime with computer people. Subjects range from cartoon characters to *Playboy* centerfolds.)

9. Write an algorithm to compute and output the volume of a box 73 centimeters long, 47 centimeters wide, and 29 centimeters high.

10. A field is 39 meters wide and 67 meters long. Write an algorithm to compute and output how many meters of fence wire will be required to enclose the field.

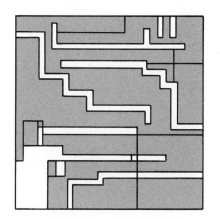

Chapter 5

Variables, Assignment, and Input

In the last chapter we saw how to instruct a computer to carry out arithmetic calculations. But all we could do with the results was to print them out. We did not provide for a *scratch pad*, a means of saving the result of one calculation to be used in a later one. In this chapter we will remedy that deficiency.

5.1 Names, Locations, and Variables

Memory. When a computer is working out a problem, it must keep the data it is working with at hand. Often it must save the results of current calculations for use in later ones and recall the results of previous calculations for use in the current one. These are the kinds of things you or I would do using a piece of scratch paper, a blackboard, or (these days) a calculator with a built-in memory.

A computer uses its main memory. We can think of this as being divided up into many individual *memory locations*. Each location can hold precisely one real number or string. We can think of the memory as a vast array of post office boxes or pigeonholes, each holding a single data value.

(The memory locations described here do not necessarily correspond one-to-one with the hardware locations described in Chapter 2. On some computers, for instance, a real number may occupy two or four hardware memory locations. A string almost always occupies more than one hardware memory location. The correspondence between hardware locations and those used in a higher level language is arranged by the translator or interpreter.)

Names. If we are going to entrust a piece of data to one of these memory locations, it will be best if we keep track of which one we put it in, so we can get it back when we need it again.

For this purpose, we give each memory location a *name* and refer to it by name when storing or retrieving data. We choose the name of a location to help us remember the kind of data that is stored in it. In an algorithm to compute a payroll, for instance, the location named HOURS__ WORKED might contain the number of hours a worker put in during a given week, while the one named HOURLY__RATE could hold the amount the worker earns each hour.

As a rule, we can make up whatever names we please for memory locations. To prevent names from being confused with other elements of the language, however, we impose a few minor restrictions on their construction. Names may contain only letters, digits, and the underline character __. A name must start with a letter. Thus,

```
BOSTON    NEW_YORK    DC9    M6800
```

are permissible, but

```
3B    111223333    NEW YORK    WEST—VIRGINIA
```

are not.

Instead of spaces or hyphens, which are not used in names, we use the underline character:

```
NEW_YORK    WEST_VIRGINIA    QUANTITY_ON_HAND
```

There is no limit on the length of a name.

Variables. A named memory location is known as a *variable*, since its contents vary as the computer stores new values in the location. The name of the location is the *variable name*; the contents of the location are the *value* of the variable. We refer to variables by their names. Thus, when we say the value of HOURS__WORKED is 40, we mean that the memory location named HOURS__WORKED contains the value 40.

Figure 5-1 shows two ways of visualizing a computer's memory. The list of variables and values at the bottom of the figure conveys the same information as the diagram of memory locations at the top.

We often use a verbal shorthand when speaking about variables and their values. Instead of saying "the contents of the memory location named HOURLY__RATE is 40" or "the value of the variable HOURLY__RATE is 40," we say "HOURLY__RATE equals 40" or "HOURLY__RATE is 40." In general, we often use a variable name to refer to the value of the variable. Thus we might say "HOURLY__RATE is greater than zero" instead of the

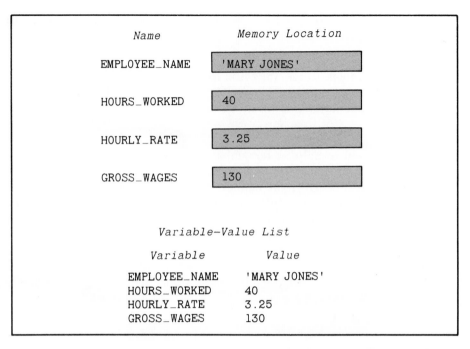

FIGURE 5-1. Two equivalent ways of visualizing a computer's memory: at top, named memory locations and their contents; at bottom, variables and their values.

longer but more precise "the value of HOURLY__RATE is greater than zero."

5.2 Assignment

The Assignment Operator. One of the simplest operations a computer can carry out is to store a certain value in a certain memory location. Now the memory location is a variable, and the value of the variable is the value stored in the location. The effect of storing a new value in the location, then, is to *assign* a new value to the variable. For this reason, the operation of storing a value in a location is called *assignment*.

We indicate the assignment with the *assignment operator*, ←. To the left of the assignment operator is a variable. To the right of it is an expression. The value of the expression on the right is stored in the location named on the left (or, the value of the expression on the right is *assigned* to the variable on the left). Thus,

EMPLOYEE_NAME ← 'MARY JONES'

causes 'MARY JONES' to be stored in the location named EMPLOYEE__ NAME. (Remember that a value such as 'MARY JONES' or 3.14 is a special case of an expression.)

The arrow ← may be read as "becomes." Thus, we could read this assignment as, "EMPLOYEE__NAME becomes 'MARY JONES'."

One way to think of the assignment operator is in terms of the effect it has on the values of variables. Suppose the following three variables have the values shown:

```
EMPLOYEE_NAME    'BOB SMITH'
HOURS_WORKED     45
HOURLY_RATE      4.25
```

After the assignment statements

```
EMPLOYEE_NAME ← 'JANE LEE'
HOURS_WORKED ← 41
HOURLY_RATE ← 5.15
```

are executed, the variables have the following values:

```
EMPLOYEE_NAME    'JANE LEE'
HOURS_WORKED     41
HOURLY_RATE      5.15
```

Figure 5-2 illustrates this in terms of memory locations.

FIGURE 5-2. The effect of assignment statements on memory.

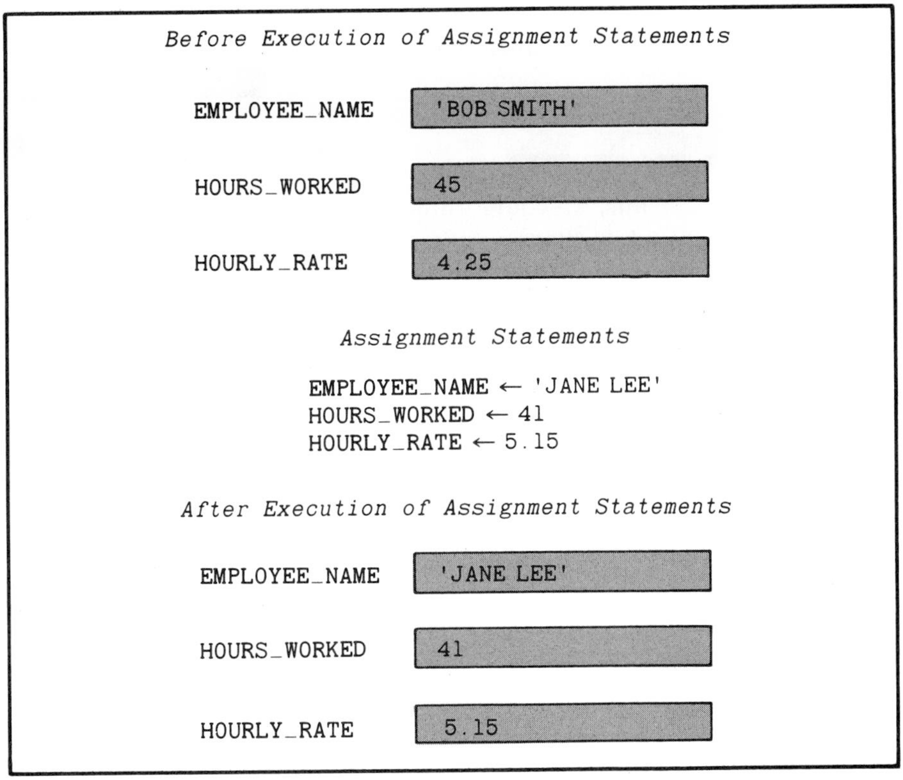

Dereferencing. We do not always want to have to write out explicitly the value we want to store in a memory location. The desired value may already be present in the computer, say, in another location. In that case, we would like to be able simply to copy the value from one location to another.

We can indicate such a copying operation in this way:

```
SECOND_LOCATION ← FIRST_LOCATION
```

The value in FIRST__LOCATION is copied in SECOND__LOCATION. Only the value of SECOND__LOCATION is changed. The value of FIRST__LO-CATION remains the same.

We can illustrate this using lists of variables and their values. Suppose that before the assignment the variable-value list is:

```
FIRST_LOCATION      50
SECOND_LOCATION     75
```

After the assignment, the new variable-value list is:

```
FIRST_LOCATION      50
SECOND_LOCATION     50
```

Figure 5-3 illustrates this in terms of memory locations.

We can reduce this copying operation to the assignment already discussed by announcing a new rule. Whenever a variable appears on the *right-hand side* of the assignment operator, that variable is replaced by its value. This operation is called *dereferencing*: a variable (or reference) is replaced by its value.

Thus, we could think of the assignment just discussed as being carried out in two steps:

FIGURE 5-3. Copying data from one memory location into another.

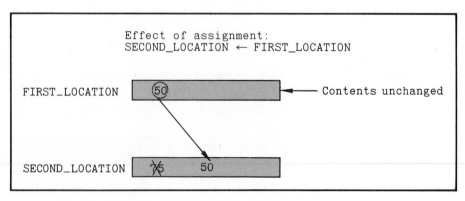

```
SECOND_LOCATION ← FIRST_LOCATION
SECOND_LOCATION ← 50                Dereference
                                    FIRST_LOCATION
                                    Assign 50 to
                                    SECOND_LOCATION.
```

Figure 5-4 illustrates dereferencing.

5.3 Expressions

When we defined assignment, we said that an expression could appear on the right-hand side of the assignment operator. So far, we have examined two special cases in which the expression was (1) a value and (2) a variable. Now let's turn to assignments involving more complicated expressions.

The expression is always evaluated before making the assignment. We can think of the assignment operator as having a lower priority than any arithmetic operator. Thus,

```
AREA ← 8*5
```

is processed as follows:

```
AREA ← 8*5
AREA ← 40       Evaluate expression.
                Assign 40 to AREA.
```

The same principle applies to more complex expressions, of course:

```
DATA ← 25+2*3**2
DATA ← 25+2*9       Exponentiation first ...
DATA ← 25+18        ... multiplication next ...
DATA ← 43           ... addition next ...
                    ... and assign 43 to DATA.
```

FIGURE 5-4. Dereferencing: replacing a variable by its value.

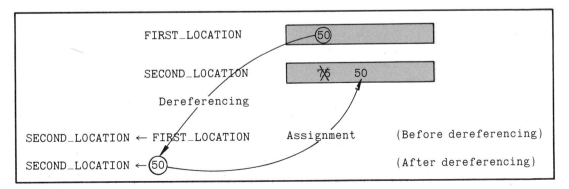

In addition to real numbers, we can use variables in our expressions. Dereferencing is done before any other operation has been carried out. When every variable has been replaced by its current value, the expression evaluation and assignment are carried out as before. For example, suppose the current variable-value list is

```
A     5
B    10
C    15
D    20
```

and we carry out the assignment

```
D ← A+B*C
```

as follows:

```
D ← A+B*C
D ← 5+10*15    Dereference variables on right side ...
D ← 5+150      ... multiplication next ...
D ← 155        ... addition next ...
               ... and assign 155 to D.
```

The new variable-value list is:

```
A      5
B     10
C     15
D    155
```

Only the value of D is changed; the value of a variable is never changed when the variable appears only on the right side of an assignment statement. Figure 5-5 illustrates this assignment.

Sometimes a variable appears on both the right and the left sides of an assignment statement. Since the expression on the right is evaluated first, the current value of the variable is used in evaluating the expression. The value of the expression then becomes the new value of the variable. For example, using the variable-value list just given and the assignment

```
A ← A+1
```

we have

```
A ← A+1
A ← 5+1    Dereference A ...
A ← 6      ... do addition ...
           ... and assign 6 to A.
```

The new variable-value list is:

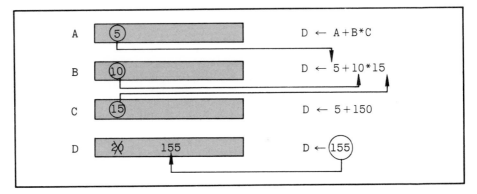

FIGURE 5-5. An assignment statement containing an expression on the right hand side specifies (a) a calculation to be carried out, (b) the memory locations containing the data for the calculation, and (c) the memory location in which the result of the calculation is to be stored.

A   6
B   10
C   15
D   155

Figure 5-6 illustrates this assignment.

5.4 Input and Output

We can now generalize the OUTPUT statement to allow variables in the expressions whose values are to be printed. The best way to do this is to think of the OUTPUT statement as a kind of assignment statement. The expressions in the OUTPUT statement are evaluated exactly as if each appeared on the right-hand side of an assignment statement. But the resulting value is printed instead of being assigned to a variable.

For example, consider these statements:

FIGURE 5-6. Adding 1 to the contents of a memory location. This operation is frequently carried out for the purpose of counting; the memory location holds a running count, which is increased by 1 each time an item is counted.

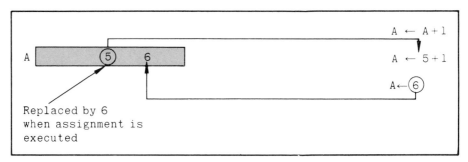

```
LENGTH ← 7
WIDTH ← 5
OUTPUT LENGTH*WIDTH, 2*(LENGTH+WIDTH)
```

The printout is:

```
35 24
```

Notice that we could have gotten the same result by writing:

```
LENGTH ← 7
WIDTH ← 5
AREA ← LENGTH*WIDTH
PERIMETER ← 2*(LENGTH+WIDTH)
OUTPUT AREA, PERIMETER
```

The expressions are evaluated the same whether they appear in an OUT-PUT statement or on the right side of an assignment statement.

In the same way, we can define an INPUT statement, which obtains a value from an input device, such as a card reader or a terminal, and assigns the value to a variable.

The word INPUT is followed by a list of variables:

```
INPUT LENGTH, WIDTH
```

Each variable is assigned a new value, just as if it had appeared on the left side of an assignment statement. But the value comes from the input device, and not from the result of evaluating an expression.

An INPUT statement, unlike an OUTPUT statement, can contain only variables. We cannot use an expression in an INPUT statement any more than we could use one on the left side of an assignment statement.

Now consider the sequence of statements:

```
INPUT LENGTH, WIDTH
AREA ← LENGTH*WIDTH
PERIMETER ← 2*(LENGTH+WIDTH)
OUTPUT 'AREA =' , AREA
OUTPUT 'PERIMETER =' , PERIMETER
```

Suppose the data typed on the input device is:

```
4, 3
```

Then, after the INPUT statement has been executed, we will have the variable-value list:

```
LENGTH      4
WIDTH       3
```

```
AREA          —
PERIMETER     —
```

where the dashes indicate that AREA and PERIMETER have not yet been assigned values. After the two assignment statements have been carried out, we get the variable-value list:

```
LENGTH        4
WIDTH         3
AREA          12
PERIMETER     14
```

Executing the OUTPUT statements gives the printout:

```
AREA = 12
PERIMETER = 14
```

5.5 Three Examples

Here are three complete algorithms that demonstrate the features of the algorithmic language we have studied so far. Flowcharts for these algorithms are given in Figures 5-7, 5-8, and 5-9.

Units Conversion. This algorithm inputs a length in feet and inches and converts it to centimeters:

```
ALGORITHM CONVERT
    INPUT FEET, INCHES
    TOTAL_INCHES ← 12*FEET + INCHES
    CENTIMETERS ← 2.54*TOTAL_INCHES
    OUTPUT FEET, 'FEET', INCHES, 'INCHES ='
    OUTPUT CENTIMETERS, 'CENTIMETERS'
END CONVERT
```

The input data

```
6, 4
```

produces the output

```
6 FEET 4 INCHES =
193.04 CENTIMETERS
```

Wage Calculation. This algorithm calculates a person's wages, given the hours worked and the amount paid for each hour:

```
ALGORITHM WAGES
    INPUT NAME, HOURS, RATE           (Get data)
```

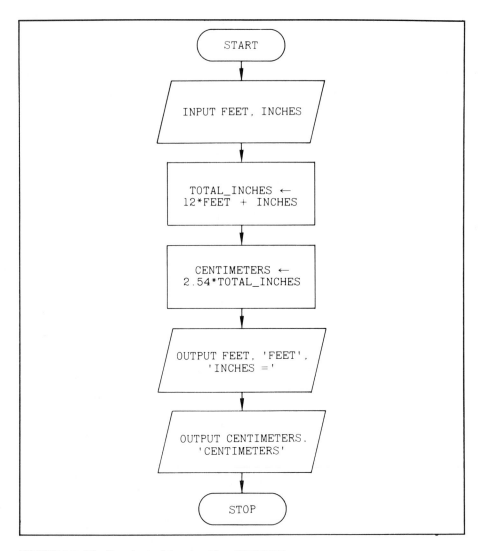

FIGURE 5-7. The flowchart of the algorithm CONVERT.

```
    GROSS_WAGES ← HOURS*RATE        (Compute wages)
    OUTPUT 'NAME:', NAME            (Output results)
    OUTPUT 'PAY:', GROSS_WAGES
END WAGES
```

Most programming languages have some provisions for inserting *comments* or *remarks* to explain the program statements. In the algorithmic language, comments will be enclosed in parentheses as shown. Since our algorithmic language is designed for easy reading, and since complicated algorithms will be explained in the surrounding text, we will not need nearly so many comments as we would for a more obscure language, with no accompanying text. Our main use for comments will be outlining an algorithm before filling in the details.

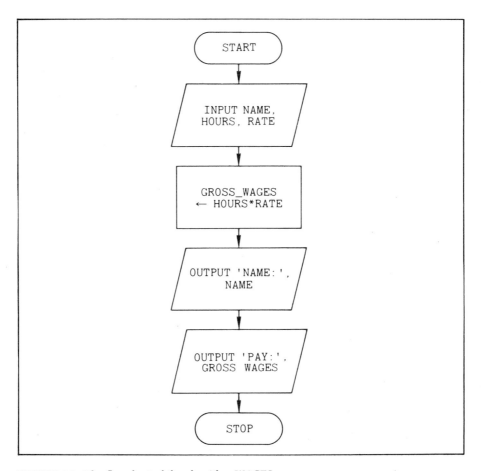

FIGURE 5-8. The flowchart of the algorithm WAGES.

Given the data

```
'MARY JONES', 30, 8.50
```

the algorithm WAGES will print

```
NAME: MARY JONES
PAY: 255
```

Discount and Tax. An item is purchased that is subject to a certain discount and a certain tax on the discounted price. Given the list price of the item, the discount rate, and the tax rate, compute the amount the purchaser must pay.

We can outline the algorithm with comments before filling in the details:

```
ALGORITHM PURCHASE
    (Input list price, discount rate, and tax rate)
```

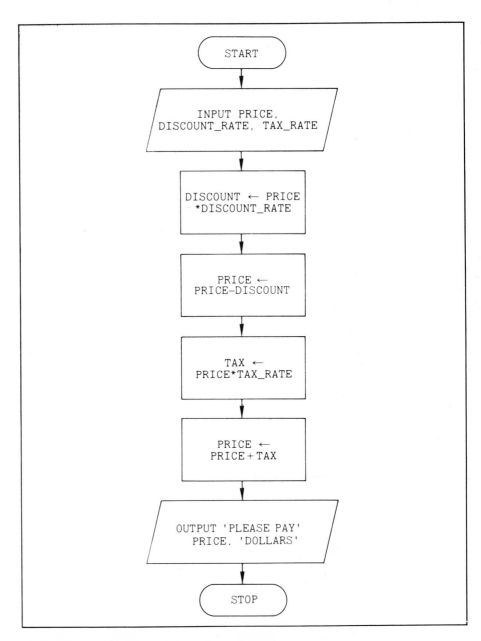

FIGURE 5-9. The flowchart of the algorithm PURCHASE.

```
        (Compute discount)
        (Subtract discount from price)
        (Compute tax)
        (Add tax to price)
        (Output price)
END PURCHASE
```

We now fill in the details:

```
ALGORITHM PURCHASE
    (Input list price, discount rate, and tax rate)
        INPUT PRICE, DISCOUNT_RATE, TAX_RATE
    (Compute discount)
        DISCOUNT ← PRICE*DISCOUNT_RATE
    (Subtract discount from price)
        PRICE ← PRICE−DISCOUNT
    (Compute tax)
        TAX ← PRICE*TAX_RATE
    (Add tax to price)
        PRICE ← PRICE+TAX
    (Output price)
        OUTPUT 'PLEASE PAY', PRICE, 'DOLLARS'
END PURCHASE
```

The comments may then be omitted if they are not needed to explain the algorithm:

```
ALGORITHM PURCHASE
    INPUT PRICE, DISCOUNT_RATE, TAX_RATE
    DISCOUNT ← PRICE*DISCOUNT_RATE
    PRICE ← PRICE−DISCOUNT
    TAX ← PRICE*TAX_RATE
    PRICE ← PRICE+TAX
    OUTPUT 'PLEASE PAY', PRICE, 'DOLLARS'
END PURCHASE
```

Given the input data

```
50,    .10,    .03
```

the algorithm PURCHASE will print

```
PLEASE PAY 46.35 DOLLARS
```

Review Questions

1. What does a computer use in place of a blackboard or scratch pad?

2. Why do we need names for memory locations?

3. What are the restrictions imposed on the spelling of names?

4. Why are memory locations often called *variables*?

5. Describe the correspondence between a variable and its value.

6. What is a *variable-value list*?

7. Sometimes we use shorthand phrases such as "EMPLOYEE__NAME is 'MARY JONES'" or "HOURS__WORKED equals 40." Explain what each of these phrases actually means.

8. What is the function of the assignment operator?

9. What is *dereferencing*?

10. Is dereferencing ever applied to the variable on the left side of an assignment statement?

11. Describe the action carried out by an assignment statement when there is a single *value* to the right of the assignment operator.

12. Describe the actions carried out by an assignment statement when there is a single *variable* to the right of the assignment operator.

13. Describe the actions carried out by an assignment statement when there is an *arithmetic expression* to the right of the assignment operator.

14. Illustrate with diagrams what happens when the following statement is executed:

```
SECOND_LOCATION ← FIRST_LOCATION
```

15. Define the OUTPUT statement as a variation on the assignment statement.

16. Define the INPUT statement as a variation on the assignment statement.

17. What are *comments* or *remarks*? How are they written in the algorithmic language?

18. Languages vary tremendously in the clarity with which they can express an algorithm. For what kinds of languages are comments most necessary?

19. Explain how a judicious choice of variable names can eliminate the need for some comments.

20. Explain how comments can be used to outline an algorithm before filling in all the fine details.

Exercises

1. Which of the following variable names are permissible in the algorithmic language?

(a) NORTH CAROLINA	(b) NORTH−CAROLINA
(c) NORTH_CAROLINA	(d) APT_24A
(e) $_AMOUNT	(f) AMOUNT_IN_$
(g) IBM−360	(h) IBM_360
(i) 315_65_9817	(j) Z9
(k) 9Z	(l) EMPLOYEE_#

2. Let the initial values of A, B, C, and D be as given by the following variable-value list:

```
A   10
B   20
C   30
D   40
```

Construct a trace of the execution of the following assignment statements:

```
A ← D
D ← B
B ← C
C ← D
```

3. Suppose the initial values of A, B, C, and D are given by the variable-value list in Exercise 2 and that the input data is

```
1
2
3
```

Construct a trace of the execution of the following statements:

```
D ← C
C ← B
B ← A
INPUT A
D ← C
C ← B
INPUT B
D ← C
INPUT C
```

4. Will the sequences of assignment statements

```
A ← B
B ← C
```

and

```
B ← C
A ← B
```

have the same effect? Comment on whether or not we can interchange the order of assignment statements without changing their effect.

5. Devise a sequence of assignment statements that will interchange the contents of A and B. (*Hint:* Another location—say, T—will be needed for temporary storage.)

6. Write an algorithm to convert from centimeters to inches.

7. Write an algorithm to convert from Fahrenheit to Celsius using the formula

$$C = \frac{5}{9}(F - 32)$$

8. The length of the diagonal of a rectangle is given by the square root of the sum of the squares of the lengths of the sides. Write an algorithm to input the length and width of a rectangle and to output the length of its diagonal.

9. Write an algorithm to input the number of items purchased, the cost per item, and the sales tax rate and to output the amount the customer must pay.

10. One can check an automobile speedometer for accuracy by noting the time required to travel a "measured mile" while maintaining a certain indicated speed. Write an algorithm that will input the time, in minutes and seconds, required to travel between two milestones, and output the speed the car was traveling.

11. Salespeople at a certain company get a 15% commission on their sales. Write an algorithm to input the amount a person sold and to print both the commission the person receives and the amount the company receives after the commission has been deducted.

12. The diameter of a circular pool and the depth to which it is filled are both given. Write an algorithm to calculate how many liters of water are needed to fill the pool to the specified depth. The diameter and depth are given in meters.

We can calculate the volume of water needed as follows:

$$\text{volume} = \frac{3.14 \times \text{depth} \times \text{diameter}^2}{4}$$

This formula gives the volume in cubic meters. Each cubic meter contains 1000 liters, so

number-of-liters = 1000 × volume

13. The *length* of a rectangular object is its longest dimension; the *girth* of the object is the distance around it, measured perpendicular to the length. The combination *length-plus-girth* occurs in postal regulations; for instance, a package cannot be sent by first class mail if its length-plus-girth exceeds 100 inches. Write an algorithm to input the length, width, and height of a package and print its length-plus-girth.

14. A bank account pays interest at the rate of i percent each year, compounded monthly. Let a be the amount currently in the account, and suppose that no further deposits are made. After n months, the amount c currently in the account is given by

$$c = a(1 + r)^n$$

where r is the monthly interest rate, expressed as a decimal:

$$r = \frac{i}{1200}$$

Write an algorithm to compute the amount currently in the account, given the starting amount, the yearly rate of interest, and the number of months the money was left in the account.

15. Suppose the situation is the same as for Exercise 14 except that an amount d is deposited in the account at the beginning of each month. With this change, the formula for the amount currently in the account becomes:

$$c = d\frac{(1 + r)^n - 1}{r}(1 + r) + a(1 + r)^n$$

Write an algorithm to compute the amount currently in the account, given the starting amount, the monthly deposit, the yearly rate of interest, and the number of months.

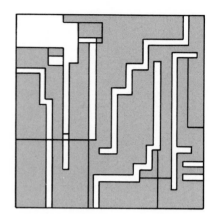

Chapter 6

Selection

The *control structures* of a language allow one to specify the order in which the statements of an algorithm will be executed. The only control structure we have used so far is *sequencing*, whereby statements are executed one after another in the order in which they are written in the algorithm. In this chapter we will study *selection*, which allows a particular set of statements to be chosen for execution, the choice depending on conditions holding when the algorithm is executed.

6.1 Conditions

Logical Values. We will be concerned with conditions that either hold or do not hold. We can consider a condition to be a statement that is either true or false. If the statement is true, the condition holds; if the statement is false, the condition does not hold.

To distinguish between these two alternatives, we introduce a new data type, which consists of exactly two *logical values*, denoted TRUE and FALSE. The symbols TRUE and FALSE are on the same footing as other value denotations such as 3.14 and 'GOOD GRIEF'.

Logical values can be inputted, assigned to variables, and outputted, just like any other values. Consider the statements:

```
INPUT P, Q
R ← FALSE
OUTPUT Q, P, R
```

If the input is

```
TRUE, FALSE
```

the output will be

```
FALSE TRUE FALSE
```

Just as we had to be careful to distinguish between 3.14 (a real number) and '3.14' (a string), so we must not confuse TRUE (a logical value) and 'TRUE' (a string).

Relational Operators. A relational operator corresponds to a relation that can exist between values, such as one number being equal to another, or one string preceding another in alphabetical order. The relational operator is applied to two values and yields a logical value. If the corresponding relation holds, the value yielded is TRUE. Otherwise, the value is FALSE.

The following relational operators apply to real numbers:

```
=    is equal to
≠    is not equal to
<    is less than
>    is greater than
≤    is less than or equal to
≥    is greater than or equal to
```

The result of applying one of these operators to two real numbers will be TRUE or FALSE, depending on whether or not the corresponding relation holds:

```
Expression       Value
   3 = 5         FALSE
   2 ≤ 3         TRUE
   5 ≥ 5         TRUE
   4 ≠ 4         FALSE
   7 < 7.5       TRUE
3.14 > 3.1416    FALSE
```

The relational operators have a lower priority than any arithmetic operator. Therefore, if we place a relational operator between arithmetic expressions, the arithmetic expressions will be evaluated first, and the relational operator will be applied to the results. Consider the following evaluations:

```
9-3*2 > 5
  9-6 > 5        Multiplication first ...
    3 > 5        ... then subtraction ...
      FALSE      ... then "greater than."
```

```
2**3+1 = 3**2
   8+1 = 9          Exponentiations first ...
     9 = 9          ... then addition ...
      TRUE          ... then "equal to."
```

We can define relational operators on strings as well as on real numbers. The same six symbols are used for the relational operators on strings, but—except for = and ≠—the corresponding relations are different:

```
=     is equal to
≠     is not equal to
<     precedes in alphabetical order
>     follows in alphabetical order
≤     precedes or is equal to
≥     follows or is equal to
```

Thus:

Expression		*Value*
'BILL'	< 'JACK'	TRUE
'TOM'	< 'DICK'	FALSE
'LARRY'	≥ 'JANE'	TRUE
'TOM'	≤ 'TOD'	FALSE

Blank spaces count when doing comparisons, so 'JACK' = 'JACK ' is FALSE. If one string forms the initial part of another, then the shorter one precedes the longer. Thus 'JACK' < 'JACKSON' is TRUE.

Conditions. We can now give a precise definition of a condition: A *condition* is an expression that evaluates to TRUE or FALSE. That is, it is an expression whose value is a logical value. Obviously, all the expressions described in this section are conditions.

6.2 One- and Two-Way Selection

The IF and END IF Statements (One-Way Selection). The simplest possible selection is to execute or not execute a group of statements, depending on whether or not some condition is TRUE or FALSE. We express this selection using the IF and END IF statements like this:

```
IF condition THEN
    statements
END IF
```

If the *condition* is TRUE, then the *statements* between IF and END IF are executed, after which execution continues with the statement following END IF. If the *condition* is FALSE, the *statements* between IF and END IF are skipped, and execution continues immediately with the statement following END IF.

Example 1:

In Chapter 1 we wrote an algorithm, WAGES, to compute an employee's salary from hours worked and hourly rate. But we did not take into account the fact that many employees get "time-and-a-half for overtime" for hours in excess of 40.

Let's modify the algorithm to compute the extra wages received for overtime work and add these to the worker's salary. First, we outline the modified algorithm:

```
ALGORITHM WAGES
    (Input data)
    (Compute GROSS_WAGES without extra pay for
     overtime)
    IF HOURS > 40 THEN
        (Compute extra pay for overtime)
        (Add extra pay for overtime to GROSS_WAGES)
    END IF
    (Output results)
END WAGES
```

Filling in the details gives us:

```
ALGORITHM WAGES
    INPUT NAME, HOURS, RATE
    GROSS_WAGES ← HOURS*RATE
    IF HOURS > 40 THEN
        EXTRA_FOR_OVERTIME ← 0.5*(HOURS−40)*RATE
        GROSS_WAGES ← GROSS_WAGES + EXTRA_FOR_OVERTIME
    END IF
    OUTPUT 'NAME:', NAME
    OUTPUT 'PAY:', GROSS_WAGES
END WAGES
```

If the value of HOURS is not greater than 40, then the statements between IF and END IF will be skipped. But if the value of HOURS is greater than 40, then the 50% extra for the overtime hours is computed and added to GROSS__WAGES. Note that if the IF and END IF statements were omitted, then the algorithm would impose a 50% *penalty* for each hour less than 40 that was worked—obviously not what was intended.

Figure 6-1 shows the flowchart version of the IF construction.

The decision symbol corresponds to the "IF *condition* THEN," and the collector circle corresponds to the "END IF." The two branches that leave the decision symbol rejoin at the collector circle. This corresponds to the fact that we always end up at the statement following the END IF, whether the *condition* is TRUE or FALSE.

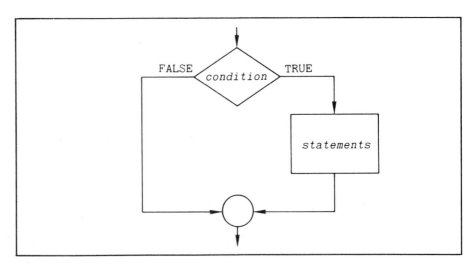

FIGURE 6-1. Flowchart of one-way selection.

Figure 6-2 shows a flowchart of the revised version of the algorithm WAGES. Note that the flowchart of Figure 6-1 forms a part of Figure 6-2.

The ELSE Statement (Two-Way Selection). With IF and END IF, we can cause a group of statements to be either executed or not executed, depending on whether a condition is TRUE or FALSE. By adding the ELSE statement, we can select one group of statements for execution when the condition is TRUE, and another when it is FALSE. Here is the construction:

```
IF condition THEN
    statements-1
ELSE
    statements-2
END IF
```

If the *condition* is TRUE, then the first group of statements, *statements–1,* is executed. Otherwise, *statements–2* are executed. In either case, execution ultimately continues with the statement following END IF.

Figure 6-3 shows a flowchart of this construction. Figure 6-3 differs from Figure 6-2 only in that there are now *statements* boxes in *both* branches leaving the decision symbol.

Example 2:
The following algorithm inputs two strings and outputs them in alphabetical order:

```
ALGORITHM ALPHABETIZE
    INPUT FIRST, SECOND
    IF FIRST ≤ SECOND
        OUTPUT FIRST, SECOND
```

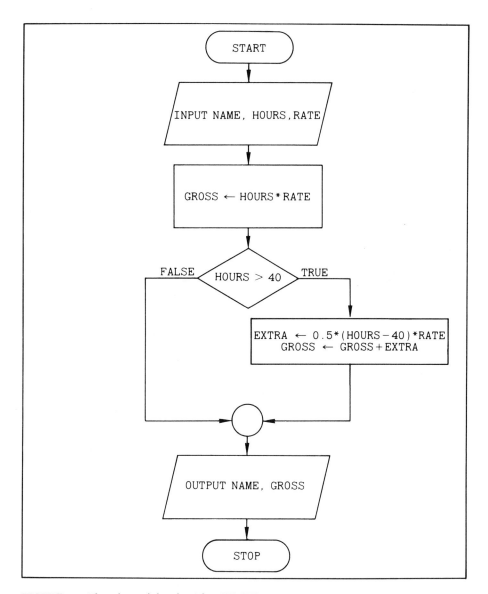

FIGURE 6-2. Flowchart of the algorithm WAGES.

```
    ELSE
        OUTPUT SECOND, FIRST
    END IF
END ALPHABETIZE
```

If the input to this algorithm is

`'TOM', 'DICK'`

the output will be

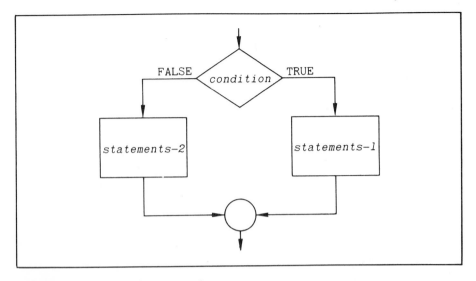

FIGURE 6-3. Flowchart of two-way selection.

```
DICK TOM
```

If the input is

```
'JACK', 'JOE'
```

the output will be

```
JACK JOE
```

Figure 6-4 shows the flowchart of ALPHABETIZE.

Nested IF Constructions. The statements that occur between IF and ELSE or between ELSE and END IF can themselves contain selection constructions. We use the word *nested* to describe the situation where one construction contains another construction of the same kind.

Example 3:
Consider a part of a "computer-assisted instruction" algorithm, where a student is asked a question and given a chance to answer. If the answer is incorrect, the student is given another chance before being told the right answer:

```
OUTPUT 'WHAT IS THE CAPITAL OF WEST VIRGINIA?'
INPUT ANSWER
IF ANSWER = 'CHARLESTON' THEN
   OUTPUT 'YOU ARE RIGHT'
ELSE
   OUTPUT 'NO, TRY AGAIN'
   INPUT ANSWER
```

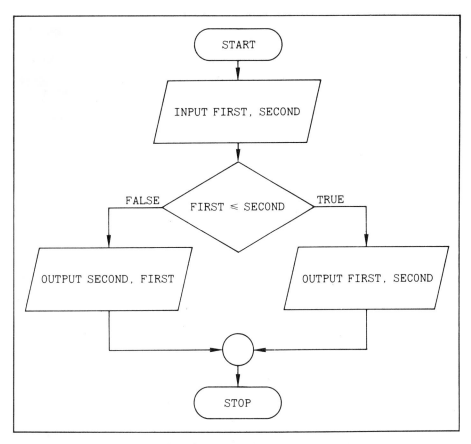

FIGURE 6-4. Flowchart of the algorithm ALPHABETIZE.

```
IF ANSWER = 'CHARLESTON' THEN
    OUTPUT 'YOU GOT IT RIGHT THIS TIME'
ELSE
    OUTPUT 'NO, CHARLESTON IS THE CAPITAL OF WEST VIRGINIA'
    END IF
END IF
```

Figure 6-5 shows how a nested IF construction appears on a flowchart.

Indentation. If an algorithm is to be easily readable, it is essential that the reader be able to see at a glance which statements are part of extended constructions such as IF . . . ELSE . . . END IF. When constructions are nested, the reader must be able to see immediately which conditions influence the execution of which statements. This is accomplished by *indenting* the statements between IF and ELSE and between ELSE and END IF (or between IF and END IF when there is no ELSE) with respect to IF, ELSE, and END IF.

This is not the first time we have used indentation, of course. All along we have been indenting the statements of an algorithm with respect

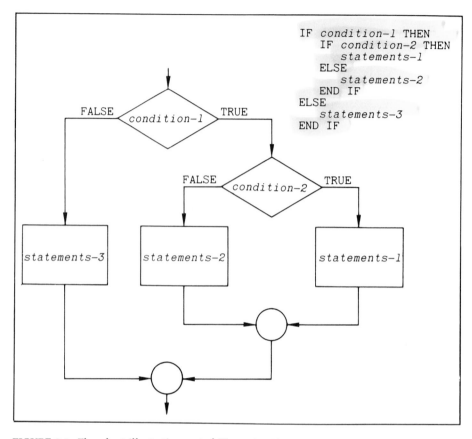

```
IF condition-1 THEN
    IF condition-2 THEN
        statements-1
    ELSE
        statements-2
    END IF
ELSE
    statements-3
END IF
```

FIGURE 6-5. Flowchart illustrating nested IF constructions.

to ALGORITHM and END. And we will find still more uses for indentation as we go further. In every case, the purpose of indentation is to render the structure of an algorithm visible at a glance.

In most programming languages, indentation is optional. In the algorithmic language, however, it is *required*. The object of the algorithmic language is to provide a means for writing algorithms in a form that is easy to read and understand. Without indentation, complex algorithms are neither easy to read nor easy to understand.

6.3 Multiway Selection

So far, we have seen how either to select or not to select one group of statements and how to select between two alternative groups of statements. Sometimes we must select from among more than two groups of statements. The algorithmic language provides two ways of doing this.

The ELSE IF statement. The first way is to extend the IF construction that we already have with the addition of an ELSE IF statement. Consider the following:

```
IF condition-1 THEN
    statements-1
ELSE IF condition-2 THEN
    statements-2
ELSE IF condition-3 THEN
    statements-3
ELSE
    statements-4
END IF
```

If condition-1 is TRUE, then statements-1 are executed. If condition-1 is not TRUE, but condition-2 is, then statements-2 are executed. If neither condition-1 nor condition-2 is TRUE, but condition-3 is, then statements-3 are executed. If none of the conditions are TRUE, then statements-4 are executed.

In other words, the conditions are examined in top-to-bottom order. When the *first* true condition is found, the following group of statements is executed. Only one group of statements is executed, even if more than one condition is TRUE.

If none of the conditions are TRUE, the group of statements following ELSE is executed. ELSE is optional. If it is omitted and none of the conditions are TRUE, then all the groups of statements are skipped and execution continues with the statement following END IF.

An IF . . . END IF construction can contain any number of ELSE IFs. It may or may not contain an ELSE.

Figure 6-6 shows a flowchart of the IF construction with ELSE IF. Note that multiway selection is the only situation in which more than two branches can join at a collector circle.

Example 4:
The algorithm letter grade in Figure 6-7 inputs a numerical grade and outputs the corresponding letter grade, using the following scale:

A   90–100
B   80–89
C   70–79
D   60–69
F   below 60

The fact that the conditions are tested in top-to-bottom order is essential to the correct functioning of this algorithm. If, for instance, NUMBER__GRADE $\geq$ 60 were tested first, then anyone making 60 or over would get a D, which is certainly not what is intended.

Figure 6-8 is a flowchart of LETTER__GRADE.

The CASE Construction. The other way to do multiway selection is to let a numerical value determine which group of statements is to be executed. If the value is 1, the first group will be executed; if the value is 2, the second group will be executed, and so on.

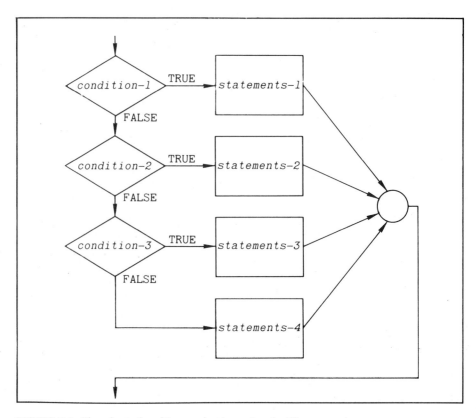

FIGURE 6-6. Flowchart of multiway selection using the IF construction.

FIGURE 6-7. The algorithm LETTER__GRADE using the IF construction.

```
ALGORITHM LETTER_GRADE
   INPUT NUMBER_GRADE
   IF  NUMBER_GRADE ≥ 90 THEN
       OUTPUT 'A'
   ELSE IF NUMBER_GRADE ≥ 80 THEN
       OUTPUT 'B'
   ELSE IF NUMBER_GRADE ≥ 70 THEN
       OUTPUT 'C'
   ELSE IF NUMBER_GRADE ≥ 60 THEN
       OUTPUT 'D'
   ELSE
       OUTPUT 'F'
   END IF
END LETTER_GRADE
```

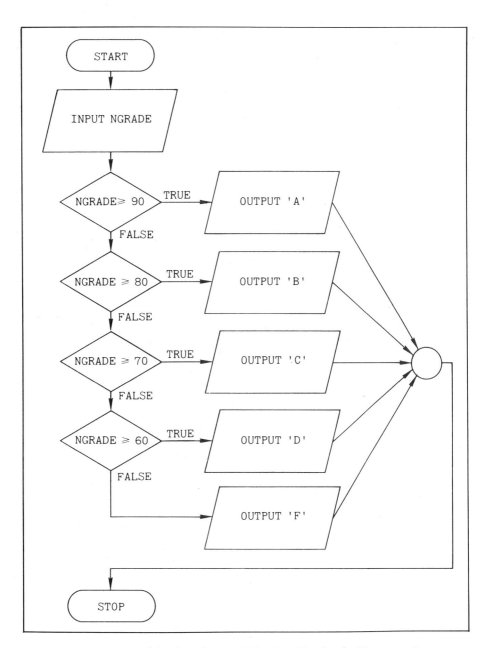

FIGURE 6-8. Flowchart of the algorithm LETTER__GRADE using the IF construction.

A variable whose value is used for this purpose is called a *switch*, since its value switches the computer to one of several groups of statements.

Here is the construction:

```
CASE SWITCH OF
1:
    statements-1
2:
    statements-2
3:
    statements-3
ELSE
    statements-4
END CASE
```

If the value of SWITCH is 1, *statements-1* will be executed. If the value of SWITCH is 2, *statements-2* will be executed. If the value of SWITCH is 3, *statements-3* will be executed. If the value of SWITCH is not 1, 2, or 3, then *statements-4* will be executed.

There may be any number of cases. These are numbered by successive integers starting at 1: 1, 2, 3, 4, and so on. The ELSE part is optional. If it is omitted, and the value of the switch is not the number of one of the cases, then the entire CASE construction is skipped, and execution continues with the statement following END CASE.

Figure 6-9 shows the flowchart of the CASE construction. Again we have more than two branches coming together at a collector circle, a sure sign of multiway selection.

Example 5:
The LETTER__GRADE algorithm can be rewritten to use the CASE construction with the help of the following expression

```
INT((NUMBER_GRADE-50)/10)
```

whose values are as follows:

NUMBER_GRADE	INT((NUMBER_GRADE-50)/10)
100	5
90–99	4
80–89	3
70–79	2
60–69	1
0–59	0 or negative

Figure 6-10 shows this version of LETTER__GRADE, and Figure 6-11 shows its flowchart.

6.4 Logical Operators and Expressions

The relational operators are not by themselves sufficient to express conveniently all the conditions we need. Sometimes we need the equivalent of English sentences containing the connectives "or," "and," and "not."

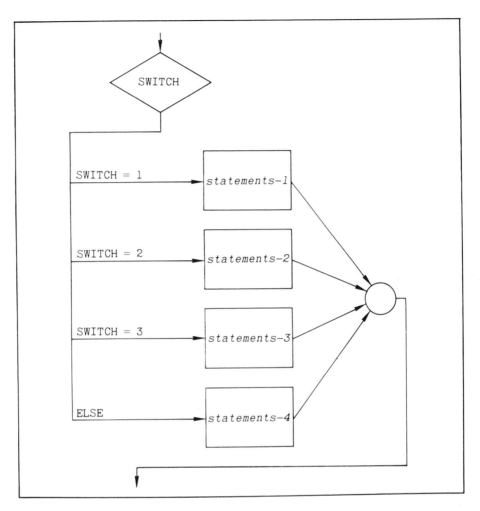

FIGURE 6-9. Flowchart of the CASE construction.

The logical operators OR, AND, and NOT correspond directly to these English connectives. We use them to form expressions such as

```
A < B AND C = 25
```

which correspond to statements such as

The value of A is less than the value of B, and the value of C equals 25.

The expression

```
P OR Q
```

```
             ALGORITHM LETTER _GRADE
                INPUT NUMBER_GRADE
                RANGE ← INT((NUMBER_GRADE-50)/10)
                CASE RANGE OF
                1:
                    OUTPUT 'D'
                2:
                    OUTPUT 'C'
                3:
                    OUTPUT 'B'
                4:
                    OUTPUT 'A'
                5:
                    OUTPUT 'A'
                ELSE
                    OUTPUT 'F'
                END CASE
             END LETTER_GRADE
```

FIGURE 6-10. The algorithm LETTER__GRADE using the CASE construction.

is TRUE if P is TRUE or Q is TRUE or *both* are true. Since the only possible values of P and Q are TRUE and FALSE, we can list every possible case of the expression P OR Q:

Expression	*Value*
FALSE OR FALSE	FALSE
FALSE OR TRUE	TRUE
TRUE OR FALSE	TRUE
TRUE OR TRUE	TRUE

The expression

P AND Q

is TRUE if and only if both P *and* Q are TRUE. Again we can write out all possible cases:

Expression	*Value*
FALSE AND FALSE	FALSE
FALSE AND TRUE	FALSE
TRUE AND FALSE	FALSE
TRUE AND TRUE	TRUE

The expression

NOT P

is FALSE if P is TRUE and vice versa:

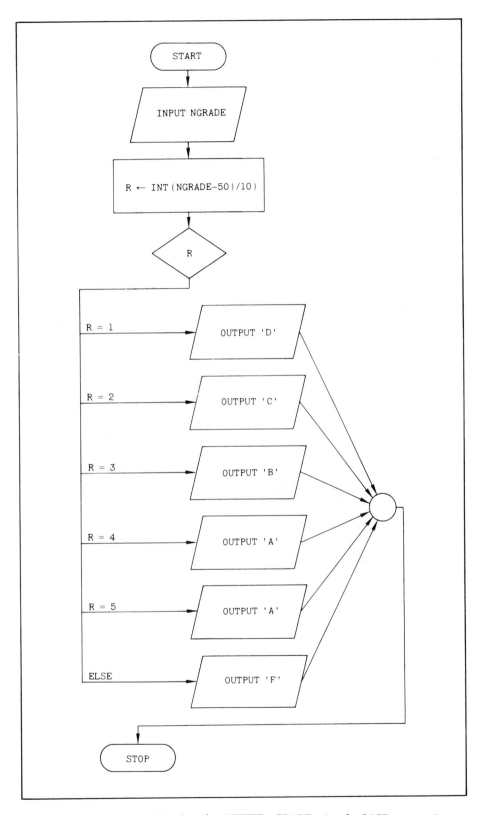

FIGURE 6-11. Flowchart of the algorithm LETTER__GRADE using the CASE construction.

```
Expression       Value

NOT TRUE         FALSE
NOT FALSE        TRUE
```

The logical operators have *lower* priorities than either the relational or arithmetic operators. This means that in a general logical expression,

- the arithmetic operators will be applied first,

- the relational operators will be applied next, and

- the logical operators will be applied last of all.

Example 6:

```
3+4 > 12 OR 3*4 = 12
3+4 > 12 OR 12 = 12
  7 > 12 OR 12 = 12
    FALSE OR TRUE
         TRUE
```

Despite these priority conventions, the liberal use of parentheses is recommended for clarity. Thus,

```
(3+4 > 12) OR (3*4 = 12)
```

is clearer than

```
3+4 > 12 OR 3*4 = 12
```

Among themselves, the logical operators have the following priorities:

```
NOT      highest priority
AND
OR       lowest priority
```

Thus,

```
NOT TRUE OR FALSE AND TRUE
```

is evaluated

```
NOT TRUE OR FALSE AND TRUE
  FALSE OR FALSE AND TRUE
  FALSE OR FALSE
      FALSE
```

As before, parentheses can save much head scratching over the original expression:

(NOT TRUE) OR (FALSE AND TRUE)

Here is a general logical expression (condition) and its evaluation:

(3 ≠ 5) AND NOT ((3 < 7) OR (4 > 9))
  TRUE AND NOT (TRUE OR FALSE)
  TRUE AND NOT TRUE
  TRUE AND FALSE
  FALSE

Review Questions

1. What is the purpose of the *control structures* of a language?

2. Describe the *sequencing* control structure.

3. Describe the *selection* control structure.

4. The symbols TRUE and FALSE denote the two possible logical values. Give some examples of similar value denotations for other data types.

5. Distinguish between TRUE and FALSE on one hand and 'TRUE' and 'FALSE' on the other.

6. Give the six relational operators that apply to real numbers and the relation corresponding to each.

7. What is the priority of the relational operators, relative to that of the arithmetic operators? Why do you suppose that this choice of priorities was made?

8. Give the six relational operators that apply to strings and the relation corresponding to each.

9. Explain why 91 = 091 is TRUE, but '91' = '091' is FALSE.

10. Give the general form of the IF construction that causes a group of statements to be either executed or not executed. Give an example of this form.

11. Give the form of the IF construction that causes one of two alternative groups of statements to be executed.

12. In the flowchart of one- or two-way selection, what corresponds to IF *condition* THEN, and what corresponds to END IF?

13. Is there anything in the flowchart of a two-way selection that corresponds to ELSE? How *do* the flowcharts of one- and two-way selections differ?

14. Why is indentation a required feature of the algorithmic language?

15. When more than two branches come together at a collector circle, this is a sure sign of what?

16. Of the two multiway selection constructions, which is an extension of the construction used for one- and two-way selection?

17. What is a *switch*?

18. Define each of the logical operators by giving a table showing the value of the expression formed with that operator for every possible value of its operands. Why could this technique not be used for defining the operators on real numbers?

19. What are the relative priorities of (a) the logical operators, (b) the relational operators, and (c) the arithmetic operators?

20. Why are parentheses strongly recommended in logical expressions, even when they are not necessary to specify the order of evaluation?

Exercises

In Exercises 1, 2, and 3, assume the following variable-value list

Variable	Value	Variable	Value
A	3	P	TRUE
B	4	Q	FALSE
C	12	R	TRUE

1. Evaluate:

(a) B > C (b) A*B = C
(c) A ≠ B (d) A + B ≤ C
(e) B − A ≥ 1 (f) B < 6

2. Evaluate:

(a) 'BIG' = 'BAD' (b) 'BIG' > 'BAD'
(c) 'BAD' ≤ 'BOY' (d) 'BOY' ≠ 'BOY'
(e) 'BOY' ≠ 'BOY ' (f) 'BILLY' < 'BILL'

3. Evaluate:

(a) NOT Q
(b) P OR Q
(c) P AND Q
(d) P AND Q OR R
(e) (B > A) AND (B > C)
(f) (B > A) OR (B > C)
(g) NOT ((A = B) OR (A = C))
(h) ('BOOK' < 'BOOKED') AND ('BOOK' = 'BOOKS')
(i) ('BOY' ≤ 'BOYS') AND (3 < 5)
(j) (A > B) OR (B > C) OR (C > A)
(k) (A > B) AND (B > C) AND (C > A)

4. Almost all algorithms can be written in more than one way. Rewrite the algorithm WAGES given in this chapter as follows: If HOURS does not exceed 40, compute GROSS__WAGES using

```
HOURS*RATE
```

If HOURS is greater than 40, compute GROSS__WAGES using

```
        40*RATE              +        1.5*(HOURS-40)*RATE
(for hours at regular rate)   (for hours at overtime rate)
```

5. A salesperson gets a 5% commission on sales of $1,000 or less and a 10% commission on sales over $1,000. (So someone who sold $1,500 worth would get a 5% commission on $1,000 and a 10% commission on $500.) Write an algorithm to input the amount of sales and compute both the salesperson's commission and the amount the company receives after the commission has been deducted.

6. A computer is often used to monitor some quantity, such as the heart rate of a patient in an intensive care unit, and sound an alarm if the quantity falls outside a predetermined range. Write an algorithm to input a test value together with the upper and lower limits of the range in which it should lie. The algorithm should print OK, LOW, or HIGH depending on whether the value lies in the desired range, is too low, or is too high.

7. Write an algorithm to input two numbers and output the smaller of the two. The algorithm should use only one OUTPUT statement.

8. Write an algorithm to input three numbers and output them in ascending numerical order, regardless of the order in which they were entered.

9. In Exercises 13 of Chapter 5 we learned that a package cannot be sent by first class mail if its length-plus-girth exceeds 100 inches. Write an algorithm to input the length, width, and height of a rectangular package; the algorithm should print OK if the package can be sent by first class mail and REJECTED otherwise.

10. Write an algorithm that inputs the length, width, and height of a box as well as the diameter and height of a cylindrical jar. The algorithm should print whether or not the jar will fit inside the box. The jar can sit upright in the box, or it can lie on its side with its top parallel to one of the sides of the box.

11. A triangle is *equilateral* if all three sides have the same length, *isosceles* if only two of its sides have the same length, and *scalene* if no two sides have the same length. Write an algorithm to input the lengths of the three sides of a triangle and print whether the triangle is equilateral, isosceles, or scalene.

12. The cost of a certain item depends on the quantity ordered, as given by the following table:

Quantity Ordered	Cost per Item
0–99	$5.95
100–199	$5.75
200–299	$5.40
300 or more	$5.15

Write an algorithm to input the quantity ordered and output the *total* cost of the order. Use the IF construction.

13. Redo Exercise 12 using the CASE construction.

14. A company wishes to hire people with the following combinations of qualifications:

Experience	Field	Degree
1 year	PROGRAMMING	BS
1 year	PROGRAMMING	MS
1 year	ENGINEERING	MS
1 year	ENGINEERING	Ph.D
5 years	PROGRAMMING	BS
5 years	ENGINEERING	BS
5 years	ENGINEERING	MS
5 years	ENGINEERING	Ph.D

Write an algorithm, using nested IF constructions, to input a person's experience, field, and degree and to indicate whether or not this company should consider him or her for hiring.

15. Rewrite the algorithm of Exercise 14 using OR and AND but not nested IF constructions.

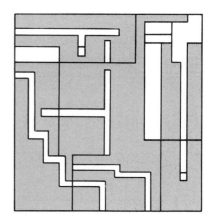

Chapter 7

Repetition

All the algorithms we have studied so far have a certain air of triviality about them. You may well have asked why it was necessary to use a computer to do the things the algorithms were written to accomplish. Would it not be just as easy to do these things by hand as it would be to program a computer to do them?

The reason these algorithms seemed trivial was that each instruction was used only once. If an instruction is to be carried out only once, then it is probably just as easy to carry it out by hand (perhaps with some aid such as a calculator) as it is to program a computer to carry it out. If a computer program is to justify its existence, some of the instructions must be executed repeatedly.

Of course, this repetition can come about because the entire program is executed more than once. But more commonly some instructions will be carried out repeatedly during a single execution of the entire program.

In this chapter, we take up the *repetition* constructions of our algorithmic language, which allow us to specify the repeated execution of groups of statements.

7.1 The While Construction

The WHILE construction causes a group of statements to be executed repeatedly as long as a certain condition holds. When the condition ceases to hold, the repetition terminates.

The WHILE construction has the following form:

```
WHILE condition DO
    statements
END WHILE
```

Figure 7–1 shows the flowchart for the WHILE construction.

The computer starts by checking the *condition*. If it is TRUE, then the *statements* are executed. Otherwise, the computer proceeds to the next statement following END WHILE. After the *statements* have been executed, the computer goes back and checks the *condition* again. This sequence of events repeats itself until eventually the *condition* tests FALSE. When that happens, the repetition is terminated, and execution continues with the statement following END WHILE.

Notice that the *condition* is checked before any executions of the *statements* take place. Therfore, the *statements* may not be executed at all if the *condition* is FALSE when the computer first arrives at the WHILE statement. This is a distinguishing feature of the WHILE construction.

Notice that in Figure 7–1 the flowchart of the repetition forms a loop. As a result, programmers often use the word "loop" interchangeably with "repetition."

Example 1: Figure 7–2 shows the algorithm AVERAGE, which inputs a sequence of numbers and computes their average. We do not know in advance how many numbers there will be in the sequence, but we do know that they will all be positive or zero. Therefore, we can use a negative

FIGURE 7-1. Flowchart for the WHILE construction. Notice that the condition is tested before any of the statements are executed.

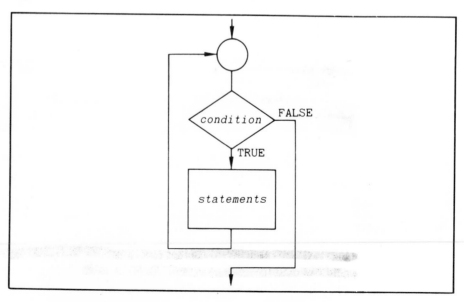

```
ALGORITHM AVERAGE
    SUM ← 0
    COUNT ← 0
    INPUT NUMBER
    WHILE NUMBER ≥ 0 DO
        SUM ← SUM + NUMBER
        COUNT ← COUNT + 1
        INPUT NUMBER
    END WHILE
    IF COUNT > 0 THEN
        OUTPUT SUM/COUNT
    ELSE
        OUTPUT 'NO NUMBERS WERE ENTERED'
    END IF
END AVERAGE
```

FIGURE 7-2. The algorithm AVERAGE.

number to indicate the end of the sequence. (A data value used to signal the end of a sequence is called a *sentinel*.)

A possible sequence might be

1
2
3
−1

and the average would be

$$\frac{1+2+3}{3} = 2$$

We will use SUM and COUNT to keep a running total and a running count of the data values inputted. Every time we input a new NUMBER, we will update SUM and COUNT as follows:

SUM ← SUM + NUMBER
COUNT ← COUNT + 1

When all the values have been inputted, the average is calculated as SUM/COUNT.

Figure 7–3 shows the flowchart for AVERAGE.

Notice that we input the first value before starting the repetition. Each succeeding value is inputted after the preceding one has been processed. The purpose of arranging things in this way is so that the sentinel will not be processed as if it were a valid data value. Immediately after a value is inputted, before any processing of it is done, it must be checked to see if it is the sentinel. In Figure 7–3, note that after each INPUT NUMBER statement is executed the computer goes directly to the decision diamond that checks whether the value just inputted is the sentinel. If it is, the repetition terminates, and the value just inputted is not processed.

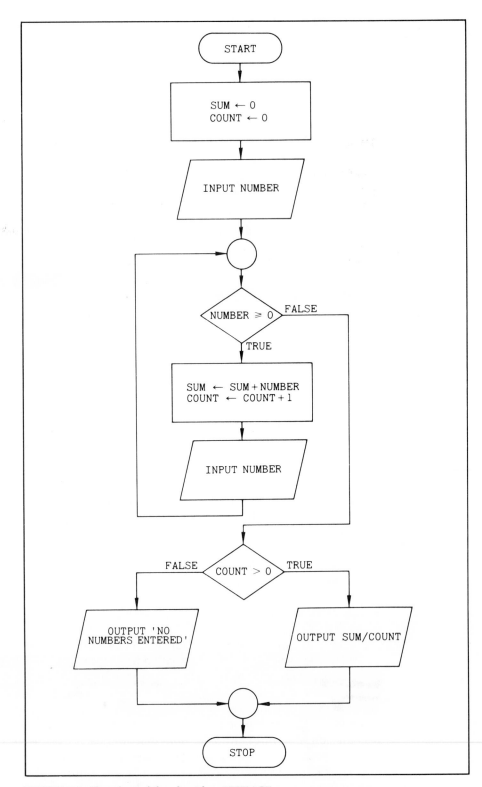

FIGURE 7-3. Flowchart of the algorithm AVERAGE.

7.2 The REPEAT Construction

The REPEAT construction has the same form as the WHILE construction:

```
REPEAT
    statements
UNTIL condition
```

The differences between REPEAT and WHILE are these:

- The *statements* are executed repeatedly *until* the *condition* becomes TRUE. The repetition continues as long as the *condition* is FALSE, and terminates when it becomes TRUE.

- The *condition* is checked after the *statements* are executed. This means that the *statements* are executed at least once, even if the *condition* is already TRUE when the computer encounters the REPEAT statement.

Figure 7–4 is a flowchart of the REPEAT construction. Compare it with the flowchart for WHILE. Make sure you can visualize why the *statements* will always be executed at least once for REPEAT, whereas they may not be executed at all for WHILE.

The REPEAT construction is most useful when it does not make sense to check the *condition* until the *statements* have been executed at least once.

For instance, suppose we wish the computer to input a series of pairs of data items. The first item of each pair is a salesperson's name; the second item is his or her monthly sales. When the first pair is found for which the

FIGURE 7-4. Flowchart for the REPEAT construction. Notice that the statements are executed before the condition is tested. Because of this, the statements are always executed at least one time even if the condition is initially true.

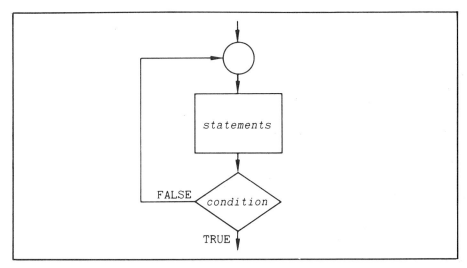

sales exceed $10,000, the salesperson's name is to be printed so he or she can be awarded a bonus.

Obviously, the repeated statement will input the pairs of data items. The repetition will stop when a sales figure over $10,000 is found. But— and this is the important point—it makes no sense to check for sales greater than 10000 until a value for sales has been inputted. In short, the repeated statement that does the input must be executed at least once before we can check the terminating condition.

Here is the algorithm:

```
ALGORITHM BONUS
    REPEAT
        INPUT NAME, SALES
    UNTIL SALES > 10000
    OUTPUT 'THE BONUS GOES TO', NAME
END BONUS
```

Figure 7–5 is the flowchart for BONUS.

FIGURE 7-5. Flowchart for the algorithm BONUS.

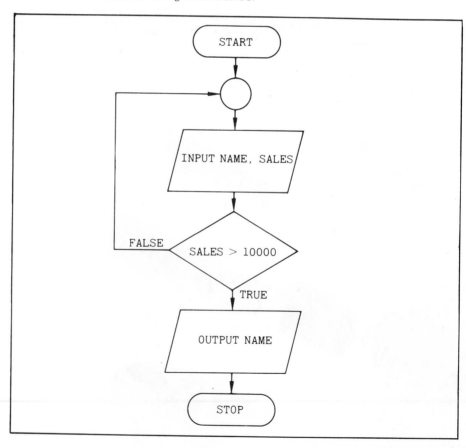

7.3. Iteration

The *iterative construction* causes a group of statements to be executed a specified number of times. Means are provided for keeping count of how many times the statements have been executed so far. The statements can use this information to do different things on different repetitions.

The general form of the iterative construction is as follows:

```
FOR variable ← expression-1 TO expression-2 [BY expression-3] DO
    statements
END FOR
```

The brackets around BY *expression-3* indicate that this phrase is optional. If omitted, the phrase BY 1 is assumed.

The general construction is somewhat complicated. We can best understand it by looking at some special cases:

```
FOR I ← 1 TO 5 BY 1 DO
    statements
END FOR
```

The *statements* will be executed five times. The first time, I will have the value 1; the second time, I will have the value 2; the third, fourth, and fifth times, I will have the values 3, 4, and 5. The *statements* can use the value of I as part of any calculation they do.

This construction is equivalent to

```
I ← 1
WHILE I > 5 DO
    statements
    I ← I + 1
END WHILE
```

When BY *expression-3* is omitted, BY 1 is assumed. So we never actually have to write BY 1. This means we can abbreviate

```
FOR I ← 1 TO 5 BY 1 DO
    statements
END FOR
```

to

```
FOR I ← 1 TO 5 DO
    statements
END FOR
```

We can use the BY phrase to count by increments other than 1. For instance,

```
FOR I ← 5 TO 25 BY 5
    statements
END FOR
```

again causes the *statements* to be executed five times, but now with I taking the values 5, 10, 15, 20, and 25.

We can even count backwards if we want to:

```
FOR I ← 5 TO 1 BY −1 DO
    statements
END FOR
```

Again we get five repetitions, but with I now taking the values 5, 4, 3, 2, and 1.

Here are three examples of the iterative construction.

Example 2:
Find the sum of all the integers from 1 through 1,000.

```
ALGORITHM INTEGER_SUM
    SUM ← 0
    FOR N ← 1 TO 1000 DO
        SUM ← SUM + N
    END FOR
    OUTPUT SUM
END INTEGER_SUM
```

Example 3:
Find the sum of all the odd integers from 1 through 999.

```
ALGORITHM ODD_INTEGER_SUM
    FOR N ← 1 TO 999 BY 2 DO
        SUM ← SUM + N
    END FOR
    OUTPUT SUM
END ODD_INTEGER_SUM
```

The successive odd integers 1, 3, 5, 7, and so on differ by 2. By starting the value of N at 1, and incrementing it by 2 each time, we cause it to step through this sequence.

Example 4:
Input a sequence of numbers and find their average. The first number inputted gives the number of values to be averaged.

For instance, the input data

```
3
1
2
3
```

tells the algorithm that there are three values to be averaged, namely, 1, 2, and 3.

```
ALGORITHM AVERAGE
    INPUT COUNT
    SUM ← 0
    FOR N ← 1 TO COUNT DO
        INPUT NUMBER
        SUM ← SUM + NUMBER
    END FOR
    OUTPUT SUM/COUNT
END AVERAGE
```

There are two ways to program a computer to process a list of data items when the number of items on the list was not known when the program was written. One is to use a special sentinel value to indicate the end of the list. The other is to start the list with a data item which gives the number of values to follow.

The sentinel method has the disadvantage that one possible data value must be reserved as the sentinel value. Also, the sentinel method is slightly harder to program. The count method has the disadvantage that the user must count the data items in advance. This may be burdensome if the number of data items is large. With the sentinel method, the computer does the counting.

Notice that the algorithm just given assumes that COUNT is not 0. As written, it will not work correctly if COUNT is 0. Can you modify it to remove this deficiency?

7.4 Five Algorithms

Repetition, more than any other control structure, opens up a whole new realm of possibilities for algorithms. Algorithms from previous chapters that may have seemed pointless and trivial become practical and useful with repetition. The following five algorithms illustrate some of the possibilities of repetition. Two of these are improvements of algorithms from the last chapter.

PAYROLL. For each employee, input employee name, hours worked, and hourly rate. An employee name of 'END OF DATA' serves as a sentinel to indicate the end of the input data. Output the name and gross wages of each employee. When all employees have been processed, output the total wages of all employees (such totals are frequently outputted, since accountants like to use them for error checking). Figure 7–6 shows the algorithm PAYROLL.

GRADES. For each student in a class, input name and number grade. The sentinel is a student name of 'END OF DATA'. For each student, output name and letter grade. (Use the grade scale given in Chapter 6.) After all

```
ALGORITHM PAYROLL
   TOTAL ← 0
   INPUT NAME, HOURS, RATE
   WHILE NAME ≠ 'END OF DATA' DO
      GROSS_WAGES ← HOURS*RATE
      IF HOURS > 40 THEN
         GROSS_WAGES ← GROSS_WAGES + 0.5*(HOURS−40)*RATE
      END IF
      TOTAL ← TOTAL + GROSS_WAGES
      OUTPUT NAME, GROSS_WAGES
      INPUT NAME, HOURS, RATE
   END WHILE
   OUTPUT 'TOTAL GROSS WAGES:', TOTAL
END PAYROLL
```

FIGURE 7-6. The algorithm PAYROLL.

students have been processed, output the "grade distribution": the number of As, the number of Bs, and so on. Figure 7–7 shows the algorithm GRADES.

HIGH__AND__LOW. Input a series of temperature readings taken throughout the day. (The sentinel for the end of the sequence is −100.) After inputting the readings, output the high and low temperature for the day. (If a person had to type in these readings, this would be a trivial program, since the person could see the high and low at a glance. But the computer might be connected directly to an electric thermometer. Or we might be analyzing records from past years stored on a data file. In those cases, the program becomes more reasonable.)

Our strategy will be to maintain a CURRENT__LOW and a CURRENT__HIGH as the temperatures are inputted. If a newly inputted temperature is smaller than the value of CURRENT__LOW, it replaces that value. If it is larger than the value of CURRENT__HIGH, it replaces *that* value. Figure 7–8 shows the algorithm HIGH__AND__LOW.

GUESS. Now that computers have become popular with hobbyists, there has been a tremendous upsurge of interest in computer games. Many of these are quite complex. The algorithm GUESS, Figure 7–9, is a very simple game in which the player tries to guess a number the computer is "thinking of." The algorithm uses the function RANDOM, whose value is a random integer between 1 and its argument. (So the value of RANDOM(100) is a random integer between 1 and 100. The limits 1 and 100 are included in the range.) Since the value is generated by an algorithm, it is not really random, but *pseudorandom*—seemingly random.

INTEREST. We are given the amount currently in a bank account, the deposit made at the beginning of each month, and the yearly interest rate (in

```
ALGORITHM GRADES
    A_COUNT ← 0
    B_COUNT ← 0
    C_COUNT ← 0
    D_COUNT ← 0
    F_COUNT ← 0
    INPUT NAME, NUMBER_GRADE
    WHILE NAME ≠ 'END OF DATA' DO
        IF NUMBER_GRADE ≥ 90 THEN
            LETTER_GRADE ← 'A'
            A_COUNT ← A_COUNT + 1
        ELSE IF NUMBER_GRADE ≥ 80 THEN
            LETTER_GRADE ← 'B'
            B_COUNT ← B_COUNT + 1
        ELSE IF NUMBER_GRADE ≥ 70 THEN
            LETTER_GRADE ← 'C'
            C_COUNT ← C_COUNT + 1
        ELSE IF NUMBER_GRADE ≥ 60 THEN
            LETTER_GRADE 'D'
            D_COUNT ← D_COUNT + 1
        ELSE
            LETTER_GRADE ← 'F'
            F_COUNT ← F_COUNT + 1
        END IF
        OUTPUT NAME, LETTER_GRADE
        INPUT NAME, NUMBER_GRADE
    END WHILE
    OUTPUT 'GRADE DISTRIBUTION'
    OUTPUT 'A:', A_COUNT, 'B:', B_COUNT, 'C:', C_COUNT
    OUTPUT 'D:', D_COUNT, 'F:', F_COUNT
END GRADES
```

FIGURE 7-7. The algorithm GRADES.

percent). Assuming the interest is compounded monthly, how much will be in the account after a given number of months?

We get the MONTHLY__INTEREST__RATE by dividing the YEARLY__ INTEREST__RATE by 100 (to convert the percent to a decimal) and by 12 (to convert the yearly rate to a monthly rate). Then, if AMOUNT is the

FIGURE 7-8. The algorithm HIGH__AND__LOW.

```
ALGORITHM HIGH_AND_LOW
    INPUT TEMPERATURE
    CURRENT_LOW ← TEMPERATURE
    CURRENT_HIGH ← TEMPERATURE
    WHILE TEMPERATURE ≠ -100 DO
        IF TEMPERATURE < CURRENT_LOW THEN
            CURRENT_LOW ← TEMPERATURE
        ELSE IF TEMPERATURE > CURRENT_HIGH THEN
            CURRENT_HIGH ← TEMPERATURE
        END IF
        INPUT TEMPERATURE
    END WHILE
    OUTPUT 'LOW:', CURRENT_LOW
    OUTPUT 'HIGH:', CURRENT_HIGH
END HIGH_AND_LOW
```

```
ALGORITHM GUESS
    OUTPUT 'I AM THINKING OF A NUMBER BETWEEN 1 AND 100'
    OUTPUT 'YOU ARE TO TRY TO GUESS THE NUMBER. I WILL TELL'
    OUTPUT 'YOU WHETHER YOUR GUESS IS RIGHT, OR WHETHER'
    OUTPUT 'IT IS TOO LARGE OR TOO SMALL.'
    REPEAT
        NUMBER ← RANDOM(100)
        OUTPUT 'I HAVE MY NUMBER. WHAT IS YOUR GUESS?'
        REPEAT
            INPUT YOUR_GUESS
            IF YOUR_GUESS > NUMBER THEN
                OUTPUT 'YOUR GUESS IS TOO LARGE. GUESS AGAIN'
            ELSE IF YOUR_GUESS < NUMBER THEN
                OUTPUT 'YOUR GUESS IS TOO SMALL. GUESS AGAIN'
            END IF
        UNTIL YOUR_GUESS = NUMBER
        OUTPUT 'YOUR GUESS IS RIGHT'
        OUTPUT 'WOULD YOU LIKE TO PLAY AGAIN (YES OR NO)?'
        INPUT PLAY_AGAIN
    UNTIL PLAY_AGAIN ≠ 'YES'
    OUTPUT 'I HAVE ENJOYED PLAYING WITH YOU'
END GUESS
```

FIGURE 7-9. The algorithm GUESS.

amount in the account at the beginning of this month, the amount at the beginning of next month is calculated by:

```
AMOUNT ← AMOUNT+DEPOSIT
AMOUNT ← AMOUNT + MONTHLY_INTEREST_RATE*AMOUNT
```

The first statement adds to AMOUNT the deposit made at the beginning of the month. The second adds the interest earned during the month. If we repeat the calculation for the number of months we are interested in, we will obtain the amount in the account after that many months. Figure 7–10 shows the algorithm INTEREST.

Review Questions

1. Why must some of the statements in an algorithm be executed more than once if the algorithm is to justify its existence?

2. Suppose that when the computer first encounters a WHILE statement, the condition following WHILE is FALSE. How many times will the repeated statements be executed?

3. Why is a repetition often referred to as a *loop*?

4. What is a *sentinel*? Give an example of one.

5. Explain why two INPUT statements are needed in the algorithm AVERAGE.

6. Give two differences between the WHILE and REPEAT constructions.

```
ALGORITHM INTEREST
  INPUT AMOUNT, DEPOSIT, YEARLY_INTEREST_RATE, NUMBER_OF_MONTHS
  YEARLY_INTEREST_RATE ← YEARLY_INTEREST_RATE/100
  MONTHLY_INTEREST_RATE ← YEARLY_INTEREST_RATE/12
  FOR N ← 1 TO NUMBER_OF_MONTHS DO
      AMOUNT ← AMOUNT+DEPOSIT
      AMOUNT ← AMOUNT + MONTHLY_INTEREST_RATE*AMOUNT
  END FOR
  OUTPUT 'AMOUNT IN ACCOUNT AFTER', NUMBER_OF_MONTHS
  OUTPUT 'MONTHS IS', AMOUNT
END INTEREST
```

FIGURE 7-10. The algorithm INTEREST.

7. Suppose that when the computer first encounters a REPEAT statement, the condition following UNTIL is TRUE. The repeated statements will be executed at least how many times? What action could result in their being executed more than this minimum number of times?

8. In the FOR statement, if BY *expression-3* is omitted, what is assumed for it?

9. Write a WHILE construction equivalent to

```
FOR I ← L TO M BY N DO
    statements
END FOR
```

10. In some programming languages, FOR is equivalent to a REPEAT instead of a WHILE. What differences would this make in the behavior of the iterative construction?

11. In

```
FOR I ← 10 TO 100 BY 5 DO
```

identify *variable, expression-1, expression-2,* and *expression-3*.

12. Give the sequence of values of I that will be generated by:

```
FOR I ← 3 TO 15 BY 3 DO
```

13. Give the sequence of values of I that will be generated by:

```
FOR I ← 9 TO 1 BY −2 DO
```

14. What problems would arise from the use of each of the two following FOR statements?

```
        (a) FOR I ← 1 TO 10 BY −1 DO
        (b) FOR I ← 10 TO 1 DO
```

15. Would WHILE or REPEAT be most appropriate in a situation where possibly no repetitions of the *statements* should be carried out at all?

16. Would REPEAT be most appropriate in a situation where the termination condition could not be meaningfully tested until the repeated action had been executed at least once?

17. Give examples of each of the two situations mentioned in Questions 15 and 16.

18. Explain in words the differences in the flowcharts of WHILE and RE-PEAT.

19. What is a *pseudorandom* number? What are the possible values of RANDOM(25)?

20. The algorithm GUESS uses two REPEAT statements. Explain for each why REPEAT was used instead of WHILE.

Exercises

1. The *factorial* of an integer greater than 0 is defined as the product of all the integers from 1 through the integer in question. Thus, 3 factorial is 1*2*3 or 6; 4 factorial is 1*2*3*4 or 24; and so on. Write an algorithm to input an integer greater than 0 and output its factorial.

2. The factorial of 0 is defined as 1, and the factorial of a negative integer is undefined. Modify the algorithm of Exercise 1: (a) to give the correct result for 0, and (b) to give an appropriate error message when the factorial of a negative integer is requested.

3. According to legend, the inventor of chess was offered a reward by his king. Invited to name his own reward, the inventor said, "My request is modest. On the first square of my chess board place 1 grain of wheat. On the second square place 2 grains, on the third 4, and so on, doubling the number of grains for each square, until all 64 squares on the board have been filled." Write an algorithm to calculate the number of grains of wheat the inventor requested.

4. *Fibonacci's Problem:* Suppose that a pair of rabbits produces exactly one new pair each month, and the new pair becomes fertile at the age of one month. If we start with one fertile pair of rabbits, and if we assume that none die, how many pairs will we have after a year's time? (*Hints:* A little thought will show that the number of pairs at the beginning of next month will be the number of pairs at the beginning of this month plus the number at the beginning of last month. Since a newborn pair takes a month to become fertile, only those alive at the beginning of last month can have offspring during this month. Throughout the calculation, then, you must keep track of two values: the number of pairs at the beginning of the current month and the number at the beginning of the month before that. How can you express the fact that the original pair is fertile?)

5. Modify Exercise 4 so that it inputs the original number of fertile pairs and the number of months they have to reproduce.

6. Modify Exercise 4 to input a number of pairs, and find how many months it takes for the population to exceed that number.

7. Modify GRADES to compute the class average as well as the grade distribution.

8. What will be the output of HIGH__AND__LOW if the input consists of the sentinel only, with no data values? Modify the algorithm to output an error message for this case.

9. Write an algorithm to simulate the rolling of a pair of dice. Each time it is executed, it will output two random numbers in the range 1–6.

10. Some banks advertise that they compound interest daily rather than monthly. Modify INTEREST to compound interest daily.

11. Modify Example 4 (AVERAGE) in the section on iteration to output an appropriate message when the data item count is 0.

12. What will the algorithm BONUS do if *no* salesperson has sales in excess of $10,000? Modify the algorithm to output an appropriate message in this case. (*Hint:* The easiest solution is to use a sentinel consisting of a particular name *and* a particular sales.)

13. Write an algorithm to input a series of numbers and to check whether or not the numbers are in nondecreasing order. Specifically, the algorithm should print any number that is less than the number that precedes it in the series. If no such number is found, the algorithm should print a message to that effect.

14. Some programming languages do not have the exponentiation operator, **. Nevertheless, if the value of N is a positive integer, we can calculate the value of X**N by repeated multiplication: X**1 is equal to X; X**2 is equal to X*X; X**3 is equal to X*X*X; and so on. Write an algorithm to input the values of X and N and to print the value of X**N computed by repeated multiplication.

15. In algebra, the *binomial coefficient*

$$\binom{n}{r}$$

is defined by

$$\frac{(r + 1)(r + 2) \ldots (n-1)n}{1 \cdot 2 \ldots (n-r-1)(n-r)}$$

where n and r are nonnegative integers and r is less than or equal to n. When r is equal to n, the value of the binomial coefficient is 1. Write an algorithm to input values for n and r, then print the value of the binomial coefficient.

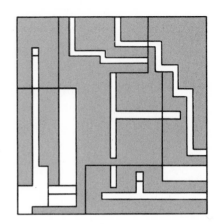

Chapter 8

Arrays

Each of the algorithms in the last chapter had this feature in common: The algorithm would input a few data items, process them, output the results, input a few more data items, process those, output the results, and so on. By continuing in this way, a large amount of data could be processed. But only a small amount would be stored in the main memory of the computer at any one time.

For many applications, however, we need to store large lists or tables of data in main memory. The computer can then refer to *any* entry in the list or table whenever it happens to need that information for the job at hand. Such lists and tables are called *arrays*.

An array is a *data structure*—a means of organizing data. One could argue that arrays should be deferred to Part 3 of this book, which is devoted to data structures. But there is a good reason for taking them up immediately after repetition: Often we want to carry out some operation on every element of an array. We do this by writing out the statements to do the desired operation once, and then arranging for their execution to be repeated for every element of the array. Thus, array processing is one of the most important applications of repetition.

8.1 One-Dimensional Arrays

So far, we have used names such as HOURS, RATE, and GROSS__WAGES to refer to single data items. Now we want to use names to refer to *lists* or *one-dimensional arrays* of data items. Figure 8-1 shows a one-dimensional array,

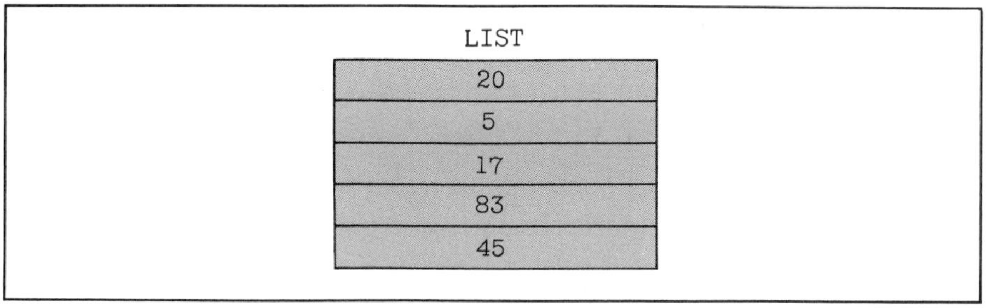

FIGURE 8-1. LIST is a one-dimensional array whose elements are the numbers 20, 5, 17, 83, and 45.

LIST, which contains the real numbers 20, 5, 17, 83, and 45.

If LIST refers to the whole array, how do we refer to the individual data items?—something we must surely be able to do if the entire concept is to be useful.

Each data item, or *element,* of the array has a number. We put the number of the element we wish to refer to in parentheses after the name of the array. Thus, LIST(1) is the name of the first element of LIST, and its value is 20; LIST(2) is the name of the second element of LIST, and its value is 5; and so on. Figure 8-2 shows LIST again, with the elements named as LIST(1), LIST(2), LIST(3), LIST(4), and LIST(5).

The value in parentheses that determines which element we are referring to is called the *subscript.* "Subscript" means "written below," and the term comes from mathematical notation. Mathematicians would write LIST(1), LIST(2), LIST(3), and so on as $LIST_1$, $LIST_2$, $LIST_3$, and so on. Most computer printers cannot print some characters below the level of the others, and so computer programmers must use the parenthesis notation. This is just as well, since the parenthesis notation is easier to read anyway. LIST(1), LIST(2), LIST(3), and so on are called *subscripted variables.* LIST itself, without a subscript, is called an *array variable.*

So far, it is not obvious what we have gained by using subscripts. Are LIST(1), LIST(2), LIST(3), and so on really better than any other sequence of names, such as say, FIRST_VALUE, SECOND_VALUE, and so on?

FIGURE 8-2. The elements of LIST are named LIST (1), LIST (2), LIST (3), LIST (4), and LIST (5).

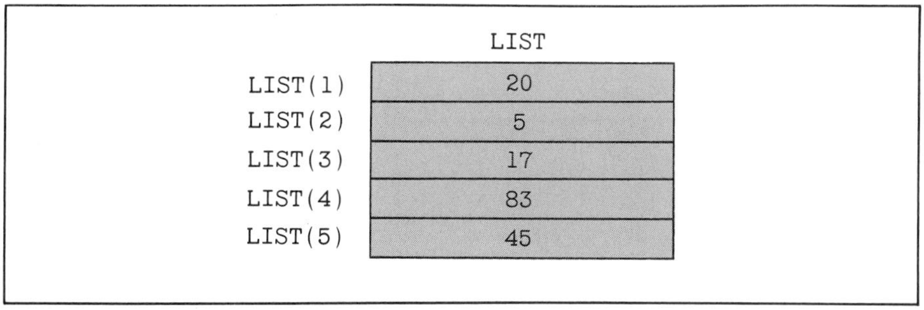

The answer is yes, because not only can we use 1, 2, 3, 4, and 5 as subscripts, we can use any expression which evaluates to 1, 2, 3, 4, or 5. This means that we can *compute* which element of the array we want to refer to. Here is where the real power of arrays lies—in the ability to compute the name of the data item we are going to manipulate, rather than having this name fixed once and for all when the algorithm is written.

Consider the simplest case of this, the expression

```
LIST(I)
```

where the value of I is 1, 2, 3, 4, or 5. This is the name of one of the elements of LIST, but which element it is depends on the value of I. We need not know this value when we write the algorithm. Indeed, we may *not be able* to know it, since it may be the result of some complicated calculation done when the algorithm is executed. Also, we can write the statements for some operation using LIST(I), and then let those statements be repeated for I equal to 1, 2, 3, 4, and 5. Thus, the operation will be applied to all the elements of LIST.

Figure 8-3 illustrates the relations among LIST, I, and LIST(I).

We can also use expressions for subscripts. All the following are valid provided the value of the expression is in the right range—1 through 5 in the case of LIST:

```
LIST(I+3)    LIST(2*J-3*I)    LIST(I*J-25)
```

8.2 Elements of Array Processing

Now we will examine some of the simpler operations we can carry out on data stored in arrays. In each example, remember that a subscripted variable can be used just like any other variable—it can occur on either the left or the right side of an assignment statement, or in an INPUT or OUTPUT statement.

We will use the five-element array LIST as an example throughout.

Averaging the Elements of an Array. We wish to find the average of the values in the array LIST. We will use basically the same technique as in our previous averaging algorithms except that, instead of inputting the values to be averaged one by one, we will use a subscripted variable to refer to the appropriate element of LIST. The following statements do the job:

```
SUM ← 0
FOR I ← 1 TO 5 DO
    SUM ← SUM + LIST(I)
END FOR
AVERAGE ← SUM/5
```

(We do not make this a complete algorithm since, for the moment, we do

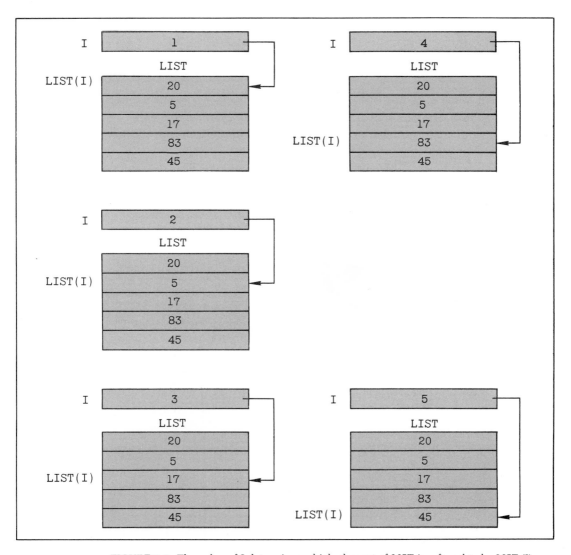

FIGURE 8-3. The value of I determines which element of LIST is referred to by LIST (I).

not wish to worry about such matters as how the values of LIST got into memory in the first place.)

The statement

```
SUM ← SUM + LIST(I)
```

will be repeated five times. On the first repetition, I will have the value 1, on the second repetition the value 2, and so on. Thus, the foregoing is equivalent to:

```
SUM ← 0
SUM ← SUM + LIST(1)
```

```
SUM ← SUM + LIST(2)
SUM ← SUM + LIST(3)
SUM ← SUM + LIST(4)
SUM ← SUM + LIST(5)
AVERAGE ← SUM/5
```

If LIST has the values given in the last section, then the successive values of SUM will be 0, 20, 25, 42, 125, and 170, as shown in Figure 8-4. The value of AVERAGE will be 170/5 or 34.

Notice how well the FOR statement works for array processing. This is one of its main uses.

Finding the Largest and Smallest Value in an Array. This works like our algorithm for finding the highest and lowest temperatures, but again we use a FOR statement to step through the elements of an array:

FIGURE 8-4. We can add up the elements of LIST by causing the statement SUM ← SUM + LIST (I) to be repeated with the value of I varying from 1 to 5.

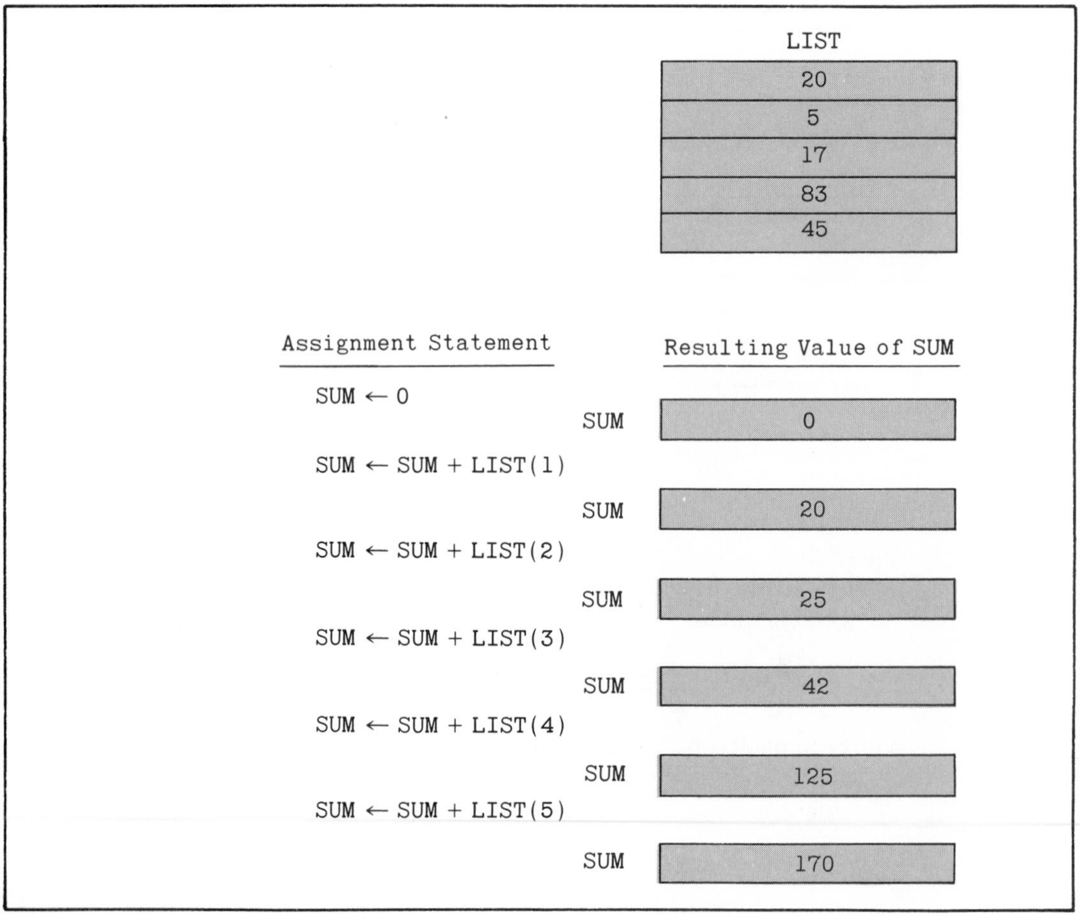

LIST

20
5
17
83
45

Assignment Statement | Resulting Value of SUM

SUM ← 0

SUM   0

SUM ← SUM + LIST(1)

SUM   20

SUM ← SUM + LIST(2)

SUM   25

SUM ← SUM + LIST(3)

SUM   42

SUM ← SUM + LIST(4)

SUM   125

SUM ← SUM + LIST(5)

SUM   170

```
SMALLEST ← LIST(1)
LARGEST ← LIST(1)
FOR I ← 2 TO 5 DO
   IF LIST(I) < SMALLEST THEN
      SMALLEST ← LIST(I)
   ELSE IF LIST(I) > LARGEST THEN
      LARGEST ← LIST(I)
   END IF
END FOR
```

These statements use both the methods we have discussed for referring to an array element. In the first two statements, we specify the element explicitly when we write LIST(1) in the algorithm. In the repeated statements, we use LIST(I) to refer to an element that will be determined at execution time.

Assigning Values to an Array. So far, we have said nothing about how the elements of an array get their values in the first place. One way is an element-by-element assignment, where each array element appears on the left side of an assignment statement. Thus, we could assign LIST its values by:

```
LIST(1) ← 20
LIST(2) ← 5
LIST(3) ← 17
LIST(4) ← 83
LIST(5) ← 45
```

To keep from having to write out long lists of assignment statements, we will use the notation

```
LIST(1:5) ← (20, 5, 17, 83, 45)
```

to mean the same thing (see Figure 8-5). Some programming languages have some similar convention for assigning a list of values to an array. (The details of the convention vary widely from one language to another.) Other languages require that all the assignment statements be written out.

If there is some computation that will yield the values we wish to place in an array, then we can use an iterative construction to do the job:

```
FOR I ← 1 TO 5 DO
   LIST(I) ← 5*I
END FOR
```

One way to get the required values would be to copy them from another array. For instance,

```
FOR I ← 1 TO 5 DO
   LIST(I) ← ANOTHER_LIST(I+3)
END FOR
```

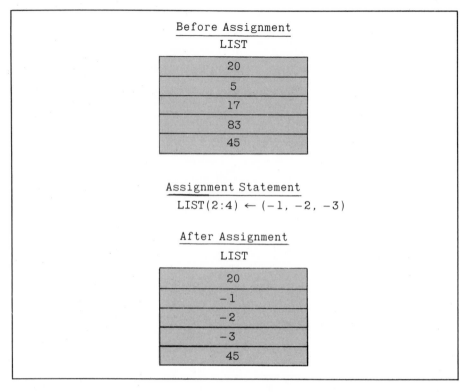

FIGURE 8-5. Assigning values to the elements of an array.

Elements 1 through 5 of LIST are copied from elements 4 through 8 of ANOTHER__LIST (as I runs from 1 through 5, I + 3 runs from 4 through 8).

Input and Output of Arrays. As usual, input and output are similar to assignment, except that the source or destination for a value is an input or output device rather than an expression or a named location.
    We can input values using an iterative construction:

```
FOR I ← 1 TO 5 DO
    INPUT LIST(I)
END FOR
```

This can be abbreviated—using the same notation as before—as

```
INPUT LIST(1:5)
```

    In the same way, we can output an array using either an iterative construction

```
FOR I ← 1 TO 5 DO
    OUTPUT LIST(I)
END FOR
```

or an abbreviated notation for the same:

```
OUTPUT LIST(1:5)
```

Grades. By using arrays, we can sometimes avoid using a CASE or other multiway selection statement. Figure 8-6 illustrates this with a version of the algorithm for converting number grades to letter grades.

We start by changing all number grades less than 50 to 50 to reduce the number of entries needed in the arrays. We then compute a value for I corresponding to the value of NUMBER__GRADE as follows:

NUMBER_GRADE	I
50–59	1
60–69	2
70–79	3
80–89	4
90–99	5
100	6

I is then used to subscript the LETTER__GRADE and COUNT arrays.

This calculation puts 100 in a class by itself, which accounts for the arrays having six entries instead of five and 'A' being treated as a special case on output. Can you think of another way of handling the "100 problem"?

8.3 Searching

One way to store a *table* in memory is to use a separate *list*—one dimensional array—for each column.

FIGURE 8-6. The algorithm GRADES.

```
ALGORITHM GRADES
    LETTER_GRADE(1:6)← ('F', 'D', 'C', 'B', 'A', 'A')
    COUNT(1:6) ← (0,0,0,0,0,0)
    INPUT NAME, NUMBER_GRADE
    WHILE NAME ≠ 'END OF DATA' DO
        IF NUMBER_GRADE < 50 THEN
            NUMBER_GRADE ← 50
        END IF
        I ← INT ((NUMBER_GRADE-40)/10)
        OUTPUT NAME, LETTER_GRADE(I)
        COUNT(I) ← COUNT(I)+1
        INPUT NAME, NUMBER_GRADE
    END WHILE
    OUTPUT 'GRADE DISTRIBUTION'
    OUTPUT 'A', COUNT(5) + COUNT(6)
    FOR I ← 4 TO 1 BY −1 DO
        OUTPUT LETTER_GRADE(I), COUNT(I)
    END FOR
END GRADES
```

Suppose, for instance, we wished to store the following tiny telephone directory containing a few of our friends' phone numbers:

Name	Number
Jane	742–8319
Jim	591–4872
Larry	984–1265
Mary	135–0465
Sue	491–2031

We could use the following two arrays:

```
NAME(1:5) ← ('JANE', 'JIM', 'LARRY', 'MARY', 'SUE')
NUMBER(1:5) ← ('742-8319', '591-4872', '984-1265',
                '135-0465', '491-2031')
```

Now *if* we know that a person's name is in a particular position in NAME, *then* we know that the person's number is in the corresponding position in NUMBER. That is, *if* we know that NAME(4) holds 'MARY', *then* we know that NUMBER(4) holds Mary's phone number.

Arrays used in this fashion can be thought of as being side by side, like the columns in an actual telephone directory (see Figure 8-7). For this reason they are called *parallel arrays*.

The question is, how do we know that 'MARY' is in NAME(4) or, in general, that the name we wish to look up is in a particular position in NAME?

The answer is that we must *search* for it. We search the array NAME to find the name we are looking up. When we find it, we look at the corresponding entry in NUMBER to find the number.

Sequential Search. The simplest—though not the fastest—way to search an array is to start at the beginning and examine the elements one by one until we find the one we are looking for. Like this:

FIGURE 8-7. Parallel arrays are arrays that, because of the way they are used, can be thought of as positioned side by side, like the columns in a telephone directory.

	NAME		NUMBER
NAME(1)	'JANE'	NUMBER(1)	'742-8319'
NAME(2)	'JIM'	NUMBER(2)	'591-4872'
NAME(3)	'LARRY'	NUMBER(3)	'984-1265'
NAME(4)	'MARY'	NUMBER(4)	'135-0465'
NAME(5)	'SUE'	NUMBER(5)	'491-2031'

```
INPUT DESIRED_NAME
I ← 1
WHILE NAME(I) ≠ DESIRED_NAME DO
    I ← I+1
END WHILE
OUTPUT NUMBER(I)
```

Since the value of I designates a particular element of the array, we can think of I as *pointing* to that element. We start with I pointing to the first element in NAME. We then run the pointer—the value of I—down the list until we find the name we are looking for. Then we output the number, which is the corresponding entry in NUMBER. Figure 8-8 illustrates this process.

No doubt at one time or another you have run your finger down a list of items while looking for a particular entry. You then probably used your finger to hold your place while you extracted the necessary information from the table. If you think of I as your finger, you will have no trouble understanding sequential search.

Unfortunately, the lookup algorithm just given has a fatal flaw. What if the name entered, the value of DESIRED__NAME, *is not an element of name?* The user might not be aware of what names are in the directory, for instance or may have misspelled the name when entering it. Either way, the algorithm just given would keep on searching until it ran off the end of the list. What would happen then would depend on the computer system used, but hopefully some kind of error message would be given.

We must have some way of stopping the search when it reaches the end of the list. The easiest way to do this is to use a sentinel. Furthermore, the best sentinel is the value we are searching for. Then, when we are going through the list, we only have to look for one thing—the value we are searching for—instead of two—the sought-after value and the sentinel.

Here is the improved version of the lookup algorithm:

```
INPUT DESIRED_NAME
NAME(6) ← DESIRED_NAME
I ← 1
WHILE NAME(I) ≠ DESIRED_NAME DO
    I ← I+1
END WHILE
IF I ≤ 5 THEN
    OUTPUT NUMBER(I)
ELSE
    OUTPUT 'THE NAME YOU REQUESTED IS NOT IN THE DIRECTORY'
END IF
```

The second statement installs the sentinel in position 6—the first free position beyond the end of the list. After the search, if the value of I is 1-5, then the sought-after item was found. But if the value of I is 6, the item was not found, and the search was prevented from running off the end of the list by the sentinel (see Figure 8-9).

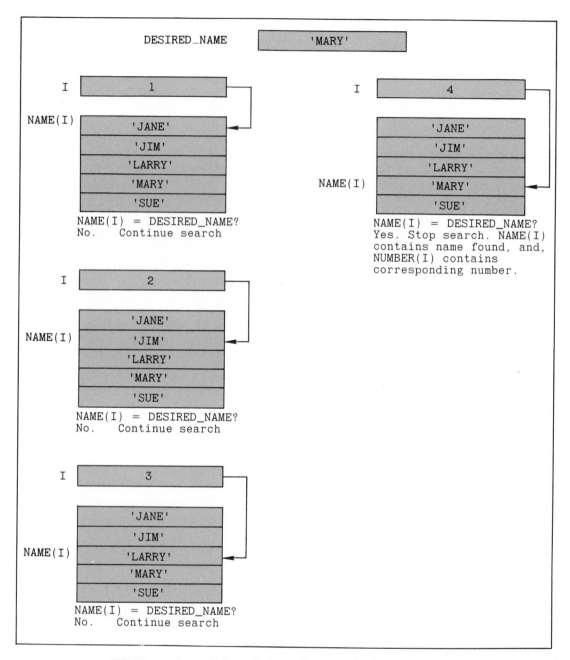

FIGURE 8-8. Sequential search. Since the value of I designates a particular element of the array, we can think of I as pointing to that element. The arrow notation shown here is widely used.

Figure 8-10 shows a complete directory lookup algorithm that works for a directory of any size. We assume that the directory is read in first. The

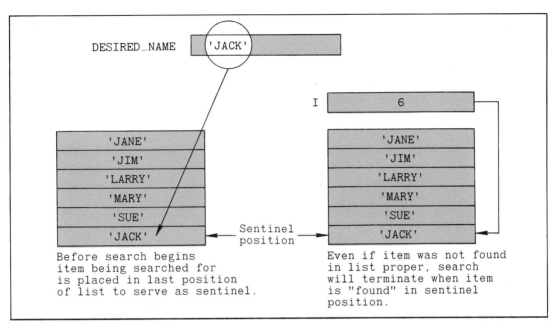

FIGURE 8-9. In this sequential search, the sought-after item was not found. The sentinel prevented the search from running of the end of the list.

data consists of the number of entries in the directory, following by all of the names, followed by all of the numbers. After reading in the directory, the algorithm accepts names and looks up numbers until the name STOP is entered.

FIGURE 8-10. The algorithm DIRECTORY using sequential search.

```
ALGORITHM DIRECTORY
    INPUT N      (N is size of directory)
    INPUT NAME(1:N)
    INPUT NUMBER(1:N)
    INPUT DESIRED_NAME
    WHILE DESIRED_NAME ≠ 'STOP' DO
        NAME(N+1) ← DESIRED_NAME      (Install sentinel)
        I ← 1
        WHILE NAME(I) ≠ DESIRED_NAME DO
            I ← I+1
        END WHILE
        IF I ≤ N THEN
            OUTPUT NUMBER(I)
        ELSE
            OUTPUT 'THE NAME YOU REQUESTED IS NOT IN THE DIRECTORY'
        END IF
        INPUT DESIRED_NAME
    END WHILE
END DIRECTORY
```

Binary Search. Although the directory in our algorithm was in alphabetical order, the sequential search did not make any use of this fact. The algorithm will work regardless of the order of the directory entries. There is some advantage to this, since getting a directory in alphabetical order—and keeping it that way when changes are made in it—entails some work.

On the other hand, a sequential search is very inefficient compared to any search that takes alphabetical (or numerical or any other) order into account. Looking up a name in a telephone directory using sequential search would mean starting with the As and going through the *entire directory* until we found the name we were looking for—even if the name was "Zellman." Needless to say, no person would ever look up a telephone number that way.

The simplest algorithm that takes alphabetical order into account is *binary search*. "Binary" refers to "two." At each step, a binary search divides the part of the list that remains to be searched into two parts. One part contains the entry we are looking for; the other part does not, and need not be searched further.

Figure 8-11 illustrates binary search. LOW and HIGH are pointers to the beginning and end of that part of the list remaining to be searched. Initially, LOW is set to 1 and HIGH to the subscript of the last entry in the list.

MIDDLE is set to point approximately halfway between LOW and HIGH by means of

```
MIDDLE ← INT((LOW+HIGH)/2)
```

The name being sought is compared with the entry NAME(MIDDLE), the entry pointed to by MIDDLE. If the sought-after name *precedes* NAME(MIDDLE), then that name is in the first half of the part of the list being searched (and therefore we can confine all further searching to the first half). If the sought-after name *follows* NAME(MIDDLE), then that name is in the second half of the part of the list being searched (and therefore, we can confine all further searching to the second half). This process is repeated until the part of the list remaining to be searched closes down on a single name—the one we are looking for.

The preceding assumes that the sought-after name is actually on the list. If it is not, then eventually the pointers LOW and HIGH will pass each other, indicating that none of the list remains to be searched (and the sought-after name has not been found). Figure 8-12 illustrates this situation.

Here are the statements for searching NAME:

```
LOW ← 1
HIGH ← N
REPEAT
   MIDDLE ← INT((LOW+HIGH)/2)
   IF DESIRED_NAME < NAME(MIDDLE) THEN
      HIGH ← MIDDLE-1 (Confine further search to first half)
   ELSE IF DESIRED_NAME > NAME(MIDDLE) THEN
```

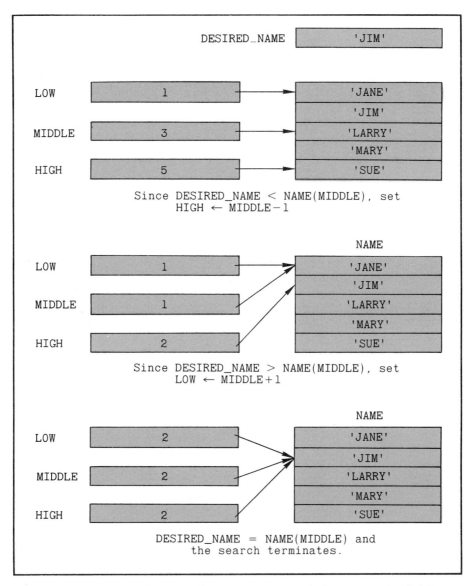

FIGURE 8-11. Binary search. LOW and HIGH are pointers to be beginning and end of the part of the list that remains to be searched. MIDDLE points roughly to the middle of this part of the list.

```
    LOW ← MIDDLE+1 (Confine further search to second half)
  END IF
UNTIL (DESIRED_NAME = NAME(MIDDLE)) OR (LOW > HIGH)
```

The repetition can terminate either because DESIRED__NAME = NAME(MIDDLE) or because LOW > HIGH. In the first case, we have found the name we are looking for. In the second, no more of the list remains to be searched: the name we were looking for was not on the list.

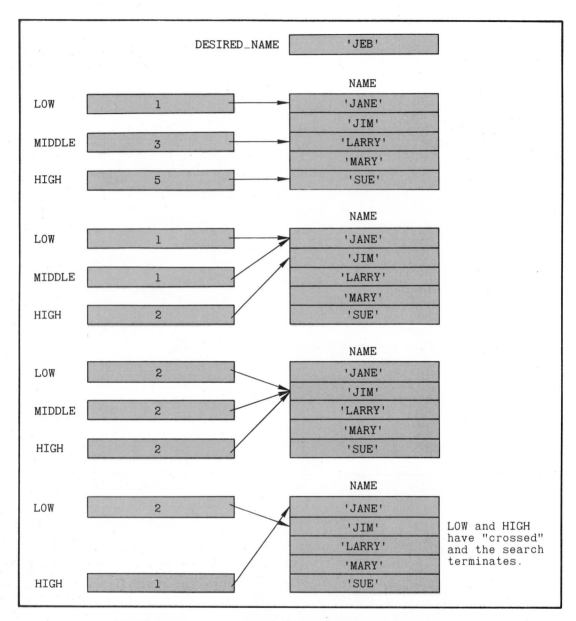

FIGURE 8-12. In a binary search, if the sought-after value is not on the list, the pointers LOW and HIGH will eventually pass one another: the value of LOW will become greater than the value of HIGH.

Figure 8-13 shows the algorithm DIRECTORY adapted for binary search. It is assumed that the entries in NAME are in alphabetical order.

If, after the search, LOW ≤ HIGH, then the sought-after name was found, and NUMBER(MIDDLE) is the corresponding number. Otherwise, the sought-after name was not in the directory.

Is binary search really better than sequential search? Suppose we had a directory with 1,000,000 entries (an extreme case if the directory was

```
ALGORITHM DIRECTORY
    INPUT N
    INPUT NAME(1:N)
    INPUT NUMBER(1:N)
    INPUT DESIRED_NAME
    WHILE DESIRED_NAME ≠ 'STOP' DO
        LOW ← 1
        HIGH ← N
        REPEAT
            MIDDLE ← INT((LOW+HIGH)/2)
            IF DESIRED_NAME < NAME(MIDDLE) THEN
                HIGH ← MIDDLE-1
            ELSE IF DESIRED_NAME > NAME(MIDDLE) THEN
                LOW ← MIDDLE+1
            END IF
        UNTIL (DESIRED_NAME = NAME(MIDDLE)) OR (LOW > HIGH)
        IF LOW ≤ HIGH THEN
            OUTPUT NUMBER(MIDDLE)
        ELSE
            OUTPUT 'THE NAME YOU REQUESTED IS NOT IN THE DIRECTORY'
        END IF
        INPUT DESIRED_NAME
    END WHILE
END DIRECTORY
```

FIGURE 8-13. The algorithm DIRECTORY using binary search.

stored as an array in main memory, but not if it were stored on some auxiliary memory device). With sequential search we would, on the average, have to examine half the entries—500,000—before finding the one we were searching for. For binary search, the average number of entries that we would have to examine is 19! Quite a difference.

8.4 Internal Sorting

Sorting consists of arranging data items in some order, normally alphabetical or numerical. Sorting is most frequently used to aid searching. We sort lists in computer memory so that the computer can search them more efficiently. We print out lists in alphabetical order so that human beings can search through the printout more easily.

In this section, we will discuss techniques for sorting arrays stored in main memory. This is known as *internal* sorting. Sorting of data stored on auxiliary memory devices is called *external* sorting and uses quite different techniques.

The Bubble Sort. We begin with a very simple sort. As with sequential search, the bubble sort is known more for its simplicity than its efficiency.

The idea of the bubble sort is this. We go through a list comparing adjacent items and exchanging those that are out of order. During such a compare-and-exchange pass, an item moves forward in the list until it "bumps up against" a larger item (see Figure 8-14). This behavior is analogous to that of a bubble rising in a liquid, and so the name "bubble sort."

7 ←	4	4	4	4	4	4	4	4
4 ←	7 ←	3	3	3	3	3	3	3
3	3 ←	7 ←	2	2	2	2	2	2
2	2	2 ←	7 ←	7	7	7	7	7
9	9	9	9 ←	9 ←	5	5	5	5
5	5	5	5	5 ←	9 ←	1	1	1
1	1	1	1	1	1 ←	9 ←	8	8
8	8	8	8	8	8	8 ←	9 ←	6
6	6	6	6	6	6	6	6 ←	9

FIGURE 8-14. A bubble sort compare-and-exchange pass. We compare adjacent items (indicated by arrows) and exchange those that are out of order.

A single compare-and-exchange pass generally will not put the list in order, but it will improve the order. The bubble sort consists of simply repeating the compare-and-exchange pass until eventually the list is in order. Figure 8-15 shows a full bubble sort.

How can we tell when the list is in order and no more compare-and-exchange passes are needed? If we can make such a pass *without having to do any exchanges*, then all the pairs of adjacent items are in order, and so the entire list is in order.

We will use a logical value named NO__EXCHANGES to indicate whether or not any exchanges have been done during a pass. Before starting a pass, we set NO__EXCHANGES to TRUE. Whenever an exchange is made during a pass, NO__EXCHANGES is set to FALSE. When we can get through a pass with NO__EXCHANGES still TRUE, the sort is complete.

(A logical value that is used in this way, to inform one part of an algorithm of something that took place in another part, is called a *flag*.)

We can outline the bubble sort as follows:

```
REPEAT
    NO_EXCHANGES ← TRUE
    (Do one compare—and—exchange pass)
UNTIL NO_EXCHANGES
```

Remember that for REPEAT the condition is checked after the repeated statements have been executed, so NO__EXCHANGES is checked *after* each compare-and-exchange pass has been done.

We now turn to the compare-and-exchange pass. N is the number of elements on the list, and TEMP is a temporary location used during an exchange:

Original List	Pass 1	Pass 2	Pass 3	Pass 4	Pass 5	Pass 6	Pass 7
7	4	3	2	2	2	1	1
4	3	2	3	3	1	2	2
3	2	4	4	1	3	3	3
2	7	5	1	4	4	4	7
9	5	1	5	5	5	5	5
5	1	7	6	6	6	6	6
1	8	6	7	7	7	7	7
8	6	8	8	8	8	8	8
6	9	9	9	9	9	9	9

No exchanges
take place on final
pass, confirming that
list is in order.

FIGURE 8-15. The bubble sort consists of repeating the compare-and-exchange pass until the list is in order. Notice how many passes are required just to get 1 in the right place.

```
FOR I ← 1 TO N−1 DO
   IF LIST(I) > LIST(I+1) THEN (Adjacent elements out of order)
      TEMP ← LIST(I)      (Exchange adjacent elements)
      LIST(I) ← LIST(I+1)
      LIST(I+1) ← TEMP
      NO_EXCHANGES ← FALSE   (Set flag to FALSE)
   END IF
END FOR
```

Putting the parts of the bubble sort together and making provisions for input and output of the list to be sorted gives us the algorithm in Figure 8-16.

The Shell Sort. As already mentioned, the bubble sort is noted more for simplicity than for efficiency. The trouble is that the bubble sort can only exchange adjacent elements of the list being sorted. If an element is far from its proper position, many exchanges are necessary to bring it to the proper position.

We can avoid this difficulty using a technique named after its inventor, Donald Shell. Figure 8-17 illustrates the principle of the Shell sort.

We start with the list to be sorted, which is shown in Figure 8-17a.

```
ALGORITHM BUBBLE_SORT
   INPUT N
   INPUT LIST(1:N)
   REPEAT
      NO_EXCHANGES ← TRUE
      FOR I ← 1 TO N-1 DO
         IF LIST(I) > LIST(I+1) THEN
            TEMP ← LIST(I)
            LIST(I) ← LIST(I+1)
            LIST(I+1) ← TEMP
            NO_EXCHANGES ← FALSE
         END IF
      END FOR
   UNTIL NO_EXCHANGES
   OUTPUT LIST(1:N)
END BUBBLE_SORT
```

FIGURE 8-16. The algorithm BUBBLE__SORT.

We choose a gap that, to begin with, is equal to one-half the size of the list. Since the list in the example contains eight elements, we start with a gap of four.

We group into sublists those elements of the list to be sorted that are separated by the chosen gap. In Figure 8-17a we have four sublists, each consisting of two elements. One sublist consists of the first and fifth ele-

FIGURE 8-17. The Shell sort. For each part of the figure, the first line shows the list being sorted, with the sublists marked. The second line shows the result of sorting the sublists.

ments of the list to be sorted; another sublist consists of the second and sixth elements; another of the third and seventh; and another of the fourth and eighth.

Each of the sublists is sorted independently of the others, with the results shown in the second line of Figure 8-17a. Since the sublists are short, the sorting proceeds rapidly. And since the gap between the elements on each sublist is large, out-of-place elements make giant strides toward their final positions.

The next step, illustrated in Figure 8-17b, is to divide the gap in half and repeat the process just described with a gap of two. Now we have two sublists, one consisting of all the odd-numbered elements of the list being sorted, and the other consisting of all the even-numbered elements. Again we sort each sublist independently, obtaining the results shown in the second line of Figure 8-17b.

Figure 8-17c shows the final step. Dividing the gap in half again gives us a gap of one. Now we have only one "sublist," the list being sorted. Sorting this single "sublist" gives us our final result, shown in the second line of Figure 8-17c.

The earlier sorts proceed rapidly because the sublists are short. As the gap becomes smaller, the sublists become longer, but they are also easier to sort because of the preliminary sorting that has already been done. For this reason, the entire sequence of sorts called for by the Shell sort take much less time than a single bubble sort applied to the original list.

So far we have said nothing about the method used to sort the sublists. Different methods give different versions of the Shell sort. We will look here at a version of the Shell sort that uses a bubble sort to sort the sublists. Let the value of GAP be the gap used to form the sublists. If we carry out a bubble sort, but compare and exchange A(I) and A(I+GAP) instead of A(I) and A(I+1), we will sort all the sublists whose elements are separated by GAP. We can outline this version of the Shell sort as follows:

```
GAP ← INT(N/2)
WHILE GAP ≠ 0 DO
    (Do a bubble sort, but compare and
     exchange A(I) and A(I+GAP) instead
     of A(I) and A(I+1))
    GAP ← INT(GAP/2)
END WHILE
```

Figure 8-18 shows the algorithm SHELL__SORT. Other, faster sorting algorithms are known, but they are often complex to program. The Shell sort is a good compromise between speed and simplicity.

8.5 Two-Dimensional Arrays

So far, we have considered the elements of an array to be arranged one after another along a straight line. For some purposes, it is better to imag-

```
ALGORITHM SHELL_SORT
    INPUT N
    INPUT LIST(1:N)
    GAP ← INT(N/2)
    WHILE GAP ≠ 0 DO
        REPEAT
            NO_EXCHANGES ← TRUE
            FOR I ← 1 TO N-GAP DO
                IF LIST(I) > LIST(I+GAP) THEN
                    TEMP ← LIST(I)
                    LIST(I) ← LIST(I+GAP)
                    LIST(I+GAP) ← TEMP
                    NO_EXCHANGES ← FALSE
                END IF
            END FOR
        UNTIL NO_EXCHANGES
        GAP ← INT(GAP/2)
    END WHILE
    OUTPUT LIST(1:N)
END SHELL_SORT
```

FIGURE 8-18. The algorithm SHELL_SORT.

ine them arranged on a plane surface, like the squares of a checkerboard. We can even think of them as arranged in three dimensions, or in some higher-dimensional space that exists only in the imagination of mathematicians.

In this section, we will concentrate on two-dimensional arrays. Figure 8-19 shows a two-dimensional array, TABLE. TABLE is a 3 × 4 array, since it has three *rows* and four *columns*.

To designate a particular element of TABLE, we must specify what *row* it is in and what *column* it is in. Thus, we need *two* subscripts to locate an element in TABLE.

The subscripts are written separated by a comma, with row number first and column number second. Thus,

TABLE(3, 2)

refers to the element in row 3, column 2, and

TABLE(2, 4)

refers to the element in row 2, column 4.

To input a two-dimensional array, we must have some convention about how the values read in are to be placed in the array. The convention we will follow is this. The array is to be "filled" with values row by row, starting with the top row, with each row being filled from left to right before going on to the next one. Figure 8-20 illustrates this.

We can accomplish this row-by-row input with two nested FOR constructions. The outermost FOR steps through the rows. The innermost one steps through the elements of each row. Thus, to input TABLE, we would write

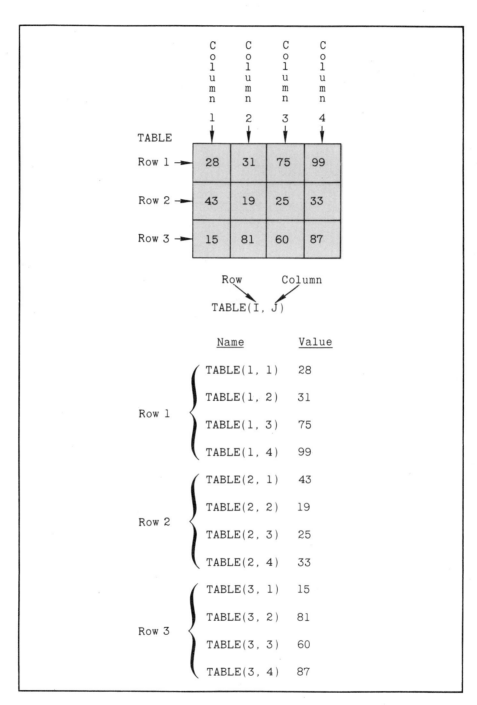

FIGURE 8-19. The two-dimensional array TABLE

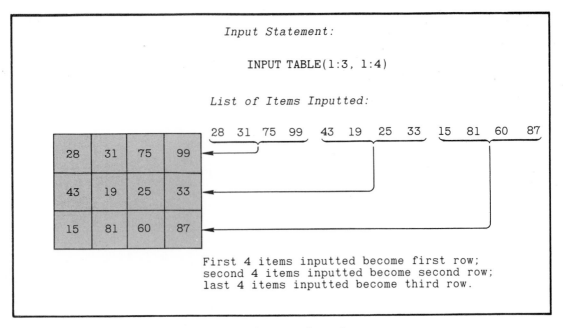

FIGURE 8-20. Inputting a two-dimensional array by rows.

```
FOR I ← 1 TO 3 DO
   FOR J ← 1 TO 4 DO
      INPUT TABLE(I, J)
   END FOR
END FOR
```

Each value of I specifies a particular row. With the value of I fixed, the value of J ranges from 1 to 4, filling in the elements of a particular row. The value of I is then increased by 1 and a new row is filled in.

In the following, we will abbreviate these statements to

```
INPUT TABLE(1:3, 1:4)
```

Output by rows is handled the same way:

```
FOR I ← 1 TO 3 DO
   FOR J ← 1 TO 4 DO
      OUTPUT TABLE(I, J)
   END FOR
END FOR
```

This, too, will usually be abbreviated:

```
OUTPUT TABLE(1:3, 1:4)
```

EXAMPLE 1:

We wish to compute the average grades of college students having particular classifications and major fields. The classifications are freshman, sophomore, junior, and senior; the major fields we are interested in are English, history, and mathematics. In our data, each student's classification and major field is coded as follows:

Classification	Code	Major Field	Code
freshman	1	English	1
sophomore	2	history	2
junior	3	mathematics	3
senior	4		

Out data consists of groups of three data items. The first item in each group is the classification code, the second is the major field code, and the third is a grade earned by a student with the given classification and major. Thus, 2, 3, 85 is a grade of 85 earned by a sophomore math major; 4, 1, 75 is a grade of 75 earned by a senior English major, and so on. The group -1, -1, -1 is the end-of-data sentinel.

The averaging will be done just as in the other averaging algorithms we have written. We will total the items to be averaged, counting their number at the same time, and then divide the total by the count to get the average.

The only problem is that we need to compute 12 totals, 12 counts, and 12 averages, one for every possible combination of classification and major. Our totals, our counts, and our averages will each form a 4 × 3 array, as shown in Figure 8-21 . In these arrays, the rows will be numbered by the classification codes, and the columns by the major field codes. Thus, the data for a junior history major will go in row 3 and column 2.

Figure 8-22 shows the algorithm AVERAGES.

It is not unusual in this kind of problem for the count to be 0 for some combinations of classification and major. An "average" of -1 is printed for those combinations to call them to the user's attention.

Review Questions

1. What is a *data structure*? Why is an array a data structure?

2. Why is array processing such an important application of repetition?

3. What is a *subscript*? How is it used?

4. How does the subscript get its name?

5. If names of array elements were always written as LIST(1), LIST(2), LIST(3), and so on, would arrays have any advantages over our previous system of naming? Why or why not?

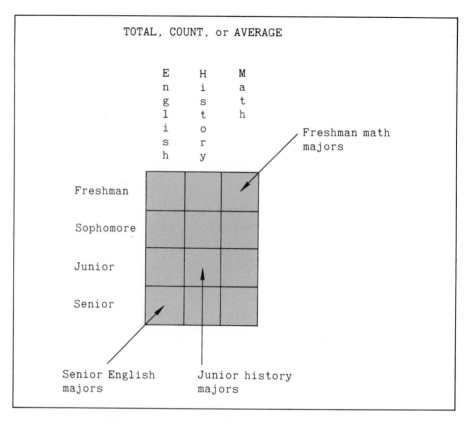

FIGURE 8-21. TOTAL, AVERAGE, and COUNT are all 4 by 3 arrays.

6. What is the importance of being able to use a variable or an expression as a subscript?

7. Which repetitive construction is most useful when we wish to carry out an operation on every element of an array?

8. Show three ways in which the elements of an array can be given values.

9. Give the statements that are abbreviated by

```
A(1:4) ← (−5, 0, 25, 100)
```

10. Give the statements that are abbreviated by

```
INPUT A(1:10)
```

11. Give the statements that are abbreviated by

```
OUTPUT A(1:N)
```

```
ALGORITHM AVERAGES
   FOR CLASS ← 1 TO 4 DO (Set totals and counts to 0)
      FOR MAJOR ← 1 TO 3 DO
         TOTAL(CLASS, MAJOR) ← 0
         COUNT(CLASS, MAJOR) ← 0
      END FOR
   END FOR
   INPUT CLASS, MAJOR, GRADE (Read data, accumulate
                                   counts and totals)
   WHILE CLASS ≠ -1 DO
      TOTAL(CLASS, MAJOR) ← TOTAL(CLASS, MAJOR) + GRADE
      COUNT(CLASS, MAJOR) ← COUNT(CLASS, MAJOR) + 1
      INPUT CLASS, MAJOR, GRADE
   END WHILE
   FOR CLASS ← 1 TO 4 DO (Compute averages)
      FOR MAJOR ← 1 TO 3 DO
         IF COUNT(CLASS, MAJOR) ≠ 0 THEN
            AVERAGE(CLASS, MAJOR) ← TOTAL(CLASS, MAJOR)
                                   /COUNT(CLASS, MAJOR)
         ELSE
            AVERAGE(CLASS, MAJOR) ← -1
         END IF
      END FOR
   END FOR
   OUTPUT AVERAGE(1:4, 1:3) (Print results)
END AVERAGES
```

FIGURE 8-22. The algorithm AVERAGES.

12. Explain sequential search, using the analogy of running your finger down a column of data.

13. After a sequential search, how can the algorithm determine whether or not the value searched for was found in the array?

14. In what way is sequential search superior to binary search? In what way is it inferior?

15. What feature of the data being searched does the sequential search ignore and the binary search take into account?

16. Explain the principle of the binary search.

17. Explain the principle of the bubble sort.

18. How is the bubble sort extended to give the Shell sort?

19. Resolve the apparent paradox that although a Shell sort consists of many bubble-sort-like passes, it is actually faster than a single bubble sort.

20. Distinguish between a one- and a two-dimensional array.

21. Though we did not discuss it in this chapter, what kind of structure do you think a *three*-dimensional array might have?

22. Which subscript of a two-dimensional array designates a particular row, and which designates a particular column?

23. What statements does the following abbreviate:

INPUT A(1:4, 1:2)

24. What statements does the following abbreviate:

OUTPUT B(1:M, 1:N)

Exercises

1. Write of an algorithm to find the largest, the smallest, and the average of all of the elements in a one-dimensional array. The algorithm should make only one pass over the array.

2. Write an algorithm to input an array of numbers and find their average. The algorithm will then output each element and one of the words ABOVE, AVERAGE, or BELOW, depending on whether the value in question is greater than, equal to, or less than the average.

3. Modify the algorithm GRADES to handle the grade 100 in the same way that grades less than 50 are handled.

4. The price list for a certain business consists of two columns. One column contains stock numbers; the other contains the corresponding prices. Write an algorithm to input the price list and then—until stopped by a sentinel (which you should devise)—input stock numbers and output the corresponding prices. Use sequential search.

5. Modify the algorithm of Exercise 4 so that it will input the stock numbers of the items ordered by a particular customer, and output an itemized statement—the number and price of each item and the total cost of all the items.

6. Assume that the price list of Exercise 4 is in alphabetical order according to stock number. Rewrite the algorithm to use binary search instead of sequential search.

7. Write an algorithm using a bubble sort to sort the telephone directory described in this chapter in alphabetical order according to name. Note that comparisons will be made between elements of NAME, but when we exchange two elements of NAME, we must do the same for the corresponding elements of NUMBER.

8. Modify the algorithm of Exercise 7 to use the Shell sort rather than the bubble sort.

9. For our telephone directory we used two one-dimensional arrays, NAME and NUMBER. We could have used a single two-dimensional array with two columns. Rewrite the two versions of DIRECTORY to use a two-dimensional array as the directory.

10. Five candidates are running for a certain office. A political pollster wishes to determine the opinions of Democrats, Republicans, and Independents toward each of the five candidates. Each input data item consists of two numbers: the political affiliation of the person questioned (coded 1 for Democrat, 2 for Republican, 3 for Independent) and the candidate that person prefers (coded 1–5). Your algorithm should input this data and output a table showing what percent of the people of a given political affiliation prefer each candidate. That is, perhaps the Democrats questioned were 50% for Candidate 1, 20% for 2, 0% for 3, 8% for 4, and 22% for 5. Your algorithm should give this kind of result for Democrats, Republicans, and Independents.

11. To compute the *median* of a list of numbers, we first arrange the values in numerical order. If the number of values is odd, then the middle value on the sorted list is the median. If the number of values is even, then the median is the average of the two middle values. Write an algorithm to input a list of numbers and output the median.

12. The *percentile rank* of a student in a class is the percentage of students in the class who received a lower grade than the student in question. Write an algorithm to input the names and grades of students in a class and output their names, grades, and percentile ranks. In the printout, the names should be in alphabetical order. *Hints:* Use three parallel arrays, one for names, one for grades, and one for percentile ranks. To compute the percentile ranks, sort the data so that the grades are in nondecreasing order. Before outputting the results, sort again so that the names are in alphabetical order. Note that students who make the same grade must have the same percentile rank.

13. Write an algorithm to input a two-dimensional array of numbers and to output the sum of the numbers in each row and the sum of the numbers in each column.

14. A *magic square* is a square array of numbers such that the numbers in each row, column, and diagonal have the same sum. Write an algorithm to input a square array of numbers and to determine whether or not it is a magic square.

15. A company has four salespeople and five products. Let the salespeople be denoted by numbers from 1 to 4 and the products by numbers from 1 to 5. Suppose we are given as data the yearly sales of each product by each salesperson. For instance, the data item

3, 5, 750

means that salesperson number 3 sold $750 worth of product number 5. Write an algorithm to input data items of this type and to output the following:

(1) the total amount sold by each person;

(2) the total amount sold of each product;

(3) the people who sold the largest and smallest amounts of each product; and

(4) the products for which each person sold the largest and smallest amounts.

If a particular combination of salesperson and product does not occur in the data, assume the person in question did not sell any of that product.

Chapter 9

Functions
and
Procedures

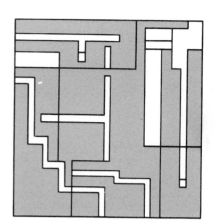

When people build a complicated machine, say an automobile, they don't start from scratch with basic raw materials such as iron ore, sand (for glass), and crude oil (for plastic). Instead, they assemble the car from previously constructed parts, such as an engine, a battery, windows, a windshield, tires, and electrical wires.

Some of these parts, such as the battery and the engine, are themselves quite complicated. Invariably, these complicated parts were not made directly from raw materials either, but were assembled out of still simpler parts.

We can apply the same principle to computer programs. Instead of trying to build every program out of the raw materials offered by a particular programming language, we can build them out of separately constructed parts. And these parts can themselves be built of still simpler parts, until we reach the level of the basic statements of a programming language. The parts out of which we build programs are called *functions* and *procedures*.

What's more, functions and procedures have two extremely desirable properties that they do not share with mechanical and electrical parts such as gears and batteries.

First, if we need to use a function or procedure many times in a program, we need only write it once. A single copy of the function or procedure suffices no matter how many times the program refers to it. It's as if we could build a car using at most one copy of each kind of part: one tire, one headlight, one spark plug, and so on.

173

Second, it would be out of the question to assemble a machine before its parts were manufactured. Yet we can do precisely that with a program. It doesn't matter whether we write the functions and procedures first and then the program, or whether we write the program first and then the functions and procedures. In the next chapter, we will see there are good arguments for writing the program before the functions and procedures.

9.1 Functions

We are already familiar with predefined or built-in functions such as INT and SQRT. We know that a function is invoked by using it in an expression and that it returns a value computed from the values of its arguments.

Thus the statement

```
X ← 3 + SQRT(16)
```

causes the function SQRT to be invoked. SQRT takes the square root of its argument, 16, obtaining 4, and returns 4 as its value. The expression on the right-hand side of ← is evaluated using 4 in place of SQRT(16). The value of the expression is 7, and this is the value assigned to X.

Now we want to learn how to define our own functions, instead of having to rely on predefined ones like INT and SQRT. Figure 9-1 shows the general form of a function definition.

Every function definition begins with a function header having the following form:

```
FUNCTION function-name(parm-1, parm-2, ..., parm-n)
```

The identifier *function-name* is the name by which the function will be invoked. Thus, *function-name* is SQRT for the square root function and INT for the integer-part function.

Parm-1, parm-2, . . ., parm-n are the formal parameters of the function. When the function is invoked, the values of the arguments are substituted for the formal parameters in the body of the function—that is, in

FIGURE 9-1. The general form of a function definition. The body of the function must contain at least one assignment to the function name.

```
    FUNCTION function-name(parm-1, parm-2, ..., parm-n)
                    .
                    .
                    .
        function-name ← expression
                    .
                    .
                    .
    END function-name
```

the statements that lie between the first line and the last line of the definition. The arguments are often called *actual parameters* since they represent the actual values that will be substituted for the formal parameters when the function is invoked.

We need some way of indicating what value the function is to return. One widely used convention is to assign the value to be returned to the function name:

function-name ← *expression*

We can think of the function name as also naming a special memory location used to hold the value of the function. When the statements in the body of the function have been executed, the value stored in this special memory location is returned as the value of the function.

A function definition may contain more than one assignment to the function name; the last such assignment that is executed determines the value that the function returns. A function definition must always contain at least one assignment to the function name, since otherwise there is no way of knowing what value the function should return.

As our first example, let's define a function to calculate the diagonal of a rectangle from its length and width using the expression

```
SQRT(LENGTH**2 + WIDTH**2)
```

The function definition is

```
FUNCTION DIAGONAL(LENGTH, WIDTH)
   DIAGONAL ← SQRT(LENGTH**2 + WIDTH**2)
END DIAGONAL
```

Figure 9-2 identifies the various parts of this definition.

FIGURE 9-2. The function DIAGONAL is used to illustrate the parts of a function definition.

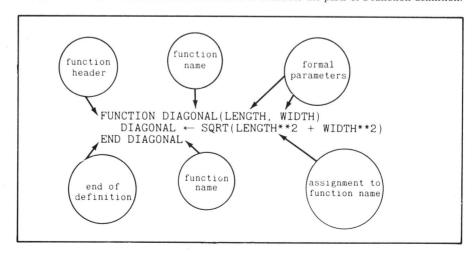

Now suppose that the function DIAGONAL is invoked by the following statements:

```
X ← 3
Y ← 4
Z ← DIAGONAL(X, Y)
```

When DIAGONAL is invoked, the body of the function is executed with the formal parameters replaced by the values of the actual parameters. The actual parameters are X and Y; because of the first two assignment statements, the value of X is 3 and the value of Y is 4. Thus the statement

```
DIAGONAL ← SQRT(LENGTH**2 + WIDTH**2)
```

is executed with 3 substituted for LENGTH and 4 substituted for WIDTH. In effect, the following statement is executed:

```
DIAGONAL ← SQRT(3**2 + 4**2)
```

Thus the value 5 is assigned to DIAGONAL. This is the value that the function returns and the value that is assigned to Z.

Note that the definition of DIAGONAL invokes another function, SQRT. For a function definition to invoke other functions is not only permissible, but commonplace.

For defining functions, we can use all the statements and constructions of the algorithmic language that we have studied so far. As an example of a function defined using selection, let's define a function MAX(M, N) whose value is the largest of its two arguments:

```
FUNCTION MAX(M, N)
   IF M > N THEN
      MAX ← M
   ELSE
      MAX ← N
   END IF
END MAX
```

Suppose we invoke this function with the following statements:

```
P ← 8
Q ← 9
R ← MAX(5*P, 4*Q + 3)
```

The values of the actual parameters are 40 and 39; these values are substituted for M and N. In effect, the following statements are executed:

```
IF 40 > 39 THEN
   MAX ← 40
```

```
ELSE
    MAX ← 39
END IF
```

Since the condition following IF is true, the statement following THEN is executed. Hence the function returns the value 40, and this is the value assigned to R.

Now let's look at a function defined using repetition. The factorial of a positive integer is the product of all the positive integers from 1 through the given number. Thus the factorial of 2 equals 1*2; the factorial of 3 equals 1*2*3; the factorial of 4 equals 1*2*3*4; the factorial of 5 equals 1*2*3*4*5; and so on. The function FACTORIAL(N) computes the factorial of its argument:

```
FUNCTION FACTORIAL(N)
    F ← 1
    FOR I ← 1 TO N DO
        F ← F*I
    END FOR
    FACTORIAL ← F
END FACTORIAL
```

Suppose we invoke FACTORIAL with the following statements

```
X ← 5
Y ← FACTORIAL(X) + 10
```

In effect, the following statements are executed:

```
F ← 1
FOR I ← 1 TO 5 DO
    F ← F*I
END FOR
FACTORIAL ← F
```

The repetition computes the product of 1, 2, 3, 4, and 5, which equals 120. This is the value assigned to FACTORIAL and the value returned by the function. The value 130 is assigned to Y.

When we are talking about a function, we often use its formal parameters to refer to its arguments. Thus, we may say that "The value of MAX(M, N) is the maximum of M and N." This is just another way of saying that "The value of MAX(M, N) is the maximum of its two arguments." We are using M to refer to the first argument of MAX and N to refer to the second argument.

The arguments of a function can be array variables as well as ordinary constants, variables, and expressions. The function SUM(A, N) returns the sum of the first N elements of the array A (notice how this sentence uses the formal parameters of SUM to refer to its arguments):

```
FUNCTION SUM(A, N)
   S ← 0
   FOR I ← 1 TO N DO
      S ← S + A(I)
   END FOR
   SUM ← S
END SUM
```

Figure 9-3 shows a version of the algorithm PAYROLL that uses a function WAGES(HOURS, RATE) to compute a worker's gross wages from the hours worked and the rate of pay. Note that by splitting up our task in this way, we separate the statements that calculate gross wages from those that read data and print results. If the rules for calculating wages change, then we only have to change the function WAGES; we don't have to make any changes in the main algorithm.

The names used for the parameters and variables of a function have nothing to do with names in other functions, procedures, or algorithms that might be spelled the same way. In Figure 9-3, for example, the names HOURS and RATE in the algorithm have nothing to do with the names HOURS and RATE in the function. In the algorithm, HOURS and RATE name variables; in the function, they name formal parameters.

9.2 Procedures

A function can only return a single value. When the calculation that we wish to do yields more than one result, we can write it as a procedure, which can return any number of results. What's more, a procedure can manipulate some variables of the invoking algorithm in arbitrary ways, so

FIGURE 9-3. The algorithm PAYROLL and the function WAGES.

```
ALGORITHM PAYROLL
   TOTAL ← 0
   INPUT NAME, HOURS, RATE
   WHILE NAME ≠ 'END OF DATA' DO
      GROSS_WAGES ← WAGES(HOURS, RATE)
      TOTAL ← TOTAL + GROSS_WAGES
      OUTPUT NAME, GROSS_WAGES
      INPUT NAME, HOURS, RATE
   END WHILE
   OUTPUT 'TOTAL GROSS WAGES', TOTAL
END PAYROLL

FUNCTION WAGES(HOURS, RATE)
   IF HOURS ≤ 40 THEN
      WAGES ← HOURS*RATE
   ELSE
      WAGES ← 40*RATE + 1.5*(HOURS−40)*RATE
   END IF
END WAGES
```

that, for instance, the same variables whose values provide the data for the calculation may also be used to store the results.

Figure 9-4 shows the general form of a procedure definition, which is similar to that of a function definition. But note that a procedure does not contain any assignment to the procedure name. The formal parameters, rather than the procedure name, are used for returning values.

The outstanding difference between functions and procedures is the way in which their formal parameters are used. For functions, the values of the actual parameters are substituted for the formal parameters. For this reason, we refer to the formal parameters of functions as *value parameters*. For procedures, the actual parameters must be variables, and these variables (not their values) are substituted for the formal parameters. For this reason, we refer to the formal parameters of procedures as *variable parameters*.

We invoke a procedure with a call statement, which has the following form:

```
CALL procedure-name(var-1, var-2, ..., var-n)
```

Var-1, var-2, . . ., var-n are the actual parameters of the procedure, and they must be variables. When the procedure is invoked, the statements in the body of the procedure are executed with the variables *var-1, var-2, . . ., var-n* substituted for the formal parameters.

To see how all of this really works, let's look at an example:

```
PROCEDURE RECTANGLE(LENGTH, WIDTH, AREA, DIAGONAL)
   AREA ← LENGTH*WIDTH
   DIAGONAL ← SQRT(LENGTH**2 + WIDTH**2)
END RECTANGLE
```

This procedure computes the area and diagonal of a rectangle from its length and width. The formal parameters LENGTH and WIDTH provide the data for the calculation; the formal parameters AREA and DIAGONAL are used to return the results.

Suppose we invoke the procedure with the following statements:

```
W ← 12
X ← 5
CALL RECTANGLE(W, X, Y, Z)
```

FIGURE 9-4. The general form of a procedure definition.

```
PROCEDURE procedure-name(parm-1, parm-2, ..., parm-n)
   .
   .
   .
END procedure-name
```

When RECTANGLE is invoked, the statements of its body are executed with the actual parameters W, X, Y, and Z substituted for the formal parameters LENGTH, WIDTH, AREA, and DIAGONAL. Thus, invoking RECTANGLE has the same effect as executing the following statements:

```
Y ← W*X
Z ← SQRT(W**2 + X**2)
```

After the subroutine has been called and has returned, the values of W and X remain unchanged, while Y has been assigned the value 60 and X the value 13.

As with functions, we sometimes use the formal parameters of a procedure to refer to its actual parameters. Thus, we may say that "RECTANGLE computes the values of AREA and DIAGONAL from the values of LENGTH and WIDTH." We sometimes go even further and use the formal parameters to refer to the values of the actual parameters. (The actual parameters have to be variables, remember.) Thus, we may say that "RECTANGLE computes AREA and DIAGONAL from LENGTH and WIDTH."

Procedures can take array variables as actual parameters. For example, Figure 9-5 shows a procedure EXTREMES(A, N, MAX, MIN) that finds the largest and smallest elements of the array A. N is the number of elements in the array. The formal parameters MAX and MIN are used to return the values of the largest and smallest elements, respectively. Note that assignments are made to MAX and MIN throughout the execution of the procedure. Therefore, the actual parameters corresponding to MAX and MIN are used not only to return results but to provide temporary storage during the execution of the procedure.

As mentioned before, the same parameters can be used both for providing data to a procedure and for returning its results. Figure 9-6 shows a procedure SORT(LIST, N) for sorting the N elements of the array LIST using a bubble sort. Note that the formal parameter LIST is used both to gain access to the data—the unsorted list—as well as to return the results—the sorted list. Put another way, the formal parameter LIST provides the procedure with access to the actual parameter A so that the procedure can manipulate the elements of A in whatever manner is needed.

FIGURE 9-5. The procedure EXTREMES.

```
PROCEDURE EXTREMES(A, N, MAX, MIN)
    MAX ← A(1)
    MIN ← A(1)
    FOR I ← 2 TO N DO
        IF A(I) < MIN THEN
            MIN ← A(I)
        ELSE IF A(I) > MAX THEN
            MAX ← A(I)
        END IF
    END FOR
END EXTREMES
```

```
PROCEDURE SORT(LIST, N)
    REPEAT
        NO_EXCHANGES ← TRUE
        FOR J ← 1 TO N-1 DO
            IF LIST(J) > LIST(J+1) THEN
                TEMP ← LIST(J)
                LIST(J) ← LIST(J+1)
                LIST(J+1) ← TEMP
                NO_EXCHANGES ← FALSE
            END IF
        END FOR
    UNTIL NO_EXCHANGES
END SORT
```

FIGURE 9-6. The procedure SORT.

Many programming languages omit the word CALL when invoking a procedure, so that, for instance, one would write just

```
SORT(A, SIZE)
```

instead of

```
CALL SORT(A, SIZE)
```

In writing your own algorithms, you can include or omit the word CALL as you wish. I have included it in the algorithms in the book (despite some suggestions that it be omitted) since its presence unmistakably signals a procedure invocation.

The use of value parameters is often referred to as *call by value*, since values are passed from the invoking algorithm to the function. The use of variable parameters is often referred to as *call-by-reference* or *call-by-location*, since variables—references to or locations of values—are passed from the invoking algorithm to the procedure.

Most modern programming languages make use of either call-by-value or call-by-reference; however, languages vary widely in the circumstances under which each method of parameter passing may be used. Some languages restrict the programmer to a single method; others allow each parameter in a function or procedure to be designated individually as a value parameter or a variable parameter.

9.3 Local and Global Variables

Unless otherwise specified, the variables used in a function or procedure definition are *local variables*. By *local* we mean that variables appearing in different algorithms, functions, and procedures are unrelated to one another even if they happen to have the same name.

In many implementations of programming languages, the memory space for local variables is allocated when a function or procedure is invoked and reclaimed for other uses after the function or procedure returns. This means that we cannot assume that local variables will retain their values from one invocation of a function or procedure to the next. Each time a function or procedure is invoked, its local variables start out undefined, regardless of what values they may have had during previous invocations.

It is sometimes convenient, however, to let an algorithm and some of the functions and procedures it invokes have some variables in common. Variables shared by an algorithm and some of the functions and procedures it invokes are called *global variables*. There are two reasons for using global variables:

1. We wish to preserve some values from one invocation of a function or procedure to the next. We have seen that this is impossible with local variables, which are created anew for each invocation. But we can achieve our goal by giving the functions or procedures access to one or more variables in the invoking algorithm. These variables will retain their values between invocations of the functions or procedures.

2. Sometimes a number of functions and procedures all require access to a common set of variables. By making these variables global, we save the programmer from having to include them as actual parameters in every function and procedure invocation.

Global variables are not without their critics. Some people maintain that it is clearer to require that all variables to which a function or procedure has access be listed as actual parameters. That way, we can see at a glance which variables affect or are affected by a particular invocation. Global variables let data in and out the back door, so to speak, and someone who is only watching the front door—the actual parameters—may have difficulty understanding what is going on.

These concerns suggest that we use global variables with caution. However, the reasons for using global variables often seem stronger than the reasons for avoiding them, so they are widely used, and we will use them later in this book.

The methods used for declaring variables to be global vary widely from one programming language to another. In our algorithmic language, we will declare global variables by listing them in a GLOBAL statement. Thus,

```
GLOBAL P, Q, R
```

declares P, Q, and R to be global variables.

Suppose that we have two variable names, X and A, each of which is used in an algorithm and in several of the functions and procedures that the algorithm invokes. Suppose that in the algorithm and in each of the functions and procedures, X appears in a GLOBAL statement

```
GLOBAL X
```

while A does not. Then X refers to the same variable whether it appears in the algorithm or in one of the functions or procedures. On the other hand, A refers to different variables in the algorithm and in each function and procedure.

To illustrate the use of a global variable, let's write a function to generate pseudorandom numbers. These, you recall, are numbers that seem to have been chosen at random, even though they were computed by a function or procedure.

Pseudorandom numbers provide the unpredictability needed by game-playing programs; few computer games would remain fun very long if the computer always made the same moves in each particular situation. In computer simulation pseudorandom numbers are important for simulating unpredictable events. Still another application is in cryptography, where messages are rendered secret by manipulating their characters in seemingly random ways.

There are many ways of generating pseudorandom numbers, some of which are adapted to the characteristics of particular computers. Since we don't have time to go deeply into the subject of pseudorandom number generation, we will be content with a "quick and dirty" method that is satisfactory for undemanding uses such as game playing.

Our pseudorandom number generator will work with a real number in the range 0–1 (not including 1). This number is called a seed, and we assign it to the global variable SEED. The starting value of SEED is supplied by the user. Thereafter, each time the pseudorandom number generator is invoked, it computes a new value of SEED from the old value of SEED. The successive values of SEED provide a sequence of pseudorandom numbers, all of which are greater than or equal to 0 and less than 1. If we need pseudorandom numbers in some other range, we can derive them from the successive values of SEED.

We compute a new value of SEED from its old value as follows:

```
SEED ← (SEED + 3.1415927)**2
SEED ← SEED - INT(SEED)
```

That is, we add a constant to the value of SEED (the mathematical constant pi was chosen here) and square the sum. The integer part of the result is dropped, leaving only the fractional part, which becomes the new value of SEED. It is largely the effect of dropping the integer part of the result and retaining only the fractional part that makes the resulting series of numbers appear to be random.

Now let's write a function that takes no arguments and yields a pseudorandom fractional value each time it is invoked:

```
FUNCTION RND
    GLOBAL SEED
    SEED ← (SEED + 3.1415927)**2
    SEED ← SEED - INT(SEED)
    RND ← SEED
END RND
```

(Note that when a function or procedure has no parameters, the entire parameter list, including the enclosing parentheses, is omitted.)

Each time RND is used in an expression, it computes a new value for SEED and yields that value as the value of the function. SEED must be a global variable, since its value has to be retained from one invocation of RND to the next.

The following algorithm uses RND to print a series of 50 pseudorandom numbers:

```
ALGORITHM CHAOS
   GLOBAL SEED
   SEED ← .8159327
   FOR I ← 1 TO 50 DO
      OUTPUT RND
   END FOR
END CHAOS
```

Note that the algorithm that uses RND has to provide a starting value for SEED. It is from this starting value that SEED gets its name; the starting value is the seed from which grows the entire sequence of pseudorandom numbers.

We often need pseudorandom numbers that are integers in a particular range. For instance, suppose we need pseudorandom integers in the range 1–100. How can we compute these from the values of RND?

We can reason as follows. Suppose our computer stores real numbers with seven-place accuracy. Then the values of RND will range from 0 through .9999999. The values of 100*RND will range from 0 through 99.99999, so the value of INT(100*RND) is an integer in the range 0–99. If we add 1 to this, we get an integer in the range 1–100.

Thus, the expression

```
INT(100*RND) + 1
```

yields pseudorandom integers in the range 1–100. In the same way,

```
INT(6*RND) + 1
```

yields pseudorandom integers in the range 1–6;

```
INT(36*RND) + 1
```

yields pseudorandom integers in the range 1–36; and so on.

We can use this principle to write our own version of the built-in function RANDOM(N), which yields pseudorandom numbers in the range 1–N:

```
FUNCTION RANDOM(N)
   GLOBAL SEED
   SEED ← (SEED + 3.1415927)**2
```

```
     SEED ← SEED − INT(SEED)
     RANDOM ← INT(N*SEED) + 1
END RANDOM
```

Figure 9-7 shows a version of the algorithm GUESS (from Chapter 7) that uses our version of RANDOM in place of the built-in function. This version of the algorithm is slightly more complicated than the one using the built-in function, since we must declare the global variable SEED and obtain an initial value for it from the player.

9.4 Recursive Functions and Procedures

We have seen that functions and procedures can be defined in terms of other functions and procedures. We can go even further and define a function or procedure partially in terms of itself. Such functions and procedures are said to be *recursive*.

The standard example of a recursive function is the FACTORIAL function. We recall that FACTORIAL(N) equals the product of all the integers from 1 through N. In particular,

```
FACTORIAL(1) = 1
FACTORIAL(2) = 2*1
```

FIGURE 9-7. The algorithm GUESS. This algorithm invokes the function RANDOM, which is defined in the text. The global variable SEED is accessible to both GUESS and RANDOM.

```
ALGORITHM GUESS
   GLOBAL SEED
   OUTPUT 'ENTER A NUMBER BETWEEN 0 AND 1'
   INPUT SEED
   OUTPUT 'I AM THINKING OF A NUMBER BETWEEN 1 AND 100'
   OUTPUT 'YOU ARE TO TRY TO GUESS THE NUMBER. I WILL TELL'
   OUTPUT 'YOU WHETHER YOUR GUESS IS RIGHT, OR WHETHER'
   OUTPUT 'IT IS TOO LARGE OR TOO SMALL.'
   REPEAT
      NUMBER ← RANDOM(100)
      OUTPUT 'I HAVE MY NUMBER. WHAT IS YOUR GUESS?'
      REPEAT
         INPUT YOUR_GUESS
         IF YOUR_GUESS > NUMBER THEN
            OUTPUT 'YOUR GUESS IS TOO LARGE. GUESS AGAIN.'
         ELSE IF YOUR_GUESS < NUMBER THEN
            OUTPUT 'YOUR GUESS IS TOO SMALL. GUESS AGAIN.'
         END IF
      UNTIL YOUR_GUESS = NUMBER
      OUTPUT 'YOUR GUESS IS RIGHT'
      OUTPUT 'WOULD YOU LIKE TO PLAY AGAIN (YES OR NO)?'
      INPUT PLAY_AGAIN
   UNTIL PLAY_AGAIN ≠ 'YES'
   OUTPUT 'I HAVE ENJOYED PLAYING WITH YOU'
END GUESS
```

```
FACTORIAL(3)  =  3*2*1
FACTORIAL(4)  =  4*3*2*1
FACTORIAL(5)  =  5*4*3*2*1
```

and so on.

Now notice that, since FACTORIAL(1) equals 1,

```
FACTORIAL(2)  =  2*1  =  2*FACTORIAL(1)
```

In the same way, we see that

```
FACTORIAL(3)  =  3*FACTORIAL(2)
FACTORIAL(4)  =  4*FACTORIAL(3)
FACTORIAL(5)  =  5*FACTORIAL(4)
```

and so on.

We can, in fact, define the FACTORIAL function by the following two statements:

```
FACTORIAL(1)  =  1
FACTORIAL(N)  =  N*FACTORIAL(N-1), N greater than 1
```

This definition is said to be recursive, since to compute the value of FACTORIAL(N) for N greater than 1, we have to use the definition repeatedly.

For instance, suppose we want to compute the value of FACTORIAL(5). From the definition, we see that

```
FACTORIAL(5)  =  5*FACTORIAL(4)
```

This doesn't help much, since we don't know the value of FACTORIAL(4). But we can go back to the definition and find that

```
FACTORIAL(4)  =  4*FACTORIAL(3)
```

Hence,

```
FACTORIAL(5)  =  5*FACTORIAL(4)  =  5*4*FACTORIAL(3)
```

Applying the definition to FACTORIAL(3), in turn, tells us that

```
FACTORIAL(5)  =  5*4*3*FACTORIAL(2)
```

and applying the definition to FACTORIAL(2) gives us

```
FACTORIAL(5)  =  5*4*3*2*FACTORIAL(1)
```

But the definition says straight out that FACTORIAL(1) equals 1, so

```
FACTORIAL(5) = 5*4*3*2*1 = 120
```

We can use the recursive definition as a basis for a function definition in the algorithmic language:

```
FUNCTION FACTORIAL(N)
    IF N = 1 THEN
        FACTORIAL ← 1
    ELSE
        FACTORIAL ← N*FACTORIAL(N−1)
    END IF
END FACTORIAL
```

Note carefully the two ways in which the word FACTORIAL is used. When FACTORIAL appears on the left-hand side of ←, we are returning a value by assigning it to the function name. When FACTORIAL appears in the expression on the right-hand side of ←, we have a new invocation of the function FACTORIAL, called a recursive invocation since FACTORIAL is being invoked by itself.

Suppose this function is invoked to compute FACTORIAL(5). During the computation of FACTORIAL(5) the function is invoked again to compute FACTORIAL(4). During the computation of FACTORIAL(4), the function is invoked again to compute FACTORIAL(3), and so on. Eventually the function is invoked to compute FACTORIAL(1).

FACTORIAL(1) can be computed without any further function invocations. (Why?) With the value of FACTORIAL(1) at hand, the computation of FACTORIAL(2) can be completed; with the value of FACTORIAL(2) at hand; the computation of FACTORIAL(3) can be completed. Proceeding in this way the computations of FACTORIAL(4) and, finally, FACTORIAL(5) are completed.

When a function calls itself, the new invocation must not change the contents of any memory locations that the old invocation is still using. This means that for each invocation of the function, a separate memory area must be set aside for holding the values of parameters and local variables.

Recursion is not always the most efficient way to solve a problem. For instance, our previous version of FACTORIAL using repetition is more efficient than the recursive version. The recursive version takes more memory because of the need for a separate memory area for each invocation. Also, for each function invocation the computer must waste a certain amount of time passing parameters to the function, setting up a new memory area for it, and returning its result after it has finished executing.

Nevertheless, some problems are inherently recursive in nature, so that the easiest and most natural way of presenting their solutions is as recursive functions or procedures. For these kinds of problems, it is worth using recursion for the sake of clarity even if some efficiency is sacrificed. We will see examples of such problems in Chapter 15.

1. Describe some everyday objects that are built out of simpler parts, whose parts are built out of still simpler parts, and so on.

2. What two properties do functions and procedures possess that are not enjoyed by the parts of which physical machines are made?

3. Give the general form of a function definition.

4. What are *formal parameters*?

5. What are *actual parameters*?

6. What is another commonly used name for actual parameters?

7. How does a function definition specify the value that the function is to return?

8. Contrast procedures and functions.

9. What are *value parameters*?

10. What are *variable parameters*?

11. What kinds of actual parameters can be substituted for value parameters? For variable parameters?

12. To what does the term *call-by-value* apply?

13. To what do the terms *call-by-reference* and *call-by-location* apply?

14. What is a *local variable*?

15. What is a *global variable*? What statement do we use to declare variables as global?

16. Give two reasons why global variables are used.

17. Why is the use of global variables sometimes criticized?

18. What do we mean by a *recursive* function or procedure?

19. Why is a recursive function or procedure sometimes less efficient than one that uses repetition in place of recursion?

20. Why, in spite of the inefficiency mentioned in Question 19, is recursion nevertheless often used?

Exercises

For each of the following you should write not only the function or procedure requested but also an algorithm that "exercises" the function or procedure by invoking it.

1. Write a function MIN(M, N) whose value is the minimum of the values of its two arguments.

2. Write a function SMALLEST(X, Y, Z) whose value is the smallest of the values of its three arguments.

3. Write a function FLOOR(X) whose value is the largest integer that is less than or equal to X. Thus, FLOOR(3.75) = 3; FLOOR(2) = 2; FLOOR(− 3.14) = − 4; FLOOR(− 8.01) = − 9. For nonnegative values of X, FLOOR(X) and INT(X) have the same value. For negative values of X, however, FLOOR(X) and INT(X) have different values.

4. We can round a value to the nearest integer by adding 0.5 to its absolute value, then discarding the fractional part of the result. Thus, to round 3.72, we add 0.5 getting 4.22. Dropping the 0.22 gives us the rounded value of 4. To round − 71.63, we add 71.63 (the absolute value of − 71.63) to 0.5 getting 72.13. Dropping the 0.13 gives 72 and restoring the minus sign gives the final rounded value of − 72. Write a function ROUND(X) whose value is its argument rounded to the nearest integer. ROUND should work for both positive and negative arguments.

5. Modify the procedure EXTREMES so that it returns not only the largest and the smallest values in the array A but also the subscripts of the element containing the smallest value and the element containing the largest value. (If the smallest value occurs more than once, the subscript of any element containing that value may be returned. The same is true for the largest value.)

6. Write a procedure ZERO(A, M, N) that sets to 0 all of the elements of the two-dimensional array A. M is the number of rows in A and N is the number of columns.

7. Let A be a two dimensional array with N rows and N columns. Write a procedure TRANSPOSE(A, N) that interchanges the rows and columns of A. After TRANSPOSE has been invoked, what was the first row of A should now be its first column, what was the second row of A should now be its second column, and so on. Put another way, for each value of I and J, TRANSPOSE exchanges the values of A(I, J) and A(J, I).

8. A procedure can contain INPUT and OUTPUT statements. Write a procedure PUT(A, M, N) to output the two-dimensional array A by rows. M is the number of rows in A and N is the number of columns.

9. Write a procedure ROLL(DIE__1, DIE__2) to simulate the rolling of a pair of dice. It should use the built-in function RANDOM to assign pseudorandom numbers from 1 through 6 to DIE__1 and DIE__2. It should also output a message informing the user of what values were rolled.

10. Write a procedure

```
FIND(LIST, COUNT, TO_BE_FOUND, LOCATION)
```

that looks up the value of TO__BE__FOUND in the one-dimensional array LIST. COUNT is the number of elements in LIST. If the sought-after value is found, LOCATION is set to the position of the value on the list. If the value is not found, LOCATION is set to − 1.

11. A few programming languages do not provide the operator ** for raising numbers to powers. For use in such languages, define a function POWER(X, N) that for any real number X and nonnegative integer N returns X raised to the Nth power. Thus POWER(X, 0) = 1; POWER(X, 1) = X; POWER(X, 2) = X*X; POWER(X, 3) = X*X*X; and so on.

12. The POWER function described in Exercise 11 can be defined recursively as follows:

```
POWER(X, 0)  =  1
POWER(X, N)  =  X*POWER(X, N-1), N greater than 1
```

Justify this definition, and use it to write a recursive version of the function POWER.

13. Write a function GCD(M, N) whose value is the greatest common divisor of the positive integers M and N. Use the technique for computing the greatest common divisor given in Chapter 1.

14. The function GCD(M, N) for computing the greatest common divisor of M and N can be defined recursively as follows:

```
GCD(M, 0)  =  M
GCD(M, N)  =  GCD(N, M MOD N), N greater than 0
```

Write a recursive version of GCD based on the recursive definition. Note that the recursive definition of GCD just expresses the two properties of the greatest common divisor that we took as the starting point for our discussion in Chapter 1. If we had known about recursive functions in Chapter 1, we could have used these properties directly, sparing ourselves some close reasoning. On the other hand, we can now view the discussion in Chapter 1 as an illustration of how to derive an algorithm that uses repetition from a recursive definition.

15. The Fibonacci sequence consists of the following numbers

0, 1, 1, 2, 3, 5, 8, 13, 21, 34, 55, . . .

The first two numbers in the sequence are 0 and 1. Each remaining number is the sum of the two immediately preceding ones. Thus 2 = 1+1, 3 = 1+2, 5 = 2+3, 8 = 3+5, and so on. We can define a function FIBONACCI(N), whose value is the Nth number in the sequence, as follows:

```
FIBONACCI(1)  =  0
FIBONACCI(2)  =  1
FIBONACCI(N)  =  FIBONACCI(N-1) + FIBONACCI(N-2),
                 N greater than 2
```

Justify these statements and use them to write a recursive function definition for FIBONACCI(N).

Chapter 10

Algorithm Design and Testing

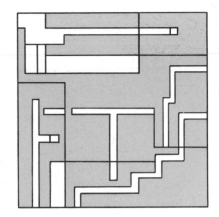

A large computer program is at least as complicated as a bridge, a building, or a battleship. We do not customarily embark on the construction of things this complex without having carefully planned them in advance. To start writing a program without having given a thought to its overall design is ridiculous—just as ridiculous as calling out a construction crew to start a new skyscraper without first giving them plans to work from.

One common feature of complicated objects is that when first completed, they seldom work as intended. There always seem to be a few "bugs" to get rid of. If the object was well-defined in the first place, then the "debugging" needed is apt to be minimal, consisting mainly of correcting a few oversights of the builders. But if the original design was bad, very substantial amounts of time, money, and effort will be required to correct the design flaws.

In this chapter, we will look at the techniques for designing and testing algorithms and programs. For these, as for other complicated systems, the more time we spend on design, the less time we are likely to spend on getting the bugs out.

10.1 Algorithm Design

Modularity. A *module* is any part of a larger, more complex system that performs a well-defined function. Many people probably first encountered the term in connection with the space program. In news reports on space exploration, there was much talk of the "command module," the "lunar module," and the "reentry module."

When we think about the functioning of any complex system, we almost invariably think in terms of the modules that make it up. We often call these modules "systems." Thus, we think of an automobile not as just a big jumble of parts, but as consisting of an electrical system, a cooling system, a steering system, a braking system, a drive system (engine and transmission), and so on. Each of these "systems" is an example of a module.

When designing or repairing a car, we invariably concentrate our attention on one of these modules to the exclusion of the others. Thus, if the engine is running too hot, we would not spend much time worrying about the battery. We would focus our attention on the cooling system. And if a tire is flat, we would not even bother to raise the hood to check the car's electrical or cooling or fuel systems. We would have the trouble localized in one small module; we could concentrate on repairing that module and no other.

Top-Down Design. An important feature of a module is that we can think of it as made up of other modules. For instance, the electrical system of an automobile is made up of the battery, the alternator, the coil, the distributor, the spark plugs, the voltage regulator, the fuses, and sundry lights and switches.

Furthermore, the modules that make up a larger module are themselves made up of still smaller modules. The battery, for instance, is made up of plates, an electrolyte, terminals, and a container. And a plate consists of . . . but you get the idea.

In short, the modules of a system form a *hierarchy,* as shown in Figure 10-1. At the top level of the hierarchy is the entire system. On the second level are those modules that are directly used by the top-level modules, and so on. Eventually we reach the bottom-level modules, which we do not find convenient to analyze further. These are usually off-the-shelf components such as batteries, which we find more convenient to buy than to make.

This hierarchical organization of modules suggests an approach to system design known as *top-down design.* We start with the top-level module and design it in terms of the modules on the next level. That is, we figure out what modules will be needed on the next level and how they should go together to make the top-level module. While we are doing this, we do not worry at all about the detailed construction of the second-level modules.

Once the top-level module has been designed, we start to work on the second-level modules. At any time during this process we will be focusing our attention on realizing a single second-level module in terms of third-level modules. We will not worry about the top-level module in terms of third-level modules. We will not worry about the top-level module; it is already designed. We will not worry about the details of the third-level modules—they will be designed later. We do not even worry about the other second-level modules; we work on one second-level module at a

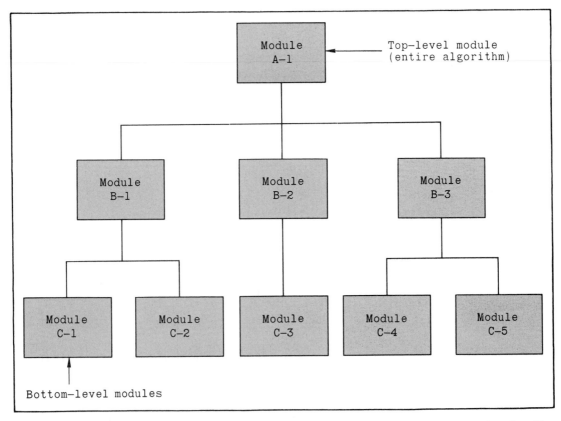

FIGURE 10-1. A hierarchy of modules. The top-level module is the entire algorithm. The bottom level modules only make use of built in operators and functions; they do not call any other user-written modules.

time. (Or different people could work on different second-level modules at the same time.)

Proceeding in this fashion, we design the modules in top-to-bottom order as they occur on the hierarchy diagram in Figure 10-1—hence the name "top-down design." Figure 10-2 illustrates top-down design.

No matter how complex the system, the design of each module can be straightforward. The reason is that we do not have to think about all of the complexities of the system at once, but only about the design of one module in terms of its immediately subordinate modules. We can think of top-down design, then, as a systematic method of focusing our attention on one small part of a complex system at a time, allowing us momentarily to ignore the rest of the system.

Functions and Procedures as Modules. One approach to applying top-down design to algorithms is to let the main algorithm be the top-level module and use functions and procedures for the various subordinate modules.

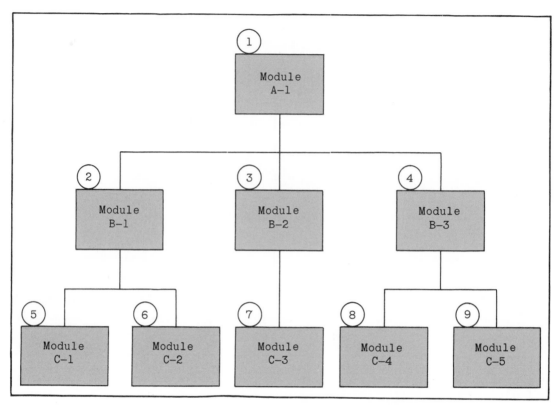

FIGURE 10-2. Top-down design. The numbers show the order in which the modules are designed.

Thus, we would start out by writing the main algorithm. But whenever the need arose to perform an operation of any complexity, we would write a function or procedure call to perform that operation. We would, of course, have to make a note of exactly what each of these functions or procedures is supposed to do, since we would have to write it later.

The procedures and functions called by the main algorithm would form the second-level modules. When writing these, we would again call on procedures and functions to perform complex operations. These procedures and functions would form the third-level modules. Eventually we will reach the bottom level. This is made up of those functions and procedures that can be expressed entirely in terms of the built-in operators and functions of the language.

As an example of top-down design using procedures we will write an algorithm to play craps with the user. The entire algorithm, called CRAPS, will form the top level of the module hierarchy, as shown in Figure 10-3.

We want to express the top-level module in terms of calls to the procedures that will form the second-level modules. A good strategy at this stage is to leave all details of the calculations to the procedures and concentrate on the overall data flow. Bearing this in mind, we come up with the following second-level modules:

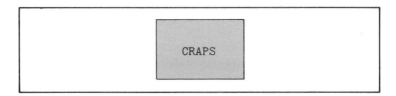

FIGURE 10-3. The top-level module for the algorithm CRAPS.

`INITIALIZE(AMOUNT)`	Find the initial amount that the player has to risk in the game, and set AMOUNT to this value.
`ACCEPT_BET(BET, AMOUNT)`	Find out how much player wishes to bet and set BET to this amount. Reject illegal bet greater than AMOUNT (player cannot bet more than he has).
`PLAY(WON)`	Play one game. Set WON to TRUE if the player wins, to FALSE if he loses.
`UPDATE(BET, AMOUNT, WON, FINISHED)`	Add BET to or subtract it from AMOUNT, depending on whether WON is TRUE or FALSE. If AMOUNT is 0, set FINISHED to TRUE. Otherwise, inquire if player wishes to continue and set FINISHED accordingly.

Using these procedures, we write the top-level module as shown in Figure 10-4. Figure 10-5 shows the hierarchy diagram with the second-level modules added.

Notice that at this point we have not said anything about the rules for craps. The algorithm just given would serve for any game where the player makes bets that are either won or lost. The rules for craps are hidden inside the module PLAY. We can change the rules of the game simply by changing PLAY, without changing any of the other modules.

INITIALIZE, Figure 10-6, merely asks the player how much money he has available for playing the game.

A module that accepts input should always check the validity of that input before returning it to the invoking module. The invoking module can then always assume that the input obtained by a lower-level module is correct.

```
ALGORITHM CRAPS
   CALL INITIALIZE(AMOUNT)
   REPEAT
      CALL ACCEPT_BET(BET, AMOUNT)
      CALL PLAY(WON)
      CALL UPDATE(BET, AMOUNT, WON, FINISHED)
   UNTIL FINISHED
   OUTPUT 'I ENJOYED PLAYING WITH YOU.'
   OUTPUT 'LET US DO IT AGAIN REAL SOON.'
END CRAPS
```

FIGURE 10-4. The algorithm CRAPS. This top-level module calls four second level modules, the procedures INITIALIZE, ACCEPT__BET, PLAY, AND UPDATE.

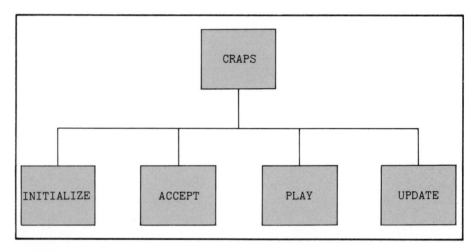

FIGURE 10-5. The top and second level modules for the algorithm CRAPS.

FIGURE 10-6. The procedure INITIALIZE.

```
PROCEDURE INITIALIZE(AMOUNT)
   OUTPUT 'HOW MUCH MONEY DO YOU HAVE TO PLAY WITH?
   INPUT AMOUNT
   WHILE AMOUNT ≤ 0 DO
      OUTPUT 'YOU CANNOT PLAY WITH A ZERO OR NEGATIVE'
      OUTPUT 'AMOUNT OF MONEY. PLEASE ENTER A POSITIVE'
      OUTPUT 'AMOUNT'
      INPUT AMOUNT
   END WHILE
END INITIALIZE
```

```
PROCEDURE ACCEPT_BET(BET, AMOUNT)
    OUTPUT 'HOW MUCH DO YOU WISH TO BET ON THIS GAME?'
    INPUT BET
    WHILE BET > AMOUNT DO
        OUTPUT 'YOU CANNOT BET MORE THAN YOU HAVE'
        OUTPUT 'PLEASE ENTER ANOTHER BET'
        INPUT BET
    END WHILE
END ACCEPT_BET
```

FIGURE 10-7. The procedure ACCEPT_BET.

ACCEPT_BET, Figure 10-7, accepts the amount that the player wishes to bet on this game. This bet must be less than the value of AMOUNT; the player cannot play on credit.

The module PLAY, Figure 10-8, causes the dice to be rolled and determines whether the player wins or loses according to the rules of craps. Those rules are:

If the player rolls a 7 or 11 on his first roll, he wins. If he rolls a 2, 3, or 12 on his first roll, he loses.

Otherwise, what he rolled on his first roll becomes his "point." The player continues rolling until he "makes his point"—rolls the same thing he got on his first roll—or "craps out"—rolls a 7. If the player makes his point, he wins; if he craps out, he loses.

At this level we are only concerned with the value rolled—the sum of the numbers on both dice. We will use the procedure

```
ROLL_DICE(VALUE)
```

FIGURE 10-8. The procedure PLAY. This second-level module calls one third-level module, the procedure ROLL_DICE.

```
PROCEDURE PLAY(WON)
    CALL ROLL_DICE(VALUE)
    IF (VALUE = 7) OR (VALUE = 11) THEN
        WON ← TRUE
    ELSE IF (VALUE = 2) OR (VALUE = 3) OR (VALUE = 12) THEN
        WON ← FALSE
    ELSE
        POINT ← VALUE
        REPEAT
            CALL ROLL_DICE(VALUE)
        UNTIL (VALUE = POINT) OR (VALUE = 7)
        IF VALUE = POINT THEN
            WON ← TRUE
        ELSE
            WON ← FALSE
        END IF
    END IF
END PLAY
```

```
PROCEDURE UPDATE(BET, AMOUNT, WON, FINISHED)
    IF WON THEN
        OUTPUT 'CONGRATULATIONS, YOU WIN!'
        AMOUNT ← AMOUNT + BET
    ELSE
        OUTPUT 'TOO BAD, YOU LOSE!'
        AMOUNT ← AMOUNT - BET
    END IF
    OUTPUT 'YOU NOW HAVE', AMOUNT, 'DOLLARS.'
    IF AMOUNT = 0 THEN
        FINISHED ← TRUE
    ELSE
        OUTPUT 'DO YOU WANT TO PLAY ANOTHER GAME?'
        INPUT ANSWER
        IF ANSWER = 'YES' THEN
            FINISHED ← FALSE
        ELSE
            FINISHED ← TRUE
        END IF
    END IF
END UPDATE
```

FIGURE 10-9. The procedure UPDATE.

to roll the dice and set VALUE to the resulting value.

UPDATE, Figure 10-9, updates the amount of money that the player has, depending on whether he won or lost the last game. UPDATE determines whether the player wants to keep on playing (if he is not broke) and sets FINISHED accordingly.

The procedures INITIALIZE, ACCEPT_BET, and UPDATE are all bottom-level modules, since none of them call any other procedures. PLAY, however, calls a third-level module, ROLL_DICE.

ROLL_DICE, Figure 10-10, simulates the rolling of two dice. It informs the player what was rolled, and assigns the total value rolled to its argument.

If we assume that RANDOM is a built-in function, then ROLL_DICE is a bottom-level module. Figure 10-11, now shows the complete hierarchy diagram for CRAPS.

Of course, this example is very much a miniature one. An actual large

FIGURE 10-10. The procedure ROLL_DICE, our only third-level module. RANDOM is assumed to be a built-in function. If it were written by the user, it would be a fourth-level module.

```
PROCEDURE ROLL_DICE(VALUE)
    DIE_1 ← RANDOM(6)
    DIE_2 ← RANDOM(6)
    VALUE ← DIE_1 + DIE_2
    OUTPUT 'YOU ROLLED A', DIE_1, 'AND A', DIE_2
END ROLL_DICE
```

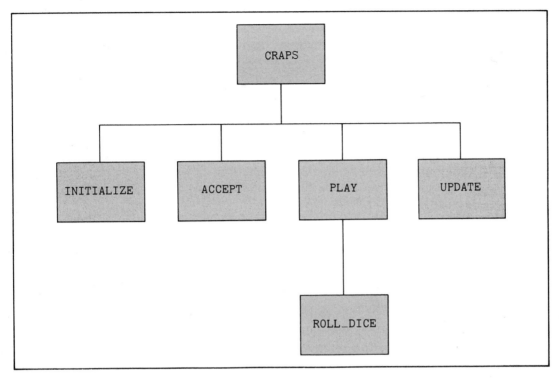

FIGURE 10-11. The complete module hierarchy for the algorithm CRAPS.

program such as an operating system, a translator, or an accounting system might fill this entire book if it were written out in the algorithmic language. Such a program might have hundreds of modules and a hierarchy diagram five to ten levels deep. But our example, small as it is, illustrates the principles that are being used more and more to design large, complex programs.

Stepwise Refinement. It is not always desirable to implement every module as a function or a procedure. In some languages, such as BASIC, the various argument-passing methods used in the algorithmic language are not available. And in many languages where they are available, they are inefficient; too much computer time is wasted passing arguments to functions and procedures.

An alternative technique is *stepwise refinement*. When we write a module, we represent each reference to a lower-level module by a comment rather than by function or procedure call. We then refine this description by replacing each comment by the statements that carry out the operation the comment describes. (These statements implement the modules on the next lower level.)

We start by writing the top-level module in a form that consists mostly of comments. We refine it by replacing some comments by statements.

Some of those statements may be comments that need further refinement, and so on. Eventually, we will eliminate all the comments and have only algorithmic language statements left. Thus, we can use a top-down approach to design without having to call functions or procedures.

We use the algorithm CRAPS again as an example. As shown in Figure 10-12, we start out with the top-level module, but using comments where we used procedure calls before.

Now we work out the statements necessary to implement each comment. For the first comment, we would have:

```
(Accept initial value for AMOUNT)
    OUTPUT 'HOW MUCH MONEY DO YOU HAVE TO PLAY WITH?'
    WHILE AMOUNT ≤ 0 DO
        OUTPUT 'YOU CANNOT PLAY WITH A ZERO OR NEGATIVE'
        OUTPUT 'AMOUNT OF MONEY. PLEASE ENTER A POSITIVE'
        OUTPUT 'AMOUNT'
        INPUT AMOUNT
    END WHILE
```

We could do the same for each of the other comments. But since the refinements of the comments are the same as the bodies of the procedures already given, we will not repeat each refinement separately. Instead, Figure 10-13 gives the result of inserting the refinement below each comment (retaining the comments for documentation).

The call to the procedure ROLL_DICE has been retained. Since ROLL_DICE is called twice, it is best to make it a procedure and call it twice rather than repeating the statements for ROLL_DICE twice. If this consideration had not intervened, a comment would have been used in place of each call to ROLL_DICE. On the next refinement, each such comment would have been replaced by the statements from the body of ROLL_DICE.

FIGURE 10-12. To construct the algorithm CRAPS by stepwise refinement, we start with an outline in which the lower-level modules are represented by comments.

```
ALGORITHM CRAPS
    (Accept initial value for AMOUNT)
    REPEAT
        (Accept BET and see that it does not exceed AMOUNT)
        (Play a game and set WON to TRUE or FALSE to
        indicate the result)
        (Update AMOUNT according to results of last
        game; set FINISHED to TRUE or FALSE depending
        on whether or not more games are to be played)
    UNTIL FINISHED
    OUTPUT 'I ENJOYED PLAYING WITH YOU'
    OUTPUT 'LET US DO IT AGAIN REAL SOON'
END CRAPS
```

```
ALGORITHM CRAPS
   (Accept initial value for AMOUNT)
       OUTPUT 'HOW MUCH MONEY DO YOU HAVE TO PLAY WITH?'
       INPUT AMOUNT
       WHILE AMOUNT ≤ 0 DO
           OUTPUT 'YOU CANNOT PLAY WITH A ZERO OR NEGATIVE'
           OUTPUT 'AMOUNT OF MONEY. PLEASE ENTER A POSITIVE'
           OUTPUT 'AMOUNT'
       END WHILE
   REPEAT
       (Accept BET and see that it does not exceed AMOUNT)
           OUTPUT 'HOW MUCH MONEY DO YOU WISH TO BET ON THIS GAME?'
           INPUT BET
           WHILE BET > AMOUNT DO
               OUTPUT 'YOU CANNOT BET MORE THAN YOU HAVE'
               OUTPUT 'PLEASE ENTER ANOTHER BET'
               INPUT BET
           END WHILE
       (Play a game and set WON to TRUE or FALSE to
        indicate the result)
           CALL ROLL_DICE(VALUE)
           IF (VALUE = 7) OR (VALUE = 11) THEN
               WON ← TRUE
           ELSE IF (VALUE = 2) OR (VALUE = 3) OR (VALUE = 12) THEN
               WON ← FALSE
           ELSE
               POINT ← VALUE
               REPEAT
                   CALL ROLL_DICE(VALUE)
               UNTIL (VALUE = POINT) OR (VALUE = 7)
               IF VALUE = POINT THEN
                   WON ← TRUE
               ELSE
                   WON ← FALSE
               END IF
           END IF
       (Update AMOUNT according to results of last
        game. Set FINISHED to TRUE or FALSE
        depending on whether or not more games are
        to be played.)
           IF WON THEN
               OUTPUT 'CONGRATULATIONS, YOU WON!'
               AMOUNT ← AMOUNT+BET
           ELSE
               OUTPUT 'TOO BAD, YOU LOSE!'
               AMOUNT ← AMOUNT-BET
           END IF
           OUTPUT 'YOU NOW HAVE', AMOUNT, 'DOLLARS.'
           IF AMOUNT = 0 THEN
               FINISHED ← TRUE
           ELSE
               OUTPUT 'DO YOU WANT TO PLAY ANOTHER GAME?'
               INPUT ANSWER
               IF ANSWER = 'YES' THEN
                   FINISHED ← FALSE
               ELSE
                   FINISHED ← TRUE
               END IF
           END IF
   UNTIL FINISHED
   OUTPUT 'I ENJOYED PLAYING WITH YOU'
   OUTPUT 'LET US DO IT AGAIN REAL SOON'
END CRAPS
```

FIGURE 10-13. We refine the outline of the algorithm CRAPS by replacing each comment with statements that carry out the operation described. Instead of actually replacing the comments, we can retain them to document the algorithm.

Designing Individual Modules. So far, we have concentrated on the hierarchical relationships among modules and have said little about the design of individual modules. There is a limit to what we can say. The design of a module is a creative act of the programmer; it cannot be completely analyzed. Nevertheless, two points can be made:

■ *A module should be short.* The whole idea of partitioning a complex program into modules is to make each module simple enough to be intellectually manageable. We defeat our purpose if we make the module so long and complex that it cannot be easily understood. When written in the algorithmic language, a module should seldom be longer than 50 to 100 lines.

■ *Simple, easy-to-understand control structures should be used.* In the preceding chapters, we have learned to use three simple, manageable control structures: *sequencing, selection,* and *repetition.* It is a matter of controversy among computer scientists whether any control structures more complicated than these three are needed. But the programming problems that cannot be solved with sequencing, selection, and repetition—if any exist at all—are very rare.

In languages such as BASIC and FORTRAN, which contain the GO TO statement, it is possible to build control structures that do not correspond to any of these three. The same result can be obtained with the unrestricted use of flowcharts. These do-it-yourself control structures sometimes seem to be slightly better than the standard ones for the particular problem at hand. But since they are inevitably more complex than the standard control structures, and since they have not been studied as extensively, their effects are less predictable and their use more risky. Confining oneself to the control structures in the algorithmic language will go a long way toward simplifying the design of reliable modules.

10.2 Program Testing

A program, just like any other complex system, must be thoroughly tested after completion and before it is turned over to its final users.

Unfortunately, this vital step if often omitted. The programmer tries the program on a few pieces of test data, and if the answers "look right," the program is pronounced ready for use. This is the kind of testing that gives rise to the adage that there are no debugged programs, only those in which the bugs have not yet been encountered!

By far the best way to test any system, be it a program or a complex mechanical or electronic device, is to test it part by part as it is constructed. That is, we test each module separately as well as various modules in combination.

The most obvious way to do this is known as *bottom-up testing.* We first test those modules on the bottom level of the hierarchy, the ones that do not call on any other modules. When we are sure that these work, we move up to the next level and test those modules that are built from the already-tested modules of the bottom level. We continue in this way until eventually we reach the top level and can test the entire program. Figure 10-14 illustrates bottom-up testing.

But bottom-up testing suffers from two problems. First, it goes in the opposite direction to top-down design and construction. Therefore, we cannot test the modules as we design and program them. Second, when we test a module, the higher level modules that will actually use it have not been tested yet. Therefore, we must construct a "test harness": a program that invokes the module under test merely for the purpose of testing it. It would be better if we could test a module "in place," letting it be called by the module that will actually call it in the finished program.

Top-down testing solves both problems. In top-down testing, we start with the top-level module and test it first. Then we test the second-level modules, and so on, until the bottom-level modules are tested (see Figure 10-15).

Now modules can be tested in the same order in which they are designed and constructed. We can design and test the top-level module before we even begin work on the second-level modules.

And when the second-level modules are tested, the already-tested top-level module provides an ideal test harness. Each module is tested in ex-

FIGURE 10-14. Bottom-up testing. The numbers show the order in which the modules are tested.

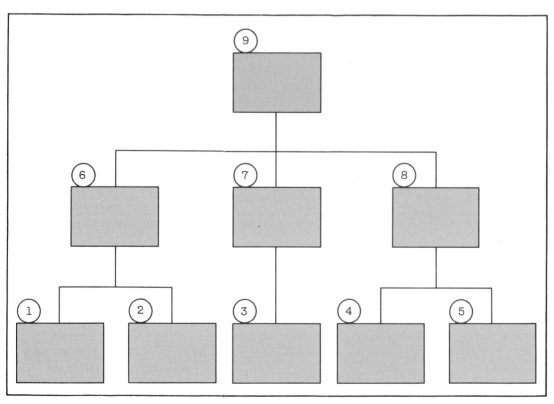

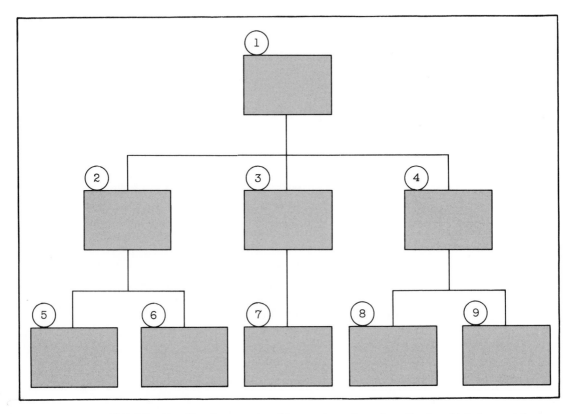

FIGURE 10-15. Top-down testing. The numbers show the order in which the modules are tested. Notice that this order is the same as for top-down design.

actly the same environment in which it will operate in the finished program.

But wait—how can we test the modules on one level when the lower level modules they must call have not been written? The answer is that we replace the unwritten modules with *program stubs*. A *program stub* is a module that prints out the fact that it has been called and prints any data values relevant to the call. By studying this printout, we can see that the higher level module is invoking the correct lower level modules under the correct circumstances and is passing them the correct arguments. Figure 10-16 illustrates the use of program stubs.

Example. As an example of top-down testing, we will take a simple payroll program. This is to process groups of three data items, each group consisting of an employee name, the number of hours the employee has worked, and the hourly rate at which the employee is paid. The sentinel is a group whose employee name is 'END OF DATA'.

We write the top-level module as follows:

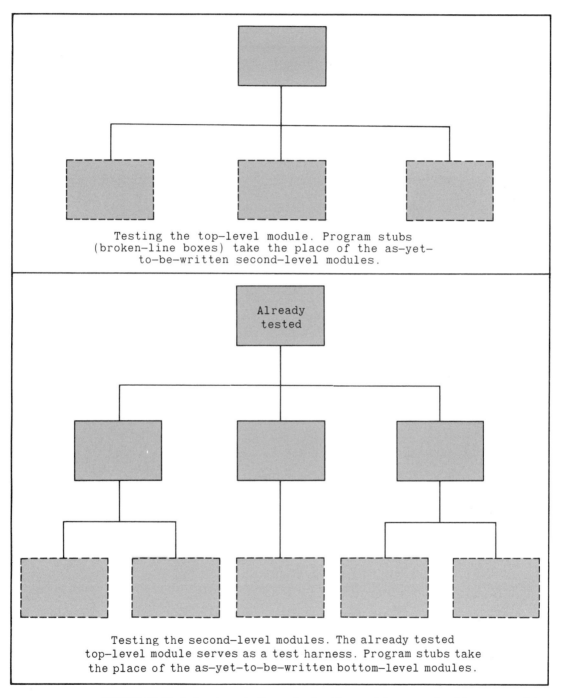

Testing the top—level module. Program stubs
(broken—line boxes) take the place of the as—yet—
to—be—written second—level modules.

Testing the second—level modules. The already tested
top—level module serves as a test harness. Program stubs take
the place of the as—yet—to—be—written bottom—level modules.

FIGURE 10-16. In top-down testing, not-yet-written modules are replaced by program stubs, which are shown here as boxes enclosed by broken lines.

```
ALGORITHM PAY
   INPUT NAME, HOURS, RATE
   WHILE NAME ≠ 'END OF DATA' DO
      CALL COMPUTE_PAY(HOURS, RATE, WAGES)
      OUTPUT NAME, WAGES
      INPUT NAME, HOURS, RATE
   END WHILE
END PAY
```

We want to test this much *before* writing COMPUTE__PAY. We therefore write a program stub as follows:

```
PROCEDURE COMPUTE_PAY(HOURS, RATE, WAGES)
   OUTPUT 'COMPUTE_PAY INVOKED WITH'
   OUTPUT 'HOURS = ', HOURS
   OUTPUT 'RATE = ', RATE
   WAGES ← 999.99
END COMPUTE_PAY
```

When this program stub is invoked, it will announce itself and print out the values that were passed to it. Also, it assigns a dummy value (999.99) to WAGES so we can check that the value which COMPUTE__PAY assigns to WAGES is being properly used by the rest of the program.

With the aid of this program stub, we can test PAY rather thoroughly. In particular, we can test that

■ COMPUTE__PAY is invoked once for each group of data, until a group with employee name equal to 'END OF DATA' is encountered.

■ For each group of data, the values of HOURS and RATE are correctly passed to COMPUTE__PAY.

■ The value of WAGES calculated by COMPUTE__PAY is printed along with the employee name.

After testing PAY, we write COMPUTE__PAY, possibly calling on still more as yet unwritten lower level modules. We test COMPUTE__PAY by replacing the lower level modules by program stubs and by invoking COMPUTE__PAY using the already tested PAY. The process continues until eventually the bottom-level modules are tested. At this point, the entire program has been tested.

Choosing Test Data. To test any module or a complete program, we must supply it with test data for which the correct output is known and compare the output the program produces with the correct output. The success of our testing efforts will rest, in large part, on our ability to construct good test cases.

Ideally, we would like to choose our test cases so as to cause the program or module to follow every conceivable path through its flowchart during testing, as shown in Figure 10-17.

But except for extremely simple modules, this is impractical. If a module contains as few as 32 decision symbols in its flowchart (or IF construc-

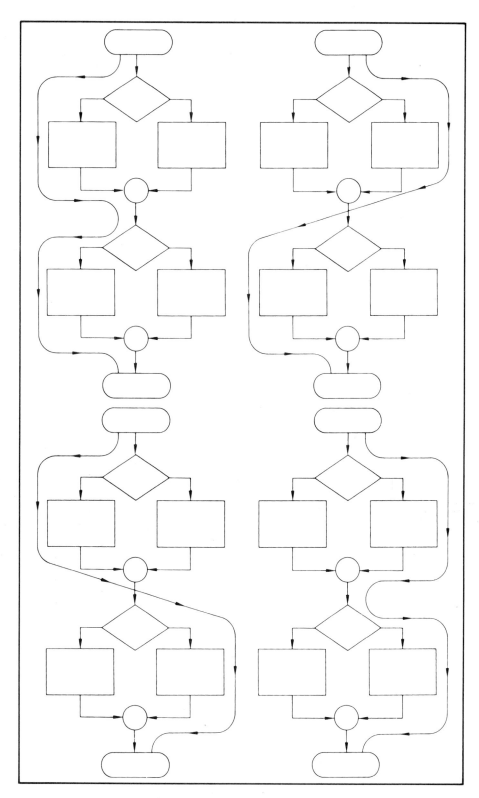

FIGURE 10-17. Ideally, we should use enough test cases to cause a program to traverse every possible path through its flowchart.

tions in its algorithm), then there can exist as many as a billion paths through the flowchart. Repetition complicates matters further by causing the computer to pass repeatedly through the same decision symbol, with possibly different paths being followed from it on different repetitions.

A more modest goal is to see that the test data causes every branch to be taken from every decision symbol during testing (see Figure 10-18). This will not be a thorough testing, since branches from different decision symbols will not be tested in every possible combination. But we will avoid the common situation in which entire sections of the flowchart remain unexplored.

FIGURE 10-18. In practice, often the best we can hope to do is to test every branch leaving each decision symbol. This does not test every branch through the entire flowchart, as we can see by comparing Figures 10-17 and 10-18.

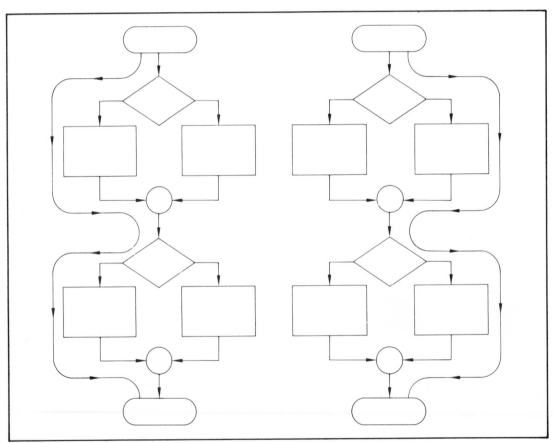

In complicated cases it may not be obvious whether or not each flow-chart branch has indeed been taken at least one time. We can check this by introducing a series of *counters*, say COUNT_1, COUNT_2, COUNT_3, and so on. These will all be set to 0 on entry to the module. In each branch leaving a decision symbol we insert a statement of the form

COUNT ← COUNT + 1

using a different counter for each branch, (see Figure 10-19). On exit from the module, the values of all the counters are printed out.

If the value of any counter is 0 when it is printed out, then the corresponding branch has not been tested. For the testing to be minimally thorough, the value of each counter must be at least 1. For greater confidence in the results of the test, the value for each counter should be greater than 1. The exact value we should hold out for will depend on the complexity of the program, the use to which it will be put, the consequences of its failing, and the cost of testing.

Review Questions

1. Give some additional examples of complex systems whose construction must be carefully planned in advance, and in which starting to work on the system without careful planning would be the height of folly.

2. Do complicated systems usually work correctly the first time they are tested?

3. How is the amount of time and effort spent in designing a system likely to be related to the amount that will be needed to debug it?

4. What is a *module*?

5. Give some examples of systems that can be decomposed into modules, telling what the modules are in each case.

6. What is the advantage of modularity when we are designing, testing, or repairing a system?

7. In what sense do the modules of a system form a *hierarchy*?

8. What characterizes the top-level module in the module hierarchy? The bottom-level modules?

9. Describe *top-down design*.

10. At any stage of a top-down design, on what will our attention be focused? What are some of the things we can forget about for the moment?

11. Explain how functions and procedures can serve as modules.

12. What are the disadvantages of using functions and procedures as modules?

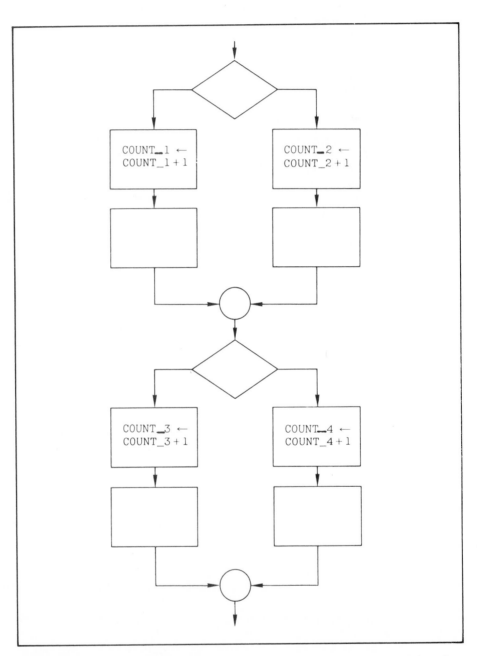

FIGURE 10-19. A flowchart with software counters inserted to make sure that each branch is tested at least once. After initializing the counters to zero, the segment shown is executed repeatedly with different sets of data. Then the values of the counters are displayed to show how many times each branch was tested.

13. Compare stepwise refinement with the use of functions and procedures as modules.

14. Under what condition would a module probably be implemented as a function or procedure, even in stepwise refinement?

15. Give two principles for the design of individual modules.

16. What control structures are recommended for the design of modules? What are the problems of using do-it-yourself control structures?

17. Contrast *bottom-up* and *top-down* testing.

18. What are two difficulties of bottom-up testing that are not present in top-down testing?

19. In top-down testing, how do we test a module even though some of the modules it calls are still unwritten?

20. Ideally, a module would be tested by testing every path through its flowchart. Why is this exhaustive testing usually impractical?

21. Distinguish between testing every branch leaving a decision symbol and testing every path through the flowchart. Why is the former usually practical while the latter usually is not?

22. How can software counters be used to assure that every branch leaving a decision symbol is tested at least once?

Problems

1. In constructing the algorithm CRAPS by stepwise refinement, we decided to leave ROLL__DICE as a procedure rather than to carry the stepwise refinement to the third level of the hierarchy diagram. As an exercise, carry the stepwise refinement to the third level. Rewrite the "refined" version given in the text with comments in place of calls to ROLL__DICE. Then refine this version by replacing the comments with appropriate statements. As in the text, the comments may be retained for documentation instead of actually being replaced.

2. Write a program to simulate your favorite game. Casino games such as roulete, slot machines, and black jack are the most straightforward to simulate. But games such as golf, bowling, baseball, a naval battle, or a space war can also be simulated.

(a) Write the *specifications* for your program by describing what the inputs and outputs will be, and how the outputs will be related to the inputs.
(b) Using top-down design, write the program in the algorithmic language.
(c) As each module is designed in (b), translate it into a programming language and test it on the computer. Use program stubs for unwritten modules needed by the module being tested.
(d) In testing each module, use software counters to verify that each

branch in the flowchart has been tested at least once (and preferably more than once).

(e) It is interesting to make this problem a team effort, with the modules on each level written simultaneously by different students. The most difficult problem here is to communicate to the person who is going to write a module *exactly* what it should do. If this communication fails, then the modules will not "fit together" properly after they have been written.

(f) It is also interesting to have the program specified by one person (the customer) and written by another (the programmer). To be realistic, the customer should go into the discussions with only a vague idea of what he or she wants. The programmer will then have to ask many leading questions to find out what the customer "really wants." It is then up to the programmer to write the detailed specifications and get the customer to agree to them in writing. Otherwise, after the program is completed, the customer is apt to complain that it is not what was "really wanted."

PART THREE

DATA STRUCTURES

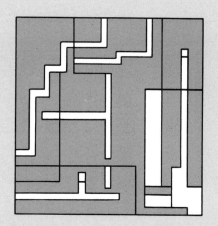

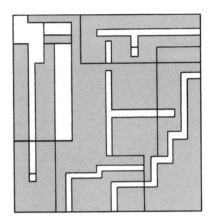

Chapter 11

Character Strings

Beginning with this chapter, we shift our emphasis from algorithms—ways of *manipulating* data—to data structures—ways of *organizing* data. Of course, we will still be concerned with algorithms, since the reason for organizing data is to make it convenient to manipulate. But we will be applying the principles of algorithm construction we have already learned. What will be new will be the techniques for organizing the data.

We have already taken up two data structures so far: arrays and character strings. Arrays were discussed thoroughly in Chapter 8. Although we will find new uses for arrays as we go along, we will not devote another chapter to arrays in general.

On the other hand, we have only been using character strings in the simplest possible ways—inputting them, outputting them, and comparing them with one another. There are many more things we can do with character strings, and this chapter will explore some of them.

11.1 Representation in Memory

Fixed-and Variable-Length Strings. A character string is normally stored in a series of adjacent memory locations, one character per location, as shown in Figure 11-1. We can give this sequence of adjacent locations a name and treat it as a single memory location capable of holding the entire string. Each "character string location" is actually made up of a number of "physical memory locations" (see Figure 11-2).

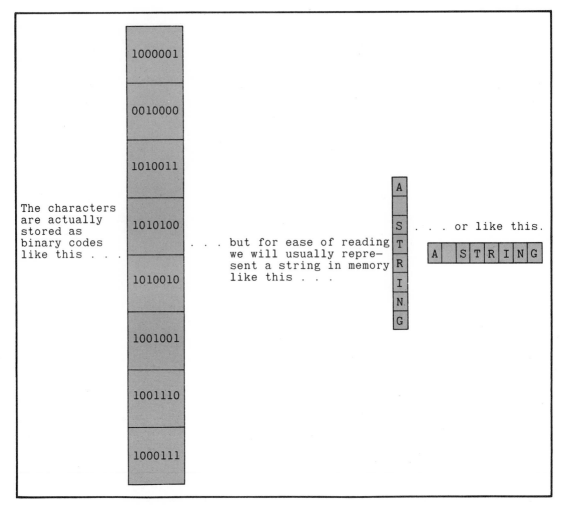

The characters are actually stored as binary codes like this . . .

1000001
0010000
1010011
1010100
1010010
1001001
1001110
1000111

. . . but for ease of reading we will usually represent a string in memory like this . . .

A
S
T
R
I
N
G

. . . or like this.

A S T R I N G

FIGURE 11-1. A character string is normally stored with the characters in adjacent memory locations.

FIGURE 11-2. One character string location is made up of many physical memory locations.

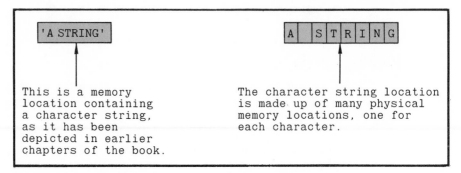

'A STRING'

This is a memory location containing a character string, as it has been depicted in earlier chapters of the book.

A S T R I N G

The character string location is made up of many physical memory locations, one for each character.

A character string location can be of fixed length, that is, it can consist of a fixed number of character locations. If a shorter character string is stored in a fixed-length location, the shorter string must be "padded" with blanks to fill out the location. The padding blanks are usually added to the right end of the shorter string.

On the other hand, a character string location can be of variable length, consisting of only enough character locations to hold the string that is stored in it. As strings of different length are stored in it, the number of character locations that make it up changes. No matter how short the string that is stored, no padding is ever needed. Figure 11-3 contrasts fixed-length and variable-length character string locations.

Memory Management for Character Strings. In programming languages that use fixed-length strings, the user is required to declare for each character string location the number of characters it contains. Thus, a statement such as

```
DECLARE STRING CHAR(20)
```

would reserve space for 20 characters and give that 20-character block the name STRING (see Figure 11-4). Throughout the program, the variable STRING would always refer to this 20-character block. If a 15-character string was stored in STRING, it would be padded with five blanks. If one attempted to store a 25-character string in STRING, five characters would not be stored.

For a variable-length string, we must have some way of specifying the number of characters that currently make up the string, since that number

FIGURE 11-3. Fixed- and variable-length character string locations.

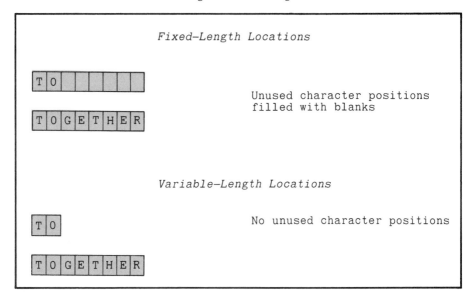

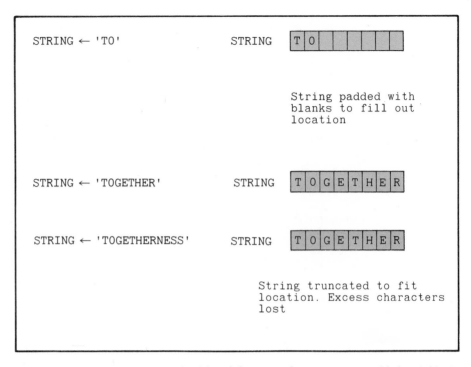

FIGURE 11-4. Storing strings in a fixed-length location. Short strings are padded with blanks to fill out the location; long strings are truncated to fit.

will vary depending on the data the program is processing. There are two ways to do this:

1. Precede the character string with a memory location containing a number that gives the number of characters in the string.

2. Follow the character string with a special "end-of-string" character. Often the ASCII null character, 0000000, is used for this purpose.

Figure 11-5 illustrates two techniques. The end-of-string character is represented by "φ."

Some languages require the user to specify the maximum size of a variable-length character string. Thus,

```
DECLARE STRING CHAR(20) VARYING
```

would make STRING the name of a location that could hold from 0 to 20 characters, but no more than 20. In this case, memory space would be set aside for 20 characters. Either a preceding character count or a trailing end-of-string character would be used to indicate the number of characters currently in use (see Figure 11-6).

In some languages, no limit is placed on the size of a character string location. A variable such as STRING can be assigned a string of any length.

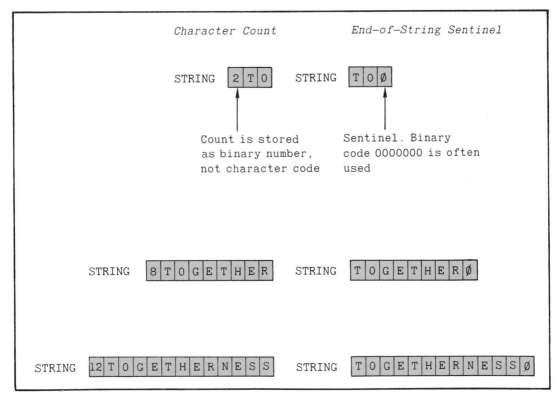

FIGURE 11-5. Two methods for storing variable-length character strings. One method uses a character count to keep track of the length of the string; the other method uses an end-of-string sentinel.

When such an assignment is made, the system must find a block of memory of the required size and store the assigned string in that block. Since the variable STRING can refer to different blocks of memory at different times, the system must keep track of which block STRING currently refers to (see Figure 11-7). Because of all these things the system must do each time a string assignment is made, strings of unlimited length are less efficient than those having a maximum length. But they are more convenient for the programmer to use.

Since the emphasis in our algorithmic language is on convenience for the programmer, it uses variable-length strings with no maximum length.

11.2 Character String Operations and Functions

Concatenation. The word *concatenate* means "chain together" or "join together." It refers to joining two strings together, one after the other, to obtain a new string. The work *join* would be just as descriptive and a lot shorter. But we seem to be stuck with "concatenate."

Just as we used the same relational operators for real numbers and for

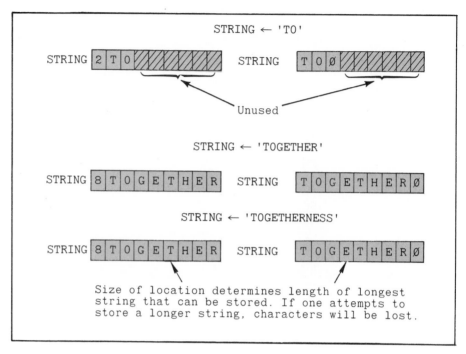

FIGURE 11-6. Storing variable-length character strings in a location of fixed length. Only part of the location is used for strings of less than the maximum length.

character strings, so we will appropriate the plus sign for the concatenation operator. The following examples illustrate concatenation:

Expression	Value
'FOR' + 'GET'	'FORGET'
'TO' + 'GET' + 'HER'	'TOGETHER'
'GOOD' + 'DAY'	'GOODDAY'
'GOOD ' + 'DAY'	'GOOD DAY'
'GOOD' + ' ' + 'DAY'	'GOOD DAY'
'GOOD' + '' + 'DAY'	'GOODDAY'

Notice that concatenation *never* introduces any blanks. If a blank is needed between the items being concatenated, it must be explicitly introduced. Also, in the last example, concatenating a string with the null string does not change it in any way. The null string is ignored in a concatenation.

Variables as well as values may occur in concatenations. If S, T, U, and V have the values

S	'FOR'	U	'TO'
T	'GET'	V	'HER'

then the following expressions have the values shown:

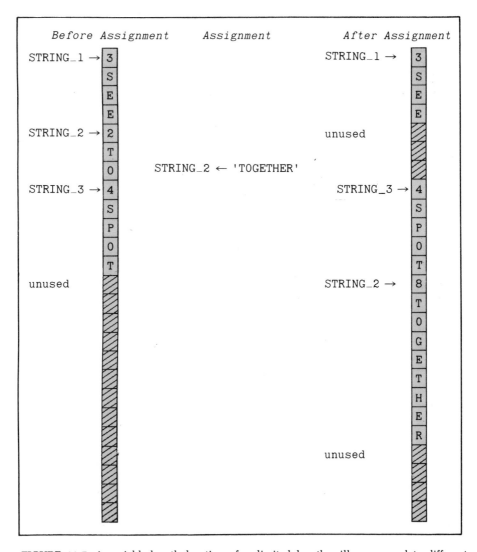

FIGURE 11-7. A variable-length location of unlimited length will correspond to different physical memory locations at different times as the computer system finds space in different parts of memory to store strings of different lengths.

Expression	Value
S + T	'FORGET'
U + T + V	'TOGETHER'
U + ' ' + T + ' ' + S + ' ' + V	'TO GET FOR HER'

Like arithmetic expressions, concatenations and other string expressions can be used in OUTPUT statements and on the right-hand side of assignment statements. Thus,

OUTPUT S + T

would output 'FORGET', and

U ← U+T+V

would assign U the value 'TOGETHER'. The values of T and V would not be changed.

Substrings. A substring is a part of a string. We specify a substring by giving its position in the string and its length.

The characters of a string are assumed to be numbered from left to right as shown in Figure 11-8. The leftmost character is number 1, the next character to the right is number 2, and so on. The *position* of a substring is the number of its first character. A substring in position 1 starts with the first character of the string. A substring in position 2 starts with the second character of the string, and so on, as illustrated in Figure 11-9.

The *length* of a substring is simply the number of characters that make it up.

The function MID(STRING, POSITION, LENGTH) has as its value the substring of STRING specified by the values of POSITION and LENGTH:

Expression	Value
MID('TOGETHER', 1, 2)	'TO'
MID('TOGETHER', 3, 3)	'GET'
MID('TOGETHER', 4, 5)	'ETHER'
MID('TOGETHER', 6, 3)	'HER'

The function MID can extract any substring from a string. Since substrings that begin at the beginning of the string or end at the end of the string are often needed, however, some languages provide additional functions LEFT and RIGHT that are more convenient for extracting these special substrings.

The function LEFT(STRING, LENGTH) has as its value the substring extracted from the left end of STRING whose length is specified by the value of LENGTH. RIGHT(STRING, LENGTH) similarly extracts a substring from the right end of STRING:

Expression	Value
LEFT('TOGETHER', 2)	'TO'
LEFT('FORGET', 3)	'FOR'
RIGHT('TOGETHER', 3)	'HER'
RIGHT('TOGETHER', 5)	'ETHER'

The LEFT, MID, and RIGHT functions can be combined with concatenation to form more complex string expressions. For instance, the statements

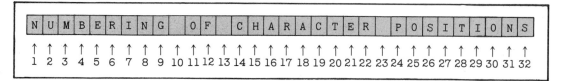

FIGURE 11-8. The numbering of character positions in a string.

```
S ← 'TOGETHER'
T ← LEFT(S, 2)+' '+MID(S, 3, 3)+' '+RIGHT(S, 3)
```

would assign T the value 'TO GET HER'.

Locating Substrings. In practice, when we write an algorithm we often do not know the actual string values we will be working with. These will come from data that was read in as the algorithm executed.

Therefore, we will not usually know the positions of the substrings we are interested in. We will have to *search* the strings to locate the substrings of interest.

The function POS(STRING, SUBSTRING) has as its value the position of SUBSTRING in STRING. If SUBSTRING does not occur in STRING, then the value of POS(STRING, SUBSTRING) is 0:

Expression	*Value*
POS('TOGETHER', 'GET')	3
POS('TOGETHER', 'TO')	1
POS('TOGETHER', 'ETHER')	4
POS('TOGETHER', 'TOGS')	0

FIGURE 11-9. The position of a substring within another string.

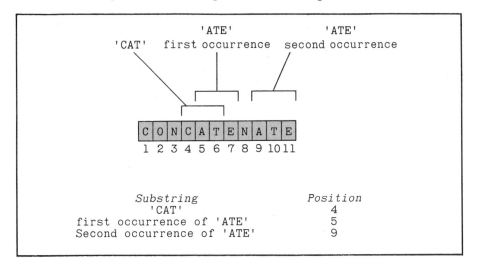

If the substring occurs in the string more than once, POS yields the position of the *first* occurrence:

Expression	Value	
POS('CONCATENATE', 'ATE')	5	(not 9)
POS('CONCATENATE', 'N')	3	(not 8)
POS('ERROR', 'R')	2	(not 3 or 5)
POS('TO GET HER', ' ')	3	(not 7)

Figure 11-10 shows how the search for the substring is carried out. An attempt is made to match the substring with the string starting at position 1. If this match fails, then the substring is shifted to position 2 and the match is attempted again, and so on. When a match is found, the current position of the substring is returned as the value of POS. If no match is found for any position of the substring, then 0 is returned as the value of POS.

Often the substrings we wish to extract are separated, terminated, or delimited by other substrings. For instance, words in a sentence are separated by spaces, a sentence is terminated by a period, and a quotation is delimited by quote marks. It is these delimiting substrings that we usually locate with POS. We use their positions to extract the delimited substrings.

FIGURE 11-10. Searching a string for a given substring.

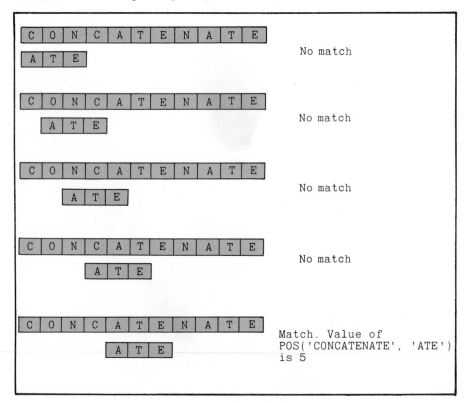

For example, to extract the first word from the value of STRING, we start by finding the first blank:

```
I ← POS(STRING, ' ')
```

The first word is everything to the left of the first blank:

```
WORD ← LEFT(STRING, I-1)
```

Extracting the first sentence is similar, except that we include the period that ends the sentence in the extracted sentence:

```
I ← POS(STRING, '.')
WORD ← LEFT(STRING, I)
```

Three Additional String Functions. The following three functions often come in handy; their equivalents are found in many programming languages.

The LEN function yields as its value the length of a string:

Expression	Value
LEN('FORGET')	6
LEN('TOGETHER')	8

Blanks are always counted in finding the length of a string. Thus, the value of LEN('TO GET HER') is 10.

With the LEN function we can extract a quotation—a substring bounded by quote marks. We begin by locating the first quote mark:

```
I ← POS(STRING, '"')
```

Now we extract all the string *following* the first quote mark:

```
REST ← RIGHT(STRING, LEN(STRING)-I)
```

Then we find the terminating quote mark in REST

```
J ← POS(REST, '"')
```

and extract everything that precedes it:

```
QUOTE ← LEFT(REST, J-1)
```

Remembering that the values of I and J are the positions of the two quote marks, we could have also extracted the quote with

```
QUOTE ← MID(STRING, I+1, J-I-1)
```

For instance, in

```
'JANE SAID, "SEE SPOT RUN."'
```

The value of I is 12, the value of J is 26, and the value of

```
MID('JANE SAID, "SEE SPOT RUN."', 13, 13)
```

is:

```
'SEE SPOT RUN.'
```

Previous chapters have stressed that real numbers such as 3.1416 and strings such as '3.1416' are different kinds of data, represented differently inside the computer and subject to different operations. Sometimes it is desired to change a string such as '3.1416' into the corresponding real number, and vice versa. The VAL and STR functions accomplish this data conversion:

Expression	Value
VAL('3.1416')	3.1416
VAL('-25')	-25
STR(3.1416)	'3.1416'
STR(-25)	'-25'

Effectively, VAL removes quote marks from around a number and STR places quote marks around a number. But what goes on inside the computer is more complicated than this. Inside the computer real numbers are normally represented in binary notation, whereas strings such as '3.1416' are in decimal notation, with each decimal digit represented by a character code. Thus, what is actually involved is decimal-to-binary conversion for VAL and binary-to-decimal conversion for STR.

11.3 Examples of String Processing

The POS Function. Some programming languages have the equivalent of the MID and LEN functions, and allow strings to be compared for equality. But they do not have any equivalent to the POS function. All is not lost, however, because we can write our own POS function.

POS(STRING, SUBSTRING) must compare SUBSTRING with every substring of STRING having the same length as SUBSTRING. Let

```
L1 ← LEN(STRING)
L2 ← LEN(SUBSTRING)
```

A match is possible only if $L2 \leq L1$. In that case, STRING has $L1 - L2 + 1$

substrings of length L2, as shown in Figure 11-11. Each of these must be compared with SUBSTRING. If a match is found, the position of the matching substring is returned. Otherwise, 0 is returned. Figure 11-12 shows the function POS.

Form Letters. Companies like to send out "personalized" form letters in which the recipient's name, and perhaps, city of residence, are inserted throughout the letter.

This is done by writing a form letter in which some special character— say, #—is used wherever the name is to be inserted. Some other character—say, %—is used wherever the city is to be inserted. A computer then prints copies of the letter—with the correct names and cities inserted—for each person on the mailing list.

The form letter—before insertions—might look something like this:

```
Dear #,
 As a person who needs to stay well informed, you, #,
cannot afford to be without a subscription to
YESTERDAY'S NEWS. If you subscribe, then as you walk
down the main street of % people will say, "There goes
#, the best-informed person in %." Wouldn't you like
that? Please, #, send me your subscription to
YESTERDAY'S NEWS right away.

                              J. S. Hardsell
                              Circulation Manager
```

The algorithm must examine each line of the letter and determine if it contains a # or a %. If it does, then the appropriate substitution is made. For simplicity, we assume that neither # nor % occurs more than once on the same line. However, a line can contain one # and one %.

Figure 11-13 shows the algorithm FORM__LETTER. I is the position of the #, LEFT(LINE, I−1) is that portion of LINE to the left of the #, and RIGHT(LINE, L−I) is that portion of the line to the right of the #. The same considerations hold for J and %.

This algorithm prints only a single copy of the letter. We leave it as an exercise to construct a version which reads in the letter once and then outputs many copies with different names and cities plugged in.

Substring Replacement. Sometimes we need to replace one substring of a string with another. In a text-editing system, for instance, we might replace an incorrect word with the correct one. A general substring replacement routine could also have been used in FORM__LETTER to replace # and % with the values of NAME and CITY.

The function REPLACE(STRING, SUB__1, SUB__2) has as its value the result of replacing SUB__1 in STRING by SUB__2. If SUB__1 does not occur in STRING, then STRING is left unchanged. Some values of RE-PLACE are as follows:

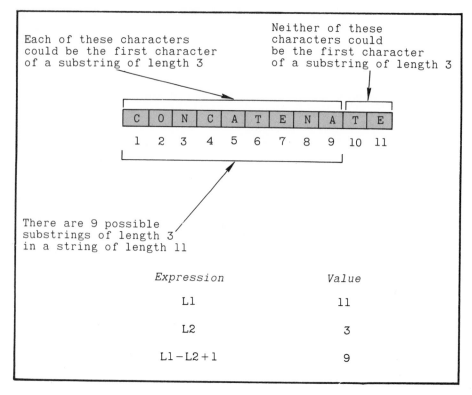

FIGURE 11-11. In a string of length L1, there are L1 − L2 + 1 possible substrings of length L2.

FIGURE 11-12. The function POS.

```
FUNCTION POS(STRING, SUBSTRING)
    L1 ← LEN(STRING)
    L2 ← LEN(SUBSTRING)
    N ← L1-L2+1
    I ← 1
    NOT_FOUND ← TRUE
    WHILE (I ≤ N) AND NOT_FOUND DO
        IF MID(STRING, I, L2) = SUBSTRING THEN
            NOT_FOUND ← FALSE
        ELSE
            I ← I+1
        END IF
    END WHILE
    IF NOT_FOUND THEN
        POS ← 0
    ELSE
        POS ← I
    END IF
END POS
```

```
ALGORITHM FORM_LETTER
    INPUT NAME, CITY
    INPUT LINE
    WHILE LINE ≠ 'THE END' DO
        I ← POS(LINE, '#')
        IF I ≠ 0 THEN
            L ← LEN(LINE)
            LINE ← LEFT(LINE, I-1) + NAME + RIGHT(LINE, L-I)
        END IF
        J ← POS(LINE, '%')
        IF J ≠ 0 THEN
            L ← LEN(LINE)
            LINE ← LEFT(LINE, J-1) + CITY + RIGHT(LINE, L-J)
        END IF
        OUTPUT LINE
        INPUT LINE
    END WHILE
END FORM_LETTER
```

FIGURE 11-13. The algorithm FORM_LETTER.

Expression	*Value*
REPLACE('FORGET', 'GET', 'GIVE')	'FORGIVE'
REPLACE('UNDISGUISED', 'DISGUIS', 'DISCOVER')	'UNDISCOVERED'

If POS(STRING, SUB_1) = 0—SUB_1 is not a substring of STRING—then the value of STRING is returned as the value of REPLACE. Otherwise, the parts of STRING which precede and follow SUB_1 must be extracted. If we let

```
I ← POS(STRING, SUB_1)
L ← LEN(STRING)
L1 ← LEN(SUB_1)
```

then the part of STRING preceding SUB_1 is

```
LEFT(STRING, I-1)
```

and the part following STRING is:

```
RIGHT(STRING, L-I-L1+1)
```

(See Figure 11-14.)
The value returned by REPLACE, then, is:

```
LEFT(STRING, I-1) + SUB_2 + RIGHT(STRING, L-I-L1+1)
```

Figure 11-15 shows the function REPLACE.

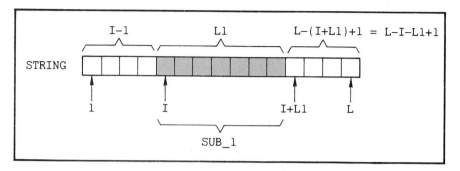

FIGURE 11-14. The substring SUB__1, which starts at position I and has a length L1, divides the string into three parts. The first part, the part that precedes SUB__1, has the length I − 1. The second part, SUB__1 itself, has length L1. The third part, the part that follows SUB__ 1, has length L − I − L1 + 1, where L is the length of the entire string.

FIGURE 11-15. The function REPLACE.

```
FUNCTION REPLACE(STRING, SUB_1, SUB_2)
   I ← POS(STRING, SUB_1)
   IF I = 0 THEN
      REPLACE ← STRING
   ELSE
      L ← LEN(STRING)
      L1 ← LEN(SUB_1)
      REPLACE ← LEFT(STRING, I-1) + SUB_2 + RIGHT(STRING, L-I-L1+1)
   END IF
END REPLACE
```

Review Questions

1. Contrast algorithms and data structures.

2. What two data structures had we already encountered before starting this chapter?

3. Distinguish between fixed-and variable-length character strings.

4. What is *padding*? Which character is most commonly used for padding?

5. Describe two ways of storing variable-length character strings.

6. In this chapter we discussed three kinds of character strings: fixed-length strings, variable-length strings with an upper limit on the length, and variable-length strings with no upper limit on the length. Which of these can the computer process most efficiently? Least efficiently? Why?

7. Give five examples of concatenation.

8. Suppose that WORD contains a word that forms its plural by adding 'S'. Write an assignment statement that will form the plural of the value of WORD and store the result back into WORD.

9. What is a *substring* of a string?

10. How is the *position* of a substring in a string defined?

11. What is the *length* of a substring?

12. Describe the action of the function MID and give several examples of its use.

13. Describe the actions of the functions LEFT and RIGHT. Give several examples of the use of each.

14. Show how each of the examples with LEFT and RIGHT could also be written using MID.

15. Describe the operation of the POS function and give several examples of its use.

16. What does POS return if the string does not contain the sought-after substring?

17. If the sought-after substring occurs more than once in the string being searched, which occurrence does POS return the position of?

18. Give several examples of the LEN function, using strings that differ only by the presence or absence of blank spaces.

19. Which function does a decimal-to-binary conversion?

20. Which function does a binary-to-decimal conversion?

Exercises

1. Suppose a programming language has MID and LEN, but does not have LEFT and RIGHT. Write the functions LEFT and RIGHT using MID and LEN.

2. Some programming languages have a function

```
POS (STRING, SUBSTRING, I)
```

which searches for SUBSTRING in STRING, starting at position I in STRING, rather than position 1. Give some examples showing how this version of POS differs from the one given in the text. Generalize the algorithm given for POS to include a starting position I.

3. Write an algorithm that will read in strings such as

```
'3.5+2.61'
'7-5'
'4.25*5'
'3.5/2'
```

carry out the arithmetic operation, and print the result.

4. Modify FORM__LETTER so that it will read in the letter containing **#** and % once and store each line as an element of an array. It will then imput names and cities, and for each name and city it will print a "person- alized" copy of the letter. The algorithm will terminate when a name of 'END OF DATA' is read.

5. Text is usually inputted to a computer line by line, where each line corresponds to one punched card or one line typed on a terminal. Some programs, notably translators, process text character by character. Write a subroutine GET__CHAR(C) that will, on each call, set C to the next char- acter on the current line. If the current line is exhausted, then GET__CHAR will input a new line, and set C to the first character on the new line.

CURRENT__LINE (value is the current line), LENGTH (of current line), and POSITION (of first unused character in current line) will be global variables. Before the first call to GET__CHAR, POSITION and LENGTH will be initialized so that POSITION > LENGTH. This will force GET__CHAR to input a new line the first time it is called.

6. Instead of MID, some programming languages offer a function SEG. SEG (STRING, FIRST, LAST) has as its value the substring of STRING specified by the values of FIRST and LAST. FIRST is the position of the first char- acter of the substring and LAST is the position of the last character of the substring. Using SEG, write an expression equivalent to MID(STRING, PO- SITION, LENGTH). Using MID, write an expression equivalent to SEG (STRING, FIRST, LAST).

7. In *Adventure* and similar computer games, the player explores a fic- tional setting such as an eerie castle. The player enters commands such as CLIMB STAIRS, OPEN DOOR, TAKE JEWELS, DRINK POTION, AND ATTACK OGRE. After each command, the computer prints what happened when the requested action was attempted. Each command consists of a verb (CLIMB, OPEN, TAKE, . . .) followed by an object (STAIRS, DOOR, JEWELS, . . .). Write a *command-interpreter* procedure that will accept a command and translate it into two code numbers, one giving the position of the verb in the list of all possible verbs and the other giving the position of the object in the list of all possible objects. If either verb or object cannot be found on the appropriate list, the procedure should inform the player that it doesn't know the word in question.

8. Write an algorithm to do the following: (a) Input lines of English text until a sentinel line consiting of a single period (.) is encountered. (b) Input the maximum number of characters that are to be in each printed line. (c) Output the text in lines that do not exceed the specified maximum length. Each line will contain as many words as possible, but no work will be broken between lines. The algorithm should do something reasonable if it encounters a word longer than the specified maximum line length.

9. Write an algorithm to input a line of English text and output a list of all the words that occur in the line. The words appear on the list in the same order that they appear in the line, and each word appears on the list the same number of times it appears in the line. The text may be punctuated with periods, commas, question marks, colons, and semicolons; the punctuation marks don't appear on the list.

10. Modify the algorithm of Exercise 9 so that the list of words produced is in alphabetical order and each word appears on the list only once no matter how many times it occurs in the line.

11. A *cipher* is a method of sending secret messages that manipulates individual characters rather than entire words or phrases. The original message is the *plaintext*; the secret message is the *ciphertext*. We *encipher* the plaintext when we convert it into ciphertext; we *decipher* the latter when we convert it back to plaintext.

A *substitution cipher* uses a correspondence between a *plaintext alphabet* and a *cipher alphabet*:

plaintext alphabet: ABCDEFGHIJKLMNOPQRSTUVWXYZ
cipher alphabet: VJMQDSBGKYAZPWETXCNLHORFUI

Each character in the plaintext alphabet is to be replaced by the corresponding character in the cipher alphabet. For example, A will be replaced by V, B will be replaced by J, C will be replaced by M, and so on.

A substitution cipher is *monoalphabetic* if we use the same cipher alphabet for each character of plaintext. For example, if we encipher ATTACK AT NOON by monoalphabetic substitution, using the alphabets just given, we get VLLVMA VL WEEW. If we assume that plaintext alphabet to be the normal one, only the cipher alphabet needs to be given. Write an algorithm to encipher and decipher messages using monoalphabetic substitution. The algorithm should obey three commands: A (accept a new cipher alphabet), E (encipher the following message), and D (decipher the following message).

12. The algorithm of Exercise 11 leaves spaces in the ciphertext where there were spaces in the plaintext. This provides too many clues for someone trying to break the cipher. Modify the algorithm of Exercise 11 to print the cipher in groups of five letters. Thus ATTACK AT NOON would be enciphered as VLLVM AVLWE EW.

13. Since cipher alphabets are hard to remember, we would like to be able to generate a cipher alphabet from an easily remembered *key*. One approach is to use a key word or phrase such as SCHOOL ZONE. First, write down the letters of the key, omitting any repetitions:

SCHOLZNE

Next, write down the remaining letters of the alphabet in their normal order, but omit any letters that are already in the key:

SCHOLZNEABDFGIJKMPQRTUVWXY

This is our cipher alphabet. Modify the algorithm of Exercise 12 to accept a key and generate the cipher alphabet in the manner just explained.

14. A polyalphabetic substitution cipher uses more than one cipher alphabet. One type of polyalphabetic substitution uses the following 26 cipher alphabets:

ABCDEFGHIJKLMNOPQRSTUVWXYZ
BCDEFGHIJKLMNOPQRSTUVWXYZA
CDEFGHIJKLMNOPQRSTUVWXYZAB

.
.
.

XYZABCDEFGHIJKLMNOPQRSTUVW
YZABCDEFGHIJKLMNOPQRSTUVWX
ZABCDEFGHIJKLMNOPQRSTUVWXY

To encipher, a key is written repeatedly above the plaintext. If the key is CUB and the plaintext is ATTACK AT NOON, we write

repeated key: CUBCUB CU BCUB
plaintext: ATTACK AT NOON

We encipher each letter of the plaintext using the cipher alphabet that begins with the corresponding letter of the repeated key. With the key CUB, for instance, we encipher the first letter of the plaintext using the cipher alphabet that begins with C, the second letter of the plaintext using the cipher alphabet that begins with U, and so on. The ciphertext for ATTACK AT NOON is CNUCW LCNOQ IO. Write an algorithm to encipher and decipher messages using this technique. Can you think of a way to write the algorithm that avoids having to generate and store 26 cipher alphabets?

15. In Exercise 14, the sequence in which the different cipher alphabets is used repeats itself throughout the plaintext. This repetition provides a method of breaking the cipher. One way to avoid this problem is to use a pseudorandom number generator to determine which cipher alphabet will be used for each plaintext character. Suppose the 26 cipher alphabets given in Exercise 14 are numbered 1 through 26. For each character to be enciphered or deciphered, we can use the value of RANDOM(26) to select the cipher alphabet. Write an algorithm to encipher and decipher in this way. You can use the implementation of RANDOM given in Chapter 9, although practical cipher programs use much more complex ways of generating pseudorandom numbers. The starting value of SEED will serve as a key; the same starting value must be used for deciphering a message as was used for enciphering it.

Chapter 12

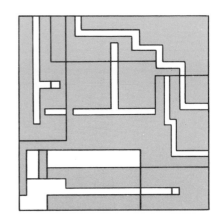

Stacks

A *stack* is a data structure that behaves like a stack of physical objects, such as a stack of papers, a stack of cards, or a stack of books.

We can carry out two operations on a stack. We can add a new item to the top of the stack, or we can remove the item currently on top of the stack. But we are forbidden from adding, removing, or inspecting any item other than the top one.

A stack is ofter called a *push-down stack* or a *push-down list*. This terminology is intended to bring to mind the spring-operated mechanisms used to hold stacks of plates in cafeterias. The top plate on the stack is at the level of the counter and is the only one that is accessible. When a plate is removed, the remaining plates "pop up" so that the new topmost plate is accessible. When a plate is added, the plates already on the stack are "pushed down."

The cafeteria analogy gives rise to the terminology for adding an item to or removing an item from the top of the stack. When an item is placed on top of the stack, we say that it is *pushed* onto the stack. When an item is removed from the top of the stack, we say that it is *popped* off the stack. Figure 12-1 illustrates a stack and the PUSH and POP operations.

This analogy is faulty in one respect, however. When an item is pushed on or popped off a stack, the remaining items on the stack do not move, as the cafeteria plates do. The only item affected is the one pushed on or popped off.

Items are popped off a stack in the reverse of the order in which they were pushed on.

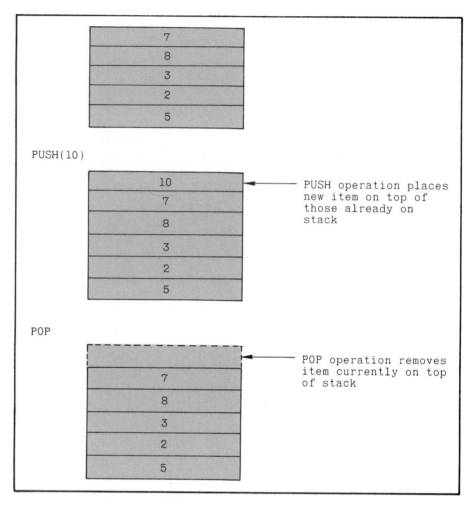

PUSH(10)

PUSH operation places new item on top of those already on stack

POP

POP operation removes item currently on top of stack

FIGURE 12-1. A stack. PUSH places a new item on top of the stack; POP removes the top item from the stack.

12.1 Representation of Stacks in Memory

A stack is represented in memory by means of an array and a pointer to the top element of the stack (see Figure 12-2). A pointer, remember, is a variable whose value designates a particular element of an array. The element pointed to can be accessed by using the pointer as a subscript.

As shown in Figure 12-2, the pointer points to the top element of the stack. All array elements from the start of the array through the top element are in use and hold items currently on the stack. All array elements following the top element are currently unused. They will be used as new items are pushed on the stack.

Let SIZE be the number of elements in the array used for the stack. When the value of the pointer equals the value of SIZE, then the stack is *full*, and no more items can be pushed on. An attempt to push another item onto a full stack causes an error condition, known as *overflow*.

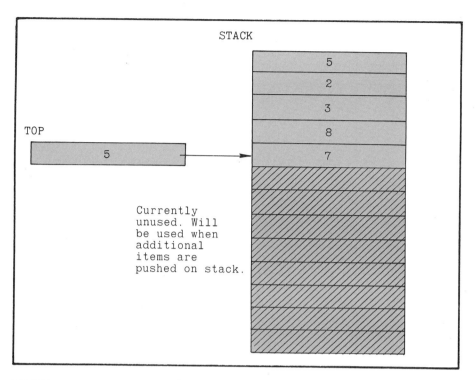

FIGURE 12-2. Representing a stack in memory. TOP points to the top item on the stack. Note that the stack in this diagram is upside down compared to the one in Figure 12-1.

When the value of the pointer is 0, the stack is *empty*. An attempt to pop another item off an empty stack causes an error condition, known as *underflow*. In some situations, underflow may not be an error but merely an indication that all the items that were on the stack have been removed and processed, so the algorithm can proceed to other matters.

Figure 12-3 illustrates full and empty stacks as well as the overflow and underflow conditions.

We can easily write procedures PUSH and POP to push items onto and pop them off of a stack. The call

```
CALL PUSH(ITEM)
```

pushes the value of ITEM onto the stack, and

```
CALL POP (ITEM)
```

pops the top value off the stack and assigns it to ITEM.

Let the array STACK as well as TOP and SIZE be global variables. TOP is the pointer to the top of the stack. SIZE is the number of elements in the array STACK or, alternatively, the pointer to the last element of the array STACK.

For the procedure PUSH, we have:

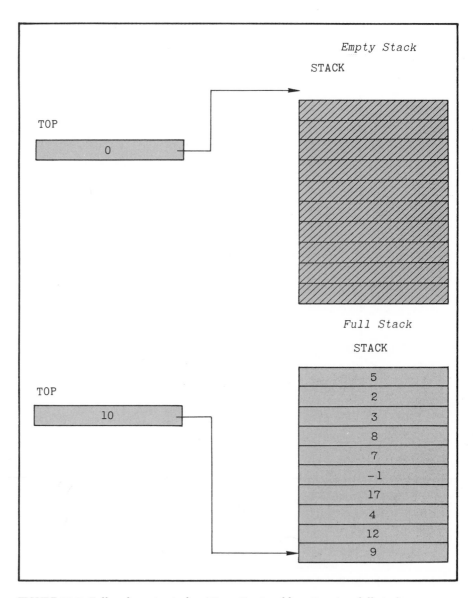

FIGURE 12-3. Full and empty stacks. Attempting to add an item to a full stack causes overflow. Attempting to remove an item from an empty stack causes underflow.

```
PROCEDURE PUSH(ITEM)
    GLOBAL STACK, TOP, SIZE
  IF TOP = SIZE THEN
    CALL ERROR('STACK OVERFLOW')
  ELSE
    TOP ← TOP+1
    STACK(TOP) ← ITEM
  END IF
END PUSH
```

The procedure ERROR(MESSAGE) is assumed to output the error message supplied as its argument, then to offer the user the option of either continuing or terminating the algorithm. If the user chooses to continue, ERROR will return normally. Otherwise, it will not.

POP is essentially the reverse of PUSH:

```
PROCEDURE POP(ITEM)
   GLOBAL STACK, TOP, SIZE
   IF TOP = O THEN
      CALL ERROR('STACK UNDERFLOW')
   ELSE
      ITEM ← STACK(TOP)
      TOP ← TOP-1
   END IF
END POP
```

12.2 Evaluating Arithmetic Expressions

The most common application of stacks is the evaluation of arithmetic expressions. Every BASIC interpreter, for instance, contains a stack for this purpose. Many advanced pocket calculators also feature stacks for expression evaluation.

The notation we ordinarily use for arithmetic expressions—the one we took up in Chapter 4—is not the best notation for evaluating an expression using a stack. Another notation, called variously *postfix notation, reverse Polish notation,* or *RPN,* is better suited to stack evaluation.

Therefore, we will start by seeing how to evaluate expressions in RPN using a stack. The we will see how to translate from the ordinary notation—which is more convenient to humans—to RPN. The translation and the evaluation can be combined into a single process. But conceptually they are best treated separately.

RPN. Consider a simple arithmetic expression such as $3+5$. There are three possible positions for the operator:

We can place the operator before the numbers:

```
+ 3 5
```

This is called *prefix* notation.

We can place the operator between the numbers:

```
3+5
```

This is called *infix* notation. "Ordinary" notation, then, is infix notation.

We can place the operator after the numbers:

```
3 5 +
```

This is called *postfix* notation.

Prefix notation was invented by the Polish logician Lukasiewicz. It was thus first known as "Lukasiewicz notation." But since "Lukasiewicz" is neither easy to pronounce nor easy to spell, the notation came to be known as "Polish notation." It is now known as either "prefix notation" or "Polish notation."

Postfix notation is similar to prefix notation except that the operator follows the operands instead of preceding them. Thus, postfix notation is also known as "reverse Polish notation." This is often abbreviated to "RPN." It is RPN which is most useful for expression evaluation.

Prefix and postfix notation share a property that infix notation does not have: *In prefix and postfix notations, neither parentheses nor operator priorities are required to determine the order in which the operators are to be applied.*

Consider the infix expression

3 + 4*5

which can be parenthesized as either

3 + (4*5)

or

(3 + 4)*5

In the absence of parentheses, we use operator priorities to determine that the multiplication should be done before the addition.

Now let us translate each of these into RPN. The rule is that the operator always follows its operands. The operands of + are 3 and (4*5). Thus, as a first step we can write

3 (4*5) +

Now we translate (4*5). Again the operator must follow the operands, so (4*5) translates into 4 5 *. Substituting this for (4*5), we get

3 4 5 * +

On the other hand, if we translate (3 + 4)*5 in the same way, we get first

(3 + 4) 5 *

and finally

3 4 + 5 *

Notice two things:

First, the two expressions, which differ only in the placement of parentheses, translate into two different RPN expressions. *We do not need parentheses to distinguish between the two.*

Second, each RPN expression determines the order in which the operators will be applied. In 3 4 5 * +, for instance, we cannot apply + first, since an operator can apply only to two immediately preceding numbers. But + is preceded by a number and an operator, rather than by two numbers. Only * is preceded by two numbers, and hence it must be applied first.

In the same way, in 3 4 + 5 *. only + is immediately preceded by two numbers, and so it must be applied first.

We can evaluate RPN expressions using the following rule: *Scan the expression from left to right. When an operator is encountered, apply it to the two immediately preceding operands. Replace operator and operands by the result of the operation. Continue scanning to the right.*

Here are the two expressions just given evaluated using this rule:

```
3  4 5 * +        3 4 + 5 *
   3 20 +             7 5 *
       23                 35
```

Here are some more examples of infix expressions and their RPN translations:

Infix	*RPN*
3*5**2	3 5 2 ** *
(2+4)*(5-3)	2 4 + 5 3 - *
3**2+2*3*5+5**2	3 2 ** 2 3 * 5 * + 5 2 ** +
2+3*(4+5*(6+7))	2 3 4 5 6 7 + * + * +
((2+3)*4+5)*6+7	2 3 + 4 * 5 + 6 * 7 +

As another example of evaluation, let us evaluate 2 3 4 5 6 7 + * + * +:

```
2 3 4 5 6 7 + * + * +
2 3 4 5 13 * + * +
  2 3 4 65 + * +
    2 3 69 * +
      2 207 +
          209
```

Evaluation Using a Stack. The rule for evaluating an RPN expression using a stack is this: *Scan the expression from left to right. When an operand is encountered, push it on the stack. When an operator is encountered, apply it to the top two elements of the stack. Replace those elements by the result of the operation.*

This is really the same as the rule previously given. We are just using the stack to hold everything to the left of the next operator to be applied.

Since each operator is applied to the two immediately preceding operands, it will be applied to the top two stack elements.

The following shows the evaluation of 2 3 4 5 6 7 + * + * + using a stack. The stack is depicted horizontally; its right end is its top:

```
Stack                 Expression

             2 3 4 5 6 7 + * + * +
2              3 4 5 6 7 + * + * +
2 3              4 5 6 7 + * + * +
2 3 4              5 6 7 + * + * +
2 3 4 5              6 7 + * + * +
2 3 4 5 6              7 + * + * +
2 3 4 5 6 7              + * + * +
2 3 4 5 13                * + * +
2 3 4 65                    + * +
2 3 69                        * +
2 207                           +
209
```

Figure 12-4 shows several other examples of expression evaluation using a stack.

Let's write an algorithm to input and evaluate an expression such as 3 4 + 5 *. We will assume that each operand is a single digit. We will ignore the possibility of stack underflow or overflow. (Underflow can be caused only by an incorrectly formed RPN expression, such as 3 4 + *. Overflow can be caused by a correct expression that is too complex to be evaluated with the stack space available.) It will be left as an exercise for the student to improve the algorithm by removing these limitations.

The expression to be evaluated is inputted as a string. Thus, 3 4 + 5 * would be inputted as '3 4 + 5 *'. The operands and operators may be separated by any number of blanks. The VAL function is used to change strings such as '3', '4', and '5' into the corresponding real numbers, 3, 4, and 5.

Figure 12-5 shows the algorithm EVALUATE. For simplicity, the algorithms in this chapter assume that exponentiation is represented by the single character ↑, instead of the two characters **. We will continue to use ** in illustrations, however.

Notice that any character other than a digit or one of the five operators is ignored. Thus, the blank spaces between the operators and the operands are ignored.

12.3 Translating Arithmetic Expressions

People usually find it easier to write expressions in infix notation than in RPN. Thus, we need some way to translate from infix notation to RPN. This is the usual purpose of translation: to go from a human-oriented to a machine-oriented notation.

If we examine the RPN expressions in the last section, we notice that

```
Expression--        Infix: 3*5**2        RPN: 3  5  2  **  *

        Stack                    Expression

                                 3  5  2  **  *
        3                           5  2  **  *
        3  5                           2  **  *
        3  5  2                          **  *
        3  25                              *
        75


Expression--        Infix:  (2 + 4)*(5 - 3)   RPN:  2  4  +  5  3  -  *

        Stack                    Expression

                                 2  4  +  5  3  -  *
        2                           4  +  5  3  -  *
        2  4                           +  5  3  -  *
        6                              5  3  -  *
        6  5                             3  -  *
        6  5  3                            -  *
        6  2                                 *
        12

Expression--   Infix:  3**2 + 2*3*5 + 5**2

        RPN:  3  2  **  2  3  *  5  *  +  5  2  **  +

        Stack                         Expression

                          3  2  **  2  3  *  5  *  +  5  2  **  +
        3                    2  **  2  3  *  5  *  +  5  2  **  +
        3  2                      **  2  3  *  5  *  +  5  2  **  +
        9                            2  3  *  5  *  +  5  2  **  +
        9  2                            3  *  5  *  +  5  2  **  +
        9  2  3                            *  5  *  +  5  2  **  +
        9  6                               5  *  +  5  2  **  +
        9  6  5                               *  +  5  2  **  +
        9  30                                   +  5  2  **  +
        39                                         5  2  **  +
        39  5                                         2  **  +
        39  5  2                                        **  +
        39  25                                             +
        64
```

FIGURE 12-4. Using a stack to evaluate expressions.

```
ALGORITHM EVALUATE
   INPUT EXPRESSION
   TOP ← 0    (Stack is initially empty)
   FOR I ← 1 TO LEN(EXPRESSION) DO
      CHAR ← MID(EXPRESSION, I, 1)
      IF (CHAR ≥ '0') AND (CHAR ≤ '9') THEN     (CHAR is a digit)
         TOP ← TOP+1
         STACK(TOP) ← VAL(CHAR)
      ELSE IF CHAR = '+' THEN
         STACK(TOP-1) ← STACK(TOP-1)+STACK(TOP)
         TOP ← TOP-1
      ELSE IF CHAR = '-' THEN
         STACK(TOP-1) ← STACK(TOP-1)-STACK(TOP)
         TOP ← TOP-1
      ELSE IF CHAR = '*' THEN
         STACK(TOP-1) ← STACK(TOP-1)*STACK(TOP)
         TOP ← TOP-1
      ELSE IF CHAR = '/' THEN
         STACK(TOP-1) ← STACK(TOP-1)/STACK(TOP)
         TOP ← TOP-1
      ELSE IF CHAR = '↑' THEN
         STACK(TOP-1) ← STACK(TOP-1)**STACK(TOP)
         TOP ← TOP-1
      END IF
   END FOR
   OUTPUT STACK(TOP)
END EVALUATE
```

(if none of these then it must be a ↑)

FIGURE 12-5. The algorithm EVALUATE.

the *operands* are in the same order in the RPN expression as they were in the infix expression. The order of the *operators,* however, has been changed, so that the operators follow their operands and so that they are in the order in which they will be applied.

Our job, then, is to reorder the operators. It turns out that we can do this by using a stack. Each operator from the infix expression is pushed on the stack before being placed in the RPN expression. But before an operator is pushed on the stack, any operators having higher priorities are popped off the stack. Thus, the operators are reordered into the order in which they will be applied, as dictated by the priorities. (We are forgetting about parentheses for the moment.)

More explicitly, the rules for translating an infix expression into an RPN expression are as follows (still ignoring parentheses for the moment): *Scan the infix expression from left to right. When an operand is encountered, move it immediately to the RPN expression. When an operator is encountered, first remove operators from the stack and place them in the RPN expression, until either the stack is empty or the priority of the top operator is less than the priority of the operator encountered in the expression. Then push the operator just encountered onto the stack.*

When the entire infix expression has been processed, remove any remaining operators from the stack and place them in the RPN expression.

Figure 12-6 illustrates these rules. The following examples will clarify them further:

1. When an operand is encountered, move it immediately
   to the RPN expression.

RPN	Stack	Infix
4 2	+ *	3 − 5
4 2 3	+ *	− 5

2. When an operator is encountered, remove operators
   from the stack and place them in the RPN expression
   until (a) the stack is empty or (b) the priority of
   the top operator is less than that of the operator
   encountered in the expression. Then push the operator
   just encountered onto the stack.

RPN	Stack	Infix
4 7 3 2	+ * **	*5
4 7 3 2 **	+ *	
4 7 3 2 ** *	+	*5
4 7 3 2 ** *	+ *	5

3. When the entire infix expression has been processed,
   remove any remaining operators from the stack and place
   them in the RPN expression.

RPN	Stack	Infix
3 2 5 4	+ * **	
3 2 5 4 **	+ *	
3 2 5 4 ** *	+	
3 2 5 4 ** * +		

FIGURE 12-6. The rules for translating infix expressions into RPN, where the infix expressions do not contain parentheses.

RPN	Stack	Infix
		3+4*5
3		+4*5
3	+	4*5
3 4	+	*5
3 4	+ *	5
3 4 5	+ *	
3 4 5 *	+	
3 4 5 * +		

Since the priority of * is higher than that of +, * is stacked on top of +. When the operators are unstacked, * comes off first and so precedes + in the RPN expression.

If the expression had been 3*4+5, on the other hand, we would have:

RPN	Stack	Infix
		3*4+5
3		*4+5
3	*	4+5
3 4	*	+5
3 4 *		+5
3 4 *	+	5
3 4 * 5	+	
3 4 * 5 +		

Since * has a higher priority than +, * must be removed from the stack and placed in the RPN expression before + can be pushed on. Thus, again, the higher priority * comes first in the RPN expression, and the lower priority + comes second.

Now for parentheses. An expression in parentheses is to be evaluated independently of anything outside the parentheses. Only when the expression inside the parentheses has been completely evaluated can its value be used to evaluate the expression outside the parentheses. This means that when a left parenthesis is encountered, the evaluation of the current expression must be suspended, to be continued only after the expression inside the parentheses has been evaluated.

To our translation rules, then, we add the following: *When a left parenthesis is encountered, push it on the stack. When unstacking operators with greater or equal priority than the operator encountered in the infix expression, if a left parenthesis comes to the top of the stack, terminate the unstacking. When a right parenthesis is encountered in the expression, unstack operators until a matching left parenthesis is found on the stack. Discard both parentheses and continue.*

When a left parenthesis is put on the stack, a new ministack is started whose bottom is at the left parenthesis. The expression inside the parentheses is translated using this ministack. When the matching right parenthesis is found, the ministrack is emptied and the parentheses are discarded.

Figure 12-7 illustrates these rules.

The following is an example of a translation of an infix expression containing parentheses:

RPN	Stack	Infix
		2*(3+4*5)*6
2		*(3+4*5)*6
2	*	(3+4*5)*6
2	* (	3+4*5)*6

4. When a left parenthesis is encountered, push it onto the stack.

RPN	Stack	Infix
4	*	(3+2)
4	* (	3+2)

5. When unstacking operators as a result of Rule 2, if a left parenthesis is encountered on the stack, stop the unstacking and push the operator encountered in the infix expression onto the stack. (Note that the left parenthesis is treated as if it were the bottom of the stack.)

RPN	Stack	Infix
4 3 2 4	− (* **	+5)
4 3 2 4 **	− (*	+5)
4 3 2 4 ** *	− (	+5)
4 3 2 4 ** *	− (+	5)

6. When a right parenthesis is encountered in the infix expression, unstack operators and place them in the RPN expression until a left parenthesis is encountered. Discard both parentheses.

RPN	Stack	Infix
2 3 4 5	* (+ *	)+6
2 3 4 5 *	* (+	)+6
2 3 4 5 * +	* (	)+6
2 3 4 5 * +	*	+6

FIGURE 12-7. The additional rules needed to handle parentheses when translating infix expressions into RPN.

2 3	* (	+4*5)*6
2 3	* (+	4*5)*6
2 3 4	* (+	*5)*6
2 3 4	* (+ *	5)*6
2 3 4 5	* (+ *	)*6
2 3 4 5 *	* (+	)*6
2 3 4 5 * +	* (	)*6
2 3 4 5 * +	*	*6
2 3 4 5 * + *		*6

```
2 3 4 5 * + *        *                    6
2 3 4 5 * + * 6      *
2 3 4 5 * + * 6 *
```

Notice that the parenthesized expression 3 + 4*5 is translated on a ministack extending from the left parenthesis to the top of the operator stack. The * below the left parenthesis remains undisturbed until the entire parenthesized expression has been translated. The left parenthesis shields higher priority operators such as the * from lower priority operators such as the +, preventing the higher priority operators from being unstacked too soon.

Now let us write an algorithm to translate from infix notation to RPN. As before, we will assume that operands are single digits, and we will ignore the possibility that the infix string may contain errors. These simplifications will prevent the fundamental algorithm from being buried in a wealth of detail. Also, removing these limitations makes a good exercise. Figure 12-8 shows an outline of the algorithm INFIX-TO-RPN.

Before filling in the details in Figure 12-8, we must think a moment about assigning numerical priorities to the operators. Let us assign priorities to characters in the infix expression as follows (remember that in the algorithms we are using ↑ in place of **):

FIGURE 12-8. Outline of the algorithm INFIX__TO__RPN.

```
ALGORITHM INFIX-TO_RPN
    (Input the infix expression INFIX; initialize
    the stack to be empty and the reverse Polish
    expression, RPN, to be the null string)
    FOR I ← 1 TO LEN(INFIX) DO
        (Set CHAR to the Ith character of INFIX)
        IF (CHAR is a digit) THEN
            (Append CHAR to RPN)
        ELSE IF (CHAR is an operator) THEN
            (Unstack operators and append them to RPN
            until (a) the bottom of the stack is
            reached, (b) a left parenthesis is
            encountered, or (c) an operator is
            encountered whose priority is less than
            the priority of CHAR)
            (Push CHAR onto stack)
        ELSE IF CHAR = '(' then
            (Push '(' onto stack)
        ELSE IF CHAR = ')' THEN
            (Unstack operators and append them to RPN
            until a left parenthesis is encountered.
            Unstack the left parenthesis and discard
            it.)
        END IF
    END DO
    (Unstack all remaining operators and append them
    to RPN)
    (Output RPN)
END INFIX_TO_RPN
```

Character	Priority
↑	4
* and /	3
+ and −	2
0 through 9	1
other	0

Priorities 0 and 1 are not used as priorities but to classify nonoperators as digits or other characters. We will assume a function PRIORITY(CHAR) whose value is the priority of CHAR. It is left as an exercise to write the function PRIORITY.

Figure 12-9 shows the complete algorithm INFIX__TO__RPN.

12.4 Stacks and Subalgorithms

When a subalgorithm—a procedure or function—is invoked, the address of the next instruction in the calling algorithm must be saved, so that the subalgorithm can return to the proper point when it has finished its work.

FIGURE 12-9. The algorithm INFIX__TO__RPN.

```
ALGORITHM INFIX_TO_RPN
   INPUT INFIX
   TOP ← 0
   RPN ← ''
   FOR I ← 1 TO LEN(INFIX) DO
      CHAR ← MID(INFIX, I, 1)
      P ← PRIORITY(CHAR)
      IF P = 1 THEN            (CHAR is digit)
         RPN ← RPN+' '+CHAR
      ELSE IF P > 1 THEN       (CHAR is operator)
         WHILE (TOP > 0) AND (PRIORITY(STACK(TOP)) ≥ P) DO
            RPN ← RPN+' '+STACK(TOP)
            TOP← TOP-1
         END WHILE
         TOP ← TOP+1
         STACK(TOP) ← CHAR
      ELSE IF CHAR = '(' THEN
         TOP ← TOP+1
         STACK(TOP) ← '('
      ELSE IF CHAR = ')' THEN
         WHILE STACK(TOP) ≠ '(' DO
            RPN ← RPN+' '+STACK(TOP)
            TOP ← TOP-1
         END WHILE
         TOP ← TOP-1
      END IF
   END FOR
   WHILE TOP > 0 DO
      RPN ← RPN+' '+STACK(TOP)
      TOP ← TOP-1
   END WHILE
   OUTPUT RPN
END INFIX_TO_RPN
```

Now the subalgorithm can invoke another subalgorithm, giving another return address to be saved. And that subalgorithm can invoke still another one, and so on. Figure 12-10 illustrates this situation.

When several subalgorithms have been invoked, then these will return in exactly the opposite order to that in which they were invoked. That is, if A invokes B which invokes C which invokes D, then D must return before C can return, and C must return before B can return (see Figure 12-11).

Thus, return addresses are used in exactly the reverse of the order in

FIGURE 12-10. Subalgorithm (function and procedure) calls can be nested. One subalgorithm can invoke another, which can in turn invoke still another, and so on.

```
                                                    ALGORITHM A
                                                         .
                                                         .
                                                         .
   When B is called, location of                    CALL B
   instruction following CALL B must  ----------------->.
   be saved, so B can return to proper                  .
   point                                                .

                                                    END A

                                                    PROCEDURE  B
                                                         .
                                                         .
   When C is called, location of                    CALL C
   instruction following CALL C must  ---------------->.
   be saved, so C can return to proper                  .
   point                                                .

                                                    END B

                                                    PROCEDURE  C
                                                         .
                                                         .
   When D is called, location of                    CALL D
   instruction following CALL D must  ---------------->.
   be saved, so D can return to proper                  .
   point                                                .

                                                    END C

                                                    PROCEDURE  D
                                                         .
                                                         .
                                                         .
                                                         .

                                                    END D
```

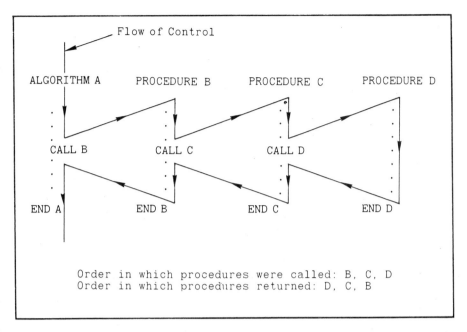

FIGURE 12-11. The order in which subalgorithms return is the reverse of the order in which they are called.

which they were saved. Since items are popped from a stack in the reverse of the order in which they were pushed on, a stack can be used to store subalgorithm return addresses. Figure 12-12 illustrates this use of a stack.

In some systems, storage for the values of the local variables of a subalgorithm is allocated when the algorithm is called and freed when the algorithm returns. This scratch pad storage can be organized as a stack.

When an algorithm is called, a block of storage called a *stack frame* is created on top of the stack. The stack frame contains storage for:

- the return address of the subalgorithm

- the addresses of the arguments of the subalgorithm

- the value a function is to return

- the values of the local variables of the subalgorithm

Figure 12-13 illustrates a stack frame.

When a subalgorithm is called, then a new stack frame is pushed onto the stack. When a subalgorithm returns, its stack frame is popped off the stack. When several subalgorithms have been called and none have returned, then there will be several frames on the stack (see Figure 12-14).

In general, a stack can be used whenever some kind of process must be interrupted and a new process of the same kind initiated. Information must be saved so that the old process can be resumed when the new one is

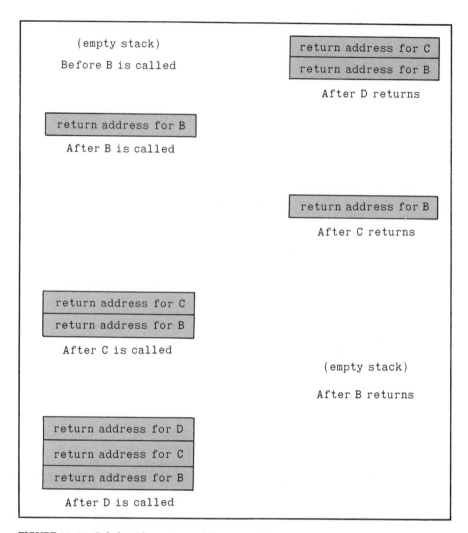

FIGURE 12-12. Subalgorithm return addresses can be saved on a stack.

completed. Evaluating parenthesized subexpressions inside larger expressions, as well as calling and returning from subalgorithms, are two examples of this use of stacks.

Review Questions

1. Explain the behavior of a stack in terms of a stack of physical objects, such as papers, books, or cards.

2. Why is a stack sometimes called a *push-down stack* or a *push-down list*?

3. What do the words *push* and *pop* refer to in connection with stacks?

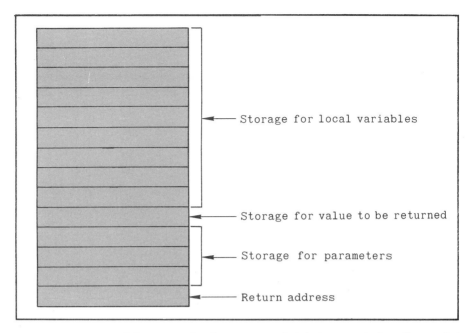

Storage for local variables

Storage for value to be returned

Storage for parameters

Return address

FIGURE 12-13. A stack frame contains the storage needed during a particular call to a subalgorithm.

4. What is the cafeteria analogy?

5. In what respect is the cafeteria analogy faulty?

6. Describe how a stack is represented in memory. How are the PUSH and POP operations implemented?

7. Distinguish among *prefix notation, infix notation,* and *postfix notation.*

8. Of prefix, infix, and postfix notations, which is ordinary algebraic notation? Which is also known as Polish notation? Which is also known as RPN?

9. What is the most important difference between infix notation on one hand and prefix and postfix on the other? (*Hint:* What does infix notation require that the other two do not?)

10. What is the connection between stacks and RPN?

11. Give the rules for evaluating an RPN expression using a stack.

12. In translating from infix to RPN, which are reordered, the operands or the operators?

13. Give the rules for translating into RPN an infix expression that does not contain parentheses.

14. Extend the rules of Question 13 to include parentheses.

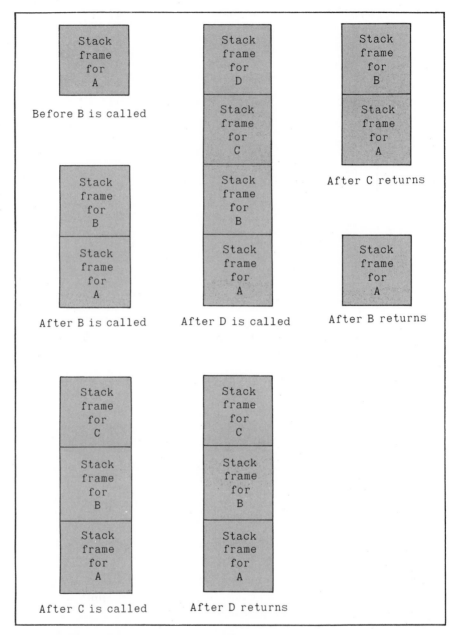

FIGURE 12-14. When a subalgorithm is called, its stack frame is pushed onto the stack. When it returns, its stack frame is popped off the stack.

15. Explain how parentheses are handled in terms of a ministack, which extends from a left parenthesis to the top of the operator stack.

16. Explain the function of a left parenthesis on a stack in terms of shielding higher priority operators from lower priority ones.

17. What property of subalgorithms allows a stack to be used for their return addresses?

18. What is a *stack frame*? What does it contain?

19. When is a stack frame created? When is it destroyed (that is, no longer used)?

20. Make a general statement about the uses of stacks. Give two examples that illustrate the general statement.

Exercises

1. In evaluating an RPN expression, the stack may overflow if the expression is too complex. If the expression is incorrectly formed, the stack may underflow, as for

3 4 2 + * +

Or, when the evaluation is finished, there may be more than one value on the stack, as for:

3 4 2 +

Modify EVALUATE to detect and report these errors.

2. Modify EVALUATE to handle expressions containing numbers with more than one digit.

3. Write the function PRIORITY(CHAR) whose value is the priority of CHAR. (*Hint:* Use two parallel arrays, CHARACTER, and RANK.)

CHARACTER	RANK
'↑'	4
'*'	3
'/'	3
'+'	2
'−'	2
'0'	1
'1'	1
'2'	1
'3'	1
'4'	1
'5'	1
'6'	1
'7'	1
'8'	1
'9'	1
(sentinel)	0

Use sequential search to locate the value of CHAR in CHARACTER.

4. A common error in infix expressions is unbalanced parentheses: more left parentheses then right, or vice versa. Modify INFIX__TO__RPN to detect unbalanced parentheses and output an appropriate error message. (*Hint:* If there are too many left parentheses, then there will still be one or more left parentheses on the stack when the end of the infix expression is encountered. If there are too many right parentheses, then a right parenthesis will be encountered in the expression with no matching left parenthesis on the stack.)

5. Another common error in infix expressions is illegal symbol combinations, such as two operands with no operator in between, or two operators with no operand in between. The following table shows the permissible symbol pairs:

Symbol	May Be Preceded by
operand	(, operator, start of expression
operator	), operand
(	(, operator, start of expression
)	), operand
end of expression	), operand

Modify INFIX__TO__RPN to detect illegal symbol pairs and issue an appropriate error message. (*Hint:* Note that there are only two kinds of entry in the "May Be Preceded by" column. Use a flag to classify each character as one kind or the other.)

Chapter 13

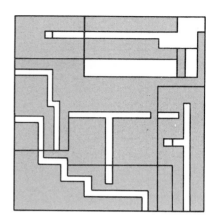

Records

So far, we have studied two kinds of data items: (a) those that can be broken down into smaller parts, and (b) those that cannot be broken down.

Arrays and strings are examples of the first kind of data item. A one-dimensional array is made up of elements. A two-dimensional array is made up of rows and columns, and each row and column is made up of elements. A string is made up of characters. These data items are called *composite*.

Real numbers and characters, on the other hand, are examples of data items of the second kind. Neither of these can be decomposed into any smaller parts. Such data items are called *elementary or atomic*, the latter coming from the Greek word for "indivisible."

(What is elementary and what is composite depends on the level at which we are working. A machine-language programmer might consider characters and real numbers as composite, since both can be decomposed into bits. But this decomposition is not made in most higher level languages. Higher level language programmers are "unaware of" the bit structure of characters and real numbers.)

An array is a uniform data structure. That is, its elements are all similar to one another. Each element is of the same data type. The elements are distinguished only by their positions in the array; otherwise, none stands out from the others. Arrays are often processed in such a way that the same operations are carried out on each element. The same remarks apply to characters in a character string.

A *record* is also a composite data item, but it may be nonuniform. The components of a record may be of different data types and may be processed in different ways for different purposes. The components are given individual names rather than being designated only by their positions.

13.1 Record Structures

Records in computer science are similar to the records we encounter in everyday life, such as school records, medical records, insurance records, employee records, and so on. Each record normally contains information about one *entity*—a particular person, place, or thing. The record is divided into components ("blanks," "boxes") each of which holds one piece of information.

For instance, consider the student record shown in Figure 13–1. We can display its structure in outline form as follows:

```
1 STUDENT
   2 NAME
   2 GPA
   2 CLASS
```

The name of the record is STUDENT. It has three *components:* NAME, GPA (grade point average), and CLASS.

The numbers 1 and 2 are called *level numbers;* their function will become clearer as we talk about more complex records. For the present, 1 designates the entire record, and 2 designates a subdivision of the entire record.

A record can have a value just like any other variable. A record is given a value by assigning values to its components, just as an array is assigned a value by assigning values to its elements.

For instance, if we make the assignments

```
NAME  ← 'MARY JOHNSON'
GPA  ← 3.5
CLASS  ← 'JUNIOR'
```

then STUDENT will have the value shown in Figure 13–2. On the other hand, if we make the assignments

FIGURE 13-1. The record STUDENT.

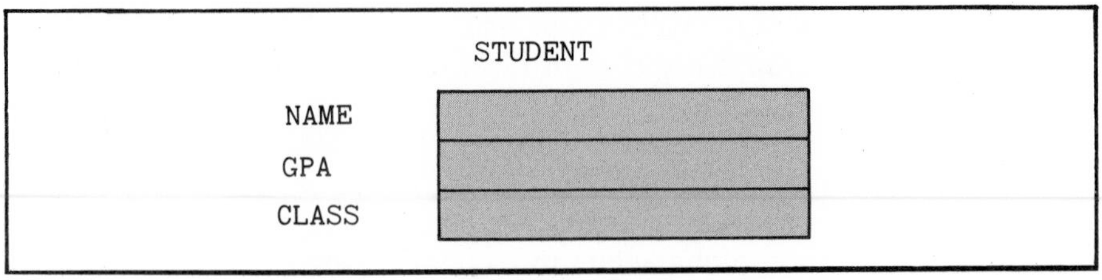

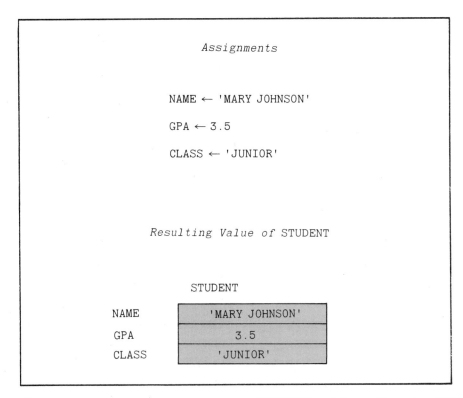

FIGURE 13-2. Assignments to the components of STUDENT and the resulting value of STUDENT.

```
NAME  ← 'JACK JONES'
GPA   ← 2.8
CLASS ← 'FRESHMAN'
```

then STUDENT will have the value shown in Figure 13–3.

As with an array, we can assign values to more than one component in the same statement. Thus,

```
STUDENT ← ('MARY JOHNSON', 3.5, 'JUNIOR')
```

gives STUDENT the value shown in Figure 13–2, and

```
STUDENT ← ('JACK JONES', 2.8, 'FRESHMAN')
```

gives it the value shown in Figure 13–3.

Sometimes it is convenient to use the same name for components of different records. Suppose, for instance, we wished to read in an employee's name, hours worked, and hourly rate, and print out the employee's name, hours worked, hourly rate, and gross wages. We might read

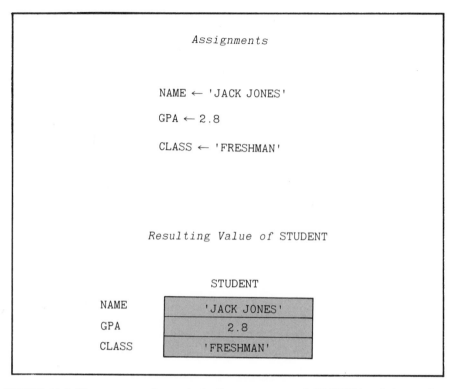

Assignments

NAME ← 'JACK JONES'

GPA ← 2.8

CLASS ← 'FRESHMAN'

Resulting Value of STUDENT

STUDENT

NAME	'JACK JONES'
GPA	2.8
CLASS	'FRESHMAN'

FIGURE 13-3. Three more assignments to the components of STUDENT and the resulting value of STUDENT.

```
1 EMPLOYEE_RECORD
  2 NAME
  2 HOURS
  2 RATE
```

and print out

```
1 PAYROLL_RECORD
  2 NAME
  2 HOURS
  2 RATE
  2 GROSS_WAGES
```

We can use GROSS_WAGES as a name with no problems, since it names a component of only one record. But what about NAME, HOURS, and RATE? When we make an assignment to NAME, do we refer to NAME in EMPLOYEE_RECORD or NAME in PAYROLL_RECORD? When HOURS óccurs in an expression, should the value from EMPLOYEE_REC-ORD or the value from PAYROLL_RECORD be used?

When a name appears as a component of more than one record, that name must be *qualified* by the name of the record. The record name is written first and the component name second; the two are separated by a dot.

Thus, instead of NAME we must write either EMPLOYEE__ RECORD.NAME or PAYROLL__RECORD.NAME; instead of HOURS we must write either EMPLOYEE__RECORD.HOURS or PAYROLL__ RECORD.HOURS, and so on. But we can write just plain GROSS__ WAGES, since GROSS__WAGES occurs in only one record (though PAY-ROLL__RECORD.GROSS__WAGES is legal if we wish to remind the reader that GROSS__WAGES is a component of PAYROLL__RECORD).

Qualified names tend to be long and clumsy to write, a fact that discourages using the same name as a component of more than one record.

Note that the word "record" can be used in two different ways. In the first usage, "record" refers to a *form* or *structure*. Thus, the "record"

```
1 STUDENT
  2 NAME
  2 GPA
  2 CLASS
```

gives the form or structure that a value of STUDENT must have. On the other hand, we can use "record" to refer to a particular set of data. Thus, ('MARY JONES', 3.5, 'JUNIOR') is the "student record" for Mary Jones.

To be precise, we could call the form of a record a *record structure* or a *record type* and the data for a particular individual a *record value*. But to keep from being so long-winded, we will usually just speak of a record and let the context show whether we are speaking of a structure or a value.

13.2 Declarations

Many programming languages require the programmer to declare the kinds of values each variable may have. Thus, a program using X to name a real number and S to name a string would have to contain the statement:

```
DECLARE X: REAL, S: STRING
```

(The exact form of the statement would vary from one language to another.)

Also, we are usually required to declare the sizes of arrays and the data types of their elements. Thus,

```
DECLARE A(100): REAL
```

would declare A to be a one-dimensional array with 100 elements, all real numbers, and

```
DECLARE B(25, 40): STRING
```

would declare B to be a two-dimensional array with 25 rows and 40 columns. Each element of B is a string.

So far, we have not required such declaration statements in the algorithmic language. For one thing, it is usually obvious what kind of values a variable can have from the words that make up the variable name and the context in which the variable is used. EMPLOYEE__NAME surely has string values, and HOURLY__RATE surely has real-number values. Deciding on the number of elements in an array is a meaningless exercise when we are composing an algorithm and have yet to decide on how much data is to be processed or even exactly what the array is to be used for.

But the DECLARATION statement has caught up with us at last. There is no way we can guess what the structure of a record is. Thus, every record name, such as STUDENT, must appear in a declaration statement such as the following:

```
DECLARE 1 STUDENT
          2 NAME
          2 GPA
          2 CLASS
```

We could specify the data types of the components of the record as follows:

```
DECLARE 1 STUDENT
          2 NAME: STRING
          2 GPA: REAL
          2 CLASS: STRING
```

Most programming languages require this data type specification. But, following the philosophy just given, we will usually omit the data types, letting context or comments in the text clarify the data type of each component.

13.3 More Complicated Records

Sometimes it is useful to let the components of a record be composite data items that can themselves be further subdivided. Consider the following version of STUDENT:

```
DECLARE 1 STUDENT
          2 NAME
            3 FIRST
            3 INITIAL
            3 LAST
          2 ADDRESS
            3 STREET
            3 CITY
            3 STATE
            3 ZIP
          2 GPA
          2 CLASS
```

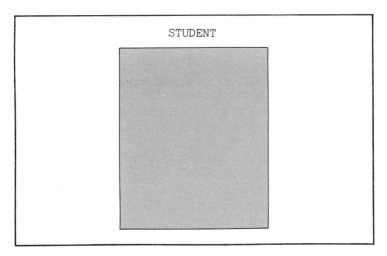

FIGURE 13-4. The name STUDENT refers to the entire record. On level 1, the record is considered as a whole and is not divided into parts.

STUDENT contains two types of components: *elementary items*, FIRST, INITIAL, LAST, STREET, CITY, STATE, ZIP, GPA and CLASS, which cannot be further subdivided; and *group items*, NAME and ADDRESS, which can be. The entire record, STUDENT, can also be considered a group item.

The name STUDENT refers to the entire record, as shown in Figure 13-4. STUDENT can be subdivided into NAME, ADDRESS, GPA, and CLASS, as shown in Figure 13-5. Finally, NAME can be further subdi-

FIGURE 13-5. Level 2 is the first level of subdivision of student.

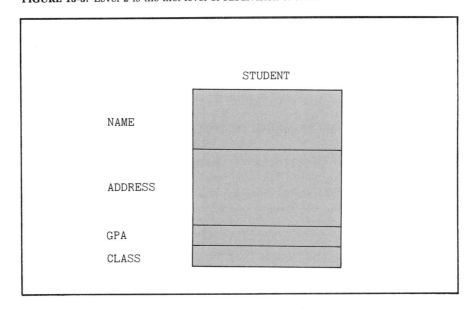

vided into FIRST, INITIAL, and LAST; and ADDRESS can be further subdivided into STREET, CITY, STATE, and ZIP, as shown in Figure 13-6.

The level numbers designate different levels of subdivision. Level 1 refers to the situation of Figure 13-4, where the entire record is considered as a whole and no subdivision whatever is done. Level 2 refers to the subdivisions of the entire record. Level 3 refers to subdivisions of level 2 items. Higher level numbers refer to still further subdivisions.

Group items such as NAME and ADDRESS are records in their own right. That is, they are composite data structures that can be subdivided into named components. If we take this point of view, we can think of a record such as STUDENT as consisting of a *hierarchy of records,* just as in Chapter 10 we viewed an algorithm as a hierarchy of modules. Figure 13-7 shows a hierarchy diagram for STUDENT similar to the ones we drew for algorithms in Chapter 10. STUDENT is the top-level record in the hierarchy. The bottom-level items are the elementary items, which cannot be further subdivided. (We include the elementary items in the hierarchy although they are not records.) The intermediate-level records are the group items other than STUDENT itself.

Every group or elementary item in a record has a *completely qualified name.* Each completely qualified name consists of a name from level 1, a name from level 2, and so on through the level of the item itself. The various names are joined by dots to form the completely qualified name. The completely qualified names of the group and elementary items in STUDENT are:

```
STUDENT
STUDENT.NAME
STUDENT.NAME.FIRST
STUDENT.NAME.INITIAL
STUDENT.NAME.LAST
```

FIGURE 13-6. On level 3, some of the level-2 items of STUDENT are further subdivided.

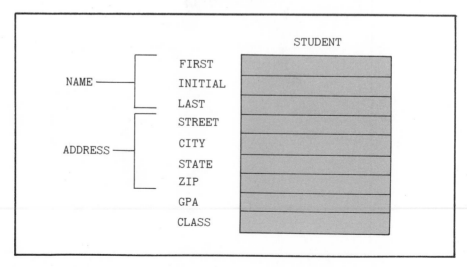

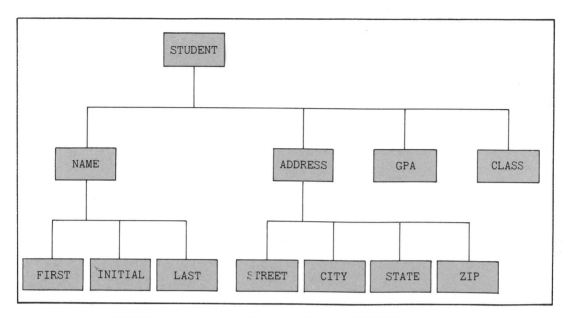

FIGURE 13-7. A hierarchy diagram for the record STUDENT.

```
STUDENT.ADDRESS
STUDENT.ADDRESS.STREET
STUDENT.ADDRESS.CITY
STUDENT.ADDRESS.STATE
STUDENT.ADDRESS.ZIP
STUDENT.GPA
STUDENT.CLASS
```

In a completely qualified name, names other than the final one are called *qualifiers*. In STUDENT.NAME.FIRST, for instance, STUDENT and NAME are qualifiers.

We may abbreviate a completely qualified name by omitting qualifiers, provided no confusion results. No confusion will result if the name is an abbreviation of, at most, one completely qualified name. An abbreviated name that can be an abbreviation of more than one completely qualified name is ambiguous and hence illegal.

For instance, consider the record defined by:

```
DECLARE 1 A
         2 B
           3 X
           3 Y
         2 C
```

If there is no other record with subdivisions B, X, Y, and C, then we can refer to the items in A as

```
        A                       Y
        B                       C
        X
```

No further qualification is necessary.

Suppose that in the same algorithm that uses A, however, there is also the declaration

```
DECLARE 1 E
          2 B
             3 X
             3 Y
          2 C
```

Now the names B, X, Y, and C are insufficient. We do not know whether X, for instance, is an abbreviation of A.B.X or E.B.X. On the other hand, A.X can only be an abbreviation of A.B.X, and E.X, an abbreviation of E.B.X. Hence, the names A.X and E.X are permissible. B can be omitted since it contributes nothing to distinguishing between the subdivisions of A and the subdivisions of E.

Here are the most abbreviated possible forms of the group and elementary items in A and E;

Record A	*Record E*
A	E
A.B	E.B
A.X	E.X
A.Y	E.Y
A.C	E.C

It is possible to use a name more than once in the *same record*. As long as each item in the record has a unique completely qualified name, no confusion will result. Such duplications may seem like an invitation to confusion, but they can reasonably occur in records such as:

```
DECLARE 1 ENROLLMENT
          2 STUDENT
             3 NAME
             3 ADDRESS
          2 PARENTS
             3 FATHER
                4 NAME
                4 ADDRESS
             3 MOTHER
                4 NAME
                4 ADDRESS
```

NAME and ADDRESS each occurs three times in this record. The completely qualified names for each occurrence of NAME are

```
ENROLLMENT.STUDENT.NAME
ENROLLMENT.PARENTS.FATHER.NAME
ENROLLMENT.PARENTS.MOTHER.NAME
```

The most abbreviated form of the first occurrence is

```
STUDENT.NAME
```

The second and third occurrences have the following most abbreviated forms:

```
FATHER.NAME
MOTHER.NAME
```

You should convince yourself that such names as

```
ENROLLMENT.NAME
PARENTS.NAME
NAME
```

are all invalid, since each abbreviates more than one completely qualified name.

ADDRESS in this record is qualified in the same way as NAME.

Notice that the record definition

```
DECLARE 1 A
          2 B
            3 X
            3 Y
          2 B
            3 U
            3 V
```

is invalid, since the two level-2 items have the same completely qualified name, A.B A record definition is valid if each component has a unique completely qualified name.

13.4 Arrays of Records

Just as we can have arrays whose elements are real numbers and strings, we can have arrays whose elements are records. We can declare such an array of records as follows:

```
DECLARE 1 BOOK(5)
          2 TITLE
          2 AUTHOR
          2 PUBLISHER
```

This declares BOOK to be a one-dimensional array with five elements. Each element is subdivided into three components, TITLE, AUTHOR, and PUBLISHER (see Figure 13-8).

Thus, BOOK(1) refers to all of the information about the first book, BOOK(2) refers to all of the information about the second book, and so on. In the same way, BOOK(1).TITLE is the title of the first book, BOOK(2).AUTHOR is the author of the second book, BOOK(3).PUBLISHER is the publisher of the third book, and so on (see Figure 13-9).

There is a problem, however, with names such as BOOK(1).TITLE and BOOK(2).AUTHOR. When no confusion will result, we would like to abbreviate the completely qualified name by omitting BOOK. But that would leave our subscript with nothing to be a subscript of. As an option, therefore, we will allow a subscript to be written to the right of the completely qualified name. Thus, the following are equivalent:

```
BOOK(1).TITLE        BOOK.TITLE(1)
BOOK(2).AUTHOR       AUTHOR(2)
BOOK(3).PUBLISHER    BOOK.PUBLISHER(3)
```

The advantage of the second form is that we can drop unneeded qualifiers without interfering with the subscripting. Thus, BOOK.TITLE(1) can be abbreviated to TITLE(1), BOOK.AUTHOR(2) can be abbreviated to AUTHOR(2), and BOOK.PUBLISHER(3) can be abbreviated to PUBLISHER(3). The following table shows three equally valid ways of referring to the components of BOOK(1).

```
BOOK(I).TITLE        BOOK.TITLE(I)        TITLE(I)
BOOK(I).AUTHOR       BOOK.AUTHOR(I)       AUTHOR(I)
BOOK(I).PUBLISHER    BOOK.PUBLISHER(I)    PUBLISHER(I)
```

FIGURE 13-8. BOOK is an array of five elements. Each element is a record with three components.

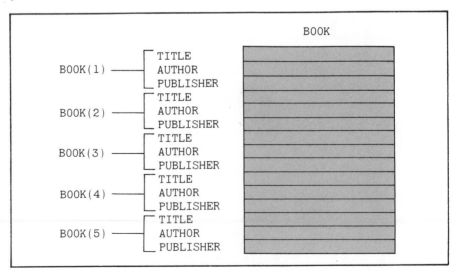

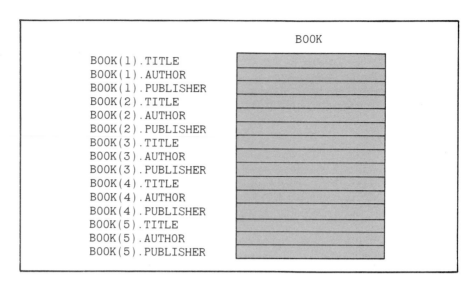

```
                                                    BOOK
              BOOK(1).TITLE
              BOOK(1).AUTHOR
              BOOK(1).PUBLISHER
              BOOK(2).TITLE
              BOOK(2).AUTHOR
              BOOK(2).PUBLISHER
              BOOK(3).TITLE
              BOOK(3).AUTHOR
              BOOK(3).PUBLISHER
              BOOK(4).TITLE
              BOOK(4).AUTHOR
              BOOK(4).PUBLISHER
              BOOK(5).TITLE
              BOOK(5).AUTHOR
              BOOK(5).PUBLISHER
```

FIGURE 13-9. We can refer to the elementary items of BOOK by combining qualification with subscripting.

As an example of the use of such subscripted components, suppose we wished to print the title of every book on our list by a given author. The following statements accomplish this:

```
INPUT AUTHORS_NAME
FOR I ← 1 TO 5 DO
    IF AUTHOR(I) = AUTHORS_NAME THEN
        OUTPUT TITLE(I)
    END IF
END FOR
```

It's possible for any component of a record to be an array. Consider the following:

```
DECLARE 1 AUTHOR
           2 NAME
           2 BOOKS(5)
              3 TITLE
              3 PUBLISHER
```

As shown in Figure 13-10, AUTHOR has two components, NAME and BOOKS. BOOKS is an array of five elements, each element of which comprises a TITLE and a PUBLISHER.

We can refer to individual titles and publishers using the completely qualified names:

```
AUTHOR.BOOKS(I).TITLE
AUTHOR.BOOKS(I).PUBLISHER
```

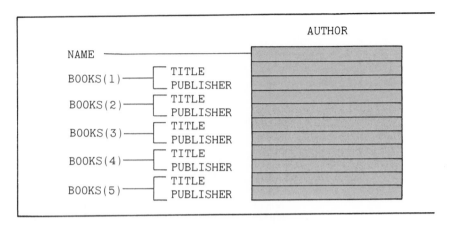

FIGURE 13-10. A component of a record can itself be an array.

As before, we can move the subscript to the right of the entire completely qualified name:

```
AUTHOR.BOOKS.TITLE(I)
AUTHOR.BOOKS.PUBLISHER(I)
```

This gives us the freedom to omit unneeded qualifiers:

```
TITLE(I)
PUBLISHER(I)
```

Finally, we may have an array of records, each record of which contains one or more arrays components:

```
DECLARE 1 AUTHOR(3)
         2 NAME
         2 BOOKS(5)
            3 TITLE
            3 PUBLISHER
```

Figure 13-11 illustrates this array.

We can refer to the various components of AUTHOR using the completely qualified names:

```
AUTHOR(I).NAME
AUTHOR(I).BOOKS(J).TITLE
AUTHOR(I).BOOKS(J).PUBLISHER
```

As always, we can move the subscripts to the right of the completely qualified names. When more than one subscript is moved to the right, the subscripts are listed in the same order in which they occur in the completely qualified name:

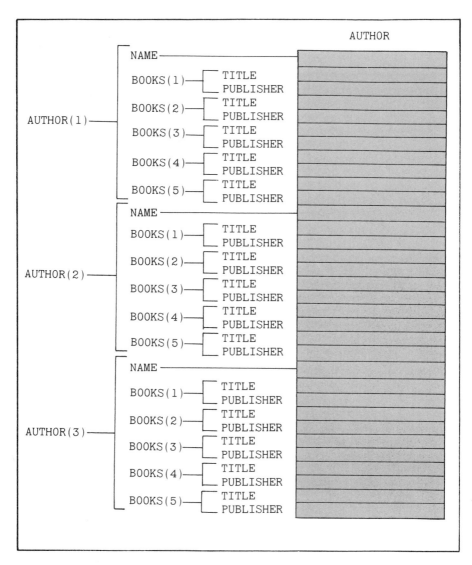

FIGURE 13-11. An array, each of whose elements contains another array as a component.

```
AUTHOR.NAME(I)
AUTHOR.BOOKS.TITLE(I, J)
AUTHOR.BOOKS.PUBLISHER(I, J)
```

Now we can drop unneeded qualifiers:

```
NAME(I)
TITLE(I, J)
PUBLISHER(I, J)
```

When we declare an array in an algorithm, it is sometimes unimportant how many elements the array will have. On the other hand, we do need to know which components of a record are arrays and which are not, particularly if we are to use abbreviated names. For this reason, we sometimes write declarations with the array sizes omitted but with the surrounding parentheses included to indicate which components are arrays:

```
DECLARE 1 AUTHOR( )
          2 NAME
          2 BOOKS( )
            3 TITLE
            3 PUBLISHER
```

This notation indicates that AUTHOR and BOOKS are arrays, but does not tell how many elements are in each array.

Another possibility is the following:

```
DECLARE 1 AUTHOR(3)
          2 NAME
          2 NUMBER_WRITTEN
          2 BOOKS(NUMBER_WRITTEN)
            3 TITLE
            3 PUBLISHER
```

In each element of AUTHOR, the size of the array BOOKS depends on the value of NUMBER_WRITTEN. In different elements, NUMBER_WRITTEN will have different values and BOOKS will have different sizes. The elements of AUTHOR are called *variable-length records*, since the size varies from one record to another. Figure 13-12 illustrates variable-length records.

13.5 Input, Output, and Assignment

One advantage of records is that a large number of values can be transferred from one place to another in a single operation. Thus,

```
INPUT STUDENT
```

would read in values for all the elementary items in STUDENT, while

```
OUTPUT AUTHOR
```

would print out the values of all the elementary items of AUTHOR.

Since the data read in or printed out is simply a list of values, we must specify a correspondence between those values and the elementary items of a record. The correspondence rule is simple: *Elementary items are read in or printed out in the same order in which they appear in the record declaration.* Thus, the first data value read or printed corresponds to the

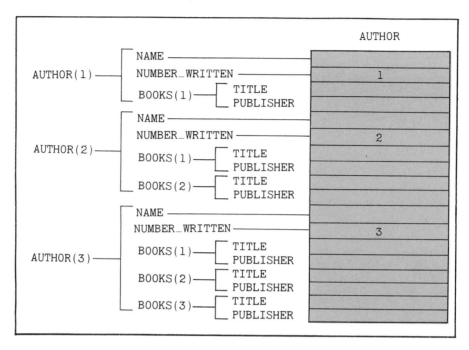

FIGURE 13-12. An array of variable-length records. In each element of AUTHOR, the value of NUMBER__WRITTEN determines the size of the array BOOKS.

first elementary item in the record declaration, the second data value read or printed corresponds to the second elementary item, and so on.

Consider the following:

```
DECLARE 1 INVENTORY_ITEM
          2 STOCK_NUMBER
          2 PRICE
          2 QUANTITY_ON_HAND
```

The statement

```
INPUT INVENTORY_ITEM
```

is then equivalent to

```
INPUT STOCK_NUMBER, PRICE, QUANTITY_HAND
```

and the statement

```
OUTPUT INVENTORY_ITEM
```

is equivalent to

```
OUTPUT STOCK_NUMBER, PRICE, QUANTITY_ON_HAND
```

The same rule holds for more complicated structures. If A is defined by

```
DECLARE 1 A
          2 B
            3 C
              4 D
              4 E
            3 F
              4 G
              4 H
          2 I
```

then INPUT A is equivalent to

```
INPUT D, E, G, H, I
```

and OUTPUT A is equivalent to

```
OUTPUT D, E, G, H, I
```

Note that values are inputted and outputted for the *elementary items only.* The same principle applies to assignment. Thus,

```
A ← (5, 10, 15, 20, 25)
```

is equivalent to

```
D ← 5
E ← 10
G ← 15
H ← 20
I ← 25
```

Also, if P is defined by

```
DECLARE 1 P
          2 Q
          2 R
            3 S
            3 T
          2 U
          2 V
```

then

```
P ← A
```

is equivalent to

```
Q  ←  D
S  ←  E
T  ←  G
U  ←  H
V  ←  I
```

Review Questions

1. Distinguish between composite and elementary data items.

2. Why might a machine-language programmer consider a certain data item to be composite, while a higher-level-language programmer might consider it elementary?

3. What is a *record?*

4. Contrast arrays and strings with records.

5. What are the numbers that appear before each item in a record description called? What function do they serve?

6. What is a *qualified name?* How is it written? What is it used for?

7. Why is it desirable to avoid qualified names when possible? How can this goal be accomplished?

8. What is a *declaration?*

9. In programming languages, declarations are frequently required so that the translator can reserve storage for the values of the declared variables. Why are declarations for this purpose not needed in an algorithmic language?

10. Distinguish between a *group item* and an *elementary item*. Which of these is a record in its own right?

11. What is a *completely qualified name?* Describe how to construct the completely qualified name of any component of a record from the record declaration.

12. What is the rule for abbreviating a completely qualified name? Under what conditions would an abbreviation be invalid?

13. Give two alternate ways in which BOOK(I).TITLE can be written.

14. Give two alternate ways in which

```
AUTHOR(I).BOOKS(J).TITLE
```

can be written.

15. What is the purpose of "moving subscripts to the right" in a qualified name?

16. How can we write a record declaration to show which components of a record are arrays without committing ourselves to specifying the number of elements in each array?

17. What are *variable-length records*? Give an example of a declaration of an array of variable-length records.

18. On input, what is the rule for assigning the values read to the elementary items of a record?

19. On output, what is the rule for printing out the elementary items of a record?

20. When record names appear on both sides of the assignment operator, give the rule by which the values of the elementary items of the record on the right are assigned to the elementary items of the record on the left.

Exercises

The following record is referred to in Exercises 1–6:

```
DECLARE 1 H
          2 I
            3 X
            3 Y
          2 J
          2 K
            3 X
            3 Y
```

1. Give the completely qualified name for every component of H.

2. Give the most abbreviated possible name for each component of H, assuming that the names I, J, K, X, and Y do not occur in any other record.

3. Give the most abbreviated possible names for each component of H, assuming that the names I, J, K, X, and Y do occur in other records.

4. Draw a series of diagrams similar to Figures 13-4, 13-5, and 13-6, showing how H is subdivided on the first, second, and third levels.

5. Draw a hierarchy diagram, similar to that in Figure 13-7, for H.

6. Write INPUT and OUTPUT statements for the elementary items of H equivalent to

```
INPUT H
```

and

```
OUTPUT H
```

Note that qualified names such as K.X can be used in INPUT and OUTPUT statements.

The following array of records is referred to in Exercises 7–10:

```
DECLARE 1 A( )
          2 B
          2 C( )
            3 X
            3 Y
```

7. Write the completely qualified name for each elementary item in A. Use the subscript I for A, and J for C, and write each subscript immediately after the name subscripted.

8. Rewrite each of the completely qualified names of Exercise 7 with the subscripts moved to the right.

9. Rewrite each of the completely qualified names of Exercise 8 in its most abbreviated form. Assume that B, C, X, and Y do not occur in any other record.

10. Suppose that the array A contains 100 elements and, in each element of A, C contains 25 elements. Modify the given declaration to reflect this additional information.

Chapter 14

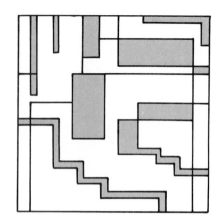

Linked Lists

Frequently the programmer is called upon to model, or represent, some portion of the outside world inside the computer's memory. The computer manipulates this model and produces results that, we hope, will be useful in dealing with the real world.

To model some portion of the world inside the computer, we must do two things. First, we must represent the entities—the persons, places, and things—in the part of the world we are trying to model. Second, we must represent the relationships among those entities.

The records we studied in the last chapter serve well to represent entities. All the data pertinent to a particular entity can be collected into a single record. And if the entity has a hierarchical structure—if it can be divided into parts that can be described separately—then the record can reflect this structure.

The only structure we have so far for representing relationships among entities is the array. The relationships represented by arrays are those present in lists, tables, books of tables, and so on. In a one-dimensional array, for instance, every element except the last is related to the element that *follows* it. And every element except the first is related to the one that *precedes* it. But while relations such as *precedes* and *follows* can be extremely useful, they fall far short of encompassing the rich and varied relationships among objects in the real world.

One way to express more complex relationships is to link together records that are related in some particular way. The linking is accomplished by including as a component of one record a pointer to the related record. (Remember, a pointer is a variable whose value can be used to locate another record. The value usually gives the position of the other record in an array.) Figure 14-1 illustrates the linking of two records in an array using a pointer.

A collection of records linked in this way is called a *plex*. In this chapter we will not study the most general possible plex but will confine ourselves to *linked lists* or *chains*—lists created using the linking mechanism. We will find that these lists are in many ways more flexible than arrays. Also, their study will prepare us for the more complicated plexes taken up in later chapters.

14.1 Singly Linked Lists

Fundamental Properties. Consider the array shown in Figure 14-2 and defined by:

```
DECLARE 1 CELL( )
          2 VALUE
          2 LINK
```

this array is made up of a series of elements which we call—following custom and for lack of a better name—*cells*. Each cell has a VALUE part and a LINK part.

The VALUE part contains all the useful information in the cell. For simplicity, we will usually think of VALUE as a character string. But nothing that follows would be changed if VALUE had subdivisions on level 3,

FIGURE 14-1. Using a pointer to link together two records in an array. The Z component of A(2) points to A(4).

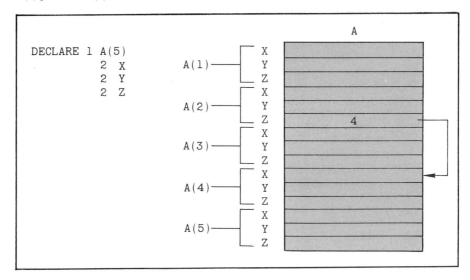

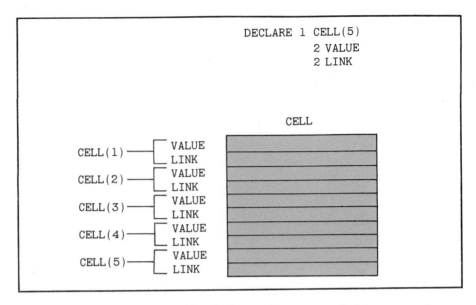

FIGURE 14-2. The array CELL. Although the text leaves unspecified how many elements CELL contains, five elements are assumed here for the sake of illustration.

level 4, and so on. Thus, VALUE could be a record of arbitrary complexity.

The LINK component of each record is used to join a set of records together into a list. For each record, LINK is a pointer to the next record on the list. More specifically, the value of LINK is the subscript of the next record.

The last record on the list has as the value of LINK some sentinel whose value cannot be confused with a subscript. A zero or negative value would serve; zero is often used. We will denote this sentinel value by NIL.

We must somehow designate the first element of the list. We use a variable FIRST whose value points to the first element of the list.

Figure 14-3 illustrates a linked list. Note the order in the linked list is not the same as the order of the cells in the array. In fact, the cells can be scattered throughout the array in a random fashion. The only purpose of organizing the cells into an array is to associate with each a unique subscript value. These subscript values are then used to link one cell to another.

In fact, it is best to forget about the array structure of the cells entirely and depict a linked list as shown in Figure 14-4. This diagram shows how the cells are linked, which is the important thing. Exactly where each cell happens to be located in the array is something we can usually forget about.

The first cell on a linked list must always be treated as a special case. The reason is that the first cell is pointed to by FIRST, which is not a component of a cell and cannot be accessed in the same way as the other LINK components. Because of this, the first cell is often singled out as the *header record*. The VALUE part of the header is not used to hold one of

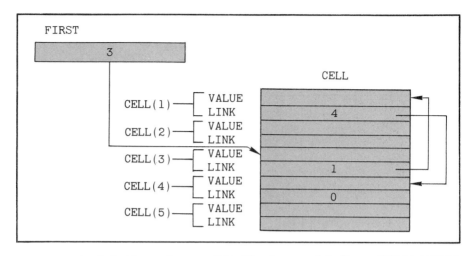

FIGURE 14-3. A linked list in the array CELL. The elements of the list are CELL(3), CELL(2), and CELL(4), in that order. FIRST contains a pointer to CELL(3), the first element of the list. CELL(4), LINK contains 0, the end-of-list sentinel.

the values on the list, although it may carry descriptive information about the list as a whole. Now every cell containing a data value is pointed to by the link of another cell and so can be treated in the same way during searches and other operations.

Figure 14-5 shows a linked list with a header. The value part of the header is shaded to indicate its unique status. Also note that a diagonal line in the LINK component of the last cell stands for NIL.

Searching a Linked List. Let us start our discussion of list processing by writing a procedure

SEARCH(F, V, Q)

to search a list for the cell containing a given value. F is the pointer to the header of the list to be searched, and V is the value sought after. When the procedure returns, Q will point to the cell whose VALUE part is V, if such

FIGURE 14-4. A linked list drawn without regard for the locations of the elements in the array CELL. The diagonal line in the LINK component of the last element represents the end-of-list sentinel, which is called NIL.

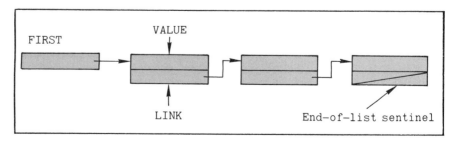

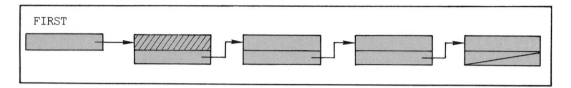

FIRST

FIGURE 14-5. A linked list with a header. The VALUE component of the header does not contain useful data. The header serves only to provide a list cell whose LINK component points to the first cell of the list that does contain useful data.

a cell was found. If no such cell was found, the value of Q will be NIL (see Figure 14-6).

We can outline the algorithm as follows:

```
PROCEDURE SEARCH(F, V, Q)
   (Set Q to point to the header of the list to be searched)
   (Initialize the flag NOT_FOUND to TRUE)
   WHILE (Q ≠ NIL) AND NOT_FOUND DO
      (Set Q to point to the next cell on the list)
      (If VALUE(Q) = V then set NOT_FOUND to FALSE)
   END WHILE
END SEARCH
```

The flag NOT__FOUND is used to stop the search when the sought-after value is found. If the end of the list is reached before the sought-after value is found, the search stops and the value NIL is returned for Q.

Since F points to the header of the list to be searched,

$$Q \leftarrow F$$

sets Q to point to the header of the list to be searched.

FIGURE 14-6. Situation after a call to the procedure SEARCH. Note that, for convenience in drawing, a pointer can be shown pointing to any part of a cell. What part of the cell it points to is not significant.

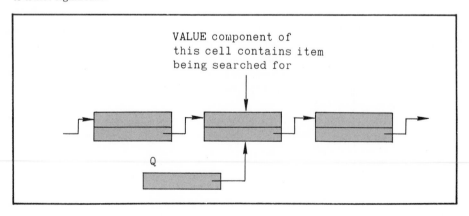

VALUE component of this cell contains item being searched for

Q

To set Q to point to the next cell, we use

```
Q ← LINK(Q)
```

Notice that this is executed once before VALUE is compared with V, thus moving Q past the header, which is not to be searched. If there were no next cell, the value of Q would be NIL. In that case, the repetition terminates, and the procedure returns with the value of Q equal to NIL.

It is assumed that CELL—and hence VALUE and LINK—was declared GLOBAL in the main algorithm, so that these names are available to the procedures. Each procedure also declares as GLOBAL whichever names it needs access to:

```
PROCEDURE SEARCH(F, V, Q)
   GLOBAL VALUE, LINK
   Q ← F
   NOT_FOUND ← TRUE
   WHILE (Q ≠ NIL) AND NOT_FOUND DO
      Q ← LINK(Q)
      IF VALUE(Q) = V THEN
         NOT_FOUND ← FALSE
      END IF
   END WHILE
END SEARCH
```

We will see presently that some operations require access to the cell *preceding* the one that is to be operated on. Deletion is an example of such an operation. But in a singly linked list we can only work through the list in a single direction, the direction in which the pointers point. There is no provision for going backwards in the list.

Therefore, the SEARCH procedure will be more useful if it returns not only a pointer to the cell found but to the preceding cell as well. We can accomplish this with a pointer P that throughout the search will always be one cell behind Q. When the procedure returns, Q will point to the cell found, and P will point to the preceding cell, as shown in Figure 14-7. The procedure SEARCH is easily modified to include P:

```
PROCEDURE SEARCH(F, V, P, Q)
   GLOBAL VALUE, LINK
   Q ← F
   NOT_FOUND ← TRUE
   WHILE (Q ≠ NIL) AND NOT_FOUND DO
      P ← Q
      Q ← LINK(Q)
      IF VALUE(Q) = V THEN
         NOT_FOUND ← FALSE
      END IF
   END WHILE
END SEARCH
```

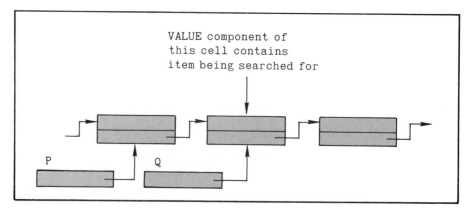

FIGURE 14-7. In addition to the pointer Q to the cell found, it's often convenient to have SEARCH also return a pointer P to the cell preceding the one found.

Suppose we want access not to the cell containing a particular value, but simply to the first cell, the second cell, the third cell, or some other particular numbered cell. It is here that linked lists are inferior to arrays. With an array, we would merely write A(1), A(2), A(3), and so on; the system would calculate the address of the requested element and obtain its value. With a linked list, we must start at the beginning of the list and work our way through, counting the cells as we go, until we reach the desired cell.

The procedure ACCESS(F, I, P, Q) does this job. F points to the list in question. I is the number of the cell we wish to access. (The header is not counted; the cell following the header is numbered 1.) As in SEARCH, Q is set to point to the requested cell, and P is set to point to the preceding cell (see Figure 14-8). An error occurs if the value of I is greater than the number of cells on the list.

ACCESS is a straightforward modification of SEARCH:

FIGURE 14-8. The procedure ACCESS returns a pointer Q to the Ith cell on the list as well as a pointer P to the preceding cell.

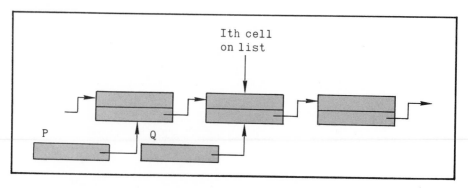

```
PROCEDURE ACCESS(F, I, P, Q)
   GLOBAL LINK
   Q ← F
   FOR J ← 1 TO I DO
      P ← Q
      Q ← LINK(Q)
   END FOR
END ACCESS
```

Memory Management. We may regard the array CELL as a reservoir of list cells. When a new cell is needed for a particular list, an unused element of CELL is added to the list. Any unused element may be used, regardless of its position in CELL. When an element is no longer needed in a list, it is removed and becomes an unused cell available for further use when needed.

Note that several linked lists can exist in CELL at the same time, so that a cell removed from one list can later be added to another.

To implement these ideas, we need some way of keeping track of the currently unused elements of CELL. We do this by linking all of the unused elements together in a *free-space list*. A global variable FREE points to the first cell of the free space list. (The free space list has no header.) Figure 14-9 shows the free space list as it might actually exist in CELL.

At the beginning of a list-processing algorithm, all of the elements of CELL are linked together in one free-space list (see Figure 14-10). As lists are built and modified, all needed cells are obtained from the free-space list. When a cell is no longer needed, it is returned to the free-space list.

The procedure NEW(P) obtains a new cell from the free-space list and

FIGURE 14-9. The free-space list. Shaded cells are currently in use. Unshaded ones are available for use. The available cells are linked together to form the free-space list.

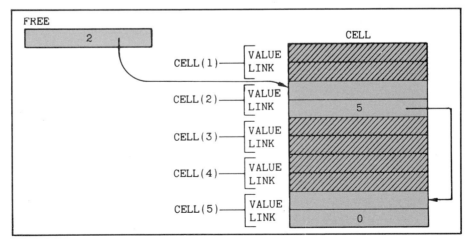

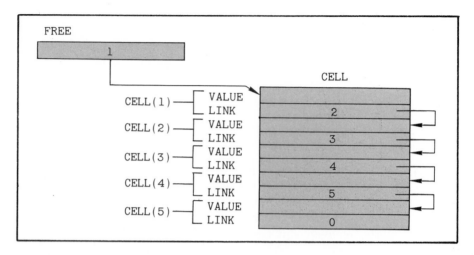

FIGURE 14-10. At the start of a list processing algorithm, all the cells of CELL are linked together to in a single free-space list.

sets P to point to it. (NEW prints an error message if there are no cells left on the free-space list.)

Figure 14-11 illustrates the operation of the procedure NEW:

```
PROCEDURE NEW(P)
   GLOBAL LINK, FREE
   IF FREE = NIL THEN    (Free-space list is empty)
      CALL ERROR('FREE SPACE EXHAUSTED')
   ELSE
      P ← FREE
      FREE ← LINK(FREE)
   END IF
END NEW
```

The procedure RECYCLE(P) returns the cell pointed to by P to the free-space list. Figure 14-12 illustrates its operation.

```
PROCEDURE RECYCLE(P)
   GLOBAL LINK, FREE
   LINK(P) ← FREE
   FREE ← P
END RECYCLE
```

Insertion and Deletion. Perhaps the most important advantage of linked lists is that new cells may be easily inserted, and ones that are no longer needed may be deleted, at any point in the list. This is *not* true for arrays. To insert a new element in the middle of an array, we must move all of the following elements up one place to make room. To delete an element, we must move all of the following elements back one place to take up the space.

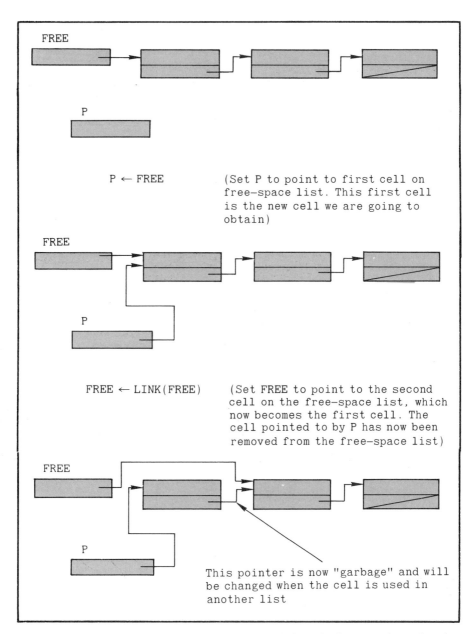

FIGURE 14-11. The procedure NEW(P) gets a new cell from the free-space list and sets P to point to it. The illustration shows the effect of each of the two statements of NEW(P) that manipulate the free-space list. P ← FREE sets P to point to the same cell that is pointed to by FREE. FREE ← LINK(FREE) is trickier to interpret. First find the cell pointed to by FREE. Follow the link component of this cell to find the cell pointed to by LINK(FREE). Set FREE to point to this cell.

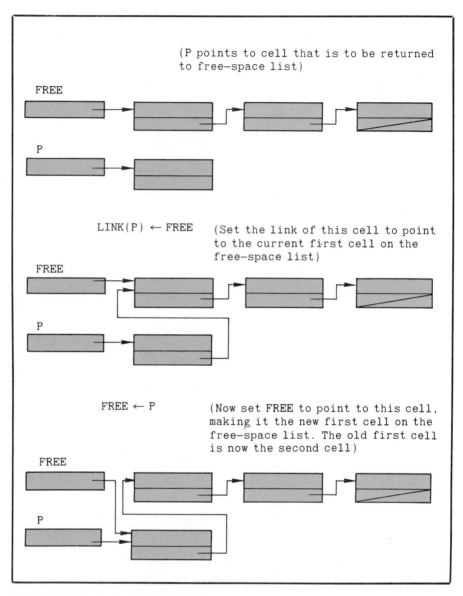

Figure 14-12. The procedure RECYCLE(P) returns the cell pointed to by P to the free-space list. To interpret the statement LINK(P) ← FREE, locate the link component of the cell pointed to by P. Set this link component to point to the same cell that is pointed to be FREE.

The procedure INSERT__AFTER(V, P) inserts a cell containing the value V *after* the cell pointed to by P. The insertion process is illustrated in Figure 14-13. We can outline the insertion procedure as follows:

```
PROCEDURE INSERT_AFTER(V, P)
    (Get a new cell and set Q to point to it)
    (Set the link of the new cell to point to the cell
     following the one pointed to by P)
```

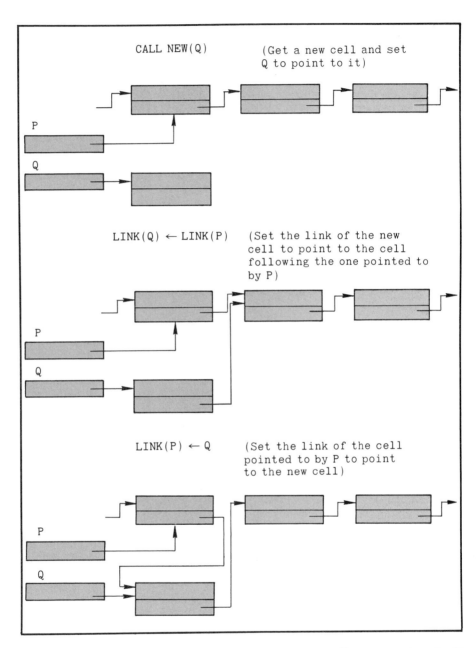

FIGURE 14-13. The procedure INSERT__AFTER(V, P) inserts a cell containing the value V after the cell pointed to by P. To interpret LINK(Q) ← LINK(P), set LINK(Q), the link component of the cell pointed to be Q, to point to the cell that is now pointed to by LINK(P), the LINK component of the cell pointed to by P.

```
(Set the link of the cell pointed to by P to point
 to the new cell)
(Set the value of the new cell to V)
END INSERT_AFTER
```

Filling in the details gives us:

```
PROCEDURE INSERT_AFTER(V, P)
   GLOBAL VALUE, LINK
   CALL NEW(Q)
   LINK(Q) ← LINK(P)
   LINK(P) ← Q
   VALUE(Q) ← V
END INSERT_AFTER
```

The procedure DELETE__AFTER(P) deletes the cell *following* the one pointed to by P.

Normally we will have found the cell we wish to delete using SEARCH. To delete it with DELETE__AFTER, we need a pointer to the preceding cell. This is why we modified SEARCH to return a pointer not only to the cell located by the search, but to the preceding cell as well.

Figure 14-14 illustrates the operation of DELETE__AFTER. We can outline the algorithm as follows:

```
PROCEDURE DELETE_AFTER(P)
   (Set Q to point to the cell following the one pointed
    to by P; Q points to the cell to be deleted)
   IF Q ≠ NIL THEN
       (Link around cell to be deleted: Set the link of
        the cell preceding the one to be deleted to point
        to the cell following the one to be deleted)
       (Return the deleted cell to the free-space list)
   END IF
END DELETE_AFTER
```

By enclosing the deletion instructions in the IF construction, we defend against the possibility that the user may attempt to delete the "cell" following the last cell on the list!

Filling in the details in this outline, we get:

```
PROCEDURE DELETE_AFTER(P)
   GLOBAL LINK
   Q ← LINK(P)
   IF Q ≠ NIL THEN
       LINK(P) ← LINK(Q)
       CALL RECYCLE(Q)
   END IF
END DELETE_AFTER
```

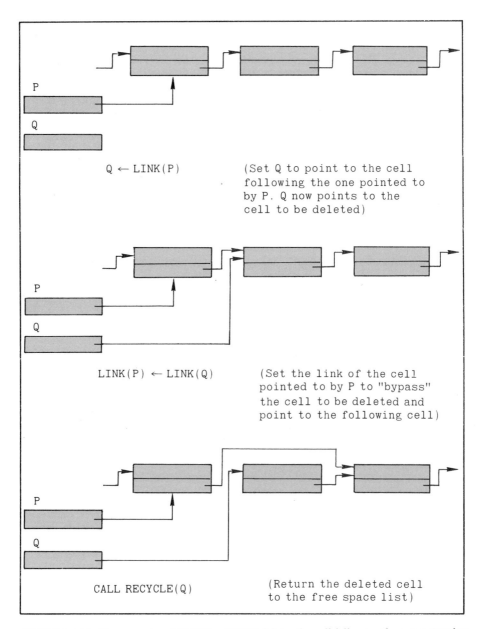

Q ← LINK(P)   (Set Q to point to the cell following the one pointed to by P. Q now points to the cell to be deleted)

LINK(P) ← LINK(Q)   (Set the link of the cell pointed to by P to "bypass" the cell to be deleted and point to the following cell)

CALL RECYCLE(Q)   (Return the deleted cell to the free space list)

FIGURE 14-14. The procedure DELETE__AFTER deletes the cell following the one pointed to by P.

14.2 Rings

An important limitation of a singly linked list is that one can only go forward in it, in the direction of the links. There is no provision for moving in the other direction.

A simple solution is to provide a link from the last cell on the list back to the header, as shown in Figure 14-15. The resulting list is called a *ring*. We can still only move in one direction in a ring. But at least when we get to the end, we can go back to the beginning and examine those cells preceding the one we started with. Specifically, we can start the search of a ring at any cell, instead of just at the header.

With a singly linked list, there is no problem in distinguishing the header from other cells. The header is always the first cell examined. In a ring, where the search may begin anywhere, we must have some way of identifying the header when we come to it. We will include in each cell a component IS_HEADER which will have the value TRUE for the header and the value FALSE for every other cell. Figure 14-16 shows a ring in which each cell has the component IS_HEADER. In the illustration, TRUE and FALSE are abbreviated to T and F.

We must redefine the array CELL for rings to include the component IS_HEADER in each record:

```
DECLARE 1 CELL( )
           2 VALUE
           2 IS_HEADER
           2 LINK
```

To search a ring for a given value, we start with an arbitrary cell and examine successive cells until we find the value we are looking for or until we get back to our starting point. When the header cell is encountered, it must be skipped over since it is not used to store an item on the list.

The procedure SEARCH(F, V, P, Q) searches a ring for the value V starting at the cell pointed to by F, which may be any cell. When SEARCH returns, Q points to the cell containing the desired value, and P points to the preceding cell. If the sought-after value is not found, the value of Q is NIL:

```
PROCEDURE SEARCH(F, V, P, Q)
    GLOBAL VALUE, IS_HEADER, LINK
    Q ← F
    FOUND ← FALSE
    REPEAT
       P ← Q
       Q ← LINK(Q)
       IF NOT IS_HEADER(Q) THEN
          IF VALUE(Q) = V THEN
             FOUND ← TRUE
          END IF
       END IF
    UNTIL (Q = F) OR FOUND
    IF NOT FOUND THEN
       Q ← NIL
    END IF
END SEARCH
```

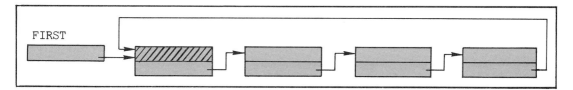

FIRST

FIGURE 14-15. A ring.

The search actually begins with the cell following the one pointed to by F and continues on around the ring. Each cell—except for the header—is examined to see if its VALUE equals the value of V. If such a cell is found, the repetition terminates, and the procedure returns with Q pointing to the cell found and P pointing to its predecessor. When we reach the cell pointed to by F, we have searched the entire ring. If the value has not been found, the repetition terminates, and the procedure returns with Q equal to NIL.

A ring is most useful when we have pointers to cells other than the header and so will not always begin a search with the header. For instance, the values on the ring could be in alphabetical order. We could maintain an index, which would contain a pointer to the first cell whose value starts with 'A', a pointer to the first cell whose value starts with 'B', and so on. Or, by giving a cell more than one LINK component, we can let it be on more than one list at the same time (see Figure 14-17). We may reach a cell by searching one list. Then we may wish to search some other list that cell is on, beginning of course with the cell at hand.

14.3 Doubly Linked Lists

A more generally useful solution to the problem of the one-way nature of singly linked lists is to include two links in each cell. One link points to the preceding cell; the other points to the following cell. The resulting list is said to be *doubly linked*.

In a doubly linked list, we can move in either direction with ease. On the other hand, a doubly linked list requires more memory than either a singly linked list or a ring, since each cell must contain two link components instead of one.

Figure 14-18 shows a doubly linked list. Note that the doubly linked list is also a ring, since the last cell is linked to the header. A doubly

FIGURE 14-16. A ring in which each cell has the component IS_HEADER. TRUE is abbreviated to T and FALSE to F.

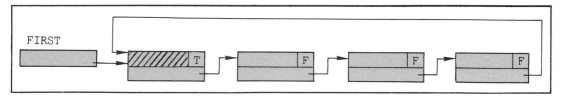

FIRST

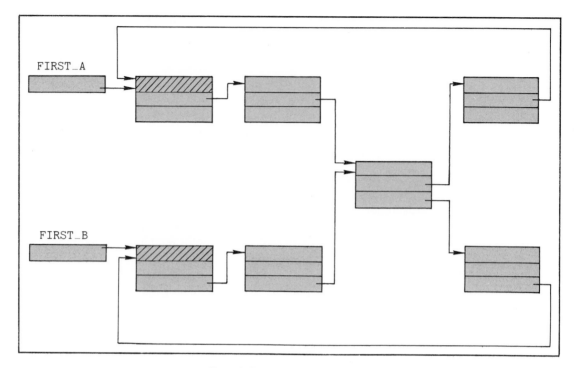

FIGURE 14-17. A cell can belong to more than one ring. A cell reached by a search along one ring can become the starting point for a search along the other ring.

linked ring provides the greatest possible flexibility in moving about on the list.

For a doubly linked list, we need two links per cell. Also, since the doubly linked list may be used as a ring, we need the flag IS__HEADER to identify the header cell:

```
DECLARE 1 CELL( )
         2 VALUE
```

FIGURE 14-18. A doubly linked list. Notice that a doubly linked list is also a ring, since the header and the last element are linked.

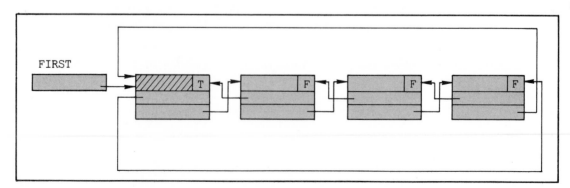

```
2 IS_HEADER
2 LEFT_LINK
2 RIGHT_LINK
```

LEFT_LINK points to the preceding cell; RIGHT_LINK points to the following one.

Searching. In searching a doubly linked list, one uses only one set of links, the right links or the left links, depending on the direction in which one wishes to search. The procedures SEARCH_LEFT(F, V, Q) and SEARCH_RIGHT(F, V, Q) differ only slightly from those already given. Writing these procedures is left as an exercise.

Notice that the search procedures for a doubly linked list do not return P, the pointer, to the preceding cell. The cell preceding or following the cell found can be obtained easily using LEFT_LINK(Q) or RIGHT_LINK(Q).

Memory Management. For doubly linked lists, we also maintain a free-space list, the first cell of which is pointed to by the global variable FREE. There is no reason for the free-space list to be doubly linked, however, since we never move around on the free-space list but just add or remove cells from its beginning. Thus, we can use only the right links to build the free-space list.

The procedures NEW and RECYCLE for doubly linked lists, then, will differ from those for singly linked lists only in notation. It is left as an exercise to write NEW and RECYCLE for doubly linked lists.

Insertion and Deletion. With insertion and deletion, we reach the point where we will need some substantially new procedures. The insertion and deletion procedures for doubly linked lists must cope with two links per cell, instead of only one, and are thus somewhat more complex than the corresponding procedures for singly linked lists.

Figure 14-19 shows the steps for inserting a cell after the one pointed to by P. We can outline the procedure INSERT_AFTER as follows:

```
PROCEDURE INSERT_AFTER(V, P)
    (Get a new cell from the free-space list, and set Q
     to point to it)
    (Let R point to the cell following CELL(P))
    (Link CELL(Q) in between CELL(P) and CELL(R))
        (Set right links in CELL(P) and CELL(Q))
        (Set left links in CELL(R) and CELL(Q))
    (Set VALUE(Q) to V)
END INSERT_AFTER
```

Replacing the comments with the appropriate algorithmic language statements gives us:

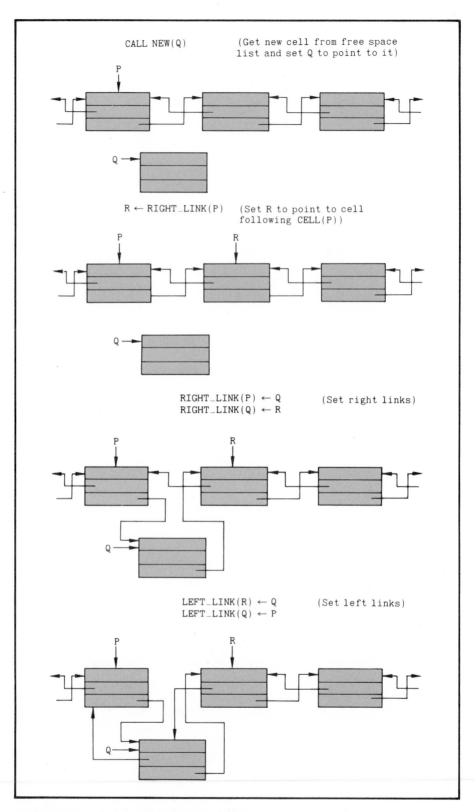

FIGURE 14-19. The procedure INSERT_AFTER(V, P) inserts a cell containing the value V after the cell pointed to by P.

```
PROCEDURE INSERT_AFTER(V, P)
   GLOBAL VALUE, LEFT_LINK, RIGHT_LINK
   CALL NEW(Q)
   R ← RIGHT_LINK(P)
   RIGHT_LINK(P) ← Q
   RIGHT_LINK(Q) ← R
   LEFT_LINK(R) ← Q
   LEFT_LINK(Q) ← P
   VALUE(Q) ← V
END INSERT_AFTER
```

For doubly linked lists, we also have INSERT__BEFORE, which inserts a cell *before* the one pointed to by P:

```
PROCEDURE INSERT_BEFORE(V, P)
   GLOBAL VALUE, LEFT_LINK, RIGHT_LINK
   CALL NEW(Q)
   R ← LEFT_LINK(P)
   RIGHT_LINK(R) ← Q
   RIGHT_LINK(Q) ← P
   LEFT_LINK(P) ← Q
   LEFT_LINK(Q) ← R
   VALUE(Q) ← V
END INSERT_BEFORE
```

Figure 14-20 illustrates the operation of INSERT__BEFORE.

For singly linked lists, we could only conveniently write a procedure DELETE__AFTER(P), which deletes the cell following the one pointed to by P. With doubly linked lists, we can write the more convenient DELETE(P).

Figure 14-21 illustrates the deletion operation. We can outline the needed procedure as follows:

```
PROCEDURE DELETE(P)
   IF (P does not point to the header cell) THEN
      (route the links from the cells before and after
       CELL(P) to bypass CELL(P))
      (Return CELL(P) to the free-space list)
   END IF
END DELETE
```

Filling in the details gives:

```
PROCEDURE DELETE(P)
   GLOBAL LEFT_LINK, RIGHT_LINK, IS_HEADER
   IF NOT IS_HEADER(P) THEN
      Q ← LEFT_LINK(P)
      R ← RIGHT_LINK(P)
      RIGHT_LINK(Q) ← R
```

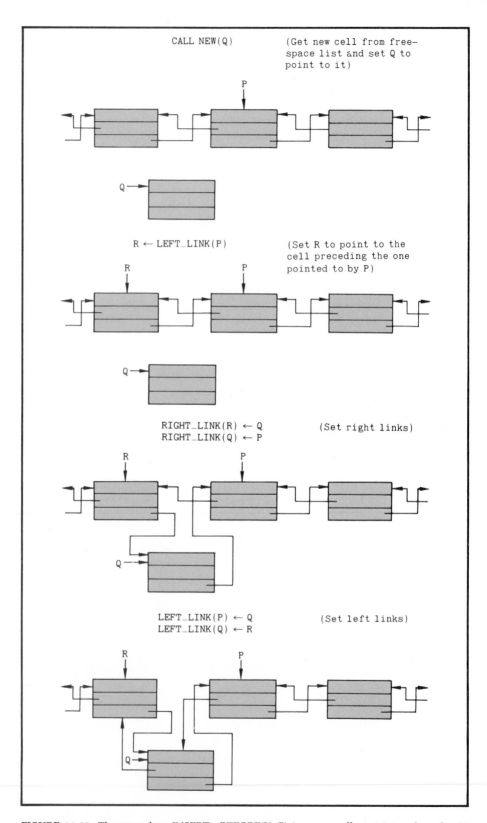

FIGURE 14-20. The procedure INSERT__BEFORE(V, P) inserts a cell containing the value V before the cell pointed to by P.

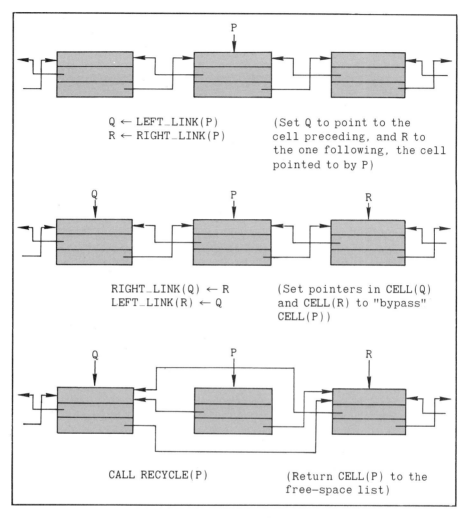

FIGURE 14-21. The procedure DELETE(P) deletes the cell pointed to by P.

```
        LEFT_LINK(R) ← Q
        CALL RECYCLE(P)
     END IF
END DELETE
```

Review Questions

1. Frequently a programmer wishes to model some portion of the real world inside the computer. Give two things that must be represented in such a model.

2. What are *entities*? How are they represented inside the computer?

3. What relations hold between the elements of a one-dimensional array? A two-dimensional array?

4. How can pointers be used to represent relationships?

5. What is a *plex*?

6. Describe in words the structure of a singly linked list.

7. What is the value NIL used for? What are some numerical values that can be used for NIL? Why those particular values?

8. What is the function of a *header record*?

9. What is the *free-space list*? Describe the operation of the procedures NEW and RECYCLE.

10. Using diagrams and words, describe the processes of insertion and deletion for a singly linked list.

11. What is a *ring*? In searching for a given value, what feature does a ring have that a singly linked list does not have?

12. Will the INSERT__AFTER procedure be the same for a ring as for a singly linked list? If not, what modification is needed?

13. Will the DELETE__AFTER procedure be the same for a ring as for a singly linked list? If not, what modification is needed? (*Hint:* Thou Shalt Not Delete the Header.)

14. Describe in words the structure of a doubly linked list.

15. What is the advantage of a doubly linked list over a singly linked list? The disadvantage?

16. Why do we have procedures INSERT__AFTER and INSERT__BEFORE for a doubly linked list, whereas we have only INSERT__AFTER for a singly linked list?

17. Using words and diagrams, describe the process of inserting a cell *before* a given cell in a doubly linked list.

18. Using words and diagrams, describe the process of inserting a cell *after* a given cell in a doubly linked list.

19. Using words and diagrams, describe the process of deleting a given cell in a doubly linked list.

20. Lists can be stored either as arrays or linked lists. Give one advantage of arrays over linked lists. Give two advantages of linked lists over arrays.

Exercises

1. Write a version of the procedure ACCESS for a ring.

2. Write the procedures SEARCH__LEFT and SEARCH__RIGHT for a doubly linked list.

3. Write a procedure ACCESS(F, I, J, Q) for a doubly linked list. F can point to any cell on the list. I is the number of the cell pointed to by F. (I is 0 for the header, 1 for the cell following the header, and so on.) J is the number of the desired cell. If J is less than I, ACCESS will move to the left until it reaches the Jth cell. If J is greater than I, ACCESS will move to the right until it reaches the Jth cell. ACCESS returns with Q pointing to the Jth cell or NIL if there was no Jth cell.

4. Write two versions of the procedure NEW for doubly linked lists. For the first version, assume that the free-space list is singly linked, using right links only. For the second, assume that the free-space list is doubly linked. (The left link of the first cell and the right link of the last one will be NIL.)

5. As in Exercise 4, write two versions of RECYCLE for doubly linked lists.

6. Suppose that a machine malfunction causes an erroneous change in the link component of a cell. With a singly linked list, all the rest of the list would be lost, since there is no way of telling where the next cell is stored. With a doubly linked list, an error in a single link—either a right link or a left link—can be detected and repaired. Write a procedure that will examine a doubly linked list in which a single link has been given an arbitrary value and that will detect and correct the error.

7. *Text Editor.* Most interactive computing systems feature a text editor, in which lines of text are stored inside the computer, and the user can insert, delete, change, and list (print out) portions of the text until satisfied with the result. Such editors often store the text as a singly linked list of lines.

Suppose the text is stored as a singly linked list, as follows:

```
DECLARE 1 CELL( )
          2 LINE_NUMBER
          2 LINE_TEXT
          2 LINK
```

The linked list of lines is kept in line number order. Thus, if the list contained lines 100, 110, and 120, and line 115 was inserted, it would be inserted between 110 and 120.

Write the following procedures:

INSERT(NUMBER, TEXT). If a line with a number equal to NUMBER is already present, then replace its text with the value of TEXT. Otherwise, insert a new line—in the proper position—with line number NUMBER and text TEXT.

Modify INSERT so that if the value of TEXT is the null string, no new line will be inserted, and if there is already a line with line number equal to NUMBER, that line will be deleted.

DELETE(FIRST, LAST) Delete all lines whose line numbers are in the range FIRST through LAST.

LIST(FIRST, LAST). Print out all lines whose line numbers lie in the range FIRST through LAST.

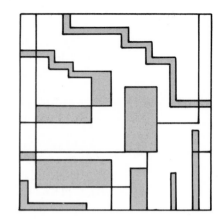

Chapter 15

Trees

A *tree* is a branching structure, as shown in Figure 15-1. The reason for the name will be evident if the figure is turned upside down: Trees in computer science are usually drawn upside down relative to their natural counterparts.

Trees have two important uses in computer science. First, a tree can represent a hierarchical structure. Second, a tree can represent a branching or forking path.

We are already familiar with trees representing hierarchical structures. The hierarchy diagrams we have used in discussing modules and records are nothing but trees. The organizational chart of a corporation is another example of a tree representing a hierarchy.

A game such as chess gives us an example of a tree used to represent a forking path. As shown in Figure 15-2, the player with the next move has a certain number of moves from the current position. Each move leads to a new position. From each new position, the opponent has a number of moves, and each of those leads to still another position. We can think of the players as moving along a forking path, each position corresponding to a fork in the path and each move corresponding to the choice of a particular path at the fork.

15.1 Definitions and Terminology

The points at which the lines come together in a tree are called *nodes*. (The word "node" comes from a word meaning "knot.") Much of the remaining

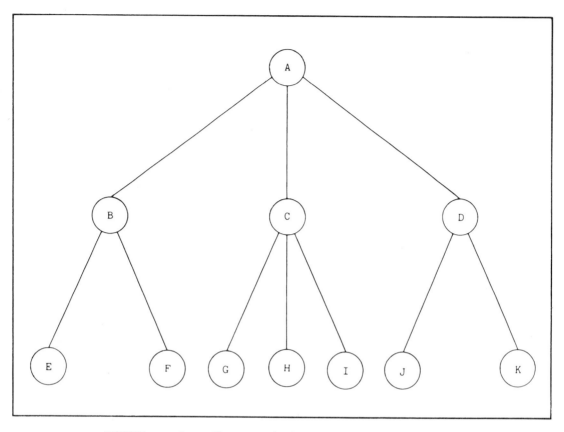

FIGURE 15-1. A tree. If you turn the drawing upside down, you will see that it resembles a natural tree.

terminology for trees comes from two sources: natural trees and family trees.

From natural trees: The topmost node of the tree is called the *root*. The bottommost nodes are called the *leaves*. The lines connecting the nodes are called the *branches*. (See Figure 15-3.)

From family trees: As shown in Figure 15-4, a node is said to be the *parent* of those immediately below it, which are said to be its children. All of the children of a given parent are said to be *twins* or *siblings*.

(*Father*, *son*, and *brother* as well as *mother*, *daughter*, and *sister* are sometimes used in place of parent, child, and twin. But rather than choose a particular "sex" for the tree, most modern writers use parent, child, and twin or sibling.)

The *descendants* of a node are the node's children, its children's children, its children's children's children, and so on.

Any node of a tree, together with all its descendants, forms a tree in its own right, as shown in Figure 15-5. This tree is said to be a *subtree* of the original tree. Note two extreme cases. The entire tree is a subtree of itself, and each leaf is a subtree consisting of only a single node.

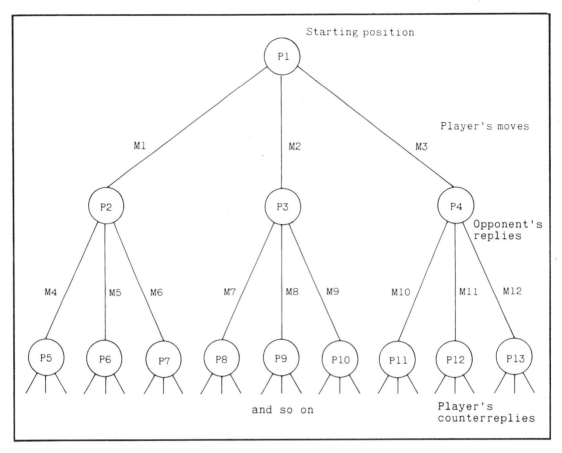

FIGURE 15-2. A game tree. The *nodes* (circles) represent game positions; the *branches* (lines) represent moves from one position to another.

So far, we haven't formulated a formal definition of a tree. We can now do so:

A tree consists of a node, called its root, and zero or more subtrees, each of which is itself a tree.

This is called a *recursive definition*, since the thing defined appears in the definition: A tree is partially defined in terms of itself. A recursive definition must be applied repeatedly to construct an example of the object being defined.

Figure 15-6 illustrates this principle for trees. Applying the definition once gives us a root and several subtrees. (The subtrees are represented by boxes.) The definition is applied again to each of the subtrees. The definition eventually terminates when all outstanding subtrees are chosen to consist of roots alone, with no further subtrees. These "root only" subtrees are the leaves of the tree.

The subtrees referred to in the definition are said to be *the subtrees of the root*. In general, the subtrees of a node are the subtrees whose roots are the children of the node.

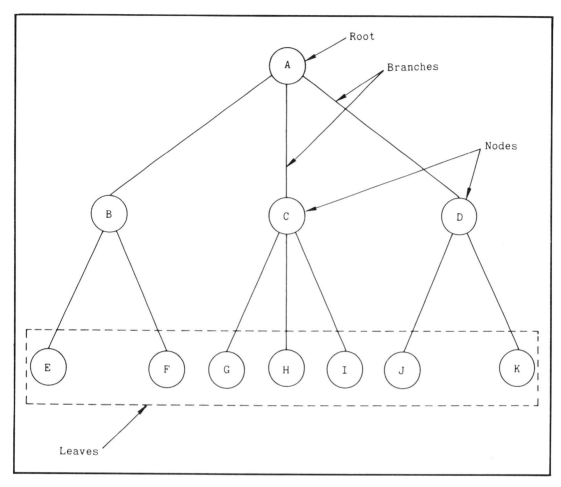

FIGURE 15-3. An illustration of the terms *root, branch, node,* and *leaf.*

Other definitions associated with trees can be put in recursive form. For instance, we can assign a *level number* to each node with the following statements:

■ *The level number of the root is 1.*

■ *The level number of a child of a node is the level number of the node plus 1.*

As shown in Figure 15-7, these statements assign a unique level number to each node.

Since the definition of a tree is recursive, we can use recursive procedures to process a tree. A recursive procedure, you remember, is one that calls itself. A recursive procedure can process every node of a tree by processing the root and then calling itself to process the nodes of each subtree.

Sometimes we would like to be able to display the structure of a tree

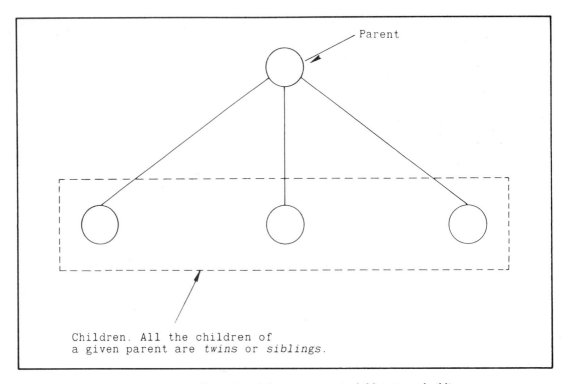

FIGURE 15-4. An illustration of the terms *parent*, *child*, *twin*, and *sibling*.

without actually having to draw a diagram. We need some *notation* for a tree. Two commonly used techniques for notating trees are *indentation* and *parentheses*.

We are already familiar with an indented tree notation from our study of records. Thus, the tree in Figure 15-8 can be represented by:

```
1 A
   2 B
      3 C
      3 D
      3 E
   2 F
      3 G
         4 H
         4 I
      3 J
```

The level numbers are not needed; the indentation displays the structure of the tree perfectly, and the reader can count off the levels:

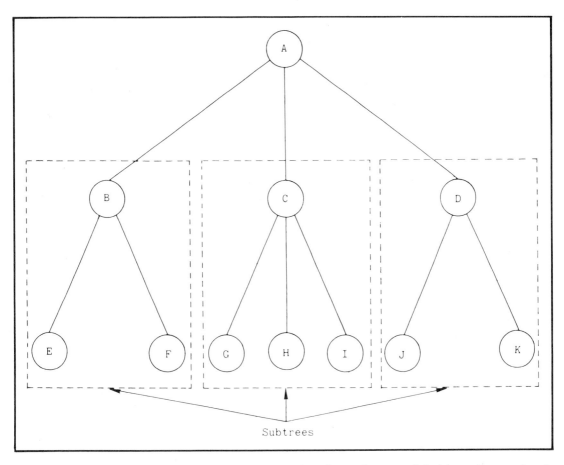

FIGURE 15-5. Subtrees. In additon to the subtrees shown, each leaf is a subtree, and so is the entire tree.

```
A
    B
        C
        D
        E
    F
        G
            H
            I
        J
```

Note that the roots of the subtrees of a given node are indented once with respect to that node.

Instead of indenting the subtrees of a node, we can enclose them in parentheses instead. This gives a more compact notation:

A(B(C D E) F(G(H I) J))

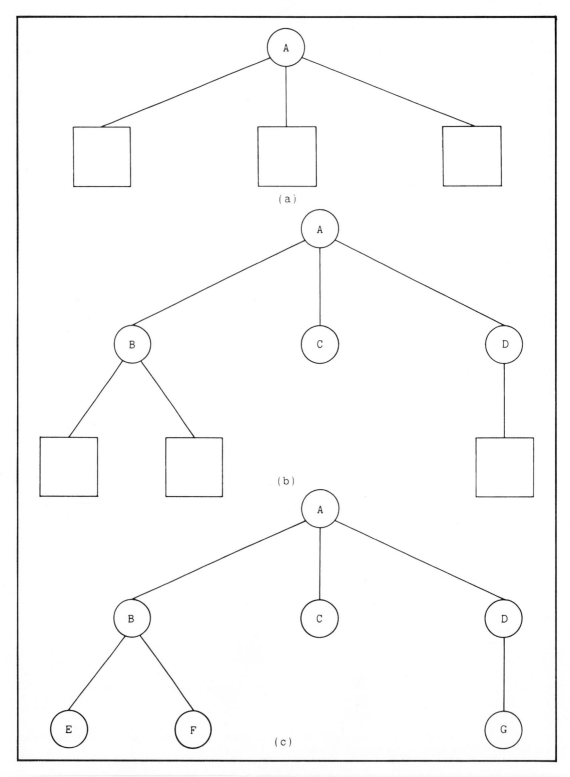

FIGURE 15-6. The recursive definition of a tree. The circles represent nodes; the squares represent subtrees.

308

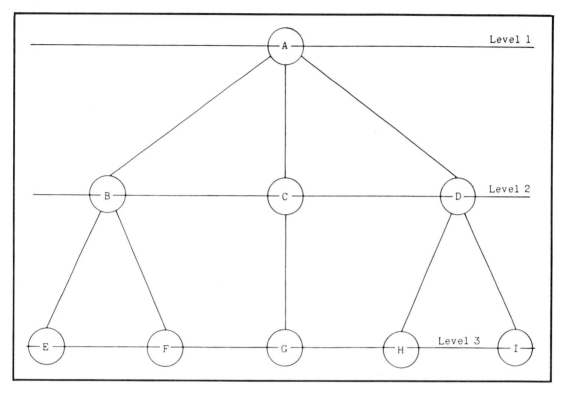

FIGURE 15-7. Level numbers. The level number of the root is 1. The level number of any other node is one greater than the level number of its parent.

Conversely, when parentheses are encountered in mathematics or computer science, especially parentheses within parentheses, then a tree structure is at hand.

15.2 Traversal and Linear Representations

To process tree-structured data, we usually either examine or carry out some operation on each node of the tree. Let's say that we *visit* a node when we examine it or manipulate it in some way. An orderly scheme for visiting each node of a tree is called a *traversal*.

A related problem is representing a tree as a list of nodes. Such a representation is said to be *linear*, since the nodes are laid out in a straight *line*.

In what order should the nodes be placed on the list? Usually, this will be the same order in which they are visited by a particular traversal scheme. We can use the traversal to construct the list from the tree. And if we later want to visit each node using the same traversal scheme, we need only scan the list from top to bottom.

Note that a linear representation constructed using one traversal scheme is of little use if we wish to visit the nodes using some other tra-

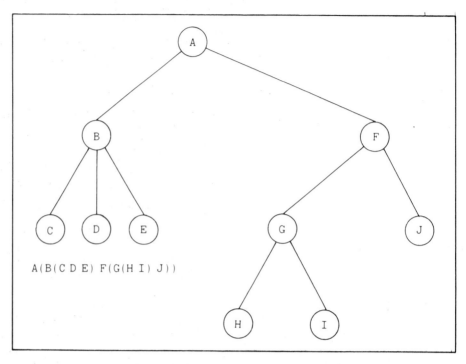

FIGURE 15-8. A tree together with its representation in parenthesis notation.

versal scheme. The choice of a linear representation, then, is determined by the order in which we wish to visit the nodes.

Preorder Traversal. In a preorder traversal, a node is visited *before* any of its descendants are visited. We can define a preorder traversal by the following two statements:

■ *Visit the root of the tree.*

■ *Do a preorder traversal of each of the subtrees of the root, taking the subtrees in left-to-right order.*

This is a recursive definition, since a preorder traversal of a tree is defined in terms of a preorder traversal of each subtree.

Figure 15-9 shows a preorder traversal of the tree:

A(B(C D) E(F(G)) H(I(J K) L(M N O)))

The order in which the nodes are visited is

A B C D E F G H I J K L M N O

The order is the same as the order in which the nodes occur in the

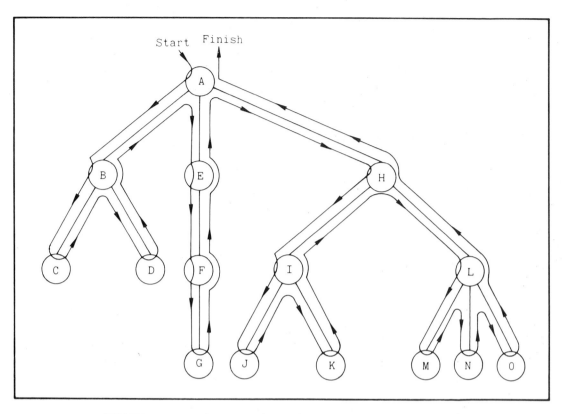

FIGURE 15-9. Preorder Traversal. A node is "visited" when the path goes through it, but not when the path goes around it.

parenthesized notation for the tree. This is no accident, for the parenthesized notation is based on a preorder traversal.

This raises the general question: What additional information must be provided, besides just the list of nodes, so that a tree can be uniquely reconstructed from a preorder list of its nodes? The answer is that we must show how the nodes are grouped into subtrees. We already know one solution. We can use parentheses, or some equivalent symbols, to enclose each subtree. This just gives us back our parenthesis notation:

A(B(C D) E(F(G)) H(I(J K) L(M N O)))

Figure 15-10 illustrates how the tree can be reconstructed from the parenthesis notation. First, remove the one node that is not inside any parentheses:

A

This is the root of the tree. Now remove the outside parentheses from the remaining nodes:

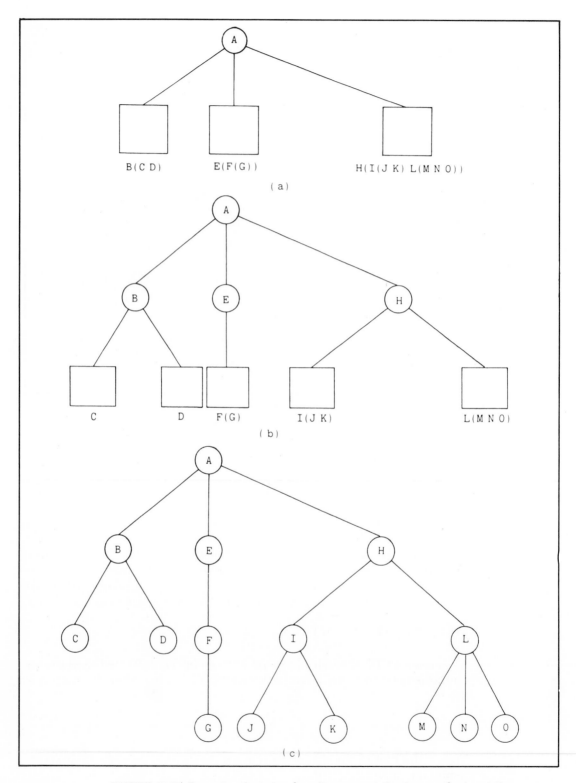

FIGURE 15-10. Reconstructing a tree from its representation in parenthesis notation.

```
B(C D)    E(F(G))    H(I(J K) L(M N O))
```

This gives the subtrees of the root, each in parenthesis notation. The construction just given is then applied recursively to the subtrees to translate them from parenthesis notation into the corresponding tree.

Another technique we have already encountered is level number notation. Suppose each node carries an indication of the level on which it occurs. Thus, C3 means node C on level 3. Our preorder list becomes:

```
Al B2 C3 D3 E2 F3 G4 H2 I3 J4 K4 L3 M4 N4 O4
```

To show that the tree can be uniquely reconstructed from this list, we convert the list to parenthesis notation. The rules for doing so are:

Whenever the level number increases by 1, insert a left parenthesis. Thus,

```
B2 C3     translates into     B (C
```

but

```
C3 D3     translates into     C D
```

Whenever the level number decreases by 1, insert a right parenthesis. Thus,

```
D3 E2     translates into     D) E
```

and

```
G4 H2     translates into     G)) H
```

At the end of the list, add enough right parentheses to bring the level number back up to 1. Thus,

```
O4        translates into     O)))
```

You should verify that these rules translate the preorder list with level numbers into the parenthesized list, from which we already know the tree can be reconstructed.

A third approach is to provide each node with an indication of how many children it has. Thus, A_3 means node A, which has three children. With this convention, our preorder list becomes:

$$A_3 \; B_2 \; C_0 \; D_0 \; E_1 \; F_1 \; G_0 \; H_2 \; I_2 \; J_0 \; K_0 \; L_3 \; M_0 \; N_0 \; O_0$$

We reconstruct the tree by reconstructing the preorder traversal, as shown in Figure 15-11. We put A down as the root and draw three "dangling branches" below it, since we know A has three children. We then place B on the leftmost dangling branch, and draw two more dangling

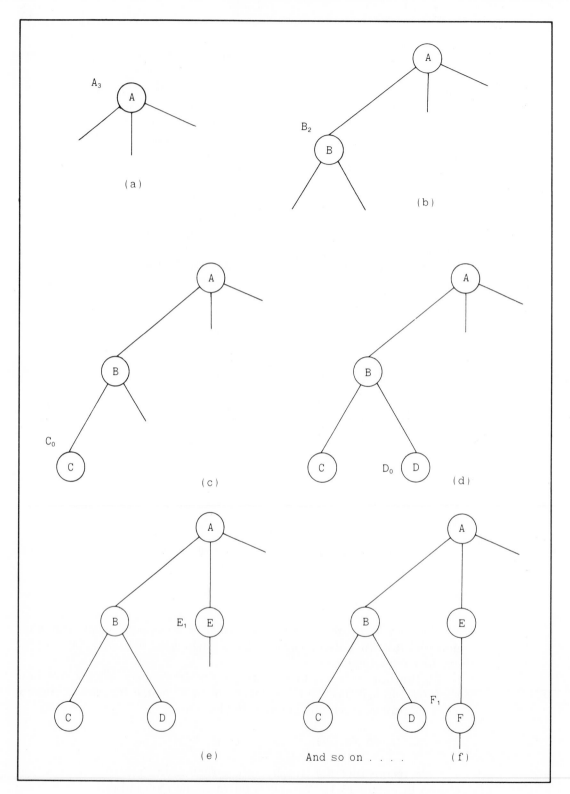

FIGURE 15-11. Reconstructing a tree from a preorder list of nodes that indicates how many children each node has.

branches below it. We continue in the same way, always hanging the next node in the preorder list onto the leftmost dangling branch.

Postorder Traversal. Instead of visiting the root before traversing its subtrees, we can traverse the subtrees first and then visit the root. This scheme is called postorder traversal; it is formally defined by:

■ *Do a postorder traversal of each of the subtrees of the root, taking the subtrees in left-to-right order.*

■ *Visit the root of the tree.*

Figure 15-12 illustrates a postorder traversal of the same tree we used for an example in preorder traversal. The nodes are now visited in the order:

C D B G F E J K I M N O L H A

As with preorder traversal, merely the list of nodes is not enough to allow us to reconstruct the original tree. But we can use any of the same techniques—enclosing subtrees in parentheses, level numbers, or num-

FIGURE 15-12. Postorder traversal. The path is the same as for preorder traversal. But the nodes (except for the leaves) are visited at different points on the path.

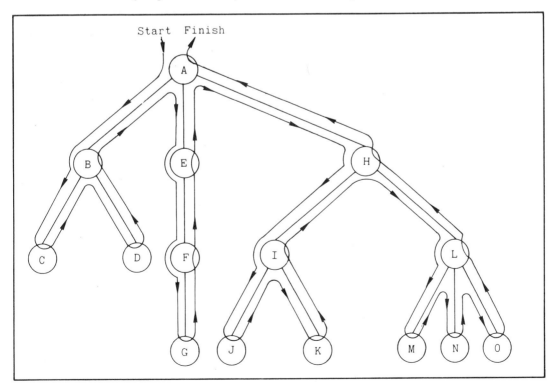

bers of children—to get lists from which the original tree can be reconstructed. The following shows each of the three forms:

```
((C D)B ((G)F)E ((J K)I (M N O)L)H)A
C3 D3 B2 G4 F3 E2 J4 K4 I3 M4 N4 O4 L3 H2 A1
C₀ D₀ B₂ G₀ F₁ E₁ J₀ K₀ I₂ M₀ N₀ O₀ L₃ H₂ A₃
```

The arguments that the original tree can be reconstructed from each of these postorder lists parallel the ones for preoder lists.

Binary Trees and Inorder Traversal. A binary tree is a tree in which each node has at most two children, as shown in Figure 15-13. The children are known as the *left child* and the *right child*, respectively. If a node has only one child, it may be either a *left child* or a *right child*.

In the same way, each node has at most two subtrees, the *left subtree* and the *right subtree*. If a node has only a single subtree, it may be either a left subtree or a right subtree.

A binary tree has another kind of traversal, *inorder traversal*, in which the root is visited in between the traversals of the two subtrees:

- *Do an inorder traversal of the left subtree, if any.*

- *Visit the root.*

- *Do an inorder traversal of the right subtree, if any.*

For the inorder traversal of the binary tree of Figure 15-13, the nodes are visited in the following order:

```
D B E A C F
```

FIGURE 15-13. A binary tree. Notice that in a binary tree a node can have a right child even though its left child is missing.

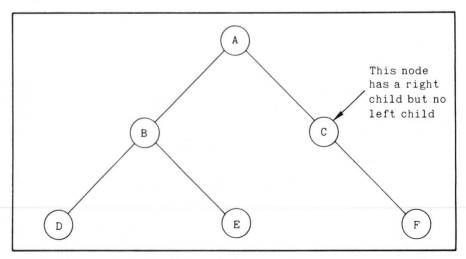

We can reconstruct the tree from the inorder list, provided the subtrees are enclosed in parentheses:

```
((D) B (E)) A (C (F))
```

15.3 Linked Representations

Linear representations of trees have two drawbacks: First, a linear representation is committed to a particular traversal scheme. Second, if the node list is stored as an array, insertion of new nodes and deletion of those no longer needed is clumsy. A linear representation is best when a tree is not to be changed frequently and when it will always be traversed in the same order.

Linked representations use pointers, rather than ordering, to delineate the tree structure. A linked representation need not be committed to a particular traversal scheme. And as we have already seen for linked lists, linked structures are easily modified through insertions and deletions.

Multiple Child Pointers. The most obvious way to represent a tree as a linked structure is to use a pointer for each branch of the tree. Most commonly, these point from parent to child and are known as *child pointers*.

Figure 15-14 shows a tree represented using multiple child pointers. The nodes of the tree come from an array, NODE, which has the following structure:

```
DECLARE 1 NODE( )
         2 VALUE
         2 NUMBER_OF_CHILDREN
         2 CHILD(NUMBER_OF_CHILDREN)
```

Thus, if P is a pointer to a node, then NODE(P).CHILD(1) points to the leftmost child of NODE(P), NODE(P).CHILD(2) points to the next to leftmost child of NODE(P), and so on.

Variable-length records are often inconvenient to implement. It's far more convenient to be able to set aside a fixed amount of memory for each record. For this reason, we often used fixed-length records for nodes, and set the unused pointers to NIL.

Suppose, for instance, we wish to represent a tree in which no node has more than three children. We can use records with three child pointers each:

```
DECLARE 1 NODE( )
         2 VALUE
         2 CHILD(3)
```

The unused child pointers are set to NIL, as shown in Figure 15-15. Note that memory space is wasted in each node in which one or more child pointers have the value NIL.

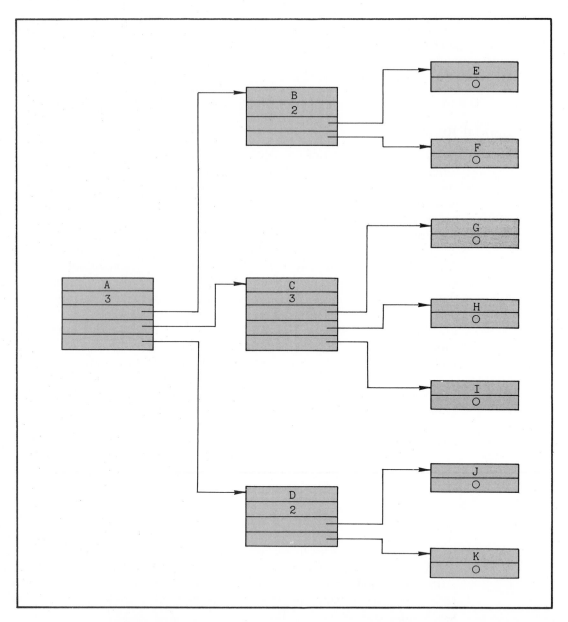

FIGURE 15-14. A representation of the tree of Figure 15-1 using multiple child pointers and variable-length records.

Child and Twin Pointers. We can overcome the problems of variable-length records or wasted space by using exactly two pointers in each node. One points to the leftmost child of that node. The other points to the next twin to the right. Figure 15-16 shows this arrangement.

Each node has the structure given by the following declaration statement:

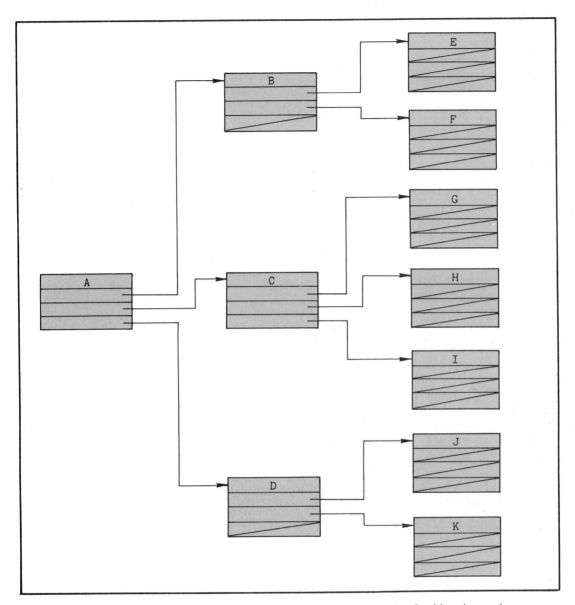

FIGURE 15-15. A multiple-child pointer representation using fixed-length records.

```
DECLARE 1 NODE( )
          2 VALUE
          2 LEFTMOST_CHILD
          2 RIGHT_TWIN
```

Thus, if P points to a node, then LEFTMOST__CHILD(P) points to the leftmost child of NODE(P), and RIGHT__TWIN(P) points to the next twin to the right of NODE(P).

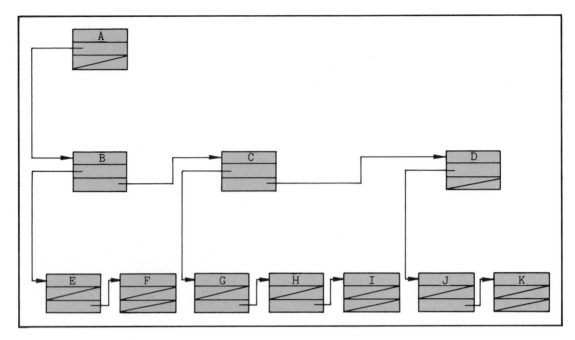

FIGURE 15-16. The child-and-twin pointers representation of the tree of Figure 15-1.

If a binary tree is represented using multiple child pointers, then each node will contain exactly two pointers, one to the left child and one to the right child. The "child-and-twin-pointers" method of representing a general tree also uses exactly two pointers per node. We can think of the child-and-twin-pointers method, then, as a method of representing any tree as a binary tree. Figure 15-17 shows the tree of Figure 15-1 redrawn as the equivalent binary tree implied by the child-and-twin-pointers representation.

Other Linking Techniques. Most linked representations of trees are based on either multiple child pointers or child and twin pointers. But just as we sometimes find rings or doubly linked lists more convenient than singly linked lists, so putting additional links in a tree may simplify processing. Some commonly used additional links are:

■ *Parent pointers.* Multiple child pointers and child and twin pointers are oriented toward top-down processing: we start with the root and work downward. If we also wish to do bottom-up processing—to work from leaves to root—we can place in each node a pointer to its parent. Occasionally, parent pointers are used by themselves, but more commonly they are used together with either multiple child pointers or child and twin pointers.

■ *Doubly linked twin lists.* In the child-and-twin-pointer method, the children of a given parent are joined by their twin pointers into a singly linked list. We can make this a doubly linked list, joining each child to a left twin

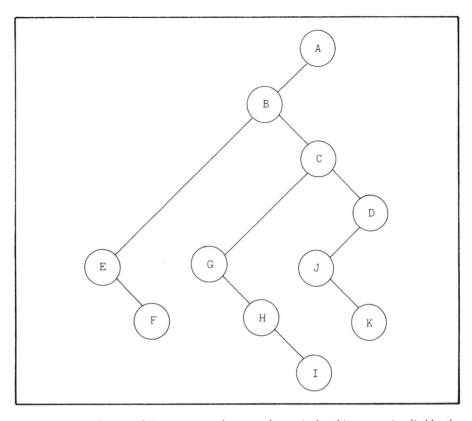

FIGURE 15-17. The tree of Figure 15–1 redrawn as the equivalent binary tree implied by the child-and-twin pointers representation.

as well as a right twin. This allows us to move either to the left or to the right in a twin list.

■ *Rings.* We can get the effect of rings in two ways. First, with child and twin pointers, we can join the leftmost twin and the rightmost twin, making the twin list into a ring. Second, with either method, we can give each leaf a pointer to the root. This gives us rings in the parent-child direction.

Figure 15-18 illustrates some of these possibilities.

15.4 Traversal Procedures

We can illustrate the use of the linked representations by writing the preorder and postorder traversal procedures for both multiple child pointers and child and twin pointers.

Multiple Child Pointers. Let P be a pointer to the root of the tree to be traversed. Let VISIT(Q) be a procedure that visits—does the required processing on—the node pointed to by Q.

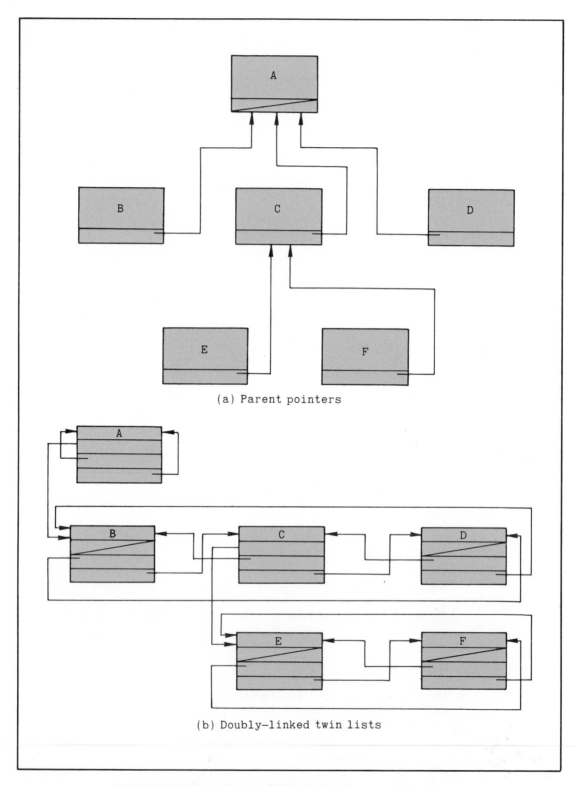

(a) Parent pointers

(b) Doubly-linked twin lists

FIGURE 15-18. Some other possibilities for linked representations.

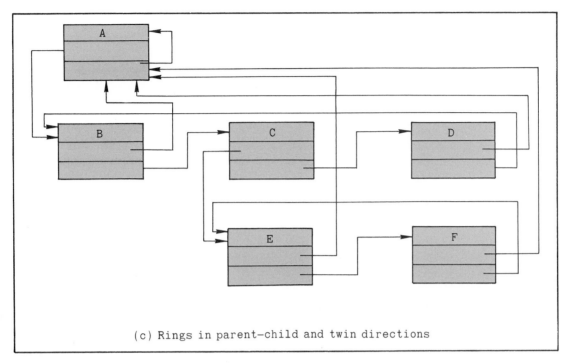

(c) Rings in parent–child and twin directions

FIGURE 15-18. (Cont.)

For preorder traversal, we visit the root of the tree to be traversed, then call the traversal procedure recursively to traverse each of its subtrees. We have:

```
PROCEDURE PREORDER_TRAVERSAL(P)
    GLOBAL NODE, NUMBER_OF_CHILDREN, CHILD
    CALL VISIT(P)
    N ← NUMBER_OF_CHILDREN(P)
    FOR I ← 1 TO N DO
        Q ← NODE(P).CHILD(I)
        CALL PREORDER_TRAVERSAL(Q)
    END FOR
END PREORDER_TRAVERSAL
```

Note that when NUMBER_OF_CHILDREN(P) is 0, the procedure does not call itself. This is what causes the recursion eventually to terminate, so that the procedure does not keep calling itself forever.

For postorder traversal, we traverse the subtrees of the root first and then visit the root:

```
PROCEDURE POSTORDER_TRAVERSAL(P)
    GLOBAL NODE, NUMBER_OF_CHILDREN, CHILD
    N ← NUMBER_OF_CHILDREN(P)
```

```
FOR I ← 1 TO N DO
   Q ← NODE(P).CHILD(I)
   CALL POSTORDER_TRAVERSAL(Q)
END FOR
CALL VISIT(P)
END POSTORDER_TRAVERSAL
```

Child and Twin Pointers. The traversal procedures using child and twin pointers are similar to those using multiple child pointers. The difference is that the children of a node form a linked list, instead of being accessed through an array of pointers.

For preorder traversal we have:

```
PROCEDURE PREORDER_TRAVERSAL(P)
   GLOBAL LEFTMOST_CHILD, RIGHT_TWIN
   CALL VISIT(P)
   Q ← LEFTMOST_CHILD(P)
   WHILE Q ≠ NIL DO
      CALL PREORDER_TRAVERSAL(Q)
      Q ← RIGHT_TWIN(Q)
   END WHILE
END PREORDER_TRAVERSAL
```

Note that if P points to a leaf, then LEFTMOST__CHILD(P) will be NIL, and the procedure will not call itself. Thus, again, the recursion is terminated, and the procedure does not call itself forever.

As before, POSTORDER__TRAVERSAL differs from PREORDER__ TRAVERSAL only in the position of CALL VISIT(P):

```
PROCEDURE POSTORDER_TRAVERSAL(P)
   GLOBAL LEFTMOST_CHILD, RIGHT_TWIN
   Q ← LEFTMOST_CHILD(P)
   WHILE Q ≠ NIL DO
      CALL POSTORDER_TRAVERSAL(Q)
      Q ← RIGHT_TWIN(Q)
   END WHILE
   CALL VISIT(P)
END POSTORDER_TRAVERSAL
```

15.5 Expression Trees

We will now look at two applications of trees. The first of these is the tree representation of expressions. This representation is basic to almost all compilers and interpreters.

An expression tree consists of two kinds of nodes: operator nodes and value nodes.

The *operator nodes* correspond to operators such as +, −, *, /, and **. An operator node has one subtree for each operand of the operator. We will only use binary operators here, so each operator node will have exactly two subtrees. But operator nodes with 1, 3, 4, and so on arguments are also possible.

The *value nodes* correspond to values to be operated upon. For simplicity, we will confine our values to real numbers, although expression trees can also be constructed for string or logical expressions. A value node has no subtrees. Thus, value nodes are the leaves of the expression tree.

Figure 15-19 illustrates operator and value nodes.

As mentioned, the subtrees of an operator node are its operands. An operand can be either a value or a subexpression that will evaluate to a value. For instance, in

3+5

the operator is +, and its operands are 3 and 5. The operator node for + will have as its subtrees the value nodes for 3 and 5, as shown in Figure 5-20a.

On the other hand, consider the expression:

(3+5)*(7−4)

The operands of the operator * are the values of 3+5 and 7−4. Thus, the subtrees of the operator node for * are the expression trees for 3+5 and 7−4 (see Figure 15-20b). Note that the parts of the expression in parentheses form subtrees.

In the expression

3+4*5

we know that the multiplication will be done before the addition because

FIGURE 15-19. Operator and value nodes.

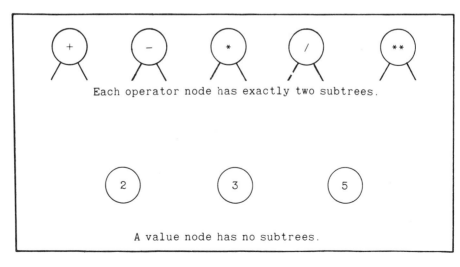

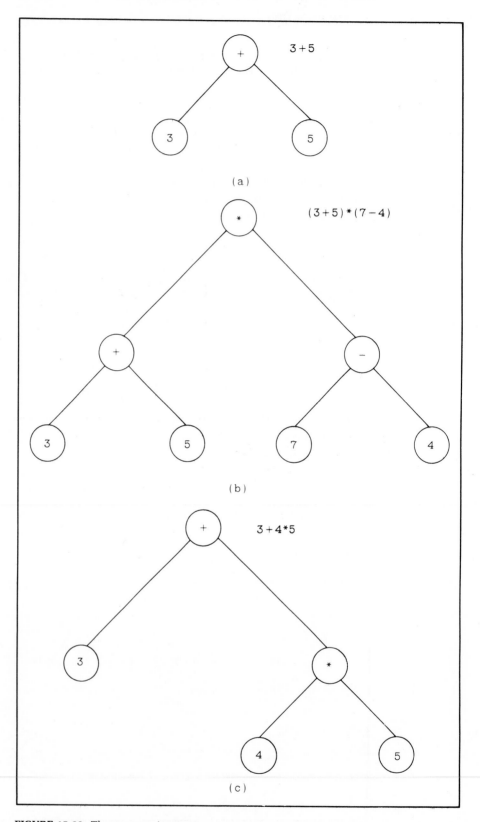

FIGURE 15-20. Three expression trees.

of the priority rules. Thus, this expression is evaluated as if it had been written:

$3 + (4*5)$

Hence, the operator node for + has two subtrees. One is the value node for 3; the other is the expression tree for 4*5 (see Figure 15-20c).

Since each operator node has exactly two subtrees, and each value node has none, our expression trees are *binary trees*. There are three ways, remember, of traversing a binary tree: preorder, postorder, and inorder. Each of these gives a linear representation of the tree. That is, each one gives a way of writing the expression as a list of symbols—a *notation* for the expression.

Consider the expression tree of Figure 15-21. If we write the operators and values as they occur in a *preorder traversal*, we get:

$* + 5 * 3 4 - 7 5$

This is the same as *prefix notation* or *Polish notation*: Each operator immediately precedes its operands.

Furthermore, we can reconstruct the expression tree from the prefix

FIGURE 15-21. The expression tree for the expression $(5 + 3*4)*(7 - 5)$.

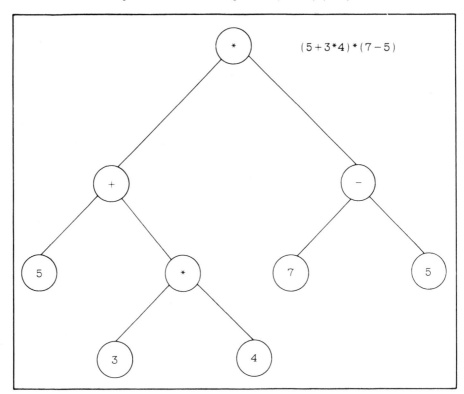

notation. The reason is that we can recognize the difference between operators and values. Each operator node has two children, each value node has none. Therefore, this expression is equivalent to

$$*_2 \ +_2 \ 5_0 \ *_2 \ 3_0 \ 4_0 \ -_2 \ 7_0 \ 5_0$$

where the subscripts give the number of children of each node. But we already know that, given a preorder list of nodes and the number of children of each node, the original tree can be reconstructed.

Now let's do a *postorder traversal* of the expression tree of Figure 15-21. The corresponding list of nodes is:

$$5 \ 3 \ 4 \ * \ + \ 7 \ 5 \ - \ *$$

This corresponds to *postfix notation*, or *reverse Polish notation*, or *RPN*, since each operator immediately follows its operands. Again, since the number of subtrees for value and operator nodes are known, the postfix expression is equivalent to

$$5_0 \ 3_0 \ 4_0 \ *_2 \ +_2 \ 7_0 \ 5_0 \ -_2 \ *_2$$

and the original tree can be reconstructed from the expression.

An *inorder traversal of the same tree gives us*

$$5 \ + \ 3 \ * \ 4 \ * \ 7 \ - \ 5$$

which corresponds to *infix notation*. However, it is now impossible to reconstruct the original tree merely by inspecting the inorder list of nodes. For instance, considering simply the part

$$5 \ + \ 3 \ * \ 4$$

it is impossible to say whether + has subtrees 5 and 3 * 4, or whether * has subtrees 5 + 3 and 4.

The original tree can be reconstructed if subtrees are enclosed in parentheses:

$$((5) \ + \ ((3) \ * \ (4))) \ * \ ((7) \ - \ (5))$$

Since we can distinguish values and operators at sight, we do not need to use parentheses around subtrees that consist of a single value, such as (5) or (3):

$$(5 \ + \ (3 \ * \ 4)) \ * \ (7 \ - \ 3)$$

Finally, we use operator priorities to permit the elimination of still more parentheses. Since * has a higher priority than +, we may eliminate the parentheses around 3 * 4, giving:

```
(5 + 3 * 4) * (7 - 3)
```

In infix notation, we do not need spaces between the items, since operators separate the operands and prevent them from running together. If we eliminate the spaces, we get the usual infix form of the expression:

```
(5+3*4)*(7-3)
```

Infix notation seems to be the most useful for human beings. When we look at an expression, we usually look for some overall pattern, instead of analyzing the expression character by character. The parentheses make the pattern of subexpressions—subtrees—apparent at a glance.

On the other hand, a computer processes an expression by scanning it character by character. The computer has no way of seeing the whole expression at a glance. What is the most useful notation for the computer? It is the one in which the operators and operands occur in the order in which the computer must scan them to evaluate the expression.

What order is most convenient for evaluation? The operands of an operator are, in general, subtrees. The operator is applied to the values of its operands, that is, to the values of the expression trees that are its subtrees. Obviously, then, an operator can be applied only after both of its subtrees have been evaluated. When the computer scans the expression tree to evaluate it, it must not scan the operator until it has scanned both of its subtrees, because only then can the operator be applied. The evaluation scan, then, is a *postorder traversal*. Thus, we confirm our statement in the chapter on stacks that postfix notation, or RPN, is the most convenient notation for expression evaluation by computer.

These considerations are fundamental to most compilers and interpreters. If an expression is to be compiled or interpreted without modification, carrying out all the operations in the same sequence specified by the programmer, then postfix notation is usually used.

Some compilers, however, attempt to *optimize* an expression, so as to make it easier to evaluate on the computer. For instance,

```
3*5+3*7
```

could be modified to

```
3*(5+7)
```

which gives same value with one less multiplication. And the statement

```
A ← 5*(C+4*D)+(C+4*D)**2
```

could be profitably replaced by

```
X ← C+4*D
A ← 5*X+X**2
```

preventing the expression C + 4*D from being evaluated twice.

Optimizing compilers must carry out more complicated manipulations of the expression than are involved in merely evaluating it. Thus, these compilers often use linked representations of the expression tree in preference to postfix notation.

15.6 Game Trees

As our second example of tree applications, let's try to see how trees are used by programs that play games, such as chess or checkers.

Consider a computer faced with a chess or checkers position and trying to decide what its next move should be. It will have a certain number of legal moves at its disposal. Each move will lead to a new game position. Like any player, the computer wishes to make the move that will lead to the position that is best for it and worst for its opponent.

The computer could attempt to make this decision by *pattern recognition*—analyzing the pattern of pieces on the board. This technique can be used to eliminate some "obviously" bad moves. But even human players find it difficult to choose a good move purely on the basis of pattern recognition. And current computer programs are considerably worse at pattern recognition than humans.

The second approach is to consider the consequences of each move. The computer "asks itself," What if I do make this move? What replies can my opponent make? And what counterreplies can I make to those? And how will my opponent reply to my counterreplies? And so on. This method of analysis is called *lookahead*. The computer looks ahead in the game to discover the possible consequences of each move.

As we mentioned at the beginning of this chapter, the lookahead process can be diagrammed as a tree, as in Figure 15-2. The root of the tree is the current position. The branches connecting the root with the level-2 nodes are the possible moves from the current position. The level-2 nodes are the positions resulting from those moves. The branches connecting the level-2 and level-3 nodes are the opponent's possible replies, and so on.

Suppose the lookahead process could always be carried through to the end of the game. That is, the leaves of the tree in Figure 15-2 would be positions in which the game was won, lost, or drawn. Then, for most games, the computer would be able to find a move that would assure it of at least a draw, regardless of its opponent's moves. And if the opponent made a single mistake, the computer would be able to find a move that would assure it of a win. This is the case for simple games such as Tic-Tac-Toe, in which you cannot beat the computer and, if you make one mistake, the computer will surely beat you.

For more complicated games such as chess, the number of nodes in the full game tree is astronomical. No computer could store all the nodes in memory or examine them all within a human lifetime. For nontrivial games, lookahead can be carried through only about five to ten levels in the tree.

We now have two problems. First, at each level, it is not possible to consider every possible move from a position for further exploration. We must somehow select the "most likely" moves, replies, counterreplies, and so on, if we are to get very far in the tree without running out of memory space or time.

Second, we must stop the lookahead long before we reach positions where the game is won, drawn, or lost. That is, the leaves of the tree in Figure 15-2 will not be positions in which the outcome of the game is known. How, then, can the computer tell which of those positions are best for it, and so are the ones to be aimed for?

One way to solve these problems is to use a so-called *static evaluation function*, which assigns a rating to a board position. "Static" means the rating assigned to a position is computed from the patterns formed by the pieces. No lookahead is done in working out the static evaluation function.

As an example of a *very simple* evaluation function for checkers, let $m_{computer}$ and $m_{opponent}$ be the number of men each side has, and $k_{computer}$ and $k_{opponent}$ the number of kings. Checkers experience shows that the relative value of kings and men is 3:2, that is, one should be willing to trade three men for two kings, or vice versa. Thus, the static evaluation function might be given by the expression:

$$3*(k_{computer} - k_{opponent}) + 2*(m_{computer} - m_{opponent})$$

In a position in which the computer had five men and two kings and the opponent has seven men and one king, the value assigned by the static evaluation function would be:

$$3*(2-1)+2*(5-7) = 3+2*(-2) = -1$$

The negative value means that this position is favorable to the opponent. Positions with positive ratings are favorable to the computer, and those with zero ratings favor neither side.

More complicated static evaluation functions are used in real checkers-playing programs, of course. These have terms for additional features of the position, such as the mobility of each side's pieces and the extent to which each side has occupied certain strategic squares.

One use of the static evaluation function is to restrict the number of moves to be explored further at each stage of the lookahead. Only a few moves leading to positions with the highest static evaluations are earmarked for further exploration.

But the most important use of the static evaluation function is to assign a rating to each leaf of the tree. These ratings are used to determine which leaf position the computer should aim for and so what its next move should be.

More specifically, we assign to each node in the tree the value of the best leaf position that can be reached from the position in question. With this done, then the correct move for the computer is the one that leads to the second-level position with the highest value. That is the position that will eventually lead to the best leaf position.

In determining the best leaf position that can be reached from a given position, we must be careful not to assume the cooperation of the opponent! Quite the contrary. Every time the opponent gets to move, he will choose a move that will lead to as poor a position as possible for the computer and as good a position as possible for himself. This must be taken into account.

We work out the value of each position from the values of the leaf positions using the following two rules:

1. When it is the computer's turn to move, it will move to the position having the best value. Therefore, the value of the current position is the largest of the values of any of its children.

2. When it is the opponent's turn to move, he or she will move to the position having the worst value for the computer. Therefore, the value of the current position is the smallest of the values of any of its children. Figure 15-22 illustrates these rules.

FIGURE 15-22. The rules for determining the value of a node from the values of its children. A circle represents a node in which it is the computer's turn to play. A triangle represents a node in which it is the opponent's turn to play.

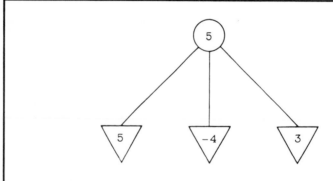

(a) The value of a node in which it is the computer's turn
to move is the *maximum* of the values of its children.

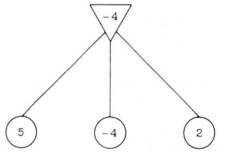

(b) The value of a node in which it is the opponent's
turn to move is the *minimum* of the values of its
children.

We can use these rules to assign a value to every position in the tree, as shown in Figure 15-23. We start with the values assigned to the leaves by the static evaluation function. We then work upwards, level by level, using the rules to calculate the values of the positions on the next highest level from the values of those on the current level. When we have assigned values to the positions on level 2, we can then determine the best move for the computer.

This method is often called the *minimax* technique, since the opponent is assumed always to choose the move that will *minimize* the value of the resulting position, while the computer chooses the move that will *maximize* it.

Although many refinements are possible, this method of position evaluation through lookahead, static evaluation functions, and the minimax technique is the foundation of most chess- and checkers-playing programs.

Review Questions

1. Give the two main areas of application for trees.

2. From what two areas is most of the terminology of trees drawn?

3. Draw a tree and indicate the *nodes*, the *branches*, the *root*, and the *leaves*.

4. Define *parent*, *child*, *twin*, and *descendant*. Illustrate your definitions with drawings.

5. Give two other sets of terms sometimes used in place of *parent*, *child*, and *twin*.

6. Give the recursive definition of a tree.

7. What feature of the definition of a tree characterizes it as recursive?

8. What is a *subtree*? What are the subtrees of a node?

9. What are the rules for assigning a level number to each node of a tree?

10. Describe and illustrate two notations for trees.

11. What is a *traversal* of a tree?

12. What is a *linear representation* of a tree?

13. What is the relation between traversals and linear representations?

14. Give the rules for a preorder traversal of a tree.

15. Give three ways in which additional information can be incorporated into a preorder or postorder list of nodes so that the tree can be reconstructed from the list.

16. Give the rules for a postorder traversal of a tree.

17. What is a binary tree?

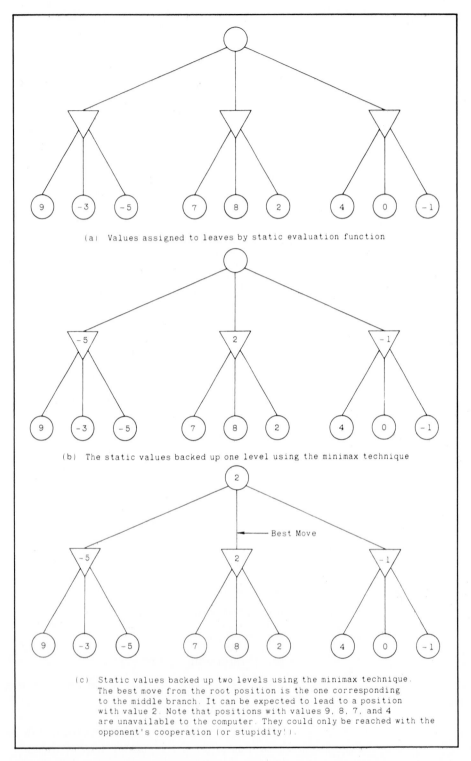

(a) Values assigned to leaves by static evaluation function

(b) The static values backed up one level using the minimax technique

Best Move

(c) Static values backed up two levels using the minimax technique. The best move from the root position is the one corresponding to the middle branch. It can be expected to lead to a position with value 2. Note that positions with values 9, 8, 7, and 4 are unavailable to the computer. They could only be reached with the opponent's cooperation (or stupidity!).

FIGURE 15-23. Assigning a value to every position in a game tree using the minimax technique. We start with the values assigned to the leaves by the static evaluation function and work upwards.

18. Define *left child, right child, left subtree,* and *right subtree* for a binary tree.

19. What are the rules for an *inorder traversal?*

20. Describe the *multiple-child-pointers* representation of trees.

21. Describe the *child-and-twin-pointers* representation of trees.

22. Describe in words the operation of each of the four traversal procedures given in this chapter.

23. Describe the relations between traversal methods and notations for algebraic expressions.

24. Give an argument that postfix notation (RPN) is best suited for expression evaluation by computer (provided that more complicated manipulations, such as rearranging the expression to simplify the calculation, are not to be attempted).

25. Describe how a game-playing program goes about determining its next move.

Exercises

1. Write a function EVALUATE(P) whose argument, P, points to the root of an expression tree, and whose value is the value of the expression.

The nodes of the expression tree are defined as follows:

```
DECLARE 1 NODE( )
           2 OPERATOR_OR_VALUE
           2 IS_VALUE
           2 LEFT_CHILD
           2 RIGHT_CHILD
```

The value of OPERATOR__OR__VALUE is a string such as '+', '*', '5', '−100', or '25.25'.

IS__VALUE is TRUE for a value node and FALSE for an operator node.

For an operator node, LEFT__CHILD and RIGHT__CHILD point to the left and right children of the node. For a value node, these components are unused.

The basic logic of EVALUATE(P) is: *If P points to a value node, then return the corresponding value. If P points to an operator node, then evaluate its left and right subtrees, apply the operator to the resulting values, and return the result.* As mentioned in the text, this logic implies a postorder traversal of the expression tree.

2. Write a function VALUE__OF(P) whose argument P points to a node of a game tree and which returns the value of the corresponding position to one player. (That player is hereafter called "the computer.")

The nodes of the game tree are defined as follows:

```
DECLARE 1 NODE( )
            2 POSITION
            2 IS_MY_MOVE
            2 LEFTMOST_CHILD
            2 RIGHT_TWIN
```

POSITION describes the current board position and will normally be either a string or an array. For this problem we will not have to worry about the details of POSITION.

IS_MY_MOVE is TRUE if it is the computer's move and FALSE if it is the opponent's move.

LEFTMOST_CHILD and RIGHT_TWIN are as described in the section on child and twin pointers. Note that a node is a leaf if and only if LEFTMOST_CHILD is NIL.

We assume that the static evaluation function, STATIC_VALUE(P), which returns the static value of the node pointed to by P, has already been written.

The logic of VALUE_OF(P) is as follows: *If the node pointed to by P is a leaf, then return STATIC_VALUE(P). Otherwise, if IS_MY_MOVE(P) is TRUE, then return the maximum of the values of the children of the node pointed to by P. If IS_MY_MOVE(P) is FALSE, return the minimum of the values of the children of NODE(P).*

In what order does this function traverse the game tree?

Chapter 16

Graphs
and Plexes

The word *graph* is the mathematician's term for a set of points connected by lines, as shown in Figure 16-1. More familiar terms for the same thing are *network*, *map*, *maze*, and *flowchart*. A tree, for instance, is a special case of a graph.

(This kind of graph has nothing to do with the kind used for plotting data. Unfortunately, the term *graph* is used in mathematics for two completely different ideas.)

A *plex*, as has been mentioned, is a collection of records, each of which contains one or more pointers to other records. The linked lists and linked representations of trees we have already studied are special cases of plexes. But the structure of the most general possible plex is that of a graph.

The most important use of a graph is to show *relationships* among entities. Each point on the graph corresponds to an entity. Each line corresponds to some relationship between the two entities connected.

16.1 Terminology

The points of a graph are called *nodes*. The lines connecting the points are called *arcs*.

If the arcs have directions associated with them, as indicated by an arrowhead on each arc, then the graph is *directed*. If there are no directions associated with the arcs, and hence no arrowheads, then the graph is *undirected*. Figure 16-2 shows directed and undirected graphs.

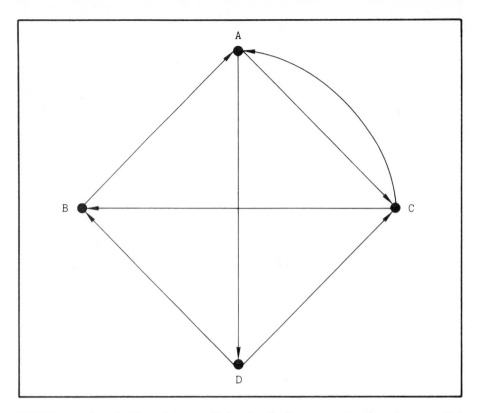

FIGURE 16-1. A graph. The points are called *nodes*; the lines connecting the points are called *arcs*.

FIGURE 16-2. Directed and undirected graphs.

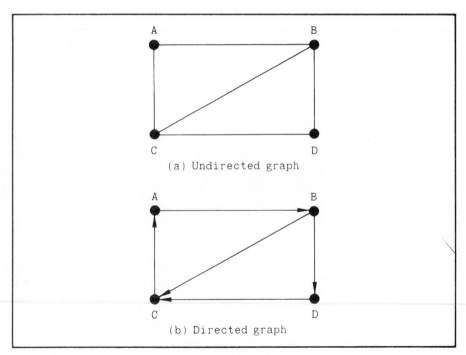

(a) Undirected graph

(b) Directed graph

The graphs used in computer science are usually directed, because the methods used for representing arcs have directions associated with them. If an undirected arc is needed, it is represented by two directed arcs joining the same nodes in opposite directions. (*Example:* A singly linked list represents the directed graph shown in Figure 16-3a. A doubly linked list represents the undirected graph shown in Figure 16-3b.)

Consider the directed arc shown in Figure 16-4. The arc joins node A to node B, with the arrowhead pointing to node B. We say that node B is the *immediate successor* of node A and that node A is the *immediate predecessor* of node B. The arc goes *from* node A *to* node B. Node A is the *initial node* of the arc; node B is the *final node*.

A graph is said to be *labeled* if the arcs carry labels as shown in Figure 16-5. Otherwise, it is *unlabeled*.

Suppose that we start at one node in a graph and move to another node, always following the arcs in the direction of the arrowheads. The nodes we pass through, including the starting and ending node, constitute a *path*. (See Figure 16-6.)

A path is a *cycle* if it begins and ends on the same node. A graph that contains no cycles is *acyclic*. Figure 16-7 illustrates a graph with cycles and an acyclic graph.

A directed graph is *strongly connected* if there exists a path between any two distinct vertices. The graph is merely *connected* if such a path exists when the directions of the arcs are ignored. If no path exists between

FIGURE 16-3. A singly linked list corresponds to the directed graph (a). A doubly linked list corresponds to the undirected graph (b). The doubly linked list is represented in memory, however, by a structure corresponding to the directed graph (c).

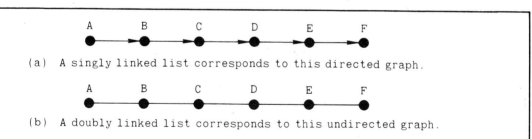

(a) A singly linked list corresponds to this directed graph.

(b) A doubly linked list corresponds to this undirected graph.

(c) To represent an undirected graph as a directed graph, we must supply two directed arcs for each undirected arc. Doing so gives a directed graph representation of a double linked list. The arcs of the directed graph correspond directly to links used to represent the list in memory.

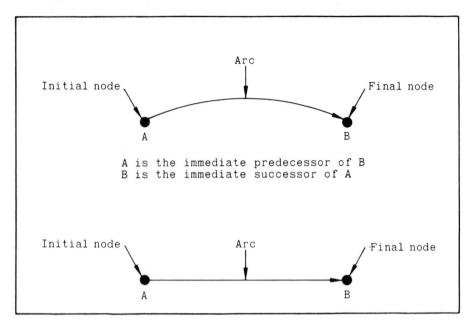

FIGURE 16-4. Arcs and nodes. An arc may be represented by either a straight line or a curve.

FIGURE 16-5. A labeled graph. Different arcs can have the same label. We can think of a label as specifying a particular kind of arc, rather than identifying an individual arc uniquely. Thus the graph shown contains two arcs of type a, two of type b, two of type c, and one of type d.

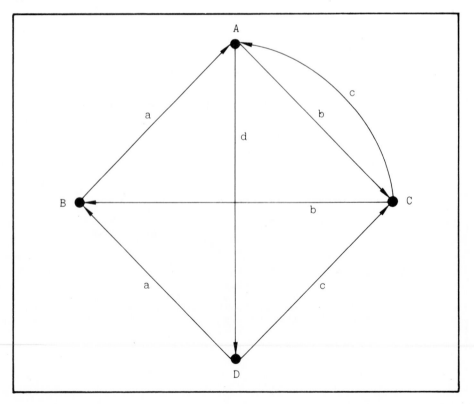

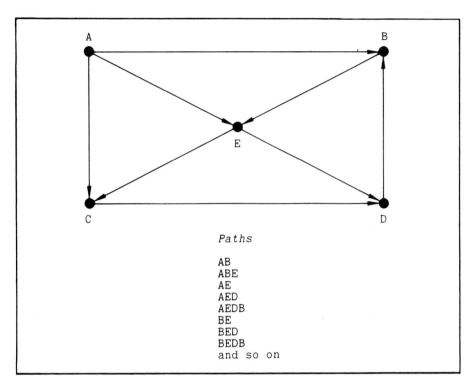

FIGURE 16-6. A graph and some of its paths.

some pair of nodes, even when the directions of the arcs are ignored, the graph is unconnected. Figure 16-8 illustrates strongly connected, connected, and unconnected graphs.

16.2 Tabular Representations

Just as trees have both linear representations and linked (or plex) representations, so there are two ways to represent graphs. In a *tabular representation*, a table specifies the arcs connecting the nodes. In a linked or plex representation, each node contains either a pointer to every node to which it is joined by an arc or a single pointer to a linked list of such pointers.

Ordered Pairs. One of the simplest ways to represent a graph is with a list of ordered pairs of nodes. The first node of each pair is joined to the second by an arc. The list contains one pair for each arc of the graph.

Such a list can be stored as a table of two columns. One column holds the initial node of each arc; the other column holds the final node. There is one row for each arc.

The following table represents the graph of Figure 16-9.

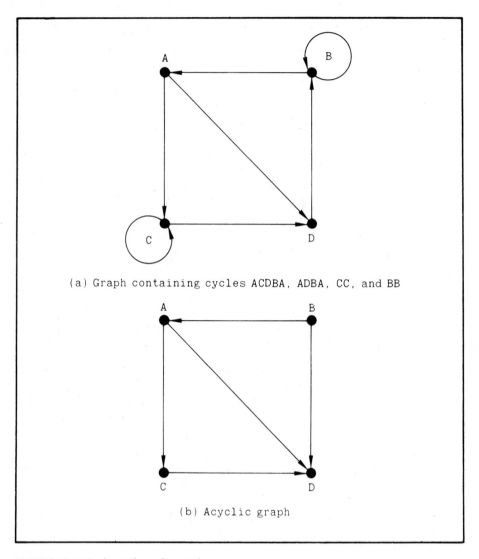

(a) Graph containing cycles ACDBA, ADBA, CC, and BB

(b) Acyclic graph

FIGURE 16-7. Cyclic and acyclic graphs.

Initial Node	Final Node
A	C
B	A
B	C
C	A
C	C
D	B
D	D
D	E
E	C

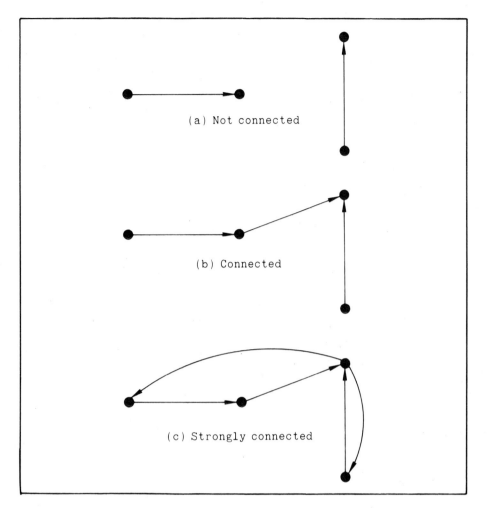

FIGURE 16-8. Unconnected, connected, and strongly connected graphs.

This table can be stored as a 9 × 2 array. The row entries can be in any order, but putting them in alphabetical order according to the names of one of the nodes may allow the entries to be accessed more efficiently.

Ordered Triples. If the graph is labeled, then the label of each arc must be specified. Thus, we must use *ordered triples* instead of ordered pairs. In the table, we need a new column for the arc labels.

Figure 16-10 shows a labeled version of Figure 16-9, where the arc labels are denoted by small letters. The table representation for this graph is:

Initial Node	Label	Final Node
A	a	C
B	a	A

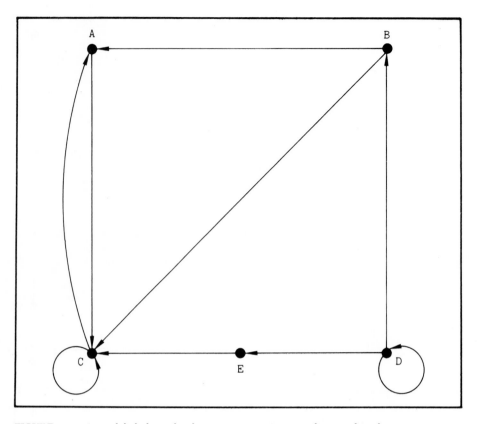

FIGURE 16-9. An unlabeled graph whose representations are discussed in the text.

B	b	C
C	b	A
C	a	C
D	c	B
D	a	D
D	b	E
E	c	C

This table can be stored as a 9 × 3 array. Such a representation is often referred to simply as a list of "triples."

Successor Lists. We can gather together all the final nodes having the same initial node and give a list of *immediate successors* for each node. Using Figure 16-9 as an example, we have:

Node	Immediate Successors
A	C
B	A C
C	A C

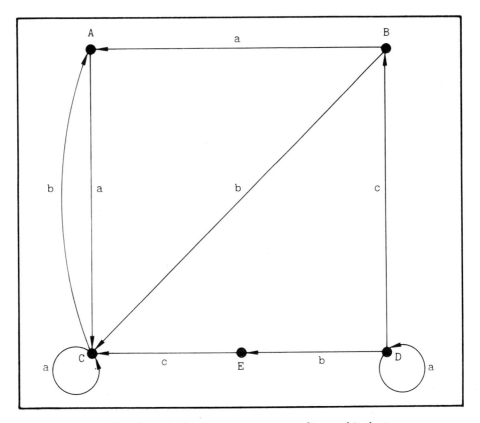

FIGURE 16-10. A labeled graph whose representations are discussed in the text.

D		B D E	
E		C	

This table can be stored as a 5 × 3 array. Note that some array elements are wasted, since not every element of every row has an entry. (The unused elements contain some special value indicating that they are unused.)

Transition Tables. Again, for labeled graphs, we must modify the table representation to show the arc labels. We can do this by labeling the immediate successor columns with the arc labels. Thus, Figure 16-10 can be represented by:

	Arcs		
Nodes	a	b	c
A	C		
B	A	C	
C	C	A	
D	D	E	B
E			C

The interpretation of this is that A is connected to C by arc a, B is connected to A by arc a and C by arc b, and so on.

This representation works best when each node is connected to only one other node by an arc with a given label. When one initial node is connected to more than one final node by arcs with the same label, then the table entry for the initial node and the arc is a *list* of final nodes. This is not so easy to store efficiently as a table in which each entry is a single node.

Such a table is often called a *transition table*. We think of the nodes as representing the *states*—the possible configurations of the parts—of some machine. The arc labels represent possible *inputs* to the machine. The table gives the *transition*—the change of state—that a particular input will cause when the machine is in a given state.

Thus, we can relabel the rows and columns of the table just given to get:

	Inputs		
States	a	b	c
A	C		
B	A	C	
C	C	A	
D	D	E	B
E			C

If the machine is in state A, then, and it receives input a, its state will change to C. If it is in state B, then input a will cause it to go to state A, input b will cause it to go to state C, and so on.

In each state there may be certain inputs that are erroneous. (*Example:* Moving the gear shift lever of a car when the clutch is not depressed is an erroneous input.) The table entries corresponding to erroneous inputs are blank.

Virtual machines such as operating systems, compilers, and interpreters are sometimes controlled by transition tables. When a transition table is used in this way, the entries corresponding to erroneous inputs contain pointers to error messages. When the user makes an error, the system uses the table to determine the appropriate error message. After the error message is printed, the virtual machine is placed in some standard starting state where it awaits further input from the user.

Connection Tables. Still another tabular representation is a table whose rows and columns are labeled by nodes. Each entry tells whether the nodes labeling that row and column are connected. If the arcs are labeled, the entry gives the label of the arc which makes the connection.

For unlabeled graphs, the entry need only be 0 if the arcs are not connected and 1 if they are. Thus, we can represent Figure 16-9 as follows:

	Final Node				
Initial Node	A	B	C	D	E
A	0	0	1	0	0
B	1	0	1	0	0
C	1	0	1	0	0
D	0	1	0	1	1
E	0	0	1	0	0

Each entry can be stored as a single bit, so the table can be stored very compactly.

The connection table for an unlabeled graph is also called an *incidence matrix*, a *bit table*, or a *bit map*.

For labeled graphs, the 1 entries are replaced with the appropriate labels:

	Final Node				
Initial Node	A	B	C	D	E
A	0	0	a	0	0
B	a	0	b	0	0
C	b	0	a	0	0
D	0	c	0	a	b
E	0	0	c	0	0

Now the table cannot be stored so compactly, since more than one bit is required to store each arc label.

16.3 Plex Representations

The most obvious way to represent a graph as a plex is directly equivalent to the multiple-child-pointers technique for trees. Each node contains a list of pointers to its immediate successors.

We can define the nodes for this representation as follows:

```
DECLARE 1 NODE( )
         2 VALUE
         2 NUMBER_OF_SUCCESSORS
         2 SUCCESSOR(NUMBER_OF_SUCCESSORS)
```

As with trees, VALUE is whatever useful information is stored in the node. NUMBER_OF_SUCCESSORS gives the size of the array SUCCES-SOR, whose elements are pointers to the immediate successors of the node in question.

Figure 16-11 shows the graph of Figure 16-9 represented using this technique.

If the graph is labeled, we must associate a label with each arc. One

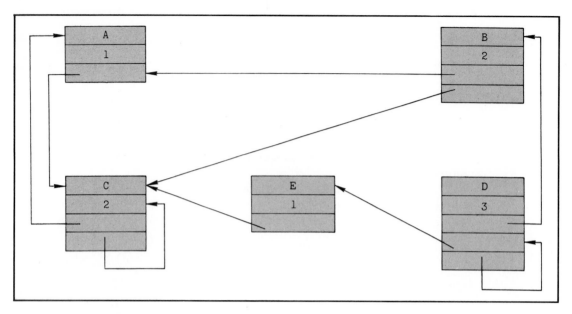

FIGURE 16-11. Plex representation of an unlabeled graph using pointers to immediate successors.

way is to make each element of SUCCESSOR a record with a LABEL component and a POINTER component:

```
DECLARE 1 NODE( )
         2 VALUE
         2 NUMBER_OF_SUCCESSORS
         2 SUCCESSOR(NUMBER_OF_SUCCESSORS)
            3 LABEL
            3 POINTER
```

SUCCESSOR has one element for each arc leaving the node in question. Each element has two components: LABEL, which is the label of the arc; and POINTER, which is the pointer to the final node of the arc in question.

Figure 16-12 shows the graph of Figure 16-10 represented using nodes of this type.

If no more than one arc with each label leaves any particular node, then we can reserve a pointer position for each label. Suppose, for instance, a graph has arcs labeled a, b, and c. We could use nodes defined as follows:

```
DECLARE 1 NODE( )
         2 VALUE
         2 SUCCESSOR_A
         2 SUCCESSOR_B
         2 SUCCESSOR_C
```

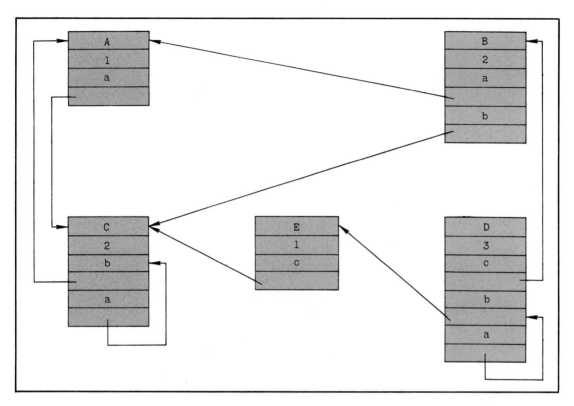

FIGURE 16-12. Plex representation of a labeled graph using pointers to immediate successors. Each pointer is preceded by a component giving the label of the corresponding arc.

SUCCESSOR__A points to the final node of the arc labeled a leaving the node in question. SUCCESSOR__B and SUCCESSOR__C point to the final nodes of the arcs labeled b and c. If no arc with a particular label leaves a node, then the value of the corresponding pointer is NIL.

Figure 16-13 shows the graph of Figure 16-10 represented in this way. Note that space is wasted in some records when pointers have NIL values. On the other hand, the records are of fixed length, and computer systems usually find fixed-length records easier to work with than variable-length records.

Our next approach may be regarded as a generalization of the child-and-twin-pointers method of representing trees. We use two kinds of records: node records and arc records. Each node contains a pointer to a linked list of arc records; each arc record contains a pointer to the final node of the arc, and possibly a label.

The node records are defined as follows:

```
DECLARE 1 NODE( )
           2 VALUE
           2 SUCCESSOR_LIST
```

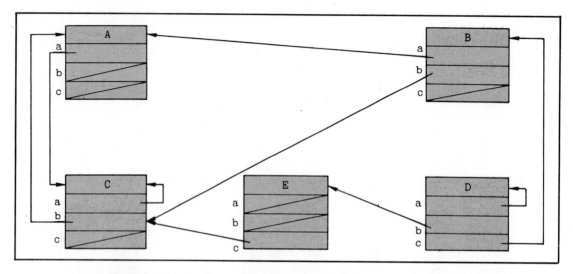

FIGURE 16-13. A plex representation of a labeled graph in which one pointer position is reserved for each label. Although the labels are shown in the drawing, they don't have to be stored in memory. The position of a pointer in the record uniquely determines the label.

SUCCESSOR_LIST points to a linked list of arc records. Each arc record contains a pointer to a successor:

```
DECLARE 1 ARC( )
          2 SUCCESSOR
          2 LINK
```

Figure 16-14 shows the graph of Figure 16-9 represented using node and arc records. Note that all the records are of fixed length. And the successor lists are easy to manipulate because they are linked lists. These are the principal advantages of this representation.

If the graph is labeled, the labels must be associated with the arcs. The most obvious way to do this is to include the labels in the arc records:

```
DECLARE 1 ARC( )
          2 LABEL
          2 SUCCESSOR
          2 LINK
```

Figure 16-15 shows the graph of Figure 16-10 represented using labeled arc records.

Occasionally, all the information in a graph is carried by the arcs; the nodes can be anonymous, with no values or labels. In this case the node records can be omitted entirely; the representation need only contain arc records.

Figure 16-16 shows a graph with anonymous nodes and its representation using arc records alone. In this kind of representation, the LABEL

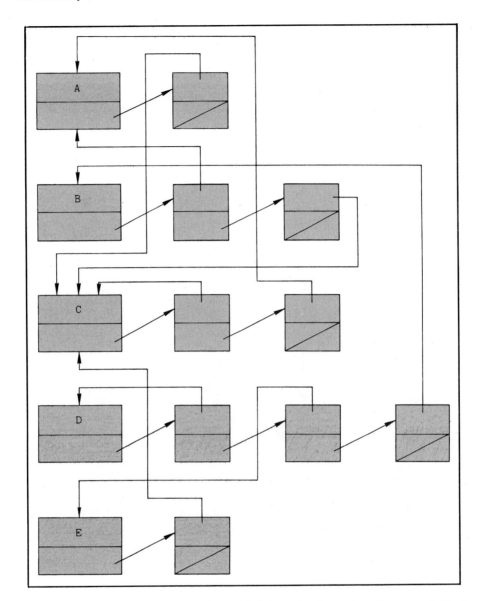

FIGURE 16-14. Plex representation of an unlabeled graph using node and arc records. Node records are shown as rectangles, arc records as squares.

components of the arcs are often replaced by VALUE components that carry more information than a mere label.

Another approach to label graphs is to have a separate successor list for each label. Suppose a graph has three labels: a, b, and c. We could represent the nodes with records defined as follows:

```
DECLARE 1 NODE( )
          2 VALUE
          2 SUCCESSOR_LIST_A
```

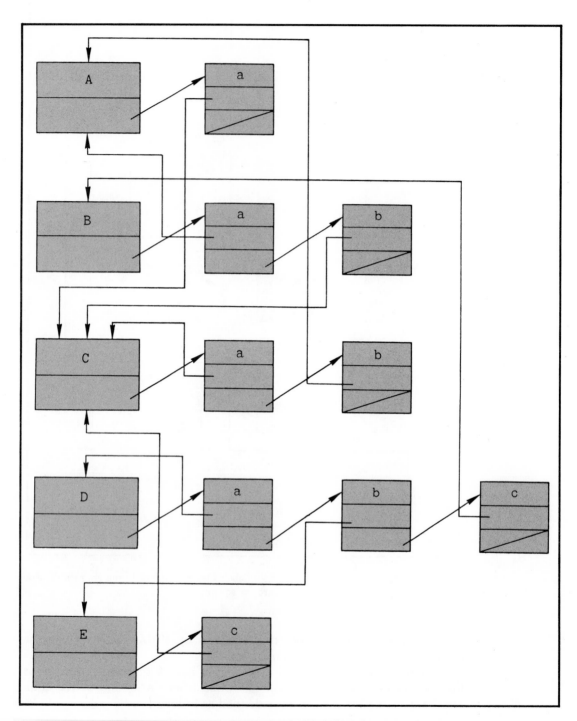

FIGURE 16-15. Plex representation of a labeled graph using node and arc records. Arc labels appear in arc records.

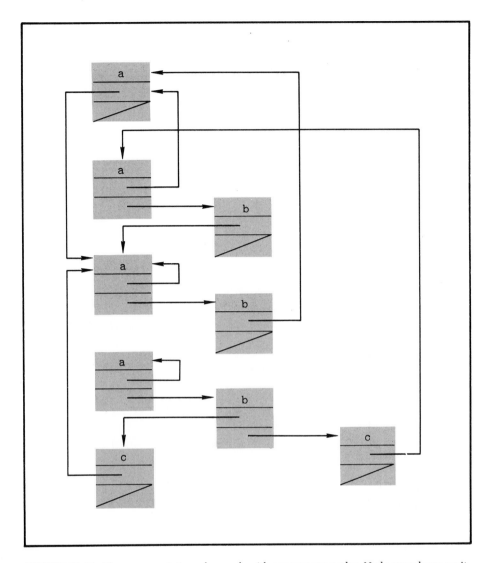

FIGURE 16-16. Plex representation of a graph with anonymous nodes. Node records are omitted. Successor pointers point to the first record of an arc list, instead of to a node record.

```
2 SUCCESSOR_LIST_B
2 SUCCESSOR_LIST_C
```

Each SUCCESSOR_LIST component points to the list of arc records for arcs having the given label. The arc records themselves need no LABEL components: The label of an arc record is determined by which list the arc record appears on. Figure 16-17 illustrates this representation.

It is possible to combine this representation with one in which the node record contains a pointer to a unique successor for each arc label. Suppose there are again three arc labels: a, b, and c. Suppose further that

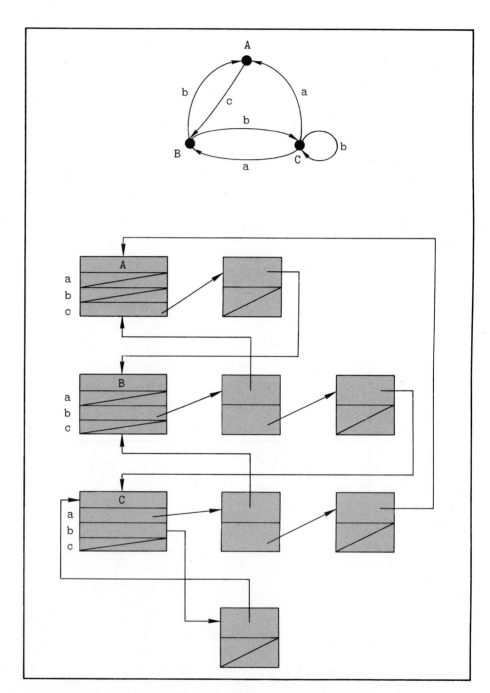

FIGURE 16-17. Plex representation of a labeled graph in which there is a separate arc list for each arc label. Notice that the arc records don't need to contain labels. Which list an arc record is on determines the label for the arc.

only one arc labeled a or b can leave a node, but that any number of arcs labeled c can do so. Then we can use the following node records:

```
DECLARE 1 NODE( )
          2 VALUE
          2 SUCCESSOR_A
          2 SUCCESSOR_B
          2 SUCCESSOR_LIST_C
```

SUCCESSOR__A and SUCCESSOR__B each point to the unique final node of the arc labeled a or b (or NIL, if no such arc leaves the node in question). SUCCESSOR__LIST__C points to a list of arc records which in turn points to the final nodes of the arcs labeled c which leave the node.

As a practical example, suppose we wished to represent the family relationships amoung people. We might have:

```
DECLARE 1 PERSON( )
          2 NAME
          2 FATHER
          2 MOTHER
          2 SPOUSE
          2 SIBLING_LIST
          2 CHILD_LIST
```

A person can have only one natural father or mother and, in our society, only one spouse at a time. Hence, FATHER, MOTHER, and SPOUSE each point to a unique record. On the other hand, a person can have more than one sibling or child, and so SIBLING__LIST and CHILD__LIST point to lists of arc records.

16.4 Applications

Data Processing and Information Retrieval. Records are ofter stored on mass storage devices, such as disks, for later retrieval and processing. When we have retrieved one record, we may find we need to examine or modify other related records. It is therefore convenient to store the records as a graph, with arcs joining related records. The labels of the arcs specify the relationships.

For instance, a record for an employee might be related to records for the department to which he is assigned, the location in which he works (large companies may have many locations, and one department can be spread over more than one location), his manager, the employees under his supervision, the equipment over which he has control, and so on. Figure 16-18 illustrates some of these relationships.

Maps and Networks. Telephone networks, computer networks, electronic circuit diagrams, maps of roads and railroads, airline routes all have a graphlike structure. When these objects are the subject of computer pro-

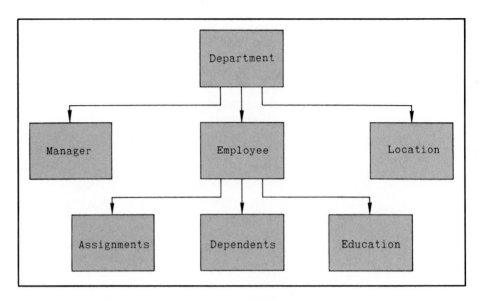

FIGURE 16-18. Relationships among records. For each department record, there are one or more employee records, one for each employee in the department. For each employee record, there are zero or more dependent records, and so on.

cessing, they are represented in memory using the techniques discussed in this chapter.

Flowcharts. A flowchart is just a graph; in fact, mathematically oriented people often call flowcharts "flowgraphs." While the usefulness of flowcharts to human beings is sometimes debated, they are usually the most straightforward way to represent a program inside a computer. Programs that manipulate other programs often store the program to be manipulated as a flowchart.

Two such "program-manipulating programs" are worth mention. First is the compiler particularly the optimizing compiler, which attempts, to modify a program to improve its efficiency, without of course changing the results that it produces. These compilers often manipulate the program in flowchart form. The compiler may add many additional labeled arcs to the flowchart, each arc specifying some relationship between different nodes. These relationships help the compiler to "understand" the operation of the program better and so to optimize it more effectively.

A second important "program-manipulating program" is the verifier, which verifies that a program will perform the function claimed by the programmer. Since in most cases we can never completely test a program in any reasonable amount of time, the verification must be based on logical analysis. Such verifiers are still highly experimental. If perfected, however, they may play as important a role in the future of programming as compilers and interpreters have played in its past.

Machine Design. We have seen that a labeled graph can be represented as a transition table. The transition table, in turn, can be thought of as describing the operation of some *abstract machine*. Transition tables and the corresponding *transition graphs* are of considerable importance in designing the various abstract machines that occur in a computer system. The implementations of these machines may be physical (implemented in hardware) or virtual (implemented in software). A hardware example is the computer's control unit. Software examples are compilers and interpreters.

Language Specification. We can think of the items of a language—keywords, signs, constants, and so on—as inputs that cause a compiler or interpreter to go from one state to another, carrying out the translation or interpretation in the process. One way to describe the grammar of the language is to give the transition graph for its interpreter or compiler.

We are not really interested in the internal states of the compiler, however. Instead, it is the *inputs* to the language processor—the arc labels—that we are trying to relate. Therefore, the graph that describes the language will have "anonymous" nodes. The mere fact that a given state exists is sufficient. It is the arc labels—the items from the language—that we are interested in relating to one another.

Figure 16-19 shows the graphs for assignment statements and arithmetic expressions in the algorithmic language. Note that *all of the named items in boxes or circles are arc labels*. The nodes are the barely visible dots where the arcs come together.

There are two kinds of arc labels—those that are enclosed in circles and those that are enclosed in boxes. The items enclosed in circles are single characters whose presence or absence the machine can detect in a single operation. The labels enclosed in squares are composite items defined by their own graphs. When a label for a composite item is encountered, the machine refers to the graph for that item to process it. The graphs for composite items function much like procedures in a programming language. Wherever a label for a composite item occurs, we can think of the corresponding graph being substituted.

The graphs are read by starting at the beginning and following the arrows. Thus, an assignment statement consists of a *variable* followed by the assignment operator followed by an *expression*.

A loop indicates that the items in the loop can occur any number of times. Thus, an expression consists of a *term* followed by *any number of* items of the form " + *term*" or " − *term*".

This kind of graph can be used for processing natural languages as well as programming languages. One feature of natural languages is that they are not so regular or consistent as programming languages. For each arc of the graph, however, we can specify arbitrarily complex tests for any special cases or features that need to be considered at that point in the processing.

Artificial Intelligence. Artificial intelligence researchers seek to improve the sophistication of the information processing that computers can carry out. They seek to program computers to do such tasks as advanced problem solving and advanced pattern recognition that can now be done only by human beings.

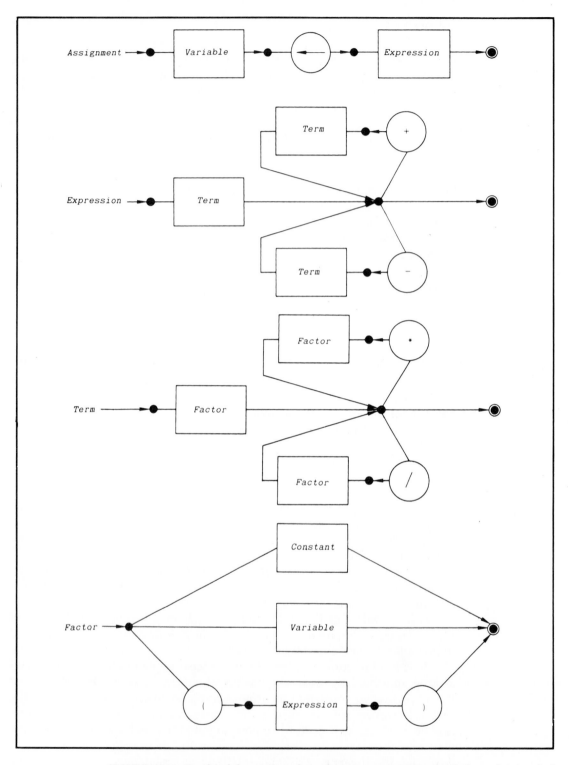

FIGURE 16-19. Graphical description of simple assignment statements. Each graph is invoked by some other graph, just as a procedure is invoked by a main algorithm or another procedure. When the circled state is reached, a return is made to the invoking graph.

An "intelligent" program must have in its memory some model of that part of the world that the program is expected to deal with. The program must deal with all the objects in that part of the world and all the relationships among them.

One popular way of representing this knowledge of the world is called a *semantic net*. Real-world objects are represented by nodes; relationships between those objects are represented by arcs. Nodes can also be used to help represent relationships that involve more than two objects.

Review Questions

1. Give four other names for graphlike structures.

2. What are the names for the points and the lines of a graph?

3. Distinguish between a directed and an undirected graph.

4. Define *initial node, final node, immediate predecessor,* and *immediate successor.*

5. Distinguish between a labeled and an unlabeled graph.

6. What is a *cycle*? What do we call a graph that contains no cycles?

7. What is a *connected graph*? A *strongly connected graph*?

8. Describe and illustrate how an unlabeled graph can be represented using ordered pairs.

9. What is the generalization of ordered pairs to labeled graphs?

10. Describe and illustrate how an unlabeled graph can be represented by successor lists.

11. Describe and illustrate the representation of a labeled graph by means of a transition table.

12. Describe the connection between a transition table and an abstract machine.

13. Describe and illustrate the representation of labeled and unlabeled graphs using connection tables.

14. Give the representations for labeled and unlabeled graphs that are (roughly) equivalent to the multiple-child-pointer representation for trees.

15. Give the representations for labeled and unlabeled graphs that are (roughly) equivalent to the child-and-twin-pointer representation for trees.

16. Describe the use of graphs in information retrieval and data processing.

17. Describe two kinds of programs that may manipulate the flowchart of another program.

18. Give some examples of real world objects that have a graphlike structure and would usually be represented inside a computer as graphs.

19. Describe the use of graphs in the design of physical and virtual machines.

20. Describe how a set of graphs may be used to describe a programming language.

21. What is one way that graphs are used in artificial intelligence research?

Exercises

1. Represent the graph of Figure 16-20 using:

(a) ordered pairs
(b) immediate successor lists
(c) a connection table
(d) records containing successor pointers

2. Represent the graph of Figure 16-21 using:

(a) ordered triples
(b) a transition table
(c) a connection table
(d) records containing successor pointers (two ways)

3. Represent the graph of Figure 16-22 using:

(a) ordered triples
(b) a connection table
(c) node records, each containing a pointer to a list of arc records

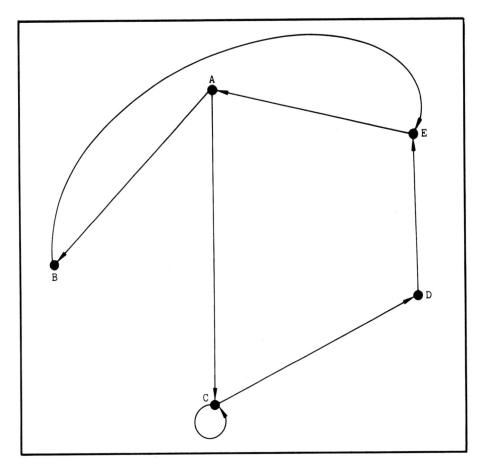

FIGURE 16-20. Graph for Exercise 1.

FIGURE 16-21. Graph for Exercise 2.

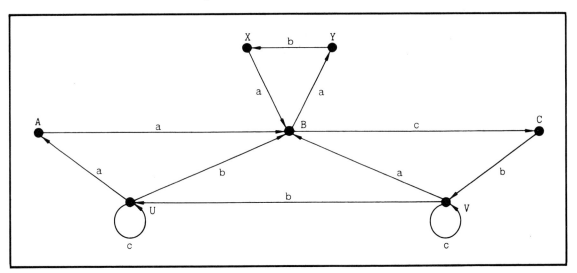

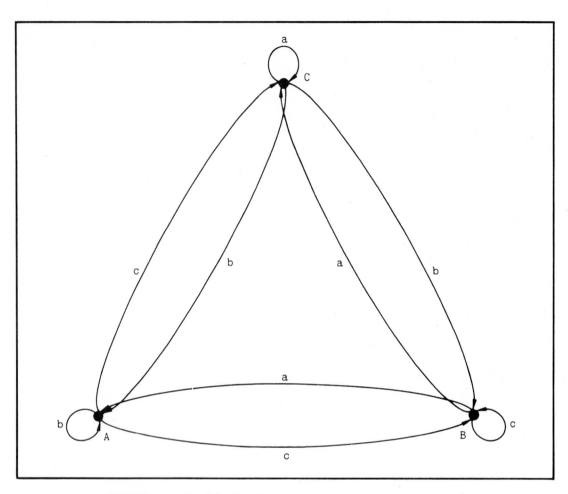

FIGURE 16-22. Graph for Exercise 3.

PART FOUR

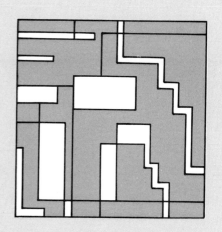

FILE
ORGANIZATION
AND PROCESSING

Chapter 17

Sequential Files

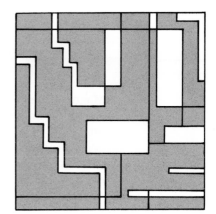

A *file* is any source of information or any place where information can be stored. A deck of punched cards is a file, as is a printed report. So are the more or less permenent files stored on tape or disk, such as employee files, inventory files, and so on.

A file may be accessed *sequentially* or *randomly*. In sequential access, the records are accessed—that is, processed—in the same order in which they are stored in the file. In random access, the records are accessed in some random order unrelated to the order in which they are stored in the file.

Some files can only be accessed sequentially. Files stored on punched cards or magnetic tape are sequenial files. So are printed reports, since the report is printed line by line in the order in which the lines will appear on the paper.

Other files can be accessed either sequentially or randomly, depending on the job at hand. Files stored on disks are the most common example of random files.

17.1 Auxiliary Memory

More or less permanent data files such as customer accounts and employee records are usually stored in auxiliary memory. At present, there are two types of auxiliary memory in widespread use: *magnetic tape* and *magnetic disk*.

The capacity of a particular *volume* of auxiliary memory (one tape reel or disk pack) will typically be in the range of 1 to 100 million characters. But since the volumes can be removed from the computer, stored away, and replaced with others, the total capacity of auxiliary memory (including the volumes not currently on the computer) is unlimited.

Magnetic Tape. Computer tape is similar to the tape used in home recorders, and works on the same principle. It is relatively inexpensive and will hold large amounts of information. The reels are easily stored when not being used on the computer.

The main disadvantage of magnetic tape is well known to every home recordist who ever searched for, say, a particular musical selection located *somewhere* on a large reel of tape. The process is time consuming. Tape is fine when you play the reel from beginning to end but very frustrating when you are looking for a particular selection.

The same thing holds for computer tape. Tape is efficient when the entire reel is to be processed from beginning to end, but inefficient otherwise. In short, tape is a *sequential-access medium*: To use it efficiently, we must process the information in the same sequence in which it is stored on the tape.

Magnetic Disk. A magnetic disk looks something like a phonograph record, but works on the same principle as magnetic tape—the information is stored magnetically rather than being engraved in grooves.

Disks vary considerably in physical form, from lightweight, flexible *floppy disks* or *diskettes* to more cumbersome *disk packs,* which may contain up to 11 individual *platters* and up to 20 recording surfaces. (Two surfaces are used on each platter except for the top and bottom platters, on which only one surface each is used.)

Information is stored on and retrieved from a disk by an *access arm,* at the end of which is a *read-write* head. Just as a phonograph needle can be put down on any part of a record, so the access arm can quickly move the read-write head to any part of the disk. Thus, disks are classified as *random-access media,* since information can be speedily retrieved regardless of where it is stored on the disk.

In this chapter we will concentrate on sequential files. These will normally be decks of punched cards, printed reports, or files stored on tape or disk. In the next chapter we will take up random files stored on disk.

17.2 Input and Output Statements for Sequential-file Processing

In the algorithmic language we will use the INPUT statement to get the next item from a sequential file, and the OUTPUT statement to put the next item into a sequential file. Our use of these statements will differ from our previous use of them in two ways, however.

First, we will not be dealing with just one input file and one output file, as we have been before. We may have several input files or several output files, and we need some way to distinguish between them. We will do this by giving each file a name and putting that name in parentheses after INPUT or OUTPUT. Thus,

```
INPUT(OLD_FILE)
```

inputs a record from the file named OLD__FILE, and

```
OUTPUT(NEW_FILE)
```

outputs a record to the file named NEW__FILE.

Second, files used in data processing are usually organized around records instead of around individual data items. Consequently, we will input or output an entire record at one time. For instance,

```
INPUT(OLD_FILE) OLD_REC
```

inputs a record from OLD__FILE and assigns this record to OLD__REC. In the same way,

```
OUTPUT(NEW_FILE) NEW_REC
```

ouputs the record NEW__REC to the file NEW__FILE.

17.3 The File Update Problem

We begin our study of sequential files with a classical data processing problem: updating a master file.

Suppose we have stored on magnetic tape a file that has to be updated each month. It could be a file of customer accounts, for instance, which has to be updated as customers make new purchases and pay for old ones. We will call this file the *master file*.

Each month, certain transactions take place. Customers make new purchases, for instance, or make payments on their accounts. New customers are added to the master file, and inactive customers are removed. The details of each transaction are punched on a card. The card containing the transactions constitute the *transaction file*.

We update the master file each month using the data in the transaction file. We can diagram this process using a system flowchart, as shown in Figure 17-1. The inputs to the computer are the old master file (the file to be updated) and the transaction file. The outputs are the new (updated) master file and perhaps some reports. The dotted line indicates that this month's new master file becomes next month's old master file.

During the update, we need some way of matching records in the transaction file with records to be updated in the master file. We must be able to tell when a transaction record and a master record refer to the same entity—to the same customer, for instance.

We can achieve this by giving each transaction record and each master

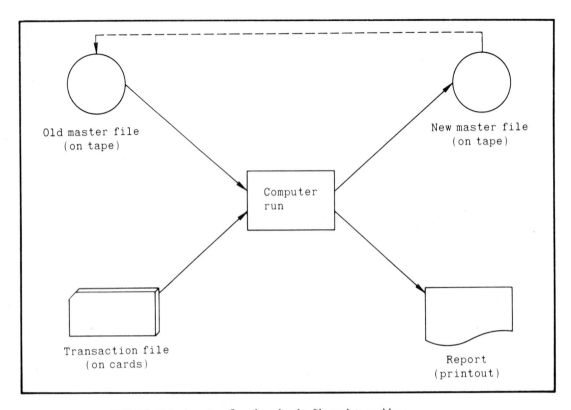

FIGURE 17-1. A system flowchart for the file-update problem.

record a *key* component. Typically, the key is an account number, a customer number, an employee number, a social security number, or some similar identifying number. (Names make bad keys: different people have the same name, and people don't always write their names the same way.) The value of the key uniquely identifies the entity to which the record refers. We will match a record in the transaction file with the record in the master file having the same key.

Since both the master and transaction files are sequential files, records can be read from them only in the order in which they are stored in each file. To be able to match the records in one file with the corresponding records in the other, the records in each file must be in alphabetical or numerical order according to their key values.

Note that the records in the master and transaction files will not correspond one to one. Many records in the master file will not be updated on a particular run, so there will be no corresponding transaction records. And the transaction file may contain some new records to be added to the master file.

Now let's write a file-update algorithm. We will name the old master file OLD__FILE and the new master file NEW__FILE. TRANS__FILE will be the name of the transaction file.

The records in the master file (both OLD__FILE and NEW__FILE) have the following structure:

```
1 OLD_REC
  2 KEY
  2 BALANCE
```

For simplicity, each record has just two fields, KEY and BALANCE.

The value of KEY identifies a particular record; we will assume that the keys are four-digit numbers, such as 3751, 4862, and 5234. The last record in OLD__FILE or NEW__FILE is a special sentinel record with a key of 9999.

The BALANCE field is a value that can be updated. It might be the amount a customer owes to a company, which will change as purchases and payments are made. It could be the amount in a person's bank account, which will change with deposits and withdrawals. Or it could refer to something having nothing to do with money, such as the number of items of a particular kind that are in stock.

The records in the transaction file, which will be used to update the records in the master file, have the following structure:

```
1 TRANS_REC
  2 KEY
  2 KIND
  2 AMOUNT
```

KEY has the same significance for a transaction record as it does for a master record. The last record in the transaction file is a special sentinel record with a key of 9999.

The value of KIND determines what kind of transaction each particular record represents. The following table shows the three possible values of KIND and the kind of transaction corresponding to each:

Value of KIND	*Kind of Transaction*
1	Add a new record to the master file
2	Update the corresponding record in the master file
3	Delete the corresponding record from the master file

The value of AMOUNT is used in different ways depending on the kind of transaction. When a new record is added, the value of AMOUNT becomes the value of BALANCE for the new record. When a record is updated, the value of AMOUNT is added to the existing value of BALANCE. The value of AMOUNT can be either positive or negative, so it can be used either to increase or decrease the balance for a record in the master file. When a record is deleted, the value of AMOUNT is not used.

We will develop the file update algorithm in top-down fashion, using procedures for the lower level modules. Figure 17-2 shows the top-level module, the algorithm FILE__UPDATE.

The algorithm begins by declaring as global those variables that will be used by all the modules. OLD__REC holds the last record read from OLD__ FILE, the old master file. NEW__REC may hold a record to be written to NEW__FILE, the new master file. TRANS__REC holds the last record read from the transaction file. CURRENT_KEY holds the key value that is currently being processed. This could be the key of a transaction record, a master record, or both. IN__USE is a flag whose value is TRUE if NEW__ REC contains a valid record to be written to the new master file. If NEW__ REC does not contain valid data, then the value of IN__USE is FALSE.

The algorithm next declares OLD__REC, NEW__REC, and TRANS__ REC to have the structures we have already discussed. Note that NEW__ REC and OLD__REC have the same structure.

Next the variable SENTINEL is set to 9999, the key value used for the sentinel record in both the master file and the transaction file.

Processing begins by reading the first record from OLD__FILE and from TRANS__FILE. The record from OLD__FILE is stored in OLD__REC; the record from TRANS__FILE is stored in TRANS__REC.

Processing of the transaction and master records is governed by the WHILE construction. Processing continues as long as either OLD__ REC.KEY or TRANS__REC.KEY does not equal the sentinel value. Put another way, processing continues as long as there remain any records to be processed from either the old master or the transaction file.

FIGURE 17-2. The algorithm FILE__UPDATE.

```
ALGORITHM FILE_UPDATE
    GLOBAL OLD_REC, NEW_REC, TRANS_REC, CURRENT_KEY, IN_USE
    DECLARE 1 OLD_REC
              2 KEY
              2 BALANCE
    DECLARE NEW_REC LIKE OLD_REC
    DECLARE 1 TRANS_REC
              2 KEY
              2 KIND
              2 AMOUNT
    SENTINEL ← 9999
    INPUT(TRANS_FILE) TRANS_REC
    INPUT(OLD_FILE) OLD_REC
    WHILE    (OLD_REC.KEY ≠ SENTINEL)
          OR (TRANS_REC.KEY ≠ SENTINEL) DO
       CALL GET_NEXT_KEY
       CALL PROCESS_TRANSACTIONS
       IF IN_USE THEN
          OUTPUT(NEW_FILE) NEW_REC
          END IF
       END WHILE
    NEW_REC.KEY ← SENTINEL
    OUTPUT(NEW_FILE) NEW_REC
END FILE_UPDATE
```

Now look at the three statements governed by the WHILE construction. The procedure GET__NEXT__KEY selects the next key value to be processed. We will postpone considering the details of how this selection is made for a moment. The value of CURRENT__KEY is set to the key value selected by GET__NEXT__KEY.

The procedure PROCESS__TRANSACTIONS processes all transaction records whose key values are equal to CURRENT__KEY, the key selected by GET__NEXT__KEY. All of these transactions refer to the same master record. For instance, they may represent various purchases and payments made by a particular customer during the month.

A newly added record may be updated by later transaction records having the same key. Although not likely, it is possible that one transaction could add a new record, several more transactions could update it, and a final one could delete it, so that the entire sequence of transactions would have no effect on the master file.

After all the transactions having a particular key have been processed, NEW__REC may or may not contain a valid record to be written to NEW__ FILE. If NEW__REC does contain a valid record, the value of IN__USE will be TRUE, and we output the value of NEW__REC to NEW__FILE. If NEW__ REC does not hold valid data, the value of IN__USE is FALSE, and no output to NEW__FILE takes place.

After all of the old master and transaction records have been processed, the last two statements of the algorithm write a sentinel record to NEW__FILE.

Figure 17-3 shows the procedure GET__NEXT__KEY, which selects the next key value to be processed.

GET__NEXT__KEY has two key values to select from: OLD__REC.KEY, the key of the last record read from OLD__FILE, and TRANS__REC.KEY, the key of the last record read from TRANS__FILE. GET__NEXT__KEY always selects the smaller of the two. By always processing the smaller key first, we assure that the records written to the new master file will be in ascending numerical order. This key-selection principle, which is the basis of *merging*, will be discussed in more detail in Section 17.4.

Also note that the values of all valid keys are less than the sentinel

FIGURE 17-3. The procedure GET__NEXT__KEY.

```
PROCEDURE GET_NEXT_KEY
    GLOBAL OLD_REC, NEW_REC, TRANS_REC, CURRENT_KEY, IN_USE
    IF OLD_REC.KEY ≤ TRANS_REC.KEY THEN
        CURRENT_KEY ← OLD_REC.KEY
        NEW_REC ← OLD_REC
        IN_USE ← TRUE
        INPUT(OLD_FILE) OLD_REC
    ELSE
        CURRENT_KEY ← TRANS_REC.KEY
        IN_USE ← FALSE
    END IF
END GET_NEXT_KEY
```

value 9999. If the sentinel record has been read for one file but not the other, GET__NEXT__KEY will always select the non-sentinel key for processing. Therefore, when the end of one file has been reached, all of the remaining records in the other file will be processed.

If OLD__REC.KEY is less than or equal to TRANS__REC.KEY, then, CURRENT__KEY is set to OLD__REC.KEY. If OLD__REC.KEY is greater than TRANS__REC.KEY, CURRENT__KEY is set to TRANS__REC.KEY.

If CURRENT__KEY is set to OLD__REC.KEY, then the old master file already contains a record—the value of OLD__REC—whose key is equal to CURRENT__KEY. The value of OLD__REC is moved to NEW__REC for further processing. IN__USE is set to TRUE to indicate that NEW__REC contains valid data. Another record from OLD__FILE is read into OLD__REC.

If CURRENT__KEY is not set to OLD__REC.KEY, then there is no record in the old master file having a key equal to CURRENT__KEY (Why?). In this case, no master record is placed in NEW__REC. IN__USE is set to FALSE to indicate that NEW__REC does not contain valid data.

The situation set up by GET__NEXT__KEY persists throughout the transaction processing. If a master record exists whose key is equal to CURRENT__KEY, that record is stored in NEW__REC and the value of IN__USE is TRUE. If no such record exists, the value of IN__USE is FALSE.

Figure 17-4 shows the procedure PROCESS__TRANSACTIONS, which controls the processing of all transactions having a particular key. The WHILE construction processes transaction records as long as their keys are equal to CURRENT__KEY. For each transaction, the CASE construction calls either ADD__RECORD, UPDATE__RECORD, or DELETE__RECORD, depending on the kind of transaction. An error message is printed if a transaction record has an invalid transaction code. After processing each transaction record, a new transaction record is read from TRANS__FILE.

Figure 17-5 shows ADD__RECORD, the procedure for adding a new record to the master file. If IN__USE is TRUE, then there is already a mas-

FIGURE 17-4. The procedure PROCESS__TRANSACTIONS.

```
PROCEDURE PROCESS_TRANSACTIONS
   GLOBAL TRANS_REC, CURRENT_KEY
   WHILE TRANS_REC.KEY = CURRENT_KEY DO
      CASE TRANS_REC.KIND OF
      1:
         CALL ADD_RECORD
      2:
         CALL UPDATE_RECORD
      3:
         CALL DELETE_RECORD
      ELSE
         OUTPUT 'INVALID TRANSACTION CODE FOR', CURRENT_KEY
      END CASE
      INPUT(TRANS_FILE) TRANS-REC
   END WHILE
END PROCESS_TRANSACTIONS
```

```
      PROCEDURE ADD_RECORD
         GLOBAL NEW_REC, TRANS_REC, CURRENT_KEY, IN_USE
         IF IN_USE THEN
            OUTPUT 'CANNOT ADD RECORD', CURRENT_KEY
            OUTPUT 'RECORD ALREADY IN MASTER FILE'
         ELSE
            NEW_REC.KEY ← TRANS_REC.KEY
            NEW_REC.BALANCE ← TRANS_REC.AMOUNT
            IN_USE ← TRUE
         END IF
      END ADD_RECORD
```

FIGURE 17-5. The procedure ADD__RECORD.

ter record having the same key as that of the record to be added. We consider it an error to add a record if a record with the same key is already present. Therefore, when IN__USE is TRUE, ADD__RECORD prints an error message.

WHEN IN__USE is false, no existing master record has the same key as the transaction record, so we are free to add a record with that key. The KEY and BALANCE components of NEW__REC are set to the KEY and AMOUNT components, respectively, of TRANS__REC. IN__USE is set to TRUE to indicate that NEW__REC now contains valid data.

Figure 17-6 shows UPDATE__RECORD, the procedure for updating a record in the master file. If IN__USE is TRUE, NEW__REC contains a master record to be updated. UPDATE__RECORD uses the AMOUNT component of TRANS__REC to update the BALANCE component of NEW__REC. If IN__USE is FALSE, the procedure complains that it cannot update a record that does not exist.

Figure 17-7 shows the procedure DELETE__RECORD, which deletes a record from the master file. If IN__USE is TRUE, NEW__REC contains the record to be deleted. The procedure deletes it by setting IN__USE to FALSE, indicating that NEW__REC no longer contains valid data. The record in NEW__REC will not be written to the new master file and so is deleted. If IN__USE is FALSE to begin with, the procedure complains that it cannot delete a record that does not exist.

FIGURE 17-6. The procedure UPDATE__RECORD.

```
   PROCEDURE UPDATE_RECORD
      GLOBAL NEW_REC, TRANS_REC, CURRENT_KEY, IN_USE
      IF IN_USE THEN
         NEW_REC.BALANCE ← NEW_REC.BALANCE + TRANS_REC.AMOUNT
      ELSE
         OUTPUT 'CANNOT UPDATE RECORD', CURRENT_KEY
         OUTPUT 'RECORD NOT IN MASTER FILE'
      END IF
   END UPDATE_RECORD
```

```
PROCEDURE DELETE_RECORD
   GLOBAL CURRENT_KEY, IN_USE
   IF IN_USE THEN
      IN_USE ← FALSE
   ELSE
      OUTPUT 'CANNOT DELETE RECORD', CURRENT_KEY
      OUTPUT 'RECORD NOT IN MASTER FILE'
   END IF
END DELETE_RECORD
```

FIGURE 17-7. The procedure DELETE__RECORD.

17.4 External Sorting

For the file-update algorithm to work, it is essential that both the master file and the transaction file be in numerical order according to the value of the key. Many other file-processing algorithms impose the same requirement.

If a file is not already in order with respect to the key to be used, it must be sorted on that key to put it in order before it can be processed.

We have already discussed *internal sorting:* the sorting of lists of items stored as arrays in main memory. Internal-sorting algorithms utilize the computer's ability to compare and exchange arbitrary elements of an array. The order in which the array elements are accessed is determined by the needs of the sorting algorithm, not by the order in which the elements are stored. In short, internal sorting algorithms demand random access to the items to be sorted.

This random access is, of course, not available for sequential files. But even so-called random access mass storage devices, such as disks, are usually not satisfactory for internal sorting. The frequent movements of the access mechanism required by the sorting algorithm just take too much time. For instance, the author knows of an attempt to sort a disk file of several thousand records using a Shell sort; The sorting time was over 30 hours.

External-sorting algorithms are designed for use with files stored on tape or disk. Normally, the files to be sorted are treated as sequential files, even if they are stored on disk.

Merging. The merge is the fundamental operation of external sorting. Two files that are already in order can be merged to yield a combined file that is already in order. And most important of all, this merge can be done by processing the files sequentially.

The algorithm for merging is very simple. At each step, we compare the keys of the next records to be processed for each of the two files being merged. The record with the smaller key is outputted to the merged file. Figure 17-8 illustrates a merge. In this and later figures, only the keys of the records are shown.

Figure 17-9 shows an algorithm for merging two files. As before, we assume each file ends with a sentinel record having a key of 9999. When

Merged File	Files Being Merged
	5 17 24
	3 19 30 35 42
3	5 17 24
	19 30 35 42
3 5	17 24
	19 30 35 42
3 5 17	24
	19 30 35 42
3 5 17 19	24
	30 35 42
3 5 17 19 24	30 35 42
3 5 17 19 24 30	35 42
3 5 17 19 24 30 35	42
3 5 17 19 24 30 35 42	

FIGURE 17-8. Merge. Two ordered files are merged to give a single merged file, which is also ordered.

the sentinel record for one input file has been read, then all of the remaining records of the other input file are copied onto the output file. This is because the key of each of these records is smaller than the sentinel key.

Note that the principle for selecting the key of the next record to be processed is the same for the merge algorithm and the file-up date algorithm. This is no accident. The file-update algorithm is a form of merge, but with the records of one file being used to update the records of the other, instead of just being placed with them in the output file.

Runs. Now let's consider a sequential file to be sorted. We will confine our attention to the keys of the records, and we will use two-digit keys for simplicity. The file might look like this:

25 38 17 65 94 59 73 87 35 76

We can break the file down into sequences of records that are already in order. These sequences are called runs:

25 38   17 65 94   59 73 87   35 76

```
ALGORITHM MERGE
    DECLARE 1 RECORD_1
              2 KEY
              2 DATA
    DECLARE RECORD_2 LIKE RECORD_1
    SENTINEL ← 9999
    INPUT(FILE_1) RECORD_1
    INPUT(FILE_2) RECORD_2
    WHILE    (RECORD_1.KEY ≠ SENTINEL)
          OR (RECORD_2.KEY ≠ SENTINEL) DO
        IF RECORD_1.KEY ≤ RECORD_2.KEY THEN
            OUTPUT(FILE_3) RECORD_1
            INPUT(FILE_1) RECORD_1
        ELSE
            OUTPUT(FILE_3) RECORD_2
            INPUT(FILE_2) RECORD_2
        END IF
    END WHILE
    RECORD_1.KEY ← SENTINEL
    OUTPUT(FILE_3) RECORD_1
END MERGE
```

FIGURE 17-9. The algorithm MERGE. Compare the method used here to select the next record to go to FILE__3 with the method used in GET__NEXT__KEY to select the next key to be processed.

The end of a run is signaled by a *stepdown*, which consists of a record with a larger key followed by a record with a smaller key. For example, the stepdown 38–17 signals the end of the first run, the stepdown 94–59 signals the end of the second run, and so on. (The end of the last run is the end of the file.)

In discussing sorting algorithms, we will illustrate files as above with extra spaces between the runs. But no such run separators actually exist in files. The sorting algorithms detect the ends of runs by looking for stepdowns.

The Merge Sort. The basic idea of merge sorting is to merge runs into larger runs until we are eventually left with just one run, which consists of the entire file. Since the runs are in order, and since merging two files that are in order yields another file that is in order, the runs obtained by merging will also be in order. When we are left with a single run consisting of the entire file, then the file is sorted.

Let us look at the process in detail. We start by *distributing* the runs onto two other files, placing the first run on one file, the next run on the other file, the next run back on the first file, and so on. The result of this distribution is:

```
25 38   59 73 87
17 65 94   35 76
```

Now we take these two files as the input to a merging algorithm. We merge the first run from the first file with the first run from the second file and place the result on the output file. Then we merge the second run from the first file with the second run from the second file and put that result on the output file, and so on. The result is:

17 25 38 65 94   35 59 73 76 87

The runs are, of course, merged record by record as the two files are processed sequentially. But it is necessary for the merging algorithm to detect the ends of the runs. When the end of the run has been detected on one file, all the records remaining in the current run on the other file are moved to the output file.

We can now distribute the runs onto two files again:

17 25 38 65 94
35 59 73 76 87

Then we merge the runs on the two files again:

17 25 35 38 59 65 73 76 87 94

Since only one run remains, the file is sorted.

The sort can be accomplished using three files, as shown in Figure 17-10. We start out with all the records on FILE__1. The runs on FILE__2 and FILE__3 are merged and the results placed on FILE__1. This process of a distribution followed by a merge is repeated until FILE__1 contains only a single run.

The Balanced Merge Sort. One problem with the merge sort just described is that each merge is preceded by a distribution. The distributions contribute nothing to the actual sorting, since they do not change the order of any records. Yet they consume as much time as the merges. If we could eliminate all distributions except the first, we could nearly halve the sorting time.

One way to do this is to use four files instead of three, as shown in Figure 17-11. As before, we start out by with a distribution: FILE__1 is distributed onto FILE__3 and FILE__4. Thereafter, merging and distribution are combined into a single merge-distribute pass. Thus, the runs on FILE__3 and FILE__4 are merged and the resulting runs distributed onto FILE__1 and FILE__2. Then the runs on FILE__1 and FILE__2 are merged and the resulting runs distributed onto FILE__3 and FILE__4. Again the process continues until only a single run is left.

The Polyphase Sort. The balanced merge sort eliminates the separate distribution passes but requires an extra file. For magnetic tape, this means an extra tape drive, which may not be available.

The polyphase sort eliminates the separate distribution passes without requiring another file. The algorithm for the polyphase sort, however, is more complex than those for the other two.

Nevertheless, the idea behind the polyphase sort is simple, as shown

```
        FILE_1:  25  38    17  65  94     59  73  87    35  76

        FILE_2:

        FILE_3:

                    Distribute

        FILE_1:

        FILE_2:  25  38    59  73  87

        FILE_3:  17  65  94    35  76

                  Merge

        FILE_1:  17  25  38  65  94    35  59  73  76  87

        FILE_2:

        FILE_3:

                    Distribute

        FILE_1:

        FILE_2:  17  25  38  65  94

        FILE_3:  35  59  73  76  87

                  Merge

        FILE_1:  17  25  35  38  59  65  73  76  87  94

        FILE_2:

        FILE_3:
```

FIGURE 17-10. The Merge sort.

in Figure 17-12. As usual, the runs of the file to be sorted are distributed onto two other files. We begin merging those files onto the original file, as in the merge sort. But, as soon as one file is empty, we immediately switch to merging the other two files onto the formerly empty one. The process continues in this way. At any time we are merging two files onto a third one. When one of the two files being merged becomes empty, we switch to merging the other two files onto it.

The initial-distribution part of the polyphase sort is complex. The reason is that only certain combinations of numbers of runs on the two files after distribution will allow the sort to "come out right in the end" with a single run. As shown in the example, one such combination is two runs

```
            FILE_1:  25  38     17  65  94     59  73  87     35  76

            FILE_2:

            FILE_3:

            FILE_4:

                        Distribute

            FILE_1:

            FILE_2:

            FILE_3:  25  38     59  73  87

            FILE_4:  17  65  94     35  76

                    Merge  and  Distribute

            FILE_1:  17  25  38  65  94

            FILE_2:  35  59  73  76  87

            FILE_3:

            FILE_4:

                    Merge  and  Distribute

            FILE_1:

            FILE_2:

            FILE_3:  17  25  38  59  65  73  76  87  94

            FILE_4:
```

FIGURE 17-11. The balanced merge sort. By using an extra file, we can combine all but one of the distributions with merges. This saves us from having to do separate passes over the files for distributions.

on one file and three runs on the other. The distribution algorithm may have to augment the real runs with imaginary *dummy runs* in order to obtain an acceptable combination.

Review Questions

1. What is a *file*?

2. Distinguish between sequentially and randomly accessed files.

```
FILE_1:  25  38    17  65  94    59  73  87    35  76    45  60  80

FILE_2:

FILE_3:

            Distribute

FILE_1:

FILE_2:  25  38    59  73  87    45  60  80

FILE_3:  17  65  94    35  76

            Merge FILE_2 and FILE_3 into FILE_1

FILE_1:  17  25  38  65  94    35  59  73  76  87

FILE_2:  45  60  80

FILE_3:

            Merge FILE_1 and FILE_2 into FILE_3

FILE_1:  35  59  73  76  87

FILE_2:

FILE_3:  17  25  38  45  60  65  80  94

            Merge FILE_3 and FILE_1 into FILE_2

FILE_1:

FILE_2:  17  25  35  38  45  59  60  65  73  76  80  87  94

FILE_3:
```

FIGURE 17-12. The polyphase sort also avoids separate distribution passes after the initial distribution—and it uses only three files. But its operation is more complicated than that of the other two sorts. (The example has been chosen to avoid most of the complications.)

3. Give two kinds of files that can only be accessed sequentially.

4. Give a kind of file that can be accessed randomly.

5. Describe the input and output statements used in the algorithmic language when more than one input and one output file are involved.

6. What does a *system flowchart* show? Contrast it with a flowchart for an algorithm.

7. Draw and give the meaning of each symbol used on the system flowchart in Figure 17-1.

8. Describe in words the operation of the file-update algorithm.

9. Why, for the file-update and merge algorithms, is the key of the sentinel chosen to follow every other key in numerical order?

10. If file update, after the sentinel has been read for the master file, any remaining records in the transaction file will be processed. But only one of the three operations is now permitted; the other two will produce error messages. What is the permitted operation?

11. Why are internal-sorting algorithms unsuitable for files stored on disk or tape?

12. Distinguish between the uses of *internal-* and *external-sorting* algorithms.

13. What is the fundamental operation of external sorting? Describe in words an algorithm for accomplishing this operation.

14. What are *runs*?

15. What is a *stepdown*?

16. Give an example showing how stepdowns are used to partition a file into runs.

17. Describe with words and illustrations the operation of the merge sort.

18. What defect of the merge sort is remedied by the balanced merge sort?

19. What defect of the balanced merge sort is remedied by the polyphase sort?

20. Why is the initial distribution part of the polyphase sort more complicated than for other sorts? Can you think of some reasons why the rest of the polyphase sort might be more complicated as well?

Exercises

1. Assuming a file to be in order is risky. This is particularly true of the transaction file; the person who drops the box of cards on the floor will probably stick the cards back in the box (in random order) quickly before someone finds out! Modify FILE__UPDATE to check that the records in both TRANS__FILE·and IN__FILE are in the correct order. If an out-of-order record is found, issue an error message, pass over the out-of-order record, and continue. (*Hint:* You will have to save the key of the previous record from each file in order to check the current one for proper order.)

2. Write an algorithm to distribute the runs of FILE__1 alternately onto FILE__2 and FILE__3. (*Hint:* The problem is to detect where one run leaves off and the next one begins. The solution is the same as for sequence checking Exercise 1.)

3. Write an algorithm to merge the runs of FILE__2 and FILE__3 and place the results onto FILE__1. (*Hint:* This is more complicated than the merge algorithm given in the text, since merging is done run by run. That is, when the end of the run occurs on one file, the remainder of the current run on the other file must be moved to FILE__1 before going on to the next pair of runs. A run can end either because a stepdown was detected or because the sentinel was read on that file. It may be helpful to have flags EOR__2 and EOR__3 that will set to TRUE if either condition occurs.)

4. Drawing on the results of Exercises 2 and 3, write a merge sort algorithm. The distributions and merges will be repeated until only one run remains on FILE__1 (so you must count the number of runs that go onto FILE__1 each time). Don't forget to write a sentinel record at the end of each file when it has been filled; the sentinel will be needed when the file is read.

Chapter 18

Random Files

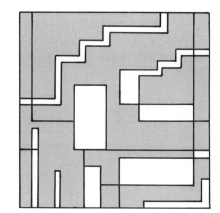

A random-access file allows us to access any record, regardless of where it is stored in the file. But how do we specify to the system which record we want to access?

Chapter 17 introduced the idea of a *key*—a component whose value uniquely identifies a record. We may request a record by giving the value of its key. Thus, we might request the record for employee '745-35-8951' or customer '284903' or inventory item '438-A-2749-AX5'.

This key, whose value uniquely identifies a record, is often called the *primary key*. Accessing a record by giving the value of its primary key is called *primary-key retrieval*. When the word *key* is used without further qualification it means *primary key*.

A record may also contain *secondary keys*: components whose values do not uniquely identify the record, but which may nevertheless be used to access the record.

For instance, AGE and SALARY could be secondary keys in an employee record. We could request from the system the records of all employees under age 30 who make more than $10,000 a year. That is, we want all records for which

```
(AGE < 30) AND (SALARY > 10000)
```

is TRUE.

Accessing records by giving values—or ranges of values—of one or more secondary keys is called *secondary-key retrieval*. Since the values of secondary keys do not identify a record uniquely, a secondary-key retrieval will usually access more than one record.

In this chapter we will look at some of the techniques for primary- and secondary-key retrieval.

18.1 The Logical Structure of Random-access Devices

A random-access mass storage device, such as a disk, is best thought of as being partitioned into compartments called *buckets,* as shown in Figure 18-1.

The buckets have the following characteristic: When trying to locate a particular record, it is easiest first to narrow the search down to a particular bucket, then locate the record inside that bucket. Because of the physical structure of the device, the alternative of examining one record in one bucket, then another record in another bucket, and so on, is much less efficient.

FIGURE 18-1. A mass storage device divided into three buckets. Each bucket can hold four records.

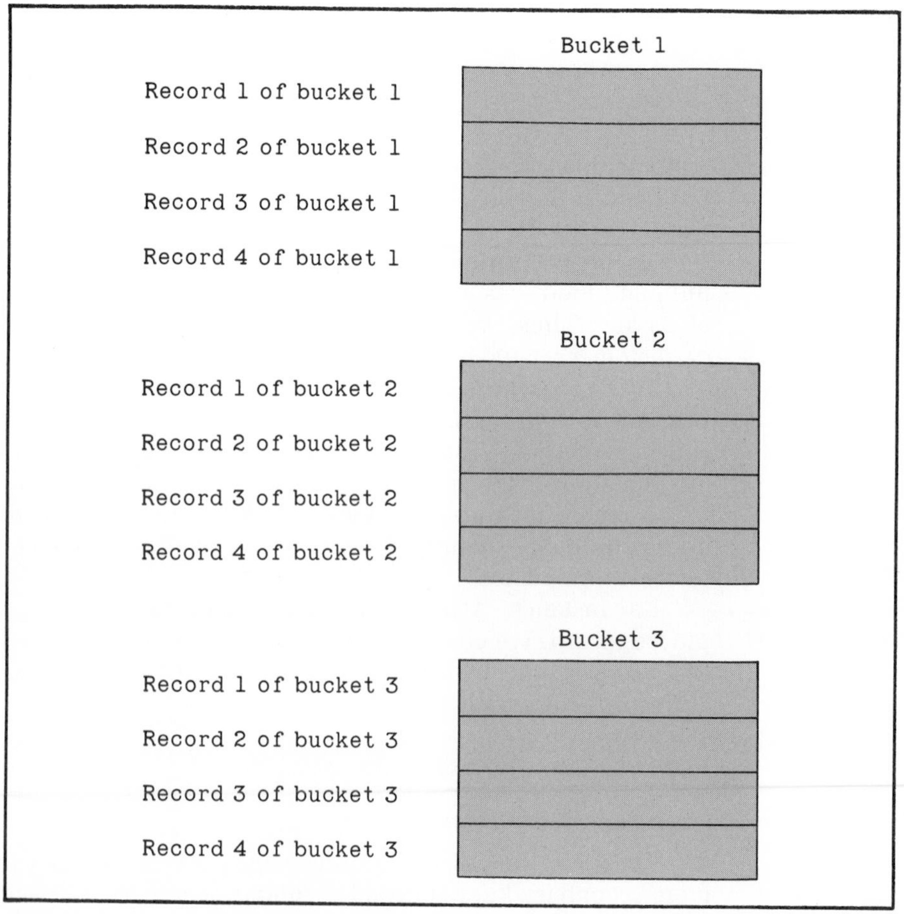

Record 1 of bucket 1

Record 2 of bucket 1

Record 3 of bucket 1

Record 4 of bucket 1

Record 1 of bucket 2

Record 2 of bucket 2

Record 3 of bucket 2

Record 4 of bucket 2

Record 1 of bucket 3

Record 2 of bucket 3

Record 3 of bucket 3

Record 4 of bucket 3

Bucket 1

Bucket 2

Bucket 3

An everyday example of this is a filing cabinet. The filing cabinet has four drawers and each drawer is a bucket. Obviously, it is easier to find a record in one drawer than it would be to examine one record in one drawer, then another record in another drawer, and so on. We would spend more time opening and closing drawers than we would spend looking at records!

For this reason, a file cabinet has a card on the front of each drawer bearing a legend such as A–F or G–L or M–R or S–Z. Each card gives the range of keys of the records stored in a particular drawer. Using the cards, we immediately narrow our search down to one drawer—one bucket—and do all our further searching inside that drawer.

A random-access device may have a hierarchical structure. That is, the buckets may be further subdivided into smaller buckets, as shown in Figure 18-2.

Again, the filing cabinet gives us an example. It would be very laborious to go through the records in a drawer of the filing cabinet record by record until we found the record we wanted. Instead, the drawer is itself partitioned into buckets by means of separators. Each separator has a tab with a label, such as AA–AM or AN–AZ or BA–BM, which gives the range of keys present in each bucket. Using these tabs, we can again narrow our search down to a particular bucket.

For a computer-oriented example, consider the *disk pack* shown in Figure 18-3. The disk pack consists of a number (typically 11) of individual

FIGURE 18-2. A filing cabinet illustrates a hierarchically structured mass storage device. Level 1 is the entire filing cabinet. On level 2, the filing cabinet is divided into drawers. On level 3, each drawer is subdivided by divider partitions.

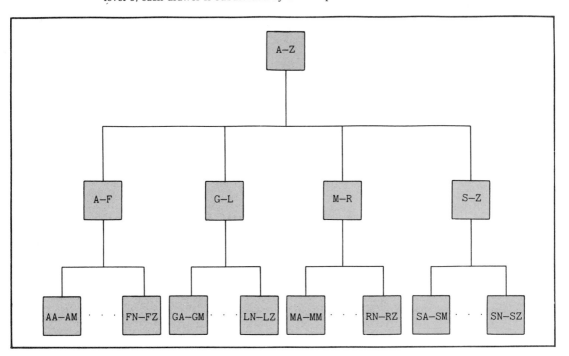

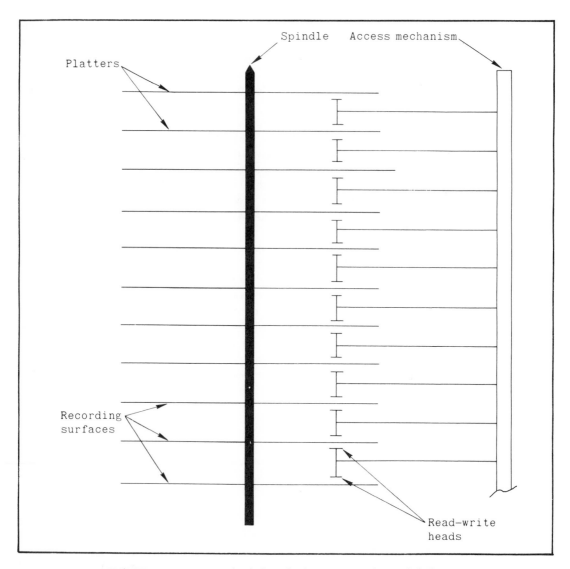

FIGURE 18-3. Structure of a disk pack (shown mounted on a disk drive).

disks or *platters*. Each platter has two *recording surfaces* on which information can be stored. The outermost recording surfaces—the top one on the top platter and the bottom one on the bottom platter—are not used.

Information is stored on and retrieved from the disks with *read-write* heads. These are mounted on a comblike *access mechanism* whose *access arms* move in and out between the platters.

Suppose the access mechanism is in a fixed position. As the disks rotate, a circular portion of each recording surface passes under the adjacent read-write head. That circular portion is called a *track*.

For any position of the access mechanism, there will be one track on each recording surface that is currently passing under a read-write head.

The set of all such tracks is called a *cylinder*. For any position of the access mechanism, we can access the tracks of one cylinder. To access a track on another cylinder, we have to move the access mechanism.

Figure 18-4 shows the hierarchical structure of a disk pack. Since moving the access mechanism is time consuming, it is best first to narrow the search down to a particular cylinder, instead of jumping from cylinder to cylinder. Thus, on level 2 of the hierarchy the disk pack is divided into cylinders.

The obvious subdivision of the cylinder is the track. For the kind of disk pack considered here, the tracks are not further subdivided. Instead, a track is searched for a given record by examining the records as they pass under the read-write head. Since we must wait for the proper record to pass under the read-write head anyway before we can retrieve it, this search consumes no additional time. On some computer systems, this search is done automatically by the hardware. We give the hardware the key of the record we wish to access and the track on which it is located. The hardware then scans the specified track for the desired record.

On some disks, a track is further subdivided into *sectors*. These disks are usually used on small computers, where the automatic track-search mechanism is not available.

FIGURE 18-4. Hierarchical structure of a disk pack. The number of cylinders and the number of tracks per cylinder vary from one type of disk pack to another.

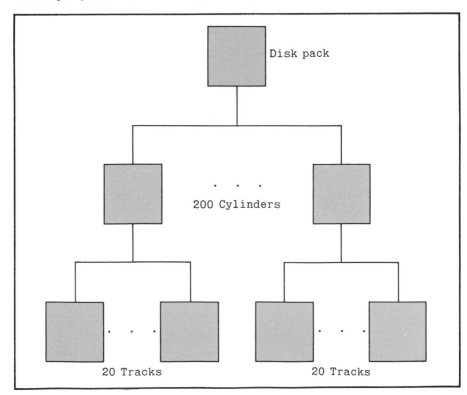

18.2 Primary-key Retrieval

We now turn to the problem of accessing a record, given its primary key. We will assume our file to be divided into buckets as shown in Figure 18-1. In a hierarchically structured file, the same access techniques would be applied on each level except the bottom one, on which the buckets would simply be searched.

Our problem, then, boils down to the following: Given the primary key of a record, find out which bucket contains the record (or should contain it if the record is being stored).

The two commonly used methods of solving this problem are *index sequential access* and *hashing*.

Indexed Sequential Files. One way to determine which bucket contains a particular record is to provide an *index* to the buckets. This is the method most commonly encountered in everyday situations. The cards on the fronts of filing cabinet drawers, for instance, constitute an index. And the index tabs on the separators inside a drawer constitute another. Or consider a dictionary. The thumb index constitutes one index, and the guide words at the top of each page constitute another.

Inside each bucket, the records are stored sequentially, with their keys in alphabetical order. The index entries are also arranged in alphabetical order. This sequential storage simplifies index construction. It also allows the file to be processed using sequential access as well as random access. An indexed sequential file can be either a sequential file or a random file, depending on the need.

Figure 18-5 shows a simple indexed sequential file. As usual in examples, only the record keys are shown. The records are laid out in alphabetical order. There is an index with one entry for each bucket.

Each index entry consists of the key of the last record that is stored in the corresponding bucket, and a pointer to the bucket. We assume the buckets to be numbered 1, 2, 3, and so on. The pointer is simply the bucket number.

To find a particular record, we scan the index from beginning to end until we find an entry whose key part is greater than or equal to the key of the record we are trying to find. That record—if it is in the file at all—is located in the corresponding bucket. Using this technique, look up several records in the file of Figure 18-5, until you are convinced that the method works.

Notice that this method works only because the records are stored in alphabetical order. In fact, if the records were stored in random order, we would need an index entry for each *record*, instead of just one for each *bucket*.

Unfortunately, our simple index sequential file has a problem. What if we want to insert a new record in the file? The new record must be inserted in its proper position in alphabetical order, of course. The only way to do that in Figure 18-5 would be to move every following record up one position. This is impractical; we must modify our simple file to allow for convenient insertions.

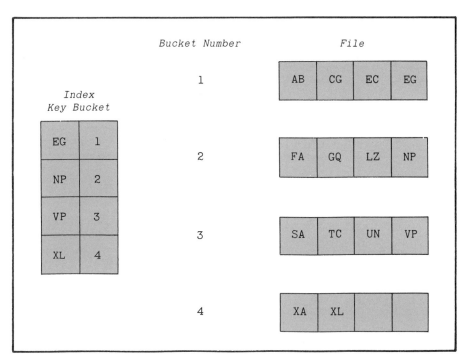

FIGURE 18-5. An indexed sequential file.

Two commonly used methods of handling insertions are *distributed free space* and *overflow areas*.

The distributed free-space technique can be observed in many libraries. Some unused space is left on each shelf, and some unused shelves are scattered throughout the stacks. Thus, a new book can be shelved in its proper place without having to reshelve every book in the library!

Figure 18-6 shows an indexed sequential file using distributed free space. When the file is created, some free space is left in each bucket. Also, some buckets are left free. Free space is left in the index for each free bucket.

When a record is inserted, the index is used to determine in which bucket it should go. If the bucket has any free space left, then the record is inserted in that bucket. Only inside that one bucket may some records have to be moved to allow the new record to be inserted in the proper position.

It may happen, however, that the bucket into which a particular record is to go is already full, its free space having been used up by previous insertions. When this happens, we must use one of the free buckets. The full bucket is *split* into two parts. Some of its records (usually half) are retained in the old bucket, and the rest are placed in the free bucket. The index entry for the original bucket must be modified, and a new index entry must be made for the formerly free bucket. The new record can now be inserted, since both parts of the original bucket now contain free space.

Figure 18-7 illustrates the overflow-area technique. The file is divided into two parts: a *prime area* and an *overflow area*. Originally, all of the

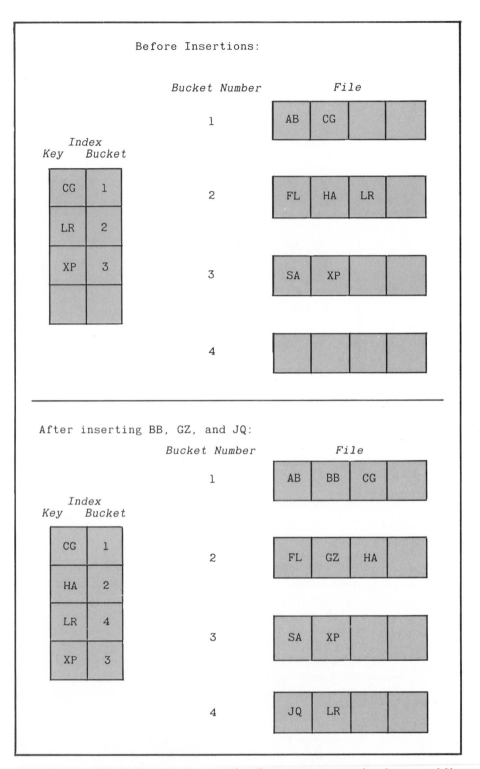

FIGURE 18-6. Using distributed free space to handle insertions in an indexed sequential file. The first new record is inserted into bucket 1 and the second into bucket 2. The third new record is also inserted into bucket 2. This causes bucket 2 to split, part of its contents staying in bucket 2 and the remainder going into bucket 4.

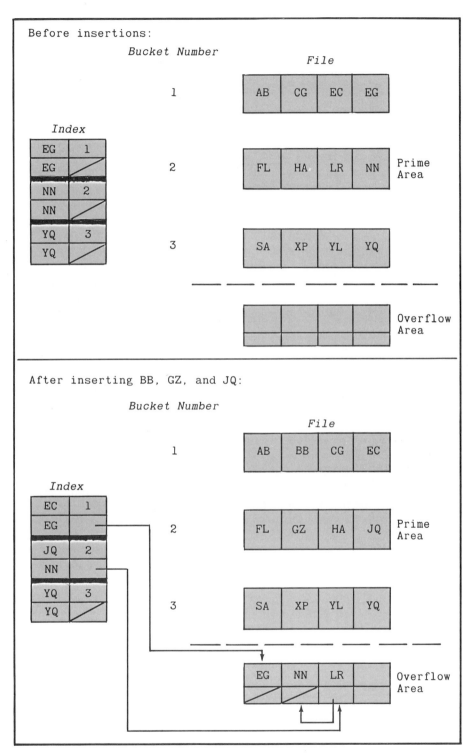

FIGURE 18-7. Using overflow areas to handle insertions in an indexed sequential file. The first new record is inserted in bucket 1 and the next two into bucket 2. This pushes one record from bucket 1 and two records from bucket 2 into the overflow area.

records of the file are placed in the prime area. No free space is left in the prime area. Instead, all of the free space is gathered together in the overflow area.

When a new record is inserted, the index is consulted to determine which bucket it should go in. The record is placed in that bucket. But since the bucket has no free space, inserting a new record will cause a record to be *pushed off the end* of the bucket. The record that is pushed off the end goes into the overflow area.

For each bucket in the prime area, there is a *pair* of index entries. The first is the usual one; it contains the key of the last record in that bucket and a pointer to the bucket.

The second entry is for those records which have been pushed off of the corresponding bucket into the overflow area. Each record in the overflow area contains a link component. These links are used to join the records that have been pushed off a given bucket into a linked list. The overflow entry for a particular bucket contains the key of the last record on the list and a pointer to the first record on the list.

If no records have been pushed off a particular bucket, then the key parts of the main and overflow index entries for that bucket are the same. The pointer part of the overflow entry is NIL. If some records have been pushed off, then the key part of the overflow entry is greater than the key part of the main entry, and the pointer part points to the list of overflow records.

The value of a pointer locates a particular record by bucket number and position in the bucket. Thus, (5, 2) refers to the second record in bucket 5, (6, 1) to the first record in bucket 6, and so on.

An overflow list may extend through several buckets. Thus, searching for a record on an overflow list is less efficient than searching for it in a single bucket. For this reason, as more and more buckets overflow and the overflow lists become longer, access will become less efficient. Eventually, the file will have to be reorganized. All the records will be copied into the prime area of a new file, and we will start all over again.

The name ISAM (Index Sequential Access Method) is applied to indexed sequential files using overflow areas. ISAM is incorporated in operating systems available from a number of computer manufacturers.

Hashing. So far, we have used an index to determine in which bucket a record with a particular key should be stored. Another approach is to carry out a *calculation* on the key that will yield the bucket number. The calculation is carried out when the record is stored and again when it is accessed. The technique is called *hashing*, since the calculation scrambles, or makes a hash out of, the key. An alternate term is *scatter storage*.

In the examples, we will assume the keys to be six-digit numbers such as 124653, 459085, and 267543. The arithmetical operations of the hashing calculation can be applied to these numeric keys. There are methods of converting alphanumeric keys such as 12-A-345-XQ into numbers for the purposes of hashing calculations, but we will not go into them. These methods often involve manipulating the bits that make up the character codes of the characters in the key and hence are machine dependent.

There are many possible ways to do the hashing calculation, but one of the simplest is also one of the most effective—a rare situation in computer science. This calculation involves dividing the key by the number of buckets in the prime area of the file and taking the remainder of the division. When 1 is added to the remainder, the result is the number of the bucket in which the record should be stored.

As we saw in Chapter 1, the operator MOD is often used to represent the operation of taking the remainder (rather than the quotient) in a division.

Expression	Value
5 MOD 3	2
11 MOD 5	1
101 MOD 25	1
1003 MOD 100	3

Using the MOD operator, we can express the hashing calculation as:

```
BUCKET_NUMBER ← (KEY MOD NUMBER_OF_BUCKETS) + 1
```

Suppose, for instance, a file has five buckets in the prime area. Then a record with key 137648 would be placed in bucket 4, since:

```
BUCKET_NUMBER ← (137648 MOD 5) + 1
BUCKET_NUMBER ← 3 + 1
BUCKET_NUMBER ← 4
```

The record with key 739645 would go in bucket number 1, since:

```
BUCKET_NUMBER ← (739645 MOD 5) + 1
BUCKET_NUMBER ← 0 + 1
BUCKET_NUMBER ← 1
```

Figure 18-8 further illustrates the use of this hashing calculation to place records in buckets.

The hashing calculation is often included in a function, called the *hashing function*, whose argument is the key and whose value is the bucket to which the record having that key is assigned. We can write the hashing function as follows:

```
FUNCTION HASH(KEY)
   GLOBAL NUMBER_OF_BUCKETS
   HASH ← (KEY MOD NUMBER_OF_BUCKETS) + 1
END HASH
```

Thus, if NUMBER_OF_BUCKETS is 5, the value of HASH(137648) is 4 and that of HASH(739645) is 1.

A hashing function should distribute the records over the buckets as

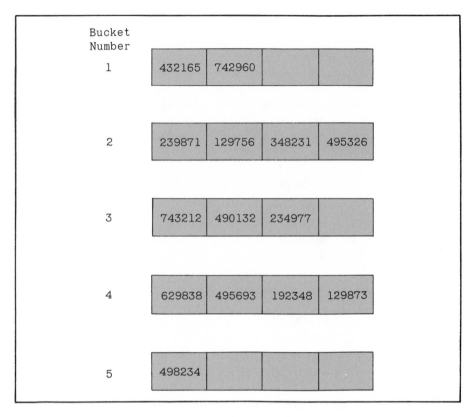

FIGURE 18-8. Distribution of records in a file using a hashing function.

evenly as possible, instead of filling up a few buckets and leaving the others empty. For HASH to have this property, we must place a restriction on NUMBER__OF__BUCKETS; its value must be a *prime number*. A prime number is one that cannot be evenly divided by any other number, expect for 1 and itself. Some prime numbers are

2 3 5 7 11 13 17 19 23 29 31 37

Nevertheless, no matter how good the hashing function, some buckets will fill up before others. To handle this problem, we divide the file into a prime area and an overflow area, as was done for index sequential files (see Figure 18-9).

Records are inserted in the prime area using the hashing function. (Note the NUMBER__OF__BUCKETS in the hashing function is the number of buckets in the *prime* area.) If the bucket whose number the hashing function yields is already full, then the record is inserted on the overflow list for that bucket. (If this is the first overflow record for that bucket, a new overflow list is started.)

When a record is to be accessed, the hashing function is first applied to the key. The bucket whose number the hashing function yields is

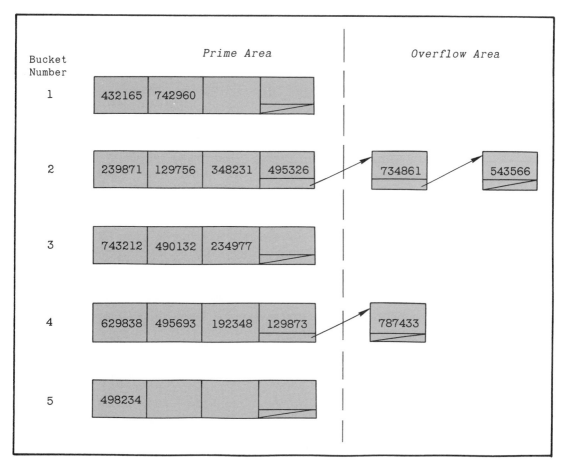

FIGURE 18-9. Use of overflow chains to handle overflow in a hashed file.

searched. If the desired record is not found in that bucket, the overflow list for that bucket is searched. Searching the overflow list will mean accessing one or more additional buckets. Thus, accessing a record in the overflow area is more time consuming than accessing one in the prime area.

The number of records in the prime area should not exceed about 75 percent of its capacity. If this *load factor* is exceeded, many buckets will overflow, and overflow lists will become long. Average access time will increase since many searches through long overflow lists will be required.

If the load factor is not exceeded, however, overflow lists will be short. In fact, a well-designed hashing scheme will usually be faster than indexed sequential access because it is faster to evaluate the hashing function than to search an index. And, of course, no storage is needed for an index.

The main drawback of hashing is that the records are not stored in order according to their keys, so sequential processing of the file is impossible. Unfortunately, for some applications this drawback is serious enough to exclude hashing from consideration.

18.3 Secondary-key Retrieval

In secondary-key retrieval, we access all the records in the file satisfying some condition on the values of the secondary keys, such as

```
(SEX = 'FEMALE') AND (MARITAL_STATUS = 'SINGLE')
```

which would yield the records of all single females.

For indexed sequential files, we stored the records in alphabetical order according to the primary key. This greatly simplified our index since we only had to include an entry for the last record in each bucket. We knew that all records following the last record in the previous bucket and preceding the last record in the current bucket would lie in the current bucket.

Unfortunately, it is not generally possible to order records according to more than one key. Thus, records are generally *not* in order according to their secondary keys. As a result, there must be an index for *every value* of a secondary key, rather than just the last value in each bucket.

Because of this, secondary-key indexes can become quite large. In advanced information-retrieval systems, it is not unusual for the indexes to be larger than the data file!

We will discuss two widely used methods of secondary-key retrieval: *multilists* and *inverted files*.

Multilists. In the multilist method, all those records in which a particular secondary key has a particular value are joined together in a linked list. The index entry for the key and value in question contains a pointer to the list.

Figure 18-10 illustrates a multilist file. The primary key is STOCK_NUMBER. The secondary keys are TYPE and COLOR.

Each record must have one link for each secondary key. Thus, the records in Figure 18-10 could be defined as follows:

```
DECLARE 1 ITEM
          2 STOCK_NUMBER
          2 TYPE
          2 TYPE_LINK
          2 COLOR
          2 COLOR_LINK
```

TYPE_LINK is used to link together all records having the same value of TYPE; COLOR_LINK is used to link together all records having the same value of COLOR.

The indexes contain one entry for each value of each secondary key. TYPE has five possible values—1, 2, 3, 4, and 5—and so the TYPE index has five entries. COLOR has four possible values—'BLUE', 'GREEN', 'RED' and 'YELLOW'—so the COLOR index has four entries.

Each index entry contains one more part in addition to the secondary

Main File

Record	STOCK_NUMBER	TYPE	TYPE_LINK	COLOR	COLOR_LINK
1	123985	1	5	'BLUE'	3
2	278943	2	7	'RED'	8
3	387465	3	NIL	'BLUE'	6
4	398732	5	10	'YELLOW'	7
5	431778	1	8	'GREEN'	NIL
6	534219	4	NIL	'BLUE'	10
7	543998	2	9	'YELLOW'	9
8	678920	1	NIL	'RED'	NIL
9	786935	2	NIL	'YELLOW'	NIL
10	794235	5	NIL	'BLUE'	NIL

TYPE Index

TYPE	Pointer	Count
1	1	3
2	2	3
3	3	1
4	6	1
5	4	2

COLOR Index

COLOR	Pointer	Count
'BLUE'	1	4
'GREEN'	5	1
'RED'	2	2
'YELLOW'	4	3

FIGURE 18-10. The multilist approach to organizing a file for secondary key retrieval.

key value and the pointer to the list of records having that value. That part gives the number of records on the list.

The reason for giving the number of records is this. Suppose we are requested to find the records satisfying:

(TYPE = 3) AND (COLOR = 'RED')

We can conduct this search in two ways. We can search the list for TYPE = 3 and select all records for which COLOR = 'RED'. Or, we can search the list for COLOR = 'RED', and select all records for which TYPE = 3.

Which list should we search? The shortest one, of course. And the number-of-records parts of the index entries tells us which list is shortest.

Inverted Files. An inverted file is not a file turned upside down, but an index for the values of a secondary key. It is said to be *inverted* since the secondary key plays the same role for the inverted file as the primary key plays for the main file. The entries in the inverted file are in alphabetical order according to the secondary key rather than the primary key.

A library, for instance, contains three inverted files in the card catalog. These are the author catalog, the title catalog, and the subject catalog. In some libraries, these are separate catalogs kept in separate drawers. In others, the author, subject, and title cards are combined in one catalog.

Thus, if we want to find the books on a given subject, we look up that subject in the subject catalog, finding a card for each book on the subject we looked up. We proceed similarly to find the books by a given author or the books with a given title.

Figure 18-11 shows the file from Figure 18-10 with two inverted files. There is one inverted file for each secondary key. Each inverted file has an entry for each possible value of the secondary key in question. That entry consists of the secondary-key value and an *occurrence list* containing the locations of all records in the main file for which the secondary key has the corresponding value.

(In Figures 18-10 and 18-11, each record is, for simplicity, designated by a single *record number*. In practice, this designation would probably consist of two parts—a *bucket number*, specifying the bucket containing the record, and a *record number*, designating a particular record in that bucket.)

Given a simple condition such as

```
COLOR = 'RED'
```

we consult the appropriate index and access all records on the occurrence list found.

For compound conditions such as

```
(TYPE = 4) OR (COLOR = 'BLUE')
```

or

```
(TYPE = 4) AND (COLOR = 'BLUE')
```

we must merge two occurrence lists and use the merged lists to select the records to be accessed.

We define two kinds of merge: the *OR-merge* and the *AND-merge*. The OR-merge of two lists yields a list of those items that occur on one or the other or both of the original lists. The AND-merge of two lists yields a list of only those items that are on both the original lists.

Main File

Record	STOCK_NUMBER	TYPE	COLOR
1	123985	1	'BLUE'
2	278943	2	'RED'
3	387465	3	'BLUE'
4	398732	5	'YELLOW'
5	431778	1	'GREEN'
6	534219	4	'BLUE'
7	543998	2	'YELLOW'
8	678920	1	'RED'
9	786935	2	'YELLOW'
10	794235	5	'BLUE'

Inverted File for TYPE

TYPE	Occurrence List
1	1 5 8
2	2 7 9
3	3
4	6
5	4 10

Inverted File for COLOR

COLOR	Occurrence List
'BLUE'	1 3 6 10
'GREEN'	5
'RED'	2 8
'YELLOW'	4 7 9

FIGURE 18-11. The inverted file approach to secondary key retrieval.

As with the merge discussed in Chapter 17, both of the lists to be merged must be ordered. We will assume the occurrence lists are numerical order according to record locations.

We can now give algorithms for the OR-merge and the AND-merge.

OR-merge. Consider the next entry to be processed on each of the two lists being merged. Compare these two entries. If they are equal, place one on the merged list and discard the other. Otherwise, place the smaller of the two on the merged list.

Repeat this procedure until one of the lists is exhausted. Then copy the remainder of the other list onto the merged list.

Figure 18-12 illustrates an OR-merge.

AND-merge. Consider the next entry to be processed on each of the two lists being merged. Compare these two entries. If they are equal, place one on the merged list and discard the other. Otherwise, discard the smaller of the two entries.

Repeat this procedure until one of the lists is exhausted. Then discard the remainder of the other list.

Figure 18-13 illustrates an AND-merge.

Notice that the lists being merged are processed sequentially. We do not need access to an entire occurrence list at one time. Instead, we can have a procedure that obtains the next item on a given occurrence list when it is needed. We can keep calling that procedure for each of the lists being merged until we get an item that is to go onto the merged list. At that time, we can access the corresponding record. Then we go back to fetching items from the occurence lists. The merged list need never exist as a list. We can create it item by item, using each item to access a record as soon as we realize it should be on the merged list.

Note that the merged list is in numerical order and so can participate in further merges as may be required by more complicated conditions.

FIGURE 18-12. The OR-merge.

Merged List	Lists Being Merged					
	17	25	35	49		
	15	20	25	30	35	50
15	17	25	35	49		
	20	25	30	35	50	
15 17	25	35	49			
	20	25	30	35	50	
15 17 20	25	35	49			
	25	30	35	50		
15 17 20 25	35	49				
	30	35	50			
15 17 20 25 30	35	49				
	35	50				
15 17 20 25 30 35	49					
	50					
15 17 20 25 30 35 49						
	50					
15 17 20 25 30 35 49 50						

Merged List	Lists Being Merged
	17 25 35 49 15 20 25 30 35 50
	17 25 35 49 20 25 30 35 50
	25 35 49 20 25 30 35 50
	25 35 49 25 30 35 50
25	35 49 30 35 50
25	35 49 35 50
25 35	49 50
25 35	 50
25 35	

FIGURE 18-13. The AND-merge.

Review Questions

1. What is the *primary key* of a record?

2. What are the *secondary keys* of a record?

3. Which kind of retrieval, primary key or secondary key, will always access just one record? Which kind will usually access more than one record?

4. Which kind of retrieval often involves conditions on more than one record component?

5. What is a *bucket*? On what basis is a random-access device partitioned into buckets?

6. Describe how a random-access device can have a hierarchical structure.

7. Using a filing cabinet as an example, illustrate the hierarchical structure of a random-access device.

8. Discuss the hierarchical structure of a disk pack.

9. Describe the organization of a simple indexed sequential file. In what order are the records stored in the buckets? Describe the index entries. In what order are the entries stored in the index?

10. Describe the procedure for locating the record with a given key in a simple indexed sequential file.

11. Describe the method of *distributed free space* for organizing an indexed sequential file so that insertions may be made.

12. Describe the *overflow-area* method of organizing an indexed sequential file.

13. In hashing, evaluation of the hashing function corresponds to what operation for indexed sequential files?

14. Describe the hashing function discussed in this chapter.

15. Give the limitations on (a) the number of buckets in the prime area and (b) the number of records stored in the prime area that are needed for the hashing scheme described in this chapter to be efficient.

16. What are two advantages of hashing? What is its main drawback?

17. In what important way does a secondary-key index usually differ from a primary-key index? What is the reason for the difference?

18. Describe the *multilist* method of organizing a file for secondary-key retrieval.

19. What is an *inverted file*? How is it used? Give an everyday example involving three inverted files.

20. What is an occurrence list?

21. Describe the OR-merge and the AND-merge. What are these merges used for?

22. Give an example of a secondary-key retrieval problem that can be solved using an OR-merge.

23. Give an example of a secondary-key retrieval problem that can be solved using an AND-merge.

Exercises

1. If the index for an indexed sequential file is small enough, the entire index may be read into main memory to speed up searching. Assume that the index is stored in main memory as an array:

```
DECLARE 1 ENTRY ( )
          2 KEY_OF_LAST_RECORD
          2 BUCKET_NUMBER
```

Write a procedure that, given the key of a record, will determine the bucket in which that record is stored. Assume a simple indexed sequential file with no provisions for overflow.

2. Extend the procedure in Exercise 1 to an indexed sequential file using

an overflow area. The procedure will return either the number of the bucket or a pointer to the overflow list containing the desired record. The index has the following structure:

```
DECLARE 1 ENTRY ( )
            2 MAIN_ENTRY
              3 KEY_OF_LAST_RECORD
              3 BUCKET_NUMBER
            2 OVERFLOW ENTRY
              3 KEY_OF_LAST_RECORD
              3 POINTER
                4 BUCKET_NUMBER
                4 RECORD_NUMBER
```

3. Consider a hash file with seven buckets, with each bucket able to hold four records. Choose 21 six-digit keys at random and, using the hashing function, insert the records with those keys into the file. Construct overflow lists when necessary. (*Hint:* To find the remainder of a division by 7 using a pocket calculator, do the following:

124735	(Key)
7)124735	(Divide by 7)
17819.28571	
−17819	(Subtract off integer part)
.28571	
× 7	(Multiply by 7)
1.99997	
2	(Round to nearest integer)

Thus, the value of 124735 MOD 7 is 2. With a little practice, this computation can be carried out very quickly on the calculator.)

4. Write an algorithm to do an OR-merge of two sequential files. This is similar to the merge algorithm discussed in Chapter 17, except that when the same record occurs in both files being merged, only one copy of that record goes into the merged file.

5. Write algorithm to do an AND-merge of two sequential files.

PART FIVE

INTRODUCTION
TO
NUMERICAL
METHODS

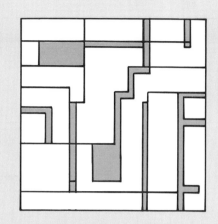

Chapter 19

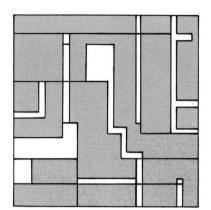

Solving Equations

One important use of computers—although by no means the only one, as some people seem to think—is solving numerical problems. The study of how to solve numerical problems using computers is called *numerical analysis.*

In this chapter and the next, we will examine some numerical problems and some algorithms for their solution. These problems were selected to illustrate some of the methods of, and give some of the feel and flavor of, numerical analysis. Anything approaching complete coverage of numerical techniques, however, is impossible in the space available. Readers primarily interested in numerical computing—physicists, chemists, engineers, applied mathematicians, and so on—should continue their study with a numerical analysis course.

The reader of this chapter is assumed to be familiar with the basic ideas and terminology taught in introductory mathematics courses.

19.1 Nonlinear equations

For the linear equation

$$ax + b = 0$$

there exists an *explicit solution*—a formula that gives the root of the equation in terms of the constants that appear in it:

x = −b/a

Given an example of a linear equation, such as

4x + 1 = 0

we have only to plug the constants into the explicit solution to get the root:

$$x = -\frac{1}{4} = -0.25$$

Even some nonlinear equations have explicit solutions. The equation of the second degree, the *quadratic equation*

$ax^2 + bx + c = 0$

has an explicit solution given by the well-known quadratic formula

$x = (-b \pm \sqrt{b^2 - 4ac})/(2a)$

Explicit solutions exist for equations of the third and fourth degrees, but they are quite complex. For the general equation of the fifth degree

$ax^5 + bx^4 + cx^3 + dx^2 + ex + f = 0$

no explicit solution exists. The same holds for the equations of the sixth, seventh, and higher degrees.

Another kind of equation for which an explicit solution rarely exists is the *transcendental equation* constructed using the trigonometric, logarithmic, or exponential functions. A few of these can be solved using special identities, such as trigonometric identities. But for most, such as

$\sin ax - b^x + c = 0$

no explicit solution exists.

When we are faced with an equation having a form for which no explicit solution exists, we must use some numerical technique to find the roots of the particular equation at hand. Usually we use an algorithm that generates *successive approximations* to a root, with each approximation better than the previous one. We let the algorithm run until the desired accuracy is obtained.

Many such algorithms exist. One of the most straightforward of them *searches* for a root of the equation much as we search an array for a particular element.

The Half-Interval Method. The half-interval method applies the principle of *binary search* to search for a root of the equation at hand.

We recall from Chapter 8 how binary search was used to find a desired element of an array. As Figure 19-1 illustrates, we started by dividing the

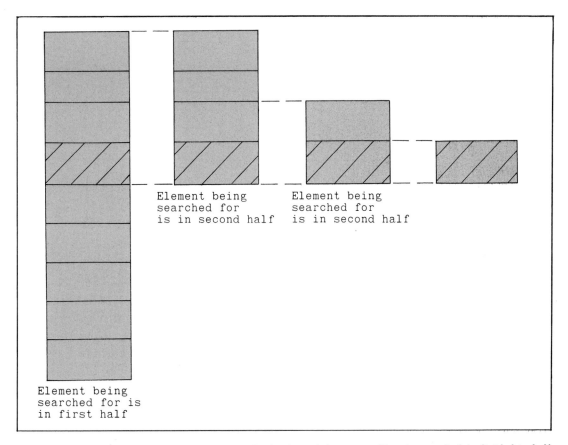

Element being
searched for
is in second half

Element being
searched for
is in second half

Element being
searched for is
in first half

FIGURE 19-1. In binary search, the part of the array still to be searched is divided in half, and only the half containing the sought-after element is retained.

array in half. We then determined if the sought-after element was in the first half or the second half. We narrowed the search down to the half containing the desired element and discarded the other half. We repeated the process on the selected half, and so on. Proceeding in this way, we quickly narrowed our search down to the element being sought.

Figure 19-2 shows how the same principle can be applied to finding the root of an equation. We start with an *interval* containing one such root. The endpoints of the interval are x_- and x_+. (We will see the reason for that notation in a moment.) We divide the interval at its midpoint

$$x_{mid} = (x_- + x_+)/2$$

giving us two intervals: one from x_- to x_{mid} and one from x_{mid} to x_+.

Now we determine in which interval the root lies. If it lies in the left interval, we set x_+ equal to x_{mid} to narrow down the search to the left interval. If the root is in the right interval, we set x_- equal to x_{mid} to narrow down the search to the right interval. Repeating this process, we get a series of smaller and smaller intervals, all containing the root. The succes-

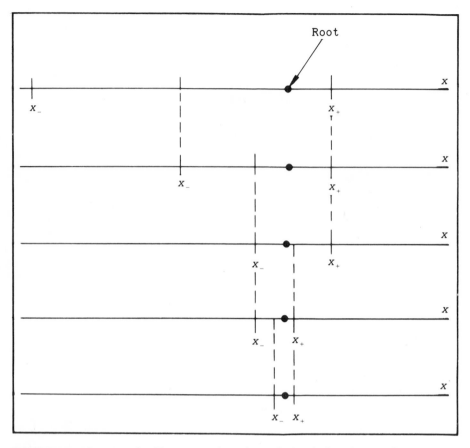

FIGURE 19-2. The principle of binary search can be applied to finding the root of an equation. An interval containing the root is divided in half and only the half containing the root is retained.

sive values of x_{mid}, the midpoints of those intervals, form a sequence of successive approximations to the root.

To apply this method, we obviously need some way of determining whether or not a given interval contains a root of an equation.

Let's write our equation in the form

$$f(x) = 0$$

where the function $f(x)$ is defined as equal to the left side of the equation. Thus, if the equation is

$$\sin ax - b^x + c = 0$$

then

$$f(x) = \sin ax - b^x + c$$

We assume that $f(x)$ is a *continuous function*: if the value of $f(x)$ passes from one value to another as x is varied, it will pass through all the intervening values as well.

Suppose, then, that we know two values of x, x_- and x_+, such that

$$f(x_-) < 0$$

$$f(x_+) > 0$$

As Figure 19-3 illustrates, as x goes from x_- to x_+, $f(x)$ goes from a negative value to a positive value. Therefore, it must pass through the value 0. Hence, there must be a value of x in the interval from x_- to x_+ such that $f(x) = 0$. Or, in other words, the interval from x_- to x_+ must contain a root of $f(x) = 0$.

Note that although the figure shows $x_- < x_+$, we could just as well have $x_+ < x_-$ if $f(x)$ goes from a positive value to a negative value as x is increased.

The interval from x_- to x_+ may contain more than one root of $f(x) = 0$. If we apply the half-interval method to an interval initially containing more than one root, the successive intervals will narrow down on one of the roots, but which one is not easily predictable in advance.

The remaining question is how long we should let the algorithm run. That is, how do we know when x_{mid} is a close enough approximation to

FIGURE 19-3. If $f(x_-) < 0$ and $f(x_+) > 0$, then there is a root of $f(x) = 0$ lying between x_- and x_+.

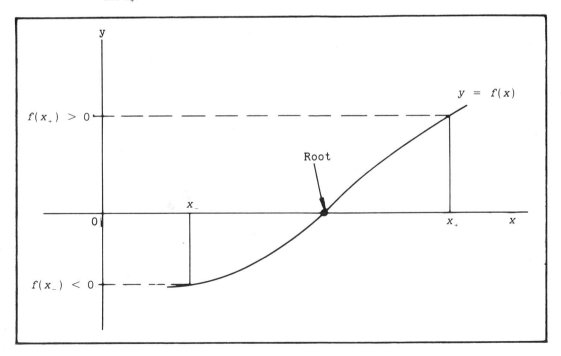

the actual root of the equation? Since we are searching for an x that will give $f(x) = 0$, a reasonable approximation would be an x_{mid} such that the absolute value of $f(x_{mid})$ is less than some maximum error. The user must specify the maximum error, since it depends on the equation and the use to which the solution is to be put.

We can now outline the algorithm:

```
PROCEDURE HALF_INTERVAL(XMINUS, XPLUS, XMID, MAX_ERROR, F)
    FMINUS ← F(XMINUS)
    FPLUS ← F(XPLUS)
    REPEAT
        (Compute XMID and FMID ← F(XMID); set either XPLUS
        or XMINUS to XMID, so that the resulting interval
        contains a root of F(X) = 0)
    UNTIL ABS(FMID) < MAX_ERROR
END HALF_INTERVAL
```

Note that the function F (corresponding to f in the foregoing discussion) is passed as an argument to the procedure. Most programming languages used for numerical programming allow functions to be passed as arguments to procedures. The function F must, of course, be defined elsewhere.

On each pass through the REPEAT loop, we first calculate XMID and FMID

```
XMID ← (XMINUS + XPLUS)/2
FMID ← F(XMID)
```

If FMID < 0, then XMINUS should be set to XMID; if FMID > 0, then XPLUS should be set to XMID. That way, F(XMINUS) will still be negative, and F(XPLUS), positive, so that the interval from XMINUS to XPLUS will still contain a root of F(X) = 0. See Figure 19-4.

```
IF FMID < 0 THEN
    XMINUS ← XMID
    FMINUS ← FMID
ELSE
    XPLUS ← XMID
    FPLUS ← FMID
END IF
```

(If FMID = 0, then the manipulations of XMINUS and XPLUS are immaterial, since the algorithm will terminate after the current pass with XMID equal to the root of the equation.)

The initial values supplied for XMINUS and XPLUS when the algorithm is called must be such that F(XMINUS) is negative and F(XPLUS) is positive. When the algorithm terminates, XMID contains the desired approximation to the root.

Figure 19-5 shows the complete procedure HALF__INTERVAL.

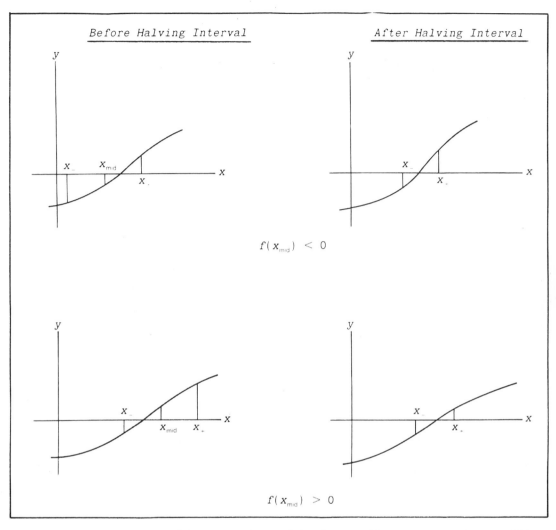

FIGURE 19-4. If $f(x_{mid}) < 0$, then we halve the interval by setting x_- equal to x_{mid}. if $f(x_{mid})$ > 0, then we set x_+ equal to x_{mid}. In each case, the new interval from x_- to x_+ contains a root of the equation.

19.2 Systems of Linear Equations

Systems of linear equations such as

$$3x_1 + 2x_2 + 4x_3 = 19$$
$$6x_1 + 5x_2 + 9x_3 = 43$$
$$9x_1 + 8x_2 + 13x_3 = 64$$

present another problem. Several explicit methods for solving such systems are taught in elementary mathematics courses. Unfortunately, systems of hundreds or even thousands of equations in as many unknowns are not uncommon in some applications. With so many equations, it is too labo-

```
PROCEDURE HALF_INTERNAL(XMINUS, XPLUS, XMID, MAX_ERROR, F)
    FMINUS ← F(XMINUS)
    FPLUS ← F(XPLUS)
    REPEAT
        XMID ← (XMINUS + XPLUS)/2
        FMID ← F(XMID)
        IF FMID < 0 THEN
            XMINUS ← XMID
            FMINUS ← FMID
        ELSE
            XPLUS ← XMID
            FPLUS ← FMID
        END IF
    UNTIL ABS(FMID) < MAX_ERROR
END HALF_INTERVAL
```

FIGURE 19-5. The procedure HALF_INTERVAL.

rious to do the calculations in the explicit solutions by hand; a computer must be used. And so many calculations are called for that round-off error becomes a problem. As a result, it is sometimes possible for a successive-approximations solution to give more accurate results than an explicit solution.

One method of solving linear equations often taught in elementary mathematics courses must be avoided at all costs. That is the method of determinants (Cramer's rule). Determinants are important for proving theorems and other theoretical analysis, but they are worthless for computation. To evaluate an $n \times n$ determinant requires more than $n!$ multiplications ($n!$ is the product of the first n integers — $5! = 1 \times 2 \times 3 \times 4 \times 5$, for example). For a 10×10 determinant, this works out to be 3,628,800. For a 50×50 determinant, over 3×10^{64} multiplications would be needed. This is more than any computer could accomplish within a human lifetime.

In this section, we will look at one explicit method for solving systems of linear equations, *Gauss-Jordan elimination*, and one successive-approximations method, the *Gauss-Seidel method*.

Gauss-Jordan Elimination. This is the method of elimination of variables that is familiar from algebra courses. In algebra problems, it is usually left up to the student to determine which variables to eliminate from which equations. To write an algorithm the computer can follow, we must, of course, specify this and all other matters explicitly. Our problem, then, will be to organize the usual method into an algorithm suitable for the computer.

Consider the system of equations shown in Figure 19-6. We can use the first equation to eliminate x_1 from the second and third equations. To do this, we multiply the first equation by $6/3 = 2$ to get

$$6x_1 + 4x_2 + 8x_3 = 38$$

$$3x_1 + 2x_2 + 4x_3 = 19$$
$$6x_1 + 5x_2 + 9x_3 = 43$$
$$9x_1 + 8x_2 + 13x_3 = 64$$

FIGURE 19-6. A set of three equations in three unknowns.

We then subtract this from the second equation and get

$$x_2 + x_3 = 5$$

The $6x_1$ terms cancel and x_1 is eliminated from the second equation.

In the same way, we can multiply the first equation by 9/3 = 3 and subtract it from the third equation. The $9x_1$ terms cancel, eliminating x_1 from the third equation.

Figure 19-7 shows the result of using the first equation to eliminate x_1 from the second and third equations.

$$3x_1 + 2x_2 + 4x_3 = 19$$
$$x_2 + x_3 = 5$$
$$2x_2 + x_3 = 7$$

FIGURE 19-7. The equations of Figure 19-6 after using the first equation to eliminate x_1 from the second and third equations.

In exactly the same way, we can now use the second equation to eliminate x_2 from the first and third equations. Figure 19-8 shows the result of these eliminations.

Finally, we can use the third equation to eliminate x_3 from the first and second equations. Figure 19-9 shows the results of these eliminations.

FIGURE 19-8. The equations of Figure 19-7 after using the second equation to eliminate x_2 from the first and third equations.

$$3x_1 + 2x_3 = 9$$
$$x_2 + x_3 = 5$$
$$-x_3 = -3$$

$$
\begin{array}{rcr}
3x_1 & = & 3 \\
x_2 & = & 2 \\
-x_3 & = & -3
\end{array}
$$

FIGURE 19-9. The equations of Figure 19-8 after using the third equation to eliminate x_3 from the first and second equations. Since each equation now contains only one unknown, the equations are easy to solve.

Now x_1 appears only in the first equation, x_2, only in the second, and x_3, only in the third. Thus, we can easily solve for x_1, x_2, and x_3, getting:

$x_1 = 3/3 = 1, x_2 = 2, x_3 = -3/-1 = 3$

Now let us write an algorithm that will carry out this elimination for N equations in N unknowns. We assume that the coefficients on the left side of the equations to be solved, as well as the constants on the right, are stored in an array A of N rows and N + 1 columns. Figure 19-10 illustrates this for three equations in three unknowns. Columns 1 through N of the array hold the left-hand-side coefficients. Column N + 1 holds the right-hand-side constants. Each row of A represents one equation, and any manipulation of equations can be carried out on the rows of A.

We will use each equation in turn to eliminate the corresponding unknown from the other equations. Equation 1 will be used to eliminate x_1 from equations 2, 3, 4, . . . ; equation 2 will be used to eliminate x_2 from equations 1, 3, 4, . . . ; and so on. Thus, we can write:

```
FOR I ← 1 TO N DO
    (Use the Ith equation to eliminate Ith unknown
     from the remaining equations)
END FOR
```

The Ith equation is used to eliminate x_1 from every equation except, of course, the Ith one. Let J be the number of the equation from which x_1 is currently being eliminated. We have:

FIGURE 19-10. A set of N equations in N unknowns is represented inside the computer as an array with N rows and N + 1 columns. Each row holds both the left-hand-side coefficients and the right-hand-side constants for a single equation.

$$
A = \begin{bmatrix}
3 & 2 & 4 & 19 \\
6 & 5 & 9 & 43 \\
9 & 8 & 13 & 64
\end{bmatrix}
$$

```
FOR I ← 1 TO N DO
   FOR J ← 1 TO N DO
      IF J ≠ I THEN
          (Use the Ith equation to eliminate the
          Ith unknown from the Jth equation)
      END IF
   END FOR
END FOR
```

To use the Ith equation to eliminate the Ith unknown from the Jth equation, we multiply the Ith equation by A(J, I)/(A(I, I), and subtract it from the Jth equation. These operations on "equations" will actually be carried out on the rows of A:

```
F ← A(J, I)/A(I, I)
FOR K ← 1 TO N+1 DO
   A(J, K) ← A(J, K) − F*A(I, K)
END FOR
```

Notice that for A(J, I) we get

```
A(J, I) ← A(J, I) − F*A(I, I)
A(J, I) ← A(J, I) − (A(J, I)/A(I, I))*A(I, I)
A(J, I) ← A(J, I) − A(J, I)
A(J, I) ← 0
```

The coefficient A(J, I) is set to 0, thus eliminating the Ith unknown from the Jth equation.

We can make the elimination somewhat more efficient as follows: We know that A(J, I) is going to be set to 0. Therefore, we can avoid calculating A(J, I) on the grounds that it is a waste of time to do a calculation if we already know the answer.

Moreover, when the Ith equation is used for purposes of elimination, all the coefficients A(I, 1), A(I, 2), . . . , A(I, I−1) will have already been set to 0. Therefore, A(I, K) will be 0 in

```
A(J, K) ← A(J, K) − F*A(I, K)
```

for K = 1, 2, 3, . . . , I−1. Hence, A(J, 1), A(J, 2), . . . , A(J, I−1) will not be changed by the elimination process, and we need not bother to calculate new values for them either.

Thus, new values need only be calculated for A(J, I+1), A(J, I+2), . . . , A(J, N+1). We can modify the elimination to read:

```
F ← A(J, I)/A(I, I)
FOR K ← I+1 TO N+1 DO
   A(J, K) ← A(J, K) − F*A(I, K)
END FOR
```

This modified calculation leaves "garbage" in those elements of A that the elimination should set to 0. But those elements do not participate in any further calculations, so no harm results.

With the eliminations complete, we can compute the values of the unknowns x_1—X(I) in algorithmic language notation—using:

```
FOR I ← 1 TO N DO
    X(I) ← A(I, N+1)/A(I, I)
END FOR
```

Combining all these results gives us the procedure GAUSS__JORDAN in Figure 19-11.

Unfortunately, this procedure contains a fatal flaw. Consider the step:

```
F ← A(J, I)/A(I, I)
```

The element we divide by—A(I, I)—is called the *pivot element*. Now what if the pivot element is 0? Dividing by 0 results in—disaster.

The system

$$x_1 + x_2 + x_3 = 6$$
$$x_1 + x_2 + 2x_3 = 9$$
$$x_1 + 2x_2 + 3x_3 = 14$$

illustrates the problem. We begin, as usual, using the first equation to eliminate x_1 from the other two equations. This gives:

$$x_1 + x_2 + x_3 = 6$$
$$0x_2 + x_3 = 3$$
$$x_2 + 2x_3 = 8$$

The next step would be to use the second equation to eliminate x_2 from the other two equations. The pivot element would be the coefficient of x_2 in the second equation. Unfortunately, that coefficient is 0.

FIGURE 19-11. The procedure GAUSS__JORDAN.

```
PROCEDURE GAUSS_JORDAN(N, X, A)
    FOR I ← 1 TO N DO
        FOR J ← 1 TO N DO
            IF J ≠ I THEN
                F ← A(J, I)/A(I, I)
                FOR K ← I+1 TO N+1 DO
                    A(J, K) ← A(J, K) − F*A(I, K)
                END FOR
            END IF
        END FOR
    END FOR
    FOR I ← 1 TO N DO
        X(I) ← A(I, N+1)/A(I, I)
    END FOR
END GAUSS_JORDAN
```

The simplest way out is to interchange the second and third equations:

$$x_1 + x_2 + x_3 = 6$$
$$x_2 + 2x_3 = 8$$
$$0x_2 + x_3 = 3$$

Now the coefficient of x_2 in the second equation is 1. This becomes the pivot element, and we proceed as before.

Even if the pivot element is not 0, we can still run into trouble. Suppose that A(I, I) is merely very small. Then F will be very large. In the calculation

```
A(J, K) ← A(J, K) − F*A(I, K)
```

we are subtracting a very large number from a much smaller one (assuming that A(J, K) and A(I, K) are of the same order of magnitude, which will usually be the case).

If our numbers could be represented with infinite precision, this situation would cause no problems. But in practice this precision is always limited.

Suppose, for instance, we subtract 983245 from .421357, and numbers can only be stored with six digits of precision. We have

```
      0.421357
-983245.000000
-983244.578643
-983245            (Round off to six places)
```

The .421357 has had no effect whatever on the answer, and the information contained in it has been lost! Thus, small pivot elements tend to increase *round-off* error—the loss of information due to rounding.

To defend against zero pivot elements, and to help defend against roundoff error caused by small pivot elements, we proceed as follows: Before using A(I, I) as a pivot element, we search the column A(I, I), A(I + 1, I), A(I + 2, I), . . . , A(N, I) to locate the A(L, I) having the largest absolute value. We then exchange the Ith and Lth equations (the Ith and Lth rows in A) so that A(L, I) becomes the pivot element. We then proceed to use the Ith equation to eliminate x_1 from the other equations, as before. This technique is called *partial pivoting*.

To find the row containing the largest of the elements A(I, I), A(I + 1, I), . . . , A(N, I), we proceed as follows:

```
MAX_A ← −1
FOR K ← I TO N DO
   IF ABS(A(K, I)) > MAX_A THEN
      MAX_A ← ABS(A(K, I))
       L ← K
   END IF
END FOR
```

When this terminates, L is the number of the row of A containing the largest element. We exchange the Ith and Lth rows as follows:

```
FOR K ← I to N+1 DO
    T ← A(I, K)
    A(I, K) ← A(L, K)
    A(L, K) ← T
END FOR
```

Inserting these statements in the GAUSS__JORDAN procedure gives us Figure 19-12.

A word about clarity of expression versus efficiency. In several places in this algorithm, we have used the expression N+1. For a large system, this could cause the value 1 to be added to the value of N many thousands of times. Yet only one addition is necessary. Since the value of N is supplied as an argument, we could have placed at the very beginning of the procedure the statement

```
NPLUS1 ← N+1
```

and then used NPLUS1 everywhere that we need N+1. The algorithm would be more efficient but not so easy to read. In the algorithmic language

FIGURE 19-12. The procedure GAUSS__JORDAN__WITH__PARTIAL__PIVOTING.

```
PROCEDURE GAUSS_JORDAN_WITH_PARTIAL_PIVOTING(N, X, A)
    FOR I ← 1 TO N DO
        MAX_A ← -1
        FOR K ← I TO N DO
            IF ABS(A(K, I)) > MAX_A THEN
                MAX_A ← ABS(A(K, I))
                L ← K
            END IF
        END FOR
        FOR K ← I TO N+1 DO
            T ← A(I, K)
            A(I, K) ← A(L, K)
            A(L, K) ← T
        END FOR
        FOR J ← 1 TO N DO
            IF J ≠ I THEN
                F ← A(J, I)/A(I, I)
                FOR K ← I+1 TO N+1 DO
                    A(J, K) ← A(J, K) - F*A(I, K)
                END FOR
            END IF
        END FOR
    END FOR
    FOR I ← 1 TO N DO
        X(I) ← A(I, N+1)/A(I, I)
    END FOR
END GAUSS_JORDAN_WITH_PARTIAL_PIVOTING
```

we stress readability, so this kind of change should be made when translating into a programming language.

Find two other places in this algorithm where easy readability has taken precedence over efficiency.

The Gauss-Seidel Method. The computations of the Gauss-Jordan method are quite complex. For large systems, they are time consuming. And, despite our best efforts to defend against it, round-off error can become a problem. For a large system, a successive-approximations method may be faster and more accurate than the explicit Gauss-Jordan method.

There are many such methods of successive approximations. We will look at one of the simplest, the *Gauss-Seidel method*.

Consider the system of equations:

$$x_1 + x_2 = 3$$
$$x_1 + 2x_2 = 5$$

You can easily verify that the exact solution to this system is $x_1 = 1$ and $x_2 = 2$. Hereafter, we will write exact and approximate solutions in the form (x_1, x_2). Thus, the exact solution to the system is $(1, 2)$.

Now let us solve this system using the Gauss-Seidel method. We start by choosing an initial approximation arbitrarily. Let us choose $(0, 0)$.

Now we solve the first equation for x_1, using the current value of x_2. We have:

$$x_1 = 3 - x_2 = 3 - 0 = 3$$

Our next approximation is $(3, 0)$. This satisfies the first equation but not the second.

Now we solve the second equation for x_2, using the current value of x_1:

$$x_2 = (5 - x_1)/2 = (5 - 3)/2 = 1$$

Thus, the next approximation is $(3, 1)$. This satisfies the second equation but not the first.

We proceed in this way, always solving the first equation for x_1 and the second equation for x_2. We get the following sequence of approximations:

$(0, 0)$, $(3, 0)$, $(3, 1)$, $(2, 1)$, $(2, 1.5)$, $(1.5, 1.5)$, $(1.5, 1.75)$, $(1.25, 1.75)$, $(1.25, 1.88)$, $(1.13, 1.88)$, $(1.13, 1.94)$, $(1.06, 1.94)$, $(1.06, 1.97)$, . . .

Obviously, the successive approximations are getting closer and closer to the exact solution $(1, 2)$. When this happens, we say that the approximations *converge* to the exact solution. More loosely, we may say that the Gauss-Seidel method "converges" for the system of equations in question.

Figure 19-13 illustrates how convergence takes place. We graph each equation as a straight line, as usual, with the intersection of the two lines being the exact solution.

Now let us start at the point (0, 0) and generate the successive approximations by the Gauss-Seidel method. Solving the first equation for x_1 means moving along a horizontal line to the point where it intersects the line representing the first equation. Solving the second equation for x_2 means following a vertical line until it intersects the line representing the second equation. If we do these two things alternately, we will follow the zig-zag path shown in Figure 19-13. The endpoint of that path approaches the exact solution.

On the other hand, convergence cannot be guaranteed for every system

FIGURE 19-13. The Gauss-Seidel method. In this case, the successive trial solutions get closer and closer to the exact solution. We say that the Gauss-Seidel method converges.

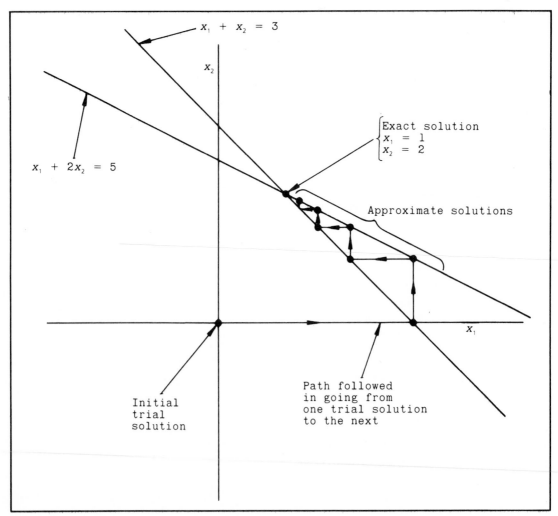

of equations. Indeed, let us take the same system as before, but interchange the two equations:

$$x_1 + 2x_2 = 5$$
$$x_1 + x_2 = 3$$

Again we will solve the first equation for x_1 and the second for x_2, but, because of the exchange, the first and second equations will not be the same ones as before.

Again we start at the point (0, 0). We obtain the following sequence of values for (x_1, x_2):

(0, 0), (5, 0), (5, −2), (9, −2), (9, −6), (17, −6), (17, −14), (33, −14), (33, −30), (65, −30), (65, −62), . . .

Obviously, we are getting further and further away from the solution (1, 2) instead of closer and closer to it. The Gauss-Seidel method *does not* converge when the equations are written in this order.

Figure 19-14 shows this graphically. Solving the first equation for x_1 means moving along a horizontal line to the point where it intersects the line for the equation $x_1 + 2x_2 = 5$. Solving the second equation for x_2 means moving along a vertical line until it intersects the line for the equation $x_1 + x_2 = 3$. Proceeding in this way, we see that our successive "approximations" are indeed moving away from the exact solution, and will never get nearer to it. You can easily show that this behavior will occur for any starting point other than the exact solution (1, 2).

Clearly, then, convergence is a somewhat tricky question for the Gauss-Seidel method. Simply changing the order of the equations—which means changing which equation is solved for which unknown—can affect whether or not convergence takes place. And even when convergence is known to take place, it is difficult to say *how many* points must be generated to obtain a solution of the desired accuracy.

Since our main interest is in the algorithm for generating the successive approximations, we will leave further considerations of convergence to numerical analysis courses.

How can we tell when we have approximated the solution of the equation to the desired accuracy? We could write our system of equations as:

$$3 - x_1 - x_2 = 0$$
$$5 - x_1 - 2x_2 = 0$$

For an approximate solution, the right-hand sides will not be exactly 0, of course. We define the *residuals* by:

$$r_1 = 3 - x_1 - x_2$$
$$r_2 = 5 - x_1 - 2x_2$$

The smaller the residuals, the more accurate is the solution. We will find MAX__R, the absolute value of the largest residual. We will consider the

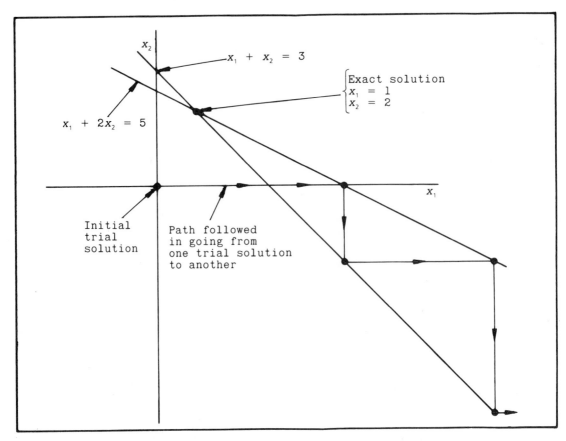

FIGURE 19-14. The Gauss-Seidel method. In this case, the successive trial solutions get further and further away from the exact solution. We say that the Gauss-Seidel method diverges. Note that the equations are the same as those in Figure 9-13. The only thing different is which equation is solved for x_1 and which for x_2.

solution to be sufficiently accurate when MAX__R is less than some MAX__ERROR specified by the user. As with the half-interval method, the choice of MAX__ERROR will depend both on the equations and the use to which the solution is to be put.

Since convergence is such an open question, however, we must take into account the possibility that convergence will not take place, or will not take place as rapidly as we hoped. We must make sure that the algorithm will ultimately terminate, whether or not a solution of the desired accuracy has been obtained.

Let one iteration consist of solving the first equation for x_1, the second for x_2, and so on through the nth for x_n. The user will specify MAX__ITERATIONS. The algorithm will terminate after this many iterations whether or not a solution of the desired accuracy has been obtained.

A flag OK will be set to TRUE if termination is due to a solution of the desired accuracy being obtained and FALSE if termination is due to MAX__ITERATIONS having been done.

Figure 19-15 shows the outline for the procedure GAUSS_SEIDEL. We begin an iteration by setting

```
MAX_R ← 0
```

so that MAX_R may be used to calculate the absolute value of the largest residual.

We now process each equation in turn:

```
FOR I ← 1 TO N DO
   (Process one equation)
END FOR
```

For each equation we calculate its residual:

```
R ← A(I, N+ 1)
FOR J ← 1 TO N DO
   R ← R - A(I, J)*X(J)
END FOR
```

If the absolute value of this residual is larger than MAX_R, we update MAX_R:

```
IF ABS(R) > MAX_R THEN
   MAX_R ← ABS(R)
END IF
```

Finally, we solve the Ith equation for X(I). This is easily done using the residual we have already calculated. This residual is the amount by which the left side of the equation falls short of the right side. If we increase A(I, I)*X(I) by R, then the two sides will be equal, and the new residual will be zero. Increasing X(I) by R/A(I, I) does the trick:

```
X(I) ← X(I) + R/A(I, I)
```

FIGURE 19-15. Outline of the procedure GAUSS_SEIDEL.

```
PROCEDURE GAUSS_SEIDEL(N, X, A, MAX_ITERATIONS, MAX_ERROR, OK)
   OK ← FALSE
   COUNT ← 1
   REPEAT
      (Do one iteration, setting MAX_R to the
       absolute value of the largest residual)
      IF MAX_R < MAX_ERROR THEN
         OK ← TRUE
      END IF
      COUNT ← COUNT+1
   UNTIL OK OR (COUNT > MAX_ITERATIONS)
END GAUSS_SEIDEL
```

We are now in a position to write the complete procedure, which is shown in Figure 19-16.

Review Questions

1. What is *numerical analysis*?

2. Give two examples of equations for which explicit solutions exist.

3. Give two examples of equations for which no explicit solutions exist.

4. Contrast the *binary search* for an element of an array with the *half-interval method* for finding a root of an equation. In what ways are they similar? In what ways do they differ? What would you say is the *idea* of both algorithms?

5. In the half-interval method, how do we determine which half interval contains the root we are searching for?

6. In the half-interval method, how do we determine when XMID is a close enough approximation to the root of the equation?

7. Describe the method of Gauss-Jordan elimination.

8. What will cause the Gauss-Jordan algorithm without partial pivoting to fail to work?

9. What can cause the Gauss-Jordan algorithm without partial pivoting to give inaccurate results?

10. Explain how partial pivoting remedies the problem mentioned in Question 8 and helps alleviate the one mentioned in Question 9.

FIGURE 19-16. The procedure GAUSS__SEIDEL.

```
PROCEDURE GAUSS_SEIDEL(N, X, A, MAX_ITERATIONS, MAX_ERROR, OK)
   OK ← FALSE
   COUNT ← 1
   REPEAT
      MAX_R ← 0
      FOR I ← 1 TO N DO
         R ← A(I, N+1)
         FOR J ← 1 TO N DO
            R ← R - A(I, J)*X(J)
         END FOR
         IF ABS(R) > MAX_R THEN
            MAX_R ← ABS(R)
         END IF
         X(I) ← X(I) + R/A(I, I)
      END FOR
      IF MAX_R < MAX_ERROR THEN
         OK ← TRUE
      END IF
      COUNT ← COUNT+1
   UNTIL OK OR (COUNT > MAX_ITERATIONS)
END GAUSS_SEIDEL
```

11. Describe the operation of the statements used to accomplish partial pivoting.

12. Why do we use expressions such as $N+1$ in positions that imply adding the unchanging value of N to the value of 1 many times?

13. The Gauss-Jordan method provides an explicit solution for any number of equations in as many unknowns. Why, then, are successive-approximations methods like the Gauss-Seidel method useful?

14. Describe the Gauss-Seidel method.

15. Sketch a graph similar to Figure 19-13, and use it to show one way in which the Gauss-Seidel can converge.

16. Sketch a graph similar to Figure 19-14, and use it to show one way in which the Gauss-Seidel method can fail to converge.

17. Using graphs, show that convergence or nonconvergence of the Gauss-Seidel method can depend on which equation is solved for x_1 and which is solved for x_2.

18. What is a *residual*?

19. How are the residuals used to determine when a solution of the desired accuracy has been obtained?

20. Why is MAX__ITERATIONS needed for GAUSS__SEIDEL but not for HALF__INTERVAL, even though both are successive-approximations methods?

Exercises

1. In the half-interval method, instead of choosing x_{mid} as the midpoint of the interval, we could use interpolation (as in trig and log tables) to get a value of x_{mid} closer to the actual root. The value of x_{mid} is then given by

$$x_{mid} - x_- = \frac{0 - f(x_-)}{f(x_+) - f(x_-)} (x_+ - x_-)$$

or

$$x_{mid} = x_- - \frac{x_+ - x_-}{f(x_+) - f(x_-)} f(x_-)$$

Rewrite HALF__INTERVAL to use this value of x_{mid}.

2. Give arguments that HALF__INTERVAL, as modified in Exercise 1, still works. Note that the size of the intervals do not now necessarily approach 0. Either x_+ or x_- may remain fixed, while the other endpoint approaches the root.

3. In Gauss-Jordan with partial pivoting, suppose that the equations are ill formed. They have no solution, or an infinite number of solutions. Then it is possible that in the column A(I, I), A(I+1, I), . . . , A(N, I) that we search for a pivot element, all of the elements might be 0. Modify GAUSS__JORDAN__WITH__PARTIAL__PIVOTING to check for this possibility. Provide for a flag OK that will be set to TRUE if the procedure returns normally and FALSE if the procedure returns because the equations were ill formed.

4. Another approach to partial pivoting is to search the row A(I, I), A(I, I+1), . . . , A(I, N) for the largest element and to interchange *columns* to make the largest element the pivot element.

When we exchange columns, we change which unknown corresponds to which column. Let SUB(I) be the subscript of the unknown corresponding to column I. Initially, we set SUB(I) to I for each I. Each time we interchange two columns, we interchange the corresponding elements of SUB. We compute the values of the unknowns using:

```
X(SUB(I)) ← A(I, N+1)/A(I, I)
```

Modify GAUSS__JORDAN__WITH__PARTIAL__PIVOTING to use this method.

5. In *full pivoting*, the entire subarray

```
A(I, I), A(I, I+1), . . ., A(I, N)
A(I+1, I)
     .
     .
     .
A(N, I), A(N, I+1), . . ., A(N, N)
```

is searched for the largest element. Then both two rows and two columns are interchanged to bring the largest element to the pivot position. Since columns are interchanged, the array SUB must be used as in Exercise 4. Modify the Gauss-Jordan procedure to use full pivoting.

6. Investigate graphically the convergence of the Gauss-Seidel method for the following systems of equations:

(a) $x - y = -1$
      $x + y = 3$

(b) $2x - y = 0$
      $x + y = 3$

Chapter 20

Numerical Integration

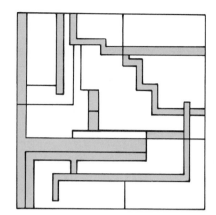

Consider this problem: We know the present position and velocity of a moving object, the forces acting on it, and the laws of physics that govern its motion. Predict the future motion of the object.

An example would be the problem of computing the orbit of a spacecraft. A more down-to-earth example would be determining the motion of an automobile suspension when the automobile hits a bump. Other examples abound in almost all branches of physics and engineering.

When we examine the laws of physics that govern moving objects, we find that they do not involve the position of the object alone. They also involve its *velocity*, which is the rate of change of its position, and its *acceleration*, which is the rate of change of its velocity. An equation describing the law of motion of an object will involve the object's velocity and acceleration as well as its position.

An equation which involves the rates of change of its variables, as well as the variables themselves, is called a *differential equation*. Finding the solution to a differential equations is called *integration*.

As with algebraic equations, some differential equations have explicit solutions. Others do not, and numerical techniques must be used. The process of solving a differential equation numerically is known as *numerical integration*.

Even if an equation has an explicit solution, we can sometimes find reasons for solving it numerically. For example, all methods of finding explicit solutions require a knowledge of calculus. With numerical methods, we can often get by with algebra and common sense. Thus, physics teachers can let noncalculus and precalculus students solve problems with the computer that would require calculus if solved explicitly.

There are many applications of differential equations other than the study of moving objects. We will stick to the moving-object problem, however, since we can visualize it, and thus we can sometimes substitute common sense for calculus.

20.1 Formulation of the Problem

We consider an object which can move along a straight line, as shown in Figure 20-1. An automobile moving along a straight highway would be an example.

We choose an arbitrary point on the line as the *origin*, 0, and specify the position of the object by its distance from the origin. The position is positive if the object is to the right of the origin and negative if the object is to the left of the origin.

We denote the position of the object by x. Since the object is in motion, the value of x will vary with time. We can express the notion of the object by

x = f(t)

FIGURE 20-1. The object shown can move along a straight line. Its position, x, is its distance from the origin. This distance is positive when the object is to the right of the origin and negative when the object is to the left of the origin.

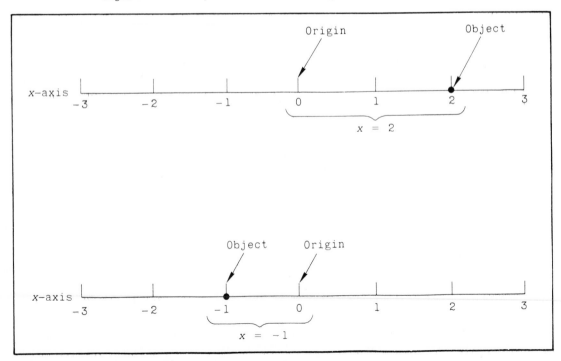

where f is some function of t. We can express this graphically by plotting x versus t, as shown in Figure 20-2.

For instance, suppose that the x-axis is turned vertically, with positive values up, negative values down, and the origin at ground level. Then the position of an object is its height above ground level. The motion of an object dropped from height h at time $t = 0$ is given by

$$x = h - \tfrac{1}{2}gt^2$$

and so $f(t) = h - \tfrac{1}{2}gt^2$.

The *velocity* (v) of the object is the rate of change of x with respect to time. Velocity in general also varies with time. For the falling body problem, for instance,

$$v = -gt$$

The *acceleration* (a) of the object is the rate of change of v with respect to time. In the falling body problem, the acceleration is given by

$$a = -g$$

FIGURE 20-2. We can show the motion of an object by graphing its position as a function of time.

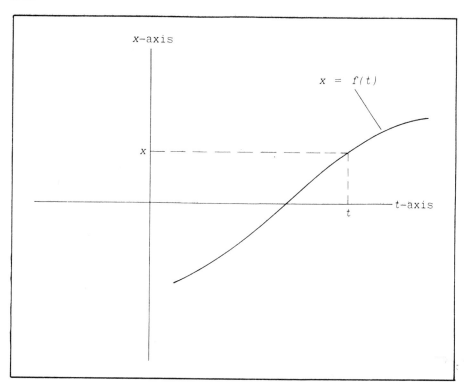

and is constant. But in other problems, acceleration is generally a function of time also.

When we translate the physical laws governing the object's motion into an equation, we will get an equation relating in general a, v, x, and t. Of course, not all of these variables need to be involved. The equation for the falling body problem, for instance, is simply:

$$a + g = 0$$

Given this equation, our aim is to find x and v as functions of t. If we were to find an explicit solution, we would give formulas for x and v in terms of t. For a numerical solution, we will give a *table of values* of x and v at various times t. This table, then, will have three columns, one for t, one for x, and one for v (see Figure 20-3).

20.2 Problems involving Only Position and Velocity

Let's ignore acceleration for the moment and consider problems involving position and velocity.

FIGURE 20-3. We can also describe the motion of an object by means of a table. The table gives the position and velocity of the object at different times.

t (sec)	x (ft)	v (ft/sec)
0	0	0
1	16	32
2	64	64
3	144	96
4	256	128
5	400	160
6	576	192
7	784	224
8	1024	256
9	1296	288
10	1600	320

Equations involving only position and velocity are not too common in mechanics, but they occur frequently in other disciplines. For instance, let the "position" x be the population of a certain environment with people or animals. If we assume the environment can support an unlimited population, then the equation for population growth is

$$v = kx$$

where k is a constant. If we assume the environment can support a maximum population b, then the equation is

$$v = cx(b - x)$$

where c and b are constants.

It is with equations such as these, but much more complicated, that the Club of Rome derives the dire predictions in the controversial book, *The Limits of Growth*. (The book is controversial because people do not agree on the principles of economics and ecology from which the equations are derived.)

In general, then, we will be given the velocity of an object as a function of position and time:

$$v = f(x, t)$$

We are to find the position of the object as a function of time.

The Euler Method. We start with a technique of numerical integration devised by the famous Swiss mathematician Leonhard Euler (pronounced *oiler*).

Suppose, for the moment, that the velocity v is constant. This would be the case, for instance, if in driving our car we kept the speedometer needle on exactly 55 mph.

With the velocity constant, there is a simple rule for figuring out how far we will travel in a given time. The rule is

distance = velocity × time

Thus, if we drive for three hours, keeping the speedometer on 55 mph all of the time, the distance we travel is given by:

distance = 55 mph × 3 hr
distance = 165 mi

Now suppose we start our trip at time t_0 and finish it at time t_1 Then the time spent traveling is $t_1 - t_0$. Moreover, if we start at position x_0 and end at position x_1, then the distance we have traveled is $x_1 - x_0$. The distance and the time are related by

$$x_1 - x_0 = v(t_1 - t_0)$$

or

$$x_1 = x_0 + v(t_1 - t_0)$$

If we let t be any time, and x our postion at that time, then we can express our position x as a function of the time t

$$x = x_0 + v(t - t_0)$$

where x_0 and t_0 are the starting position and time.

But this is only if v is constant. In most cases, v will not be constant but will be given by some function of position and time. How do we handle varying velocities?

Look at Figure 20-4. The curve shows the motion of an object moving with varying velocity. Now the equation

$$x = x_0 + v(t - t_0)$$

FIGURE 20-4. If v is the velocity of the object at time t_0, then $x = x_0 + v(t - t_0)$ is the equation of the straight line that is tangent to $x = f(t)$ at the point (t_0, v_0).

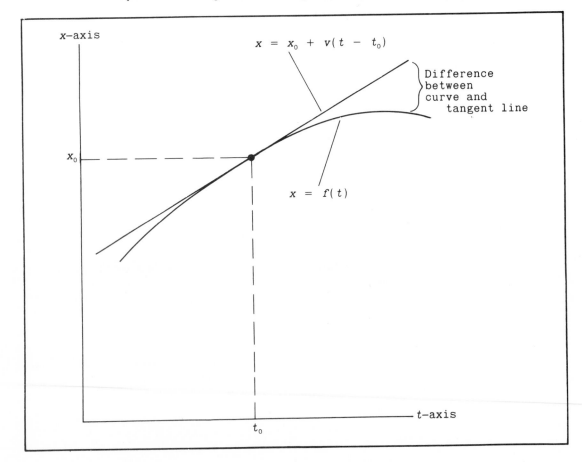

graphs as a straight line that passes through the curve at the point (t_0, x_0). Furthermore, the straight line is tangent to the curve—that is, the line and the curve are going in the same direction at time t_0. Figure 20-5 illustrates tangent and nontangent lines.

Now for times very close to t_0, the curve and the straight line nearly coincide. Therefore we can, with reasonable accuracy, use the straight line

$$x = x_0 + v(t - t_0)$$

to predict the position x of the object at time t, provided only that $t - t_0$ is not too large. The larger $t - t_0$ becomes, the greater the distance between the line and the curve becomes, and the greater becomes the error

FIGURE 20-5. Tangent and nontangent lines.

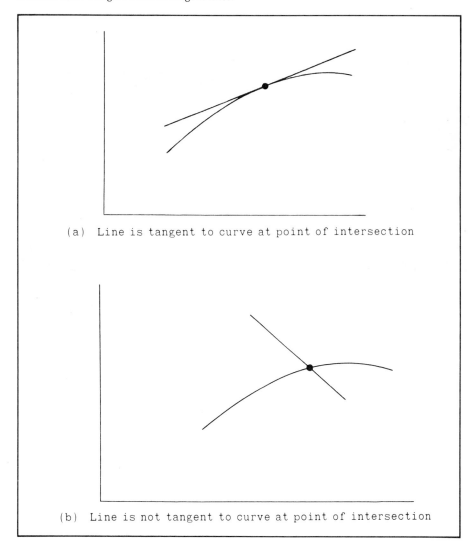

(a) Line is tangent to curve at point of intersection

(b) Line is not tangent to curve at point of intersection

of using the equation of the line to describe the motion of the body.

Thus, we found a way of calculating the postion of the moving object as a function of time, but it works only for times near t_0. Can we use this method for other times as well?

Yes, we can, and Figure 20-6 shows how. On the time axis we choose points t_0, t_1, . . . , t_n, thus dividing the t-axis between t_0 and t_n up into intervals: t_0 to t_1, t_1 to t_2, and so on.

Let

$$h = t_{i+1} - t_i$$

be the common length of all the intervals. We choose h small enough so that the curve can be acceptably approximated by the straight line in each interval. We will have to use different straight lines in different intervals, however.

More explicitly, suppose the velocity of the body is given as some function of x and t:

$$v = f(x, t)$$

Let v_0 be the velocity at the starting point:

FIGURE 20-6. We can divide the t-axis into intervals sufficiently small so that the curve can be approximated by a tangent inside each interval.

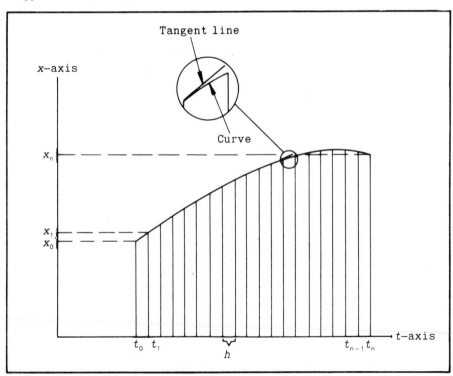

$$v_0 = f(x_0, t_0)$$

Then in the interval t_0 to t_1, the position of the body is given, with acceptable accuracy, by:

$$x = x_0 + v_0(t - t_0)$$

If we set $t - t_0$ equal to $t_1 - t_0$, which is equal to h, we can calculate the position x_1 of the object at time t_1:

$$
\begin{aligned}
x_1 &= x_0 + v_0(t_1 - t_0) \\
&= x_0 + v_0 h
\end{aligned}
$$

Now we can proceed in exactly the same way to calculate the position x_2 of the object at time t_2.

We start by defining:

$$v_1 = f(x_1, t_1)$$

In the interval t_1 to t_2, then, we can represent the motion of the body with acceptable accuracy by:

$$x = x_1 + v_1(t - t_1)$$

Setting $t - t_1$ equal to $t_2 - t_1$, which equals h, we get the position x_2:

$$x_2 = x_1 + v_1 h$$

Now we can proceed in exactly the same way to compute x_3, x_4, x_5, and so on to x_n. The table

Time	Position
t_0	x_0
t_1	x_1
.	.
.	.
.	.
t_n	x_n

constitutes the numerical solution to our differential equation $v = f(x, t)$. The x_i's are given by the equations:

$$
\begin{array}{ll}
x_1 = x_0 + v_0 h & \text{where } v_0 = f(x_0, t_0) \\
x_2 = x_1 + v_1 h & \text{where } v_1 = f(x_1, t_1)
\end{array}
$$

$$x_n = x_{n-1} + v_{n-1} h \qquad \text{where } v_{n-1} = f(x_{n-1}, t_{n-1})$$

This sequence of equations defines the Euler method.

We can easily write an algorithm for the Euler method. Let F(X, T) be the function which gives the velocity as a function of position and time. Naturally, the definition of the function F must be written out somewhere.

Now let X and T be the current values of position and time. That is, the values of X and T are x_i and t_i for some value of i. To update X and T so that their values will be x_{i+1} and t_{i+1} respectively, we do the following:

```
V ← F(X, T)
X ← X + V*H
T ← T + H
```

where H is the size of the time intervals. These statements are executed repeatedly for each new X and T value desired.

Let us write a procedure to integrate $v = f(x, t)$ using the Euler method. We will supply the procedure with the starting time and position T0 and X0, the number, N, of new points to be calculated, the time interval size H, and the function F. The procedure will return its results in two arrays, T__VALUES and X__VALUES. After the procedure executes, the value of T__VALUES(I) will be t_I, and the value of X__VALUES(I) will be x_I. Figure 20-7 shows the procedure EULER.

The Improved Euler Method. As so often happens in computer science, the simplest algorithm is not the best. There is a tendency for errors to accumulate in the Euler method. Even though the error in going from time t_i to time t_{i+1} may be small, the accumulated error in x_n may be substantial.

We can improve the accuracy, in theory, by making h smaller. In practice, this has its own pitfalls. If we make h very small, then in

$$x_{i+1} = x_i + v_i h$$

we will be adding a very small number, $v_i h$, to a much larger one, x_i. We saw in the last chapter that adding a smaller number to a much larger one aggravates round-off error. When we make h very small, we just trade

FIGURE 20-7. The procedure EULER.

```
PROCEDURE EULER(TO, XO, N, H, F, T_VALUES, X_VALUES)
    X ← XO
    T ← TO
    FOR I ← 1 TO N DO
        V ← F(X, T)
        X ← X + V*H
        T ← T + H
        X_VALUES(I) ← X
        T_VALUES(I) ← T
    END FOR
END EULER
```

round-off errors for errors that come from h being too large. We need some other plan for increasing our accuracy.

Let us go back to the equation:

$$x_{i+1} = x_i + v_i h$$

Now v_i is the velocity of the object at time t_i. This velocity will change during the time from t_i to t_{i+1}, in fact, it will be:

$$v_{i+1} = f(x_{i+1}, t_{i+1})$$

It seems reasonable that our results would be more accurate if, instead of v_i, we used the average of v_i and v_{i+1}. Then x_{i+1} will be given by:

$$x_{i+1} = x_i + \tfrac{1}{2}(v_i + v_{i+1})h$$

There is only one problem with this approach. To calculate v_{i+1}, we need to know x_{i+1}. But v_{i+1} is used in the calculation of x_{i+1}.

The solution is to estimate x_{i+1} using v_i, which we know. Thus, we write:

$$v'_{i+1} = f(x_i + v_i h, t_i + h)$$

v'_{i+1} is not exactly equal to v_{i+1}, since $x_i + v_i h$ is not exactly equal to the value we will eventually calculate for x_{i+1}. But v'_{i+1} is a good approximation to v_{i+1} and can be used in place of it.

All these considerations lead to the improved Euler method. To calculate x_{i+1}, we use:

$$v_i \leftarrow f(x_i, t_i)$$
$$v'_{i+1} \leftarrow f(x_i + v_i h, t + h)$$
$$x_{i+1} \leftarrow x_i + \tfrac{1}{2}(v_i + v'_{i+1})h$$

We can easily write an algorithm for the improved Euler method. Using V1 for v_i and V2 for v'_{i+1}, we get the procedure IMPROVED__EULER shown in Figure 20-8.

The Runge-Kutta Method. The idea behind the improved Euler method can be carried even further. We can achieve still greater accuracy by making more estimates of the velocity during the time interval t_i to t_{i+1} and using the average of these when calculating x_{i+1}.

The *Runge-Kutta method* uses four velocity estimates:

$$v_1 = v_i = f(x_i, t_i)$$

is the velocity at time t_i;

$$v_2 = f(x_i + \tfrac{1}{2}v_1 h, t_i + \tfrac{1}{2}h)$$

```
          PROCEDURE IMPROVED_EULER(TO, XO, N, H, F,
                                   T_VALUES, X_VALUES)
          X ← XO
          T ← TO
          FOR I ← 1 TO N DO
              V1 ← F(X, T)
              V2 ← F(X + V1*H, T + H)
              X ← X + 0.5*(V1 + V2)*H
              T ← T + H
              X_VALUES(I) ← X
              T_VALUES(I) ← T
          END FOR
          END IMPROVED_EULER
```

FIGURE 20-8. The procedure IMPROVED__EULER.

and

$$v_3 = f(x_i + \tfrac{1}{2}v_2h, t_i + \tfrac{1}{2}h)$$

are estimates of the velocity at time $t_i + \tfrac{1}{2}h$—midway between t_i and t_{i+1};

$$v_4 = f(x_i + v_3h, t_i + h)$$

is an estimate of the velocity at time t_{i+1}.

Figure 20-9 shows the points at which v_1, v_2, v_3, and v_4 are calculated. Note that each estimate is used in computing the next one: v_1 is used in computing v_2, v_2 is used in computing v_3, and v_3 in computing v_4.

The average

$$\frac{v_1 + 2v_2 + 2v_3 + v_4}{6}$$

is used as an estimate of the average velocity over the time interval t_i to t_{i+1}. Thus, x_{i+1} is calculated using:

$$x_{i+1} = x_i + \frac{v_1 + 2v_2 + 2v_3 + v_4}{6} h$$

It should be clear that the Runge-Kutta method is an extension of the idea of the improved Euler method; v_1, v_2, v_3, and v_4 are estimates of the velocity at various times during the interval t_i to t_{i+1}. One estimate is at time t_i, two are at time $t_i + \tfrac{1}{2}h$, and one is at time t_{i+1}.

Furthermore,

$$\frac{v_1 + 2v_2 + 2v_3 + v_4}{6}$$

is an average of v_1, v_2, v_3, and v_4. But it is a *weighted average*. The two velocities estimated at the midpoint of the interval are each given twice as much weight as those estimated at the endpoints.

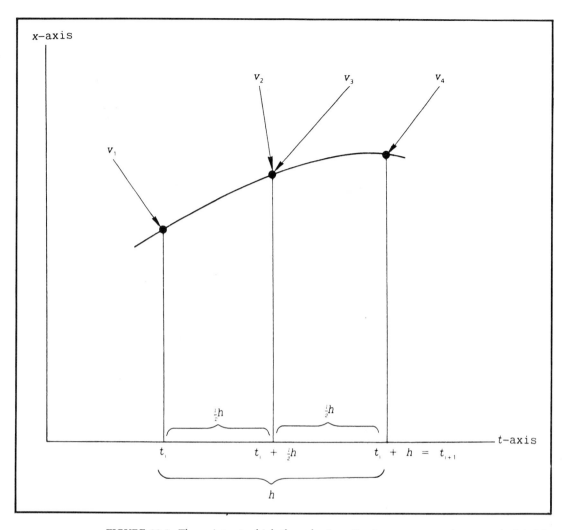

FIGURE 20-9. The points at which the velocity estimates v_1, v_2, v_3, and v_4 are calculated in the Runge-Kutta method.

An analysis of why these particular estimates are made, and why they are weighted the way they are in the average, is too complicated for this book. Even numerical analysis texts often omit this analysis, which involves lengthy and complex algebra.

Figure 20-10 shows the procedure for the Runge-Kutta method which is a straightforward extension of the one for the improved Euler method.

20.3 Problems Involving Position, Velocity, and Acceleration

The equations that describe the motion of moving objects usually involve acceleration as well as velocity and position. These equations are derived from Newton's Second Law, which states

```
           PROCEDURE RUNGE_KUTTA(TO, XO, N, H, F,
                                 T_VALUES, X_VALUES)
               X ← XO
               T ← TO
               FOR I ← 1 TO N DO
                   V1 ← F(X, T)
                   V2 ← F(X + 0.5*V1*H, T + 0.5*H)
                   V3 ← F(X + 0.5*V2*H, T + 0.5*H)
                   V4 ← F(X + V3*H, T + H)
                   X ← X + (V1 + 2*V2 + 2*V3 + V4)*H/6
                   T ← T + H
                   X_VALUES(I) ← X
                   T_VALUES(I) ← T
               END FOR
           END RUNGE_KUTTA
```

FIGURE 20-10. The procedure RUNGE__KUTTA.

mass of object $\times$ acceleration = applied force

or

$ma = F$

where m is the mass of the object, a is acceleration, and F is the net force acting on it.

If we divide both sides of this equation by m, we get:

$a = F/m$

In general, F/m depends on the position and velocity of the object, as well as on time. Thus, we have:

$a = f(x, v, t)$

This is the equation that must be integrated to find the motion of the object.

For instance, consider the *simple harmonic oscillator*, which consists of a weight hanging on a spring, as shown in Figure 20-11. The x-axis is vertical, with $x = 0$ as the equilibrium point of the system—the point at which the weight rests when it is not oscillating. The velocity axis is also vertical, with positive velocities corresponding to upward motion and negative ones to downward motion.

The net force acting on the weight is;

$F = -bv - kx$

The term kx represents the force exerted by the spring. The constant k is a measure of the stiffness of the spring. The term bv represents the frictional force exerted (mainly) by the air as the weight moves through it. The con-

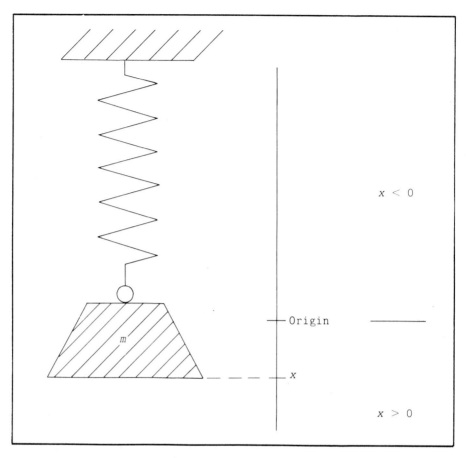

FIGURE 20-11. A simple harmonic oscillator consists of a weight suspended by a spring.

stant b is a measure of this frictional force. If b were 0, the weight would oscillate forever and would never come to rest.

Newton's Second Law gives us

$$ma = -bv - kx$$

where m is the mass of the object. The acceleration is then given by:

$$a = -(b/m)v - (k/m)x$$

In this case, the acceleration does not depend explicitly on time.

Since acceleration is the rate of change of velocity, acceleration is related to velocity in the same way that velocity is related to position (see Figure 20-12.) If a problem involved only acceleration and velocity, we could use the methods of the last section but with velocity in place of position and acceleration in place of velocity.

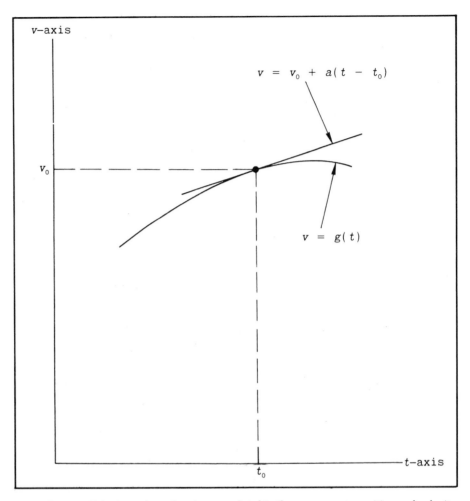

FIGURE 20-12. Velocity and acceleration are related in the same way as position and velocity. Compare this figure with Figure 20-4.

When a problem involves position, velocity, and acceleration, we must carry out the calculations for velocity in terms of acceleration and position in terms of velocity *simultaneously*.

The Euler Method. Let's generalize the Euler method to handle position, velocity, and acceleration. Suppose that the acceleration is given by:

$$a = f(x, v, t)$$

At the starting time t_0, we must specify both the starting position x_0 and the starting velocity v_0. Not only do we have to say where the object is when the calculation starts, we have to say how fast it is going.

The acceleration at time t_0 is given by:

$$a_0 = f(x_0, v_0, t_0)$$

Knowing a_0, we can calculate v_1. Remembering that velocity is calculated from acceleration just like position is calculated from velocity, we have:

$$v_1 = v_0 + a_0 h$$

We calculate x_1 from x_0, v_0, and h as usual:

$$x_1 = x_0 + v_0 h$$

This process is repeated for succeeding points:

$$
\begin{array}{lll}
x_1 = x_0 + v_0 h & v_1 = v_0 + a_0 h & a_0 = f(x_0, v_0, t_0), \\
x_2 = x_1 + v_1 h & v_2 = v_1 + a_1 h & a_1 = f(x_1\ v_1\ t_1) \\
\quad \cdot & \quad \cdot & \quad \cdot \\
\quad \cdot & \quad \cdot & \quad \cdot \\
\quad \cdot & \quad \cdot & \quad \cdot \\
x_n = x_{n-1} + v_{n-1} h & v_n = v_{n-1} + a_{n-1} h & a_{n-1} = f(x_{n-1}, v_{n-1}, t_{n-1})
\end{array}
$$

We can easily incorporate this into a procedure, as shown in Figure 20-13.

The Improved Euler Method. The improved Euler method is also easily extended to handle acceleration as well as velocity and position.
Now we make two estimates of acceleration *and* velocity:

```
A1 ← F(X, V, T)
V1 ← V
A2 ← F(X + V1*H, V + A1*H, T + H)
V2 ← V + A1*H
```

FIGURE 20-13. This version of the procedure EULER solves equations involving position, velocity, and acceleration.

```
PROCEDURE EULER(TO, XO, VO, N, H, F,
                    T_VALUES, X_VALUES, V_VALUES)
    X ← XO
    V ← VO
    T ← TO
    FOR I ← 1 TO N DO
        A ← F(X, V, T)
        X ← X + V*H
        V ← V + A*H
        T ← T + H
        X_VALUES(I) ← X
        V_VALUES(I) ← V
        T_VALUES(I) ← T
    END FOR
END EULER
```

The average of A1 and A2 is then used to estimate the next value of V; the average of V1 and V2 is used to estimate the next value of X. Figure 20-14 shows the procedure for the improved Euler method.

The Runge-Kutta Method. Again, the algorithm for the Runge-Kutta method is a straightforward generalization of the one for the improved Euler method. Now we have A1, A2, A3, and A4 in addition to V1, V2, V3, and V4. It is left as an exercise to write the procedure RUNGE__ KUTTA for problems involving acceleration as well as position and velocity.

Review Questions

1. What is a *differential equation?*

2. Define velocity and acceleration as *rates of change.*

3. Give two examples of systems whose motion can be studied by means of differential equations.

4. What do we mean by the *integration* of a differential equation?

5. Give two examples of differential equations used in the study of population growth.

6. If an object travels with constant velocity, what is the rule for finding how far it will travel in a specified amount of time?

7. An object is traveling with variable velocity. At time t_0, its position and velocity are x_0 and v_0. How is the equation

$x = x_0 + v_0t$

FIGURE 20-14. This version of IMPROVED__EULER solves equations involving position, velocity, and acceleration.

```
PROCEDURE IMPROVED_EULER(TO, XO, VO, N, H, F,
                         T_VALUES, X_VALUES, V_VALUES)
    X ← XO
    V ← VO
    T ← TO
    FOR I ← 1 TO N DO
        A1 ← F(X, V, T)
        V1 ← V
        A2 ← F(X + V1*H, V + A1*H, T + H)
        V2 ← V + A1*H
        X ← X + 0.5*(V1 + V2)*H
        V ← V + 0.5*(A1 + A2)*H
        T ← T + H
        X_VALUES(I) ← X
        V_VALUES(I) ← V
        T_VALUES(I) ← T
    END FOR
END IMPROVED_EULER
```

related to the motion of the object?

8. Describe the Euler method for a problem involving position and velocity only.

9. In theory, we could make the Euler method as accurate as we wish by making h sufficiently small. Why does this not work out in practice?

10. Give the idea behind the improved Euler method.

11. Give the procedure for the improved Euler method and explain its operation.

12. The Runge-Kutta method follows the same general idea as the improved Euler method but differs in details. How many velocity estimates (per interval) are used in the improved Euler method? In the Runge-Kutta method?

13. At what points is the velocity estimated in the improved Euler method? In the Runge-Kutta method?

14. How are the velocity estimates averaged in the improved Euler method? In the Runge-Kutta method?

15. In view of Newton's Second Law, why do the equations describing moving objects usually involve acceleration as well as position and velocity?

16. What is the significance of the constants b and k in the differential equation for the simple harmonic oscillator?

17. Describe how the Euler method is generalized to handle acceleration as well as position and velocity.

18. When dealing only with position and velocity, we need only specify the value of x_0 at time t_0. What must we specify for problems involving acceleration as well?

19. What additional estimates, corresponding to V1 and V2, must be introduced to generalize the improved Euler method to problems involving acceleration?

20. What additional estimates, corresponding to V1, V2, V3, and V4, must be introduced to generalize the Runge-Kutta method to problems involving acceleration?

Exercises

1. Generalize the Runge-Kutta method to problems involving acceleration, velocity, and position.

2. In place of the general purpose procedures given in this chapter, algorithms or procedures are often written to integrate specific equations. These can sometimes be simpler than the general procedures since the right-hand sides of the equations may not involve all the variables x, v, and t. Write procedures using the methods we have studied to integrate each of the following:

(a) $v = kx$ (b) $a = -kv$
(c) $a = -g$ (d) $a = -bv - kx$
(e) $a = \sin wt$ (f) $a = \sin wt - bv - kx$

3. Rewrite each of the procedures of this chapter as an algorithm that inputs data such as T0, X0, N and H and outputs a table of T and X values. (Add V0 and V for problems involving acceleration.) This algorithm will *not* store the values in arrays, but will output them as they are generated.

4. Often we do not wish every value generated to be outputted. Rewrite the algorithms of Exercise 3 so that they only output the values for every Mth point, where the value of M is specified by the user.

5. The solution to the equation

$a = -x$

is $x = \cos t$ if $t_0 = 0$, $x_0 = 1$ and $v_0 = 0$, and $x = \sin t$ if $t_0 = 0$, $x_0 = 0$, and $v_0 = 1$. (The arguments of sin and cos are assumed to be in radians.) For each of these cases, write and run on a computer a program to integrate the differential equation and compare the solution obtained with the exact solution. Experiment with different integration methods and different values of h and notice their effect on the accuracy of the result.

For Further Reading

Chapter 1. Further information on computer applications and the impact of computers on society can be found in

"The Computer Society." *Time,* February 20, 1978, pp. 44–59.

Evans, Christopher. *The Micro Millennium.* New York: The Viking Press, 1979.

Fedida, Sam and Malik, Rex. *The Viewdata Revolution.* New York: John Wiley & Sons, 1979.

Graham, Neill. *The Mind Tool.* St. Paul, Minn.: West Publishing Company, 1980.

Laurie, Edward J. *Computers, Automation, and Society.* Homewood, Ill.: Richard D. Irwin, 1979.

"Machines that Think." *Newsweek,* June 30, 1980, pp. 50–56.

Martin, James. *The Wired Society.* Englewood Cliffs, N.J.: Prentice-Hall, 1978.

McCorduck, Pamela. *Machines Who Think.* San Francisco: W. H. Freeman, 1979.

Nelson, Ted. *Computer Lib/Dream Machines.* Swarthmore, Pa: Ted Nelson, Publisher (distributed by The Distributers, 702 S. Michigan, South Bend, Ind., 46618), 1974.

_____. *The Home Computer Revolution.* Swarthmore, Pa.: Ted Nelson, Publisher (distributed by The Distributers, 702 S. Michigan, South Bend, Ind., 46618), 1977.

Rothman, Stanley and Mosmann, Charles. *Computers and Society.* Chicago: Science Research Associates, 1976.

Spencer, Donald H. *Computers in Society: Wheres, Whys, and Hows of Computer Use.* Rochelle Park, N.J.: Hayden Book Co., 1974.

A number of important ideas in computer science are engagingly presented in Douglas Hofstadter's Pulitzer-Prize-winning book.

Hofstadter, Douglas R. *Gödel, Escher, Bach: an Eternal Golden Braid.* New York: Basic Books, 1979.

Chapter 2. These references cover computer hardware and data representation:

American National Standard Code For Information Interchange. New York: American National Standards Institute, 1977.

Asimov, Isaac. "One, Ten, Buckle My Shoe." in *Adding a Dimension.* New York: Doubleday, 1964.

Chu, Yaohan. *Introduction to Computer Organization.* Englewood Cliffs, N.J.: Prentice-Hall, 1970.

Communications of the ACM (special issue on computer architecture), January 1978.

Computers and Computation. San Francisco: W. H. Freeman and Co., 1971.

Flores, Ivan. *Computer Organization.* Englewood Cliffs, N.J.: Prentice-Hall, 1969.

Katzen, Harry. *Computer Systems and Organization.* Chicago: Science Research Associates, 1976.

Matisoo, Juri. "The Superconducting Computer." *Scientific American,* May 1980, pp. 50–65.

Scientific American (special issue on microelectronics), September 1977.

Tannenbaum, Andrew S. *Structured Computer Organization.* Englewood Cliffs, N.J.: Prentice-Hall, 1976.

Vacroux, Andre G. "Microcomputers." *Scientific American,* May 1975, pp. 32–40.

White, Robert M. "Disk Storage Technology." *Scientific American,* August 1980, pp. 138–148.

Extensive discussion of input and output devices can be found in data processing books such as:

Mandell, Steven L. *Computers and Data Processing: Concepts and Applications.* St. Paul, Minn: West Publishing Company, 1979.

Chapter 3. The book by Tannenbaum, cited for Chapter 2, has a good discussion of the multilevel machines. Some other references on computer software are:

Denning, Peter J. "Third Generation Computer Systems." *Computing Surveys,* December 1971, pp. 175–216.

Donovan, John H. *Systems Programming.* New York: McGraw-Hill Book Company., 1972.

Holt, R. C., et al. *Structured Concurrent Programming with Operating Systems Applications.* Reading, Mass: Addison-Wesley Publishing Company, 1978.

Horning, J. J. and Randell, B. "Process Structuring." *Computing Surveys,* March 1973, pp. 5–30.

Kernighan, Brian W. and Plauger, P. J. *Software Tools.* Reading, Mass.: Addison-Wesley Publishing Company, 1976.

"Microcode: Electronic Building Blocks for Calculators." *The Hewlett-Packard Personal Computer Digest,* Volume Three 1977, pp. 4–6.

Sammet, Jean E. *Programming Languages: History and Fundamentals.* Englewood Cliffs, N.J.: Prentice-Hall, 1969.

Chapters 4–10. The approach to algorithm design and construction used in this book is called *structured programming.* The classic work on structured programming is

Dijkstra, Edsger W. "Notes on Structured Programming." in O.-J. Dahl, et al., *Structured Programming.* New York: Academic Press, 1972.

Other useful works on structured programming include:

Hearn, Albert D. "Some Words about Program Structure." *BYTE,* September 1978, pp. 68–76.

Hughes, Joan K. and Michtom, Jay I. *A Structured Approach to Programming.* Englewood Cliffs, N.J.: Prentice-Hall, 1977.

Knuth, Donald E. "Structured Programming with go to Statements." *Computing Surveys,* December 1974, pp. 261–301.

Ledgard, Henry F. and Marcotty, Michael. "A Genealogy of Control Structures." *Communications of the ACM,* November 1975, pp. 629–39.

Peterson, W. W., Kasami, T., and Tokura, N. "On the Capabilities of While, Repeat, Exit Statements." *Communications of the ACM,* August 1973, pp. 503–12.

Wirth, Niklaus. "On the Composition of Well Structured Programs." *Computing Surveys,* December 1974, 246–59.

———. *Algorithms + Data Structures = Programs.* Englewood Cliffs, N.J.: Prentice-Hall, 1975.

Yourdon, Edward J. *Techniques of Program Structure and Design.* Englewood Cliffs, N.J.: Prentice-Hall, 1975.

Some of the best down-to-earth advice on program design and construction can be found in:

Kernighan, Brian W. and Plauger, P. J. *The Elements of Programming Style.* New York: McGraw-Hill Book Company, 1974.

Chapters 11–16. The classic work on data structures is:

Knuth, Donald E. *The Art of Computer Programming.* Vol 1. 2d ed., Reading, Mass.: Addison-Wesley Publishing Company, 1969, Chapter 2.

Other useful references are:

Elson, Mark. *Data Structures*. Chicago: Science Research Associates, 1975.

Gotlieb, C. C. and Gotlieb, L. R. *Data Types and Structures*. Englewood Cliffs, N.J.: Prentice-Hall, 1978.

Harrison, Malcom C. *Data Structures and Programming*. Glenview, Ill.: Scott, Foresman, 1973.

Horowitz, Ellis and Sartaj, Sahni. *Fundamentals of Data Structures*. Potomac, Md.: Computer Science Press, 1977.

Ore, Oystein. *Graphs and their Uses*. New York: Random House and The L. W. Singer Company, 1963.

Chapters 17 and 18. The file-update algorithm given in Chapter 17, which was invented by W. H. J. Feijen, is a substantial improvement over many such algorithms found in textbooks. It is described in:

Dijkstra, Edsger W. *A Discipline of Programming*. Englewood Cliffs, N.J.: Prentice-Hall, 1976, Chapter 15.

Dwyer, Barry. "One More Time—How to Update a Master File." *Communications of the ACM*, January 1981, pp. 3–8.

In recent years there has been much interest in organizing files into data bases, which have a structure of their own apart from the programs that manipulate them. Some references in this area are:

Computing Surveys (special issue on data base management systems), March 1976.

Kroenke, David. *Database: A Professional's Primer*. Chicago: Science Research Associates, 1978.

Martin, James. *Computer Data-Base Organization*. 2d ed. Englewood Cliffs, N.J.: Prentice-Hall, 1977.

Sprowls, R. Clay. *Management Data Bases*. New York: John Wiley & Sons, 1976.

Chapters 19 and 20. Further information on numerical methods can be found in:

Arden, Bruce W. and Astill, Kenneth N. *Numerical Algorithms: Origins and Applications*. Reading, Mass: Addison-Wesley, 1970.

Smith, Jon M. *Scientific Analysis on the Pocket Calculator*. New York: John Wiley & Sons, 1975.

Pascal. Many books on Pascal are being published now; check your library and book store for recent selections. Of the following, the books by Bowles cover UCSD Pascal and the UCSD Pascal system. The user manual and report by Jensen and Wirth is the standard reference on Pascal. The remaining four references are to Pascal textbooks.

Bowles, Kenneth L. *Microcomputer Problem Solving Using Pascal*. New York: Springer-Verlag, 1977.

_____. *Beginner's Guide for the UCSD Pascal System*. New York: McGraw-Hill Book Company, 1980.

Conway, R., Gries, D., and Zimmerman, E. C. *A Primer on Pascal*. Cambridge, Mass: Winthrop Publishers, 1976.

Graham, Neill. *Introduction to Pascal*. St. Paul, Minn: West Publishing Company, 1980.

Grogono, Peter. *Programming in Pascal*. Reading, Mass: Addison-Wesley Publishing Company, 1978.

Jensen, Kathleen and Wirth, Niklaus. *Pascal User Manual and Report*. Berlin: Springer-Verlag, 1974.

Schneider, G. M., Weingart, S. W., and Perlman, D. M. *An Introduction to Programming and Problem Solving with Pascal*. New York: John Wiley & Sons, 1978.

Pascal Supplement

In the main body of this book we express our algorithms in an algorithmic language. This language emphasizes the construction of algorithms using the basic operations of sequencing, selection, and repetition. It is designed to be as simple and informal as possible, so you can express your ideas for algorithms without getting bogged down in technicalities.

The time eventually arrives, however, when you want a computer to execute some of your algorithms. Then you must translate your algorithms from the informal algorithmic language into one of the formal programming languages available for the computer system you wish to use.

Once formulated in the algorithmic language, algorithms can be translated into almost any programming language with little difficulty. Still, we can expect the job to be easier if the programming language is similar in structure to the algorithmic language and, like the latter, emphasizes the basic operations of sequencing, selection, and repetition.

A language that satisfies these requirements is Pascal. This language was specifically designed for teaching computer science. Recently, however, Pascal has moved out of the classroom and into the real world of everyday programming. Pascal is now established as one of the major programming languages.

This supplement should be used in conjunction with the main text. The topics taken up in the supplement correspond to those in the main text and are taken up in the same order. Figure P-1 shows the correspondence between sections in the main text and sections in this supplement. Each section in the supplement assumes that you have read the corre-

Supplement Section/Title		Main Text Section
P.1	Data Types and Values	4.1
P.2	Output	4.2
P.3	Arithmetic Expressions	4.3, 4.4
P.4	Functions	4.5
P.5	Writing Pascal Programs	4.6
P.6	Variables	5.1
P.7	Assignment	5.2, 5.3
P.8	Input	5.4, 5.5
P.9	Conditions	6.1
P.10	One- and Two-way Selection	6.2
P.11	Nested IF Statements	6.2
P.12	Multiway Selection	6.3
P.13	Boolean Operators	6.4
P.14	Repetition	7.1-7.4
P.15	More on Data Types	
P.16	Arrays	8.1-8.3, 8.5
P.17	Functions	9.1
P.18	Variable Parameters and Procedures	9.2
P.19	Local and Global Variables	9.3
P.20	Program Design	10.1
P.21	Packed Arrays and Fixed-length Strings	11.1
P.22	Variable-length Strings	11.2, 11.3
P.23	Records	13.1-13.3
P.24	Pointer Types and Linked Lists	14.1
P.25	Sequential Files	17.1-17.3
P.26	Random Files	18.1
P.27	Sets	

FIGURE P-1. The correspondence between sections in the supplement and those in the main text. Sections P.15 and P.27 don't correspond to any sections in the main text. Section P.15, however, should be read before going on to the following sections.

sponding section in the main text (if any) and concentrates on showing how the topic discussed in the main text is handled in Pascal.

Pascal, like most other programming languages, is available in more than one version. For Pascal, at least, the variations between versions is minor, and no one should have trouble converting programs from one version to another. The version of Pascal we will take up here is known as *UCSD Pascal*, since it was developed at the University of California at San Diego. UCSD Pascal, which was designed particularly to run on small- and medium-sized computer systems, is now one of the most widely used versions of the language. This supplement will specifically point out the few areas in which UCSD Pascal differs from other versions.

P.1 Data Types and Values

Numbers. In the algorithmic language we use only one kind of numbers, real numbers. Like many other programming languages, Pascal distinguishes between two kinds of numbers, real numbers and integers. The reason for the two types is efficiency. Integers take up less space in the computer's memory than real numbers, and the computer can manipulate them more rapidly. Another distinction between the two is that operations on integers always yield exact answers, but some operations on real numbers only give approximate results.

An integer is a whole number that does not contain a decimal point. The following are examples of integers:

25   250   100   1000

An integer can be preceded by a + or − sign:

−25   +250   −100   +1000

When the sign is omitted, the integer is assumed to be positive. Thus +25 and 25 represent the same value.

Commas are not allowed in writing integers or any other numbers. Thus, 1,375 is invalid. In Pascal, we must write 1375 instead.

A real number can be written with a decimal point:

1.25   95.0   −3.1416   +6.25

At least one digit must precede and follow the decimal point. The following are invalid:

721.   .372

Instead we must write:

721.0   0.372

We can also write real numbers in exponential notation:

3.5E25   +1.0E9   −7.62E−5   3.0E−9

When exponential notation is used, the decimal point may be omitted. When the decimal point is omitted, it is assumed to occur immediately to the left of the E. In the following, the three real numbers on each line are equivalent:

475E−1   475.0E−1   47.5
1E3   1.0E3   1000.0
1E−4   1.0E−4   0.0001

When the decimal point is present, it must be preceded and followed by at least one digit, just as in conventional notation.

To summarize, if a number contains a decimal point, the letter E, or both, then it is a real number. If it contains neither a decimal point nor the letter E, then it is an integer.

Note that although 25 and 25.0 are equivalent in ordinary arithmetic, they belong to different data types in Pascal and cannot be used interchangeably. The two values are represented differently inside the computer, and some of the operations that can be carried out on them are different.

Character Strings. Character strings in Pascal are enclosed in single quotation marks, or apostrophes, just as in the algorithmic language:

```
'GOOD MORNING'
'3.1416'
'$%#&@!?'
' '            (One blank space)
```

The quotes enclose the string but are not part of it. Thus, the string

```
'HELLO'
```

is made up of the characters H, E, L, L, and O.

A single quotes or apostrophe inside a string must be represented by two consecutive single quotes. Thus, the string that represents

```
DON'T GO NEAR THE WATER.
```

must be written

```
'DON''T GO NEAR THE WATER.'
```

and the string that represents

```
WHY AREN'T YOU IN SCHOOL TODAY?
```

must be written

```
'WHY AREN''T YOU IN SCHOOL TODAY?'
```

The reason for this convention is to prevent the computer from confusing single quotes inside a string with the single quotes that enclose the string.

Don't confuse two single quotes in succession with the double quotation mark, ", which is a single character. To represent a single quote inside a string, strike the single quote key on your computer terminal twice in succession.

P.2 Output

In the algorithmic language we don't worry about the details of how computer output is to be arranged on display screens or printed pages. When it comes time to actually give directions to a computer, however, we can no longer ignore these matters. For this reason, the operation of outputting data is a bit more complicated in programming languages such as Pascal than it is in the algorithmic language.

The WRITELN Statement. The statement in Pascal that corresponds most closely to the OUTPUT statement in the algorithmic language is the WRITELN statement. (WRITELN is an abbreviation for "WRITE LINE.") The values to be printed are listed in parentheses following the word WRITELN.

We can print integers, real numbers, and strings with WRITELN statements. Thus the statements

```
WRITELN(250);
WRITELN(3.14159);
WRITELN('HELLO!')
```

cause the computer to print

```
250
 3.14159
HELLO!
```

Note that the three statements in the example are separated by semicolons. We can see this more clearly if we write all of the statements on the same line:

```
WRITELN(250); WRITELN(3.14159); WRITELN('HELLO')
```

The semicolons separate the statements; there is no semicolon before the first statement nor following the final one. Although it's perfectly permissible to write several statements on the same line, for ease in reading we usually write each statement on a separate line.

When the word WRITELN is used by itself, it causes the printer to go to a new line. When used immediately after a another WRITELN statement, it causes the printer to skip a line. Thus

```
WRITELN('GOOD MORNING.');
WRITELN;
WRITELN('HOW ARE YOU TODAY?')
```

cause the computer to print

```
GOOD MORNING.
                        (This line skipped)
HOW ARE YOU TODAY?
```

As with the OUTPUT statement, we can provide the WRITELN statement with a list of values to print. For instance, the statements

```
WRITELN(10, 20, -30, -40, 50);
WRITELN(1.1, 2.2, -3.3, -4.4, 5.5);
WRITELN('ONE', 'TWO', 'THREE', 'FOUR', 'FIVE')
```

cause the computer to print

```
1020 − 30 − 4050
 1.10000  2.20000 − 3.30000 − 4.40000  5.50000
ONETWOTHREEFOURFIVE
```

Unfortunately, the spacing of the items (or lack of it) leaves something to be desired. What's more, the details of the spacing vary from one version of Pascal to another, so if you try the preceding three statements on your computer, you may well find that the printed items come out spaced differently.

Field-Width Parameters. Fortunately, Pascal provides a mechanism known as *field-width parameters* that allows us to control the spacing of printed items.
Consider the statement:

```
WRITELN(250:10)
```

The value to be printed is 250; the field-width parameter is 10. The latter specifies that the value 250 will be printed in a field 10 characters wide. What this means is that the printed value 250 will be preceded by seven blank spaces, so that the blank spaces, together with the three digits of 250, will together occupy 10 character positions.
To illustrate in more detail, we need some way of making blank spaces visible, so you can see exactly how many blank spaces separate printed items. We can do this by using a small b to represent a blank space. With this convention, we can say that WRITELN(250:10) causes the computer to print;

```
bbbbbbb250
```

Now consider the statement:

```
WRITELN(10:5, 20:5, −30:5, −40:5, 50:5)
```

Each of the integers is to be printed in a field five characters wide:

```
bbb10bbb20bb−30bb−40bbb50
```

To make up the five-character fields, 10, 20, and 50 are each preceded by three blank spaces, while −30 and −40 are each preceded by two blank spaces. Replacing the b's by the blank spaces they represent, we see that the actual printout looks like this:

```
   10    20   −30   −40    50
```

We can use field-width parameters with strings as well as integers. For instance,

```
WRITELN('ONE':6, 'TWO':6, 'THREE':6, 'FOUR':6, 'FIVE':6)
```

produces

```
bbbONEbbbTWObTHREEbbFOURbbFIVE
```

or, as it would actually look on the printout

```
   ONE   TWO THREE  FOUR  FIVE
```

For real numbers, if we provide only one field-width parameter for each value, then the values are printed in exponential notation. Thus the statement

```
WRITELN(105.25:15,  -73.5:15, 1000.0:15)
```

causes the computer to print

```
bbbbbb1.05250E2bbbbb-7.35000E1bbbbbb1.00000E3
```

or, as it would actually look

```
    1.05250E2      -7.35000E1        1.00000E3
```

To get a real value printed in conventional notation, we must follow it with two field-width parameters. The first of these, as usual, gives the width of the field in which the real number is to be printed. The second specifies the number of decimal places that will be printed.

Thus, the statement

```
WRITELN(2.67:7:3)
```

prints the value 2.67 in a field seven characters wide and with three digits to the right of the decimal point:

```
bb2.670
```

The statement

```
WRITELN(105.25:15:2,  -73.5:15:2, 1000.0:15:2)
```

causes the computer to print

```
bbbbbbbbb105.25bbbbbbbbb-73.50bbbbbbbbb1000.00
```

or, as it would actually appear

```
        105.25         -73.50         1000.00
```

The WRITE statement. The WRITE statement differs from WRITELN in that WRITE does not cause the printer to go to a new line after it has finished printing. Thus

```
WRITE(10:4, 20:4, 30:4);
WRITE(40:4, 50:4);
WRITE(60:4, 70:4, 80:4)
```

cause the computer to print

```
10   20   30   40   50   60   70   80
```

Since the final statement is a WRITE statement, the printer remains on the same line and the next WRITE or WRITELN statement executed will cause it to continue printing on that same line.

On the other hand, if we use WRITELN statements instead of WRITE statements

```
WRITELN(10:4, 20:4, 30:4);
WRITELN(40:4, 50:4);
WRITELN(60:4, 70:4, 80:4)
```

the computer prints

```
10   20   30
40   50
60   70   80
```

and the next WRITE or WRITELN statement begins printing on a new line.

We will use WRITELN much more frequently than WRITE, since ordinarily we want each output statement to produce a single line of output. Sometimes, however, it comes in handy to have several output statements print on the same line, and then we can put the WRITE statement to good use.

P.3 Arithmetic Expressions

The arithmetic operators in Pascal are the same as those in the algorithmic language with two exceptions: (1) Pascal does not have an exponentiation operator, so the operator ** does not occur, and (2) Pascal has two additional division operators, DIV and MOD, that are used only with integers. The following table summarizes the arithmetic operators in Pascal:

```
+                  addition
-                  subtraction
*                  multiplication
/, DIV, and MOD    division
```

The operators +, −, *, and / apply both to real numbers and integers. For +, −, and *, if both of the operands are integers, then the result is an integer. If either or both of the operands are real numbers, however, then the result is a real number. The following examples illustrate this:

```
7 + 4 = 11
7.0 + 4 = 11.0
7 + 4.0 = 11.0
7.0 + 4.0 = 11.0
```

A division can yield a result containing a decimal point if the two numbers being divided are integers. For this reason, the operator / yields a real number regardless of whether its operands are integers or real numbers:

```
3/2 = 1.5
3.0/2 = 1.5
3/2.0 = 1.5
3.0/2.0 = 1.5
```

DIV and MOD take only integers as operands and yield integers as results. These operators allow us to do quotient-remainder division, with DIV yielding the quotient and MOD the remainder. For example, 30 divided by 8 yields a quotient of 3 and a remainder of 6. Therefore,

```
30 DIV 8 = 3
30 MOD 8 = 6
```

The arithmetic operators have the same priorities in Pascal as in the algorithmic language. The priority of DIV and MOD is the same as for /. Since there is no exponentiation operator, the arithmetic operators in Pascal have only two levels, of priority:

```
*, /, DIV, and MOD     high priority
+ and −                low priority
```

As in the algorithmic language, we can write complicated expressions with the arithmetic operators, relying on operator priorities and parentheses to specify the order in which the operators are to be applied. When using DIV and MOD in such expressions, don't forget that these operators apply only to integers. For instance, the expression

```
12 / 2 DIV 3
```

is invalid. Since / and DIV have the same priority, / will be applied first, giving

```
6.0 DIV 3
```

But 6.0 is not a valid operand for DIV, whose operands must be integers.

P.4 Functions

Pascal has five built-in functions that apply to integers or real numbers:

ABS   computes the absolute value of its argument. Thus ABS(5) = 5 and ABS(−5) = 5.

SQR   computes the square of its argument. Thus SQR(5) = 25 and SQR(1.5) = 2.25.

SQRT   computes the square root of its argument. Thus SQRT(9) = 3.0 and SQRT(2.25) = 1.5.

TRUNC   converts a real number to an integer by discarding the part to the right of the decimal point. Thus TRUNC(3.25) = 3 and TRUNC(3.75) = 3.

ROUND   converts a real number to an integer by rounding the real value to the nearest integer. Thus ROUND(3.25) = 3 and ROUND(3.75) = 4.

The arguments of ABS and SQR can be either integers or real numbers. The value of the function has the same type as its argument. For SQRT, the argument can be either an integer or a real number, but the result is always a real number. For TRUNC and ROUND, of course, the argument is always an integer, and the result, a real number, since the purpose of these two functions is to convert real numbers into integers.

P.5 Writing Pascal Programs

Now let's see how to put together some of the things we have been discussing to write a complete PASCAL program. Figure P-2 shows the Pascal

FIGURE P-2. The program EXPRESSIONS.

```
PROGRAM EXPRESSIONS;
(* A SIMPLE PASCAL PROGRAM *)
BEGIN
    WRITELN('3+5  =  ',  3+5);
    WRITELN('3-5  =  ',  3-5);
    WRITELN('3*5  =  ',  3*5);
    WRITELN('3/5   = ',  3/5:4:1);
    WRITELN('SQRT(1.69)  =',  SQRT(1.69):4:1)
END.
```

program corresponding to the algorithm EXPRESSIONS in Chapter 4. The program produces the following printout:

```
3+5  =  8
3-5  =  -2
3*5  =  15
3/5  =  0.6
SQRT(1.69)  =  1.3
```

The Program Heading. Referring to Figure P-2, the first line of the program is the program heading:

```
PROGRAM EXPRESSIONS;
```

Following the word PROGRAM is the name of the program, which is EXPRESSIONS. This name was chosen by the programmer. In Pascal, names chosen by the programmer are called *identifiers* and must be constructed according to the following rules:

1. An identifier must begin with a letter of the alphabet.

2. After the first character, the remaining characters may be either letters or digits. No other characters, such as spaces or punctuation marks, may be used.

3. An identifier must not be the same as a reserved word, a word that has a specific use in the Pascal language. Examples of reserved words in our example program are PROGRAM, BEGIN, and END. Thus PROGRAM would not be a valid identifier. A list of all the reserved words is given in an appendix to this supplement.

4. To save memory, the Pascal language processor keeps track of only the first eight characters of each identifier. Identifiers that are intended to be different from one another must differ in their first eight characters. Thus the computer would confuse EXPRESSIONS, EXPRESSION, and EXPRES-SION1, considering all three to be the same identifier.

In some versions of Pascal, the program heading must include a list of all files used by the program. A file is any source from which data can be obtained or any destination to which it can be sent. Input data is ordinarily obtained from a standard file INPUT, and output data is sent to a standard file OUTPUT. If our example program were written in a version of Pascal that required the files to be listed in the program heading, its program heading would be

```
PROGRAM EXPRESSIONS(OUTPUT);
```

since the WRITELN statements use the standard file OUTPUT.

In the same way, the program heading for a program that does both input and output from the standard files would have the following form:

```
PROGRAM INANDOUT(INPUT, OUTPUT);
```

In the rest of this supplement we will follow the conventions of UCSD Pascal, which allow the file names to be omitted.

Regardless of whether or not the file names are present, the program heading ends with a semicolon.

Comments. The line

```
(* A SIMPLE PASCAL PROGRAM *)
```

is a comment. Comments are intended for human readers and are ignored by the computer; they have no effect on the compilation or execution of the program. Comments in Pascal can be enclosed either between the braces { and } or between the symbols (* and *). The latter symbols are alternatives to braces, which are frequently not available on computer terminals and printers.

The Statement Part. The statement part of the program contains the statements that the computer is to execute.

Notice that the statements are bracketed by the reserved words BEGIN and END. A group of statements bracketed by BEGIN and END is said to form a *compound statement*. The statement part of the program is always a compound statement.

The statements making up a compound statement are separated by semicolons. Note that there is no semicolon between BEGIN and the first statement nor between the last statement and END.

The statements making up a compound statement are usually indented with respect to BEGIN and END. This makes it easy to see at a glance which statements make up a particular compound statement without having to hunt through a complicated program to find the END that goes with a particular BEGIN.

The period following END indicates the end of the program.

P.6 Variables

Variable Names. Variable names in Pascal are identifiers and so must satisfy the four restrictions listed in the last section. A variable name must begin with a letter of the alphabet; its remaining characters can be letters or digits. Reserved words must not be used as variable names, and variable names intended to be different must differ in their first eight characters.

The following are some examples of valid variable names in Pascal:

```
COST    AMOUNT
X       I5
SUM     SALESTAX
```

The following variable names are invalid:

```
R2-D2        (contains hyphen)
NEW YORK     (contains space)
2X           (starts with digit)
EMPLOYEE#    (contains #)
```

Note that the two variable names

```
SALESTAX1    SALESTAX2
```

are both valid, but the computer will consider them to be identical, which is almost certainly not what the programmer wanted.

Variable Declarations. Unlike the algorithmic language, Pascal requires that we declare the data type of the values that each variable can have. Confining ourselves to numerical data, for the moment, we have two data types: *integers* and *real numbers.* Corresponding to these, we have *integer variables*, which can only have integer values; and *real variables*, which can only have real number values.

Each Pascal program that uses variables has a *variable declaration part* that lists each variable used in the program and gives the data type of the values the variable can have.

Look at the following variable declaration part:

```
VAR
    AMOUNT: REAL;
    COUNT: INTEGER;
```

These declarations specify that AMOUNT is a real variable and COUNT is an integer variable. The variable declarations are introduced by the reserved word VAR. Each declaration ends with a semicolon, and in each a colon separates the variable name from the following type identifier.

When several variables are of the same type, we can combine their declarations as follows:

```
VAR
    X, Y, Z: REAL;
    I, J, K: INTEGER;
```

These declarations specify that X, Y, and Z are real variables and I, J, and K are integer variables.

This is a good place to mention several other data types that we haven't taken up yet but will be working with later on.

The BOOLEAN data type is used to record whether or not certain statements are true or false. The type BOOLEAN has only two values, TRUE and FALSE. This type is named after the English mathematician, George Boole, who was the first to formulate an algebra of logic.

Values of type CHAR consist of letters, digits, punctuation marks, and mathematical signs. A value of type CHAR is represented by a character enclosed in single quotes. The following are values of type CHAR:

```
'A'    'B'    'C'    '0'    '1'    '2'    '.'    '+'
```

As with strings, the single quotes enclose the character values but are not part of them. The single quote or apostrophe character is represented as follows:

```
''''
```

In UCSD Pascal, variables can be declared to be of type STRING and given string values such as

```
'HAVE A NICE DAY.'
'DON''T GO NEAR THE WATER.'
```

In other versions of Pascal, the programmer must define the data types of string variables using techniques that we will take up later.

The variable declaration part

```
VAR
    P: BOOLEAN;
    C: CHAR;
    S: STRING;
```

declares P to be a Boolean variable, C, a character variable, and S, a string variable.

The variable declaration part of a program comes between the program heading and the statement part. For example, see Figure P-3 or almost any of the other programs in this supplement.

P.7 Assignment

Pascal uses the symbol := for its assignment operator instead of the left-pointing arrow used in the algorithmic language. The symbol :=, which is used in a number of programming languages, probably originated as an attempt to suggest a left-pointing arrow using symbols available on most computer printers.

For example, suppose that the variables I, X, P, C, and S are declared as follows:

```
VAR
    I: INTEGER;
    X: REAL;
    P: BOOLEAN;
    C: CHAR;
    S: STRING:
```

then the assignments

```
I : = 25;
X : = 3.14;
P : = TRUE;
C : = 'Z';
S : = 'PASCAL'
```

give I, X, P, C, and S the following values:

```
I  25          X  3.14              P  TRUE
C  'Z'         S  'PASCAL'
```

Ordinarily, the values assigned to a variable must be of the same type as the variable itself. For instance, only integer values can be assigned to an integer variable, character values, to a character variable, and so on.

There is one exception to this rule, however. To every integer there is a corresponding real number. For instance, 25.0 corresponds to 25; -73.0 corresponds to -73; 2.0 corresponds to 2; and so on. If we assign an integer to a real variable, Pascal will convert the integer to the corresponding real number before making the assignment.

Thus if X and A are real variables, the assignments

```
X : = 25;
A : = -73
```

are valid. Pascal will convert the integers to the corresponding real numbers so that X and A receive the following values:

```
X  25.0                 A  -73.0
```

Real numbers cannot be assigned to integer variables, so the assignment

```
I : = 25.0
```

is invalid. We can, however, use the functions TRUNC and ROUND to convert real numbers to integers, then assign the resulting integers to integer variables. If I and N are integer variables, the following assignments are valid:

```
I : = TRUNC(32.75);
N : = ROUND(32.75)
```

As a result of the assignments, I and N receive the following values:

```
I  32              N  33
```

P.8 Input

Pascal has two statements for input, READ and READLN, corresponding to WRITE and WRITELN for output.

READLN reads successive values from a line of input and assigns the values read to the variables listed in the READLN statement. For example, consider the statement

```
READLN(X, Y, Z)
```

where X, Y, and Z are real variables. If, when this statement is executed, the user enters

```
3.14    7.5     1.0
```

then X is assigned the value 3.14, Y the value 7.5, and Z the value 1.0. The effect is precisely the same as if the assignments

```
X := 3.14;
Y := 7.5;
Z := 1.0
```

had been executed.

The data values entered as input must have the same types as the corresponding variables in the READLN statement. For instance, suppose I is an integer variable. If, when the statement

```
READLN(I)
```

is executed, the user enters

```
3.14
```

the program will terminate with an error message, since a real value cannot be assigned to an integer variable.

Pascal will, however, convert an integer value to the corresponding real value, just as for assignment statements.

Character and string values are entered without enclosing them in quotes. For instance, suppose C is a character variable and S is a string variable. The statements

```
READLN(C);
READLN(S)
```

read a character from one line and a string from the next line. If, when these statements are executed, the user types

```
P
THIS IS A STRING
```

C and S will receive the following values:

```
C  'P'          S  'THIS IS A STRING'
```

A string value extends all the way to the end of the line on which it is typed. Therefore, no other value can follow a string on the same line, since everything else on the line is considered to be part of the string.

The READLN statement always accepts a full line of input and ignores any unneeded data. For example, consider the statements

```
READLN(X);
READLN(Y, Z)
```

Suppose the user enters the following:

```
1.8    7.3
2.5    3.9
```

X is assigned the value 1.8; the value 7.3 is ignored. Y is assigned the value 2.5 and Z is assigned the value 3.9

Occasionally, we may need to let more than one input statement read from the same line of input data. In that case we can use the READ statement, which remains on the same line of input after reading the requested data. For instance, suppose the statements

```
READ(X);
READ(Y, Z)
```

are executed. If the user enters

```
1.8    7.3
2.5    3.9
```

then X is assigned the value 1.8, Y the value 7.3, and Z the value 2.5. The value 3.9 is still available for use by the next READ or READLN statement.

In interactive versions of Pascal, where the user types in data as the program needs it, the program should print a message requesting each line of data. Such messages are call *prompts*. For instance, suppose a program wants the user to enter the length, width, and height of a box. It could use the following statements:

```
WRITE('ENTER LENGTH, WIDTH, AND HEIGHT: ');
READLN(L, W, H)
```

The WRITE statement prints the prompt; the READLN statement accepts the data. Using WRITE rather than WRITELN allows the data to be entered on the same line as the prompt. The dialog with the user might go like this:

```
ENTER LENGTH, WIDTH, AND HEIGHT: 25.3  8.7  3.9
```

```
      PROGRAM CONVERT;
      (* CONVERT FEET AND INCHES TO CENTIMETERS *)
      VAR
          FEET, INCHES, TOTALINCHES: INTEGER;
          CENTIMETERS: REAL;
      BEGIN
          WRITE('ENTER FEET AND INCHES:');
          READLN(FEET, INCHES);
          TOTALINCHES := 12*FEET + INCHES;
          CENTIMETERS := 2.54*TOTALINCHES;
          WRITE(FEET, ' FEET ', INCHES, ' INCHES =');
          WRITELN(CENTIMETERS:7:2, ' CENTIMETERS')
      END.
```

FIGURE P-3. The program CONVERT.

The prompt was typed by the computer, the remainder of the line by the user. The variables L, W, and H receive the values 25.3, 8.7, and 3.9, respectively.

If your version of Pascal does not allow you to interact with a program while it is executing, then prompts serve no useful purpose and should be deleted from the program examples.

Figure P-3 shows a Pascal program corresponding to the algorithm CONVERT in Chapter 5. Note the prompt for the length to be converted. The following is a typical dialog between the user and the program:

```
ENTER FEET AND INCHES: 6 4
6 FEET 4 INCHES = 193.04 CENTIMETERS
```

Figure P-4 shows a Pascal program corresponding to the algorithm PURCHASE in Chapter 5. The following is a typical dialog between the user and this program:

```
ENTER PRICE, DISCOUNT RATE, AND TAX RATE: 50 0.10 0.03
PLEASE PAY    46.35 DOLLARS
```

FIGURE P-4. The program PURCHASE.

```
   PROGRAM PURCHASE;
   (* COMPUTE COST OF PURCHASE *)
   VAR
      PRICE, DISCNTRATE, TAXRATE, DISCOUNT, TAX: REAL;
   BEGIN
      WRITE('ENTER PRICE, DISCOUNT RATE, AND TAX RATE: ');
      READLN(PRICE, DISCNTRATE, TAXRATE);
      DISCOUNT := PRICE*DISCNTRATE;
      PRICE := PRICE-DISCOUNT;
      TAX := PRICE*TAXRATE;
      PRICE := PRICE+TAX;
      WRITELN('PLEASE PAY ', PRICE:7:2, ' DOLLARS')
   END.
```

The algorithm PURCHASE uses the variables DISCOUNT and DIS-
COUNT__RATE. The obvious translations into Pascal are DISCOUNT and
DISCOUNTRATE. Yet the Pascal program uses DISCNTRATE instead of
DISCOUNTRATE. Why?

P.9 Conditions

Boolean values in Pascal correspond to logical values in the algorithmic
language. In each language the values in question are represented by TRUE
and FALSE. TRUE and FALSE represent Boolean values in the same way
that 3.14 represents a real number, 25 represents an integer, and 'PASCAL'
represents a string.

Three of the relational operators in Pascal are identical to their counterparts in the algorithmic language. Two others are similar:

```
Algorithmic Language  Pascal

        =                 =
        ≠                 <>
        <                 <
        >                 >
        ≤                 <=
        ≥                 >=
```

As in the algorithmic language, the relational operators have a lower
priority than any of the arithmetic operators, so that in expressions such
as

```
3*4+1 > 6/3
```

the arithmetic operators will be applied before the relational operators. If
we incorporate the relational operators into our table of priorities for Pascal, we get

```
*, /, DIV, MOD                highest priority
+, -
=, <>, <, >, <=, >=    lowest priority
```

Any expression that yields a Boolean value may be called a *Boolean
expression*. The following are all Boolean expressions, since each has a
value of either TRUE or FALSE:

```
3 < 5
6*4 = 7*3
'JOE' <= 'JIM'
```

What we call a condition in the algorithmic language corresponds to a
Boolean expression in Pascal.

P.10 One- and Two-way Selection

The IF Statement. For one-way selection, we use the following form of the Pascal IF statement:

```
IF condition THEN statement
```

If the condition is true, then the statement is executed. If the condition is false, no action is taken, and the computer goes on to the next statement in the program.

Note that the IF statement contains another statement as a part. This is characteristic of Pascal; a number of Pascal statements can contain other statements as parts.

Although we can write the controlled statement on the same line as IF *condition* THEN, readability is usually improved if we write the statement on the line below, indented with respect to IF *condition* THEN to show that it is a continuation of the IF statement:

```
IF condition THEN
   statement
```

For example, if I, J, and K are integer variables, then

```
IF I = J THEN
   J := K
```

causes the computer to compare the values of I and J. If the two are equal, the value of K is assigned to J. Otherwise, no action is taken, and the computer goes on to the next statement in the program.

When an IF statement is followed by another statement, the semicolon separating the two comes after the complete IF statement, NOT after the IF-THEN part:

```
I := 5;
IF I = J THEN
   J := K;          (* NOTE SEMICOLON *)
K := K-1
```

In the algorithmic language, we can write any number of statements between IF *condition* THEN and END IF; either all or none of the statements are executed depending on whether the condition is true or false. But the Pascal IF statement only provides for a single controlled statement. What do we do if we want to control the execution of several statements with the same condition?

Compound statements come to the rescue. A compound statement, you recall, is a sequence of statements bracketed by BEGIN and END:

```
BEGIN
   I := I-1;
   J := J+1;
   K := 0
END
```

The entire compound statement is considered to be a single statement and can be used anywhere that a single statement is allowed. (A compound statement is another example of a Pascal statement that contains other statements as parts.) In particular, the controlled statement part of an IF statement can be a compound statement:

```
IF I < J THEN
   BEGIN
      I := I-1;
      J := J+1;
      K := 0
   END
```

When this statement is executed, if the value of I is less than the value of J, then all three statements between BEGIN and END are executed. Otherwise, no action is taken, and the computer goes on to the next statement in the program.

When an IF statement containing a compound statement is followed by another statement, the semicolon separating the IF statement from the following statement comes after the word END of the compound statement:

```
IF I > 5 THEN
   BEGIN
      I := 1;
      WRITELN(J)
   END;              (* NOTE SEMICOLON *)
J := J+1
```

Figure P-5 gives a Pascal program corresponding to the algorithm WAGES in Chapter 5. Note that NAME is a string variable; if your version of Pascal doesn't have string variables, you can use an integer employee number in place of the employee's name, or you can just do away with NAME altogether, since it plays no role in the computation the program carries out.

The ELSE Part. The IF statement in Pascal has two forms. We have already seen one form, which has only one controlled statement. The other form has two controlled statements:

```
IF condition THEN statement-1 ELSE statement-2
```

This form allows two-way selection. If the condition is true, then *statement-1* is executed; if the condition is false, then *statement-2* is exe-

```
PROGRAM WAGES;
(* COMPUTE EMPLOYEE'S GROSS WAGES *)
VAR
    NAME: STRING;
    HOURS, RATE, GROSS, EXTRA: REAL;
BEGIN
    WRITE('NAME? ');
    READLN(NAME);
    WRITE('HOURS AND RATE? ');
    READLN(HOURS, RATE);
    GROSS := HOURS*RATE;
    IF HOURS > 40 THEN
        BEGIN
            EXTRA := 0.5*(HOURS-40.0)*RATE;
            GROSS := GROSS+EXTRA
        END;
    WRITELN('GROSS WAGES FOR ', NAME, ' ARE ', GROSS:7:2)
END.
```

FIGURE P-5. The program WAGES.

cuted. One statement or the other is always executed, but never both. After the selected statement has been executed, the computer goes on to the next statement in the program.

For ease of reading, *statement-1* and *statement-2* are usually written on separate lines, indented with respect to IF and ELSE:

```
IF condition THEN
    statement-1
ELSE
    statement-2
```

Statement-1 and *statement-2* can be either simple or compound statements.

Let's look at an example:

```
IF I = 0 THEN
    I := J
ELSE
    I := K;        (* NOTE SEMICOLON *)
WRITELN(I)
```

If the value of I is zero, then the value of J is assigned to I. Otherwise, the value of K is assigned to I. No matter which assignment is made, the statement following the IF statement, WRITELN(I), is always executed.

Note that the semicolon separating the IF statement from the following statement comes after *statement-2*, the statement in the ELSE part. IF *statement-2* is a compound statement, then the semicolon comes after the word END:

```
IF I = 0 THEN
    I := J
```

```
ELSE
   BEGIN
      I := K;
      K := 0
   END;              (* NOTE SEMICOLON *)
WRITELN(I)
```

Figure P-6 gives a Pascal program corresponding to the algorithm AL-
PHABETIZE. If your version of Pascal doesn't have the STRING data type,
you may modify the program to put integers in numerical order instead of
strings in alphabetical order. You may wish to try a more challenging version of the program that puts three values into alphabetical or numerical
order.

P.11 Nested if Statements

We know that some Pascal statements can contain other statements as
parts. When a statement contains another statement of the same kind, we
say that the statements are *nested*.

IF statements can be nested. For example, consider the general form
of the IF statement with ELSE part:

```
IF condition-1 THEN
   statement-1
ELSE
   statement-2
```

Either *statement-1* or *statement-2* can itself be an IF statement. If *state-
ment-1* is an IF statement, then we have

FIGURE P-6. The program ALPHABETIZE.

```
PROGRAM ALPHABETIZE;
(* PRINT TWO STRINGS IN ALPHABETICAL ORDER *)
VAR
   FIRST, SECOND: STRING;
BEGIN
   WRITE('FIRST STRING? ');
   READLN(FIRST);
   WRITE('SECOND STRING? ');
   READLN(SECOND);
   IF FIRST <= SECOND THEN
      WRITELN(FIRST, ' ', SECOND)
   ELSE
      WRITELN(SECOND, ' ', FIRST)
END.
```

```
IF condition-1 THEN
   IF condition-2 THEN
      statement-3
   ELSE
      statement-4
ELSE
   statement-2
```

Under what conditions will each statement be executed? We reason this way: If *condition-1* is false, then *statement-2* will be executed. If *condition-1* is true, then the nested IF statement will be executed. This means that if *condition-1* is true and *condition-2* is true, then *statement-3* will be executed. But if *condition-1* is true and *condition-2* is false, then *statement-4* will be executed.

We can summarize the results of our reasoning in the following table

condition-1	condition-2	statement executed
FALSE	FALSE	statement-2
FALSE	TRUE	statement-2
TRUE	FALSE	statement-4
TRUE	TRUE	statement-3

The statement in the ELSE part of an IF statement can also be another IF statement:

```
IF condition-1 THEN
    statement-1
ELSE
   IF condition-2 THEN
      statement-3
   ELSE
      statement-4
```

If *condition-1* is true then *statement-1* is executed. Otherwise, *condition-2* determines whether *statement-3* or *statement-4* will be executed. Again, we can summarize our results in a table:

condition-1	condition-2	statement executed
FALSE	FALSE	statement-4
FALSE	TRUE	statement-3
TRUE	FALSE	statement-1
TRUE	TRUE	statement-1

If nested IF statements don't seem tricky enough already, look at the following IF statement (the words *condition* and *statement* have been abbreviated to get the IF statement all on one line):

```
IF cond-1 THEN IF cond-2 THEN stmnt-1 ELSE stmnt-2
```

The question is, to which of the two IF-THEN parts does the ELSE part go? Put another way, if we write the statement in indented form, in which of the following two ways should we indent it?

```
IF cond-1 THEN                  IF cond-1 THEN
    IF cond-2 THEN                  IF cond-2 THEN
        stmnt-1                        stmnt-1
    ELSE                        ELSE
        stmnt-2                        stmnt-2
```

We cannot answer this question based on what we already know. We just have to be told the rule that Pascal compilers follow when processing IF statements. The rule is this: each ELSE part goes with the nearest preceding IF-THEN part that doesn't already have a matching ELSE part. According to this rule, the ELSE part in the example goes with the second IF-THEN part, not the first. The indentation on the left is correct; the one on the right is highly misleading since it doesn't reflect the way in which the Pascal compiler will actually process the statement.

The Pascal compiler pays no attention to indentation, but analyzes statements according to rules such as the one just given. If we should mistakenly indent the statement as shown on the right, we would manage only to confuse ourselves as to how the statement will actually be executed. Incorrect indentation is worse than none at all, for it almost forces upon us a misunderstanding of how the computer will execute the improperly indented statement.

Figure P-7 illustrates nested IF statements in a Pascal program. This program corresponds to Example 3 in Chapter 6.

P.12 Multiway Selection

There are two ways to realize multiway selection in Pascal. One is with nested IF statements. The other is with a CASE statement especially designed for multiway selection.

Nested IF Statements. We saw in the last section that nested IF statements allow us to select one of a number of statements for execution. We also saw that there are many ways of arranging nested IF statements, and for some of these ways it can be tricky to determine which statement will be executed under each particular set of conditions.

For this reason, it's helpful to adopt one standard arrangement of nested IF statements for multiway selection, an arrangement for which it is particularly easy to see how the truth or falsity of the conditions determine which controlled statement will be executed. The standard form usually adopted is the following:

```
IF condition-1 THEN
    statement-1
```

```
PROGRAM QUESTION;
(* ASK A QUESTION AND CHECK THE ANSWER *)
VAR
    ANSWER: STRING;
BEGIN
    WRITE('WHAT IS THE CAPITOL OF WEST VIRGINIA? ');
    READLN(ANSWER);
    IF ANSWER = 'CHARLESTON' THEN
        WRITELN('YOU ARE RIGHT')
    ELSE
        BEGIN
            WRITE('NO, TRY AGAIN: ');
            READLN(ANSWER);
            IF ANSWER = 'CHARLESTON' THEN
                WRITELN('YOU GOT IT RIGHT THIS TIME')
            ELSE
                BEGIN
                    WRITE('NO, CHARLESTON IS THE CAPITOL OF ');
                    WRITELN('WEST VIRGINIA')
                END
        END
END.
```

FIGURE P-7. The program QUESTION.

```
ELSE
    IF condition-2 THEN
        statement-2
    ELSE
        IF condition-3 THEN
            statement-3
        ELSE
            statement-4
```

How is this statement to be interpreted? If *condition-1* is true, then *statement-1* will be executed. Otherwise, we must check *condition-2*.

If *condition-1* is false but *condition-2* is true, then *statement-2* is executed. Otherwise, we must check *condition-3*.

If *condition-1* and *condition-2* are both false but *condition-3* is true, then *statement-3* is executed. Otherwise, all three conditions are false, and *statement-4* is executed.

We can state the results of our analysis quite simply. Note that for each of the three conditions there is a corresponding statement: *statement-1* corresponds to *condition-1*, *statement-2* corresponds to *condition-2*, and *statement-3* corresponds to *condition-3*. One statement, *statement-4* doesn't correspond to any condition. We can make a list of the conditions and their corresponding statements:

condition-1   statement-1
condition-2   statement-2
condition-3   statement-3
                    statement-4

With the aid of this table, we can state a very simple rule for interpreting the IF statement: *Start from the top of the list of conditions and go down the list. When you find the first true condition, execute the corresponding statement. If all of the conditions are false, execute the last statement, the one that doesn't correspond to any condition.*

We wrote our IF statement in such a way as to emphasize the nesting of the various IF statements making it up. Usually, it's clearer to write the statement in such a way as to emphasize the correspondence between the conditions and the controlled statements:

```
IF condition-1 THEN
    statement-1
ELSE IF condition-2 THEN
    statement-2
ELSE IF condition-3 THEN
    statement-3
ELSE
    statement-4
```

This is the Pascal version of the multiway IF construction in the algorithmic language. We can extend it to include as many condition-statement pairs as we wish. Naturally, each of the controlled statements can be a compound statement made up of any number of other statements.

Figure P-8 gives a complete Pascal program using nested IF statements for multiway selection. This program corresponds to the first version of the algorithm LETTER__GRADE in Chapter 6.

FIGURE P-8. The program LETTERGRADE using IF statements.

```
PROGRAM LETTERGRADE;
(* CONVERT NUMBER GRADE TO LETTER GRADE *)
VAR
    NUMBERGRADE: INTEGER;
BEGIN
    WRITE('NUMBER GRADE? ');
    READLN(NUMBERGRADE);
    WRITE('LETTER GRADE IS ');
    IF NUMBERGRADE >= 90 THEN
        WRITELN('A')
    ELSE IF NUMBERGRADE >= 80 THEN
        WRITELN('B')
    ELSE IF NUMBERGRADE >= 70 THEN
        WRITELN('C')
    ELSE IF NUMBERGRADE >= 60 THEN
        WRITELN('D')
    ELSE
        WRITELN('F')
END.
```

The CASE Statement. The Pascal CASE statement is very similar to the
CASE construction in the algorithmic language. We can best illustrate the
Pascal case statement with an example:

```
CASE I OF
   1: statement-1;
   2: statement-2;
   3: statement-3;
   4: statement-4
END
```

I is an integer variable. The value of I determines which statement will
be executed. If the value of I is 1, then *statement-1* is executed; if the value
of I is 2, then *statement-2* is executed; and so on. If the value of I is less
than 1 or greater than 4, then the execution of the program will terminate
with an error message.

Pascal allows us to label a statement with more than one value:

```
CASE I-3 OF
   1, 2, 3: statement-1;
   4, 5: statement-2;
   6, 7, 8: statement-3
END
```

If the value of I−3 is 1, 2, or 3, then *statement-1* is executed. If the
value of I−3 is 4 or 5, then *statement-2* is executed. And if the value of
I−3 is 6, 7, or 8, then *statement-3* is executed. The value of I−3 must lie
in the range 1 through 8, or an error occurs.

The expression whose value determines which statement will be executed is called the *selector*. The value of the selector isn't restricted to
being an integer. It can belong to any of the data types we have studied
except REAL. In theory it could be BOOLEAN, but if we want a BOOLEAN
expression to determine which statement should be executed, we are better off using an IF statement instead of a CASE statement.

This leaves CHAR as the other data type we have studied so far for
which the CASE statement is practical. For example, if LETTERGRADE is
of type CHAR, we can use the following statement to convert a letter grade
to a numerical score:

```
CASE LETTERGRADE OF
    'A': SCORE := 4;
    'B': SCORE := 3;
    'C': SCORE := 2;
    'D': SCORE := 1;
    'F': SCORE := 0
END
```

Figure P-9 gives a Pascal program using the CASE statement. This program corresponds to the second version of the algorithm LETTER__GRADE in Chapter 6.

P.13 The Boolean Operators

The logical operators OR, AND, and NOT are known as *Boolean operators* in Pascal, since they operate on Boolean values and yield Boolean values as results.

Most unfortunately, the priorities of these operators are not the same in Pascal as they are in the algorithmic language (or in just about any other programming language). If we extend our table of operator priorities to include the Boolean operators, we get the following:

```
NOT                           highest priority
*, /, DIV, MOD, AND
+, -, OR
=, <>, <, >, <=, >=      lowest priority
```

Ordinarily, the effect of these priorities is to require that the operands of Boolean operators be enclosed in parentheses.

For instance, if A, B, and C are integer variables, the expression

```
A < B AND C = 25
```

is erroneous. Since AND has a higher priority than < and =, the computer will start out by trying to evaluate:

```
B AND C
```

FIGURE P-9. The program LETTERGRADE using a CASE statement.

```
PROGRAM LETTERGRADE;
(* CONVERT NUMBER GRADE TO LETTER GRADE *)
VAR
   NUMBERGRADE, RANGE: INTEGER;
BEGIN
   WRITE('NUMBER GRADE? ');
   READLN(NUMBERGRADE);
   RANGE := NUMBERGRADE DIV 10;
   WRITE('LETTER GRADE IS ');
   CASE RANGE OF
      0, 1, 2, 3, 4, 5: WRITELN('F');
      6: WRITELN('D');
      7: WRITELN('C');
      8: WRITELN('B');
      9, 10: WRITELN('A')
   END
END.
```

Aside from not being what we intended, this is erroneous because B and C are integer variables, and the Boolean operators can only operate on Boolean values.

Instead, we must write:

```
(A < B) AND (C = 25)
```

Now the computer will apply the relational operators before attempting to apply the Boolean operator. Since the relational operators yield Boolean values, all will be well.

Thus, Example 6 of Chapter 6 must be written:

```
(3+4 > 12) OR (3*4 = 12)
```

When it is written in this way, evaluation proceeds as shown in the text.

Example 7 in Chapter 6 can be carried over into Pascal directly, since the parts of the expressions containing relational operators are already parenthesized. Note that in Pascal, as in the algorithmic language, NOT has a higher precedence than AND, which in turn has a higher precedence than OR.

P.14 Repetition

The Repetition Statements. The repetition statements in Pascal are very similar to the corresponding constructions in the algorithmic language. Corresponding to the WHILE construction, we have the WHILE statement:

```
WHILE condition DO statement
```

Usually, the statement begins on the line following WHILE and DO:

```
WHILE condition DO
    statement
```

The statement can be simple or compound. As in the algorithmic language, the statement is executed while the condition remains true. The condition is checked before each repetition. If the condition is false the first time it is checked, then the repeated statement won't be executed at all.

The following is an example of the WHILE statement:

```
I := 0;
WHILE I <= 20 DO
    BEGIN
        WRITE(I:4);
        I := I+5
    END
```

These statements cause the computer to print:

```
0    5  10  15  20
```

(Note the use of WRITE, as opposed to WRITELN, to cause all five values to be printed on the same line.)

Pascal has a REPEAT statement that is precisely the same as the RE-PEAT-UNTIL construction in the algorithmic language:

```
REPEAT
   statements
UNTIL condition
```

This statement is unusual for Pascal in that we may place any number of statements between REPEAT and UNTIL. (The statements are separated by semicolons.) We don't have to use a compound statement in order for a number of statements to be controlled by the REPEAT statement.

As in the algorithmic language, the repeated statements are executed until the condition becomes true. The condition is checked after each repetition, so the repeated statements are always executed at least once, even if the condition is initially true.

The following two examples contrast the WHILE and REPEAT statements:

```
I := 21;                 I := 21;
WHILE I <= 20 DO         REPEAT
   BEGIN                     WRITE(I:4);
      WRITE(I:4);           I := I+5
      I := I+5          UNTIL I > 20
   END
```

In the example on the left, the condition I $\leq$ 20 is false when it is checked the first time. Therefore, the repeated statement is not executed. Nothing is printed, and the value of I remains 21.

In the example on the right, the repeated statements are executed once before checking the condition I $>$ 20. Therefore, the value 21 is printed, and the value of I is increased to 26. Now the condition is checked. It is found to be true, so no more repetitions take place.

The iterative statement in Pascal is similar in form to the iterative construction in the algorithmic language. However there is no BY clause that allows us to specify the amount by which the controlled variable will be increased or decreased on each repetition. Instead, the Pascal FOR statement has two forms. In the first

```
FOR I := L TO M DO statement
```

the value of I is increased by 1 on each repetition. In the second

```
FOR I := L DOWNTO M DO statement
```

the value of I is decreased by 1 on each repetition.

In these general forms, I is a variable, but L and M can be constants, variables, or expressions. I, L, and M must all be of the same data type. The data type may not be REAL. For the present, we will use only integer variables for I; later we will note some other permissible data types.

For example, the statement

```
FOR I := 5 TO 10 DO
   WRITE(I:4)
```

causes the computer to print

```
5    6    7    8    9  10
```

The statement

```
FOR I := 10 DOWNTO 5 DO
   WRITE(I:4)
```

causes the computer to print

```
10    9    8    7    6    5
```

Figures P-10 through P-13 show Pascal programs corresponding to the following algorithms from Chapter 7: PAYROLL, GRADES, HIGH_AND_ LOW, and INTEREST. Note that some of our early programs, such as HIGHANDLOW, seem trivial when small amounts of data are entered from

FIGURE P-10. The program PAYROLL.

```
PROGRAM PAYROLL;
(* COMPUTE EMPLOYEES' GROSS WAGES *)
VAR
    NAME: STRING;
    HOURS, RATE, GROSS, TOTAL: REAL;
BEGIN
    TOTAL := 0;
    WRITE('NAME? ');
    READLN(NAME);
    WHILE NAME <> 'END OF DATA' DO
        BEGIN
          WRITE('HOURS AND RATE? ');
          READLN(HOURS, RATE);
          GROSS := HOURS*RATE;
          IF HOURS > 40 THEN
             GROSS := GROSS + 0.5*(HOURS-40.0)*RATE;
          TOTAL := TOTAL+GROSS;
          WRITELN('GROSS WAGES FOR ', NAME, ' ARE ', GROSS:7:2);
          WRITE('NAME? ');
          READLN(NAME)
        END;
    WRITELN;
    WRITELN('TOTAL GROSS WAGES ARE ', TOTAL:7:2)
END.
```

```
PROGRAM GRADES;
(* CONVERT NUMBER GRADES TO LETTER GRADES AND DISPLAY
   GRADE DISTRIBUTION *)
VAR
   NAME: STRING;
   LETTERGRADE: CHAR;
   NUMBERGRADE, ACOUNT, BCOUNT,
   CCOUNT, DCOUNT, FCOUNT: INTEGER;
BEGIN
   ACOUNT := 0;
   BCOUNT := 0;
   CCOUNT := 0;
   DCOUNT := 0;
   FCOUNT := 0;
   WRITE('NAME? ');
   READLN(NAME);
   WHILE NAME <> 'END OF DATA' DO
      BEGIN
         WRITE('NUMBER GRADE? ');
         READLN(NUMBERGRADE);
         IF NUMBERGRADE >= 90 THEN
            BEGIN
               LETTERGRADE := 'A';
               ACOUNT := ACOUNT+1
            END
         ELSE IF NUMBERGRADE >= 80 THEN
            BEGIN
               LETTERGRADE := 'B';
               BCOUNT := BCOUNT+1
            END
         ELSE IF NUMBERGRADE >= 70 THEN
            BEGIN
               LETTERGRADE := 'C';
               CCOUNT := CCOUNT+1
            END
         ELSE IF NUMBERGRADE >= 60 THEN
            BEGIN
               LETTERGRADE := 'D';
               DCOUNT := DCOUNT+1
            END
         ELSE
            BEGIN
               LETTERGRADE := 'F';
               FCOUNT := FCOUNT+1
            END;
         WRITELN('GRADE FOR ', NAME, ' IS ', LETTERGRADE);
         WRITE('NAME? ');
         READLN(NAME)
      END;
   WRITELN('GRADE DISTRIBUTION');
   WRITE('A: ':8, ACOUNT, 'B: ':8, BCOUNT, 'C: ':8, CCOUNT,
         'D: ':8, DCOUNT, 'F: ':8, FCOUNT)

END.
```

FIGURE P-11. The program GRADES.

the keyboard, since we can see the results just by glancing through the data. But if we imagine large amounts of data stored, say, on a disk file, where we can't just glance through it, then the program becomes more reasonable.

```
        PROGRAM HIGHANDLOW;
        (* FIND HIGH AND LOW TEMPERATURES *)
        VAR
           HIGH, LOW, TEMPERATURE: INTEGER;
        BEGIN
           WRITE('TEMPERATURE? ');
           READLN(TEMPERATURE);
           LOW := TEMPERATURE;
           HIGH := TEMPERATURE;
           WHILE TEMPERATURE <> -100 DO
              BEGIN
                 IF TEMPERATURE < LOW THEN
                    LOW := TEMPERATURE
                 ELSE IF TEMPERATURE > HIGH THEN
                    HIGH := TEMPERATURE;
                 WRITE('TEMPERATURE? ');
                 READLN(TEMPERATURE)
              END;
           WRITELN('LOW: ', LOW);
           WRITELN('HIGH: ', HIGH);
        END.
```

FIGURE P-12. The program HIGHANDLOW.

```
        PROGRAM INTEREST;
        (* COMPUTE INTEREST ON SAVINGS ACCOUNT *)
        VAR
           AMOUNT, DEPOSIT, YEARLYRATE, MONTHLYRATE: REAL;
           N, MONTHS: INTEGER;
        BEGIN
           WRITE('AMOUNT IN YOUR ACCOUNT NOW? ');
           READLN(AMOUNT);
           WRITE('MONTHLY DEPOSIT? ');
           READLN(DEPOSIT);
           WRITE('YEARLY INTEREST RATE? ');
           READLN(YEARLYRATE);
           WRITE('NUMBER OF MONTHS? ');
           READLN(MONTHS);
           YEARLYRATE := YEARLYRATE/100.0;
           MONTHLYRATE := YEARLYRATE/12.0;
           FOR N := 1 TO MONTHS DO
              BEGIN
                 AMOUNT := AMOUNT+DEPOSIT;
                 AMOUNT := AMOUNT + MONTHLYRATE*AMOUNT
              END;
           WRITELN('AMOUNT IN ACCOUNT AFTER ', MONTHS,
                   ' MONTHS IS ', AMOUNT:8:2)
        END.
```

FIGURE P-13. The program INTEREST.

P.15 More on Data Types

One of the virtues of Pascal is its well-organized system of data types. A small number of data types are built into the language. The programmer is given the capability of defining many more. So far we have confined ourselves to the built-in data types. In this section we will begin to look at some of the data types that the programmer can define. We will be using programmer-defined data types extensively in later sections.

To begin with, Pascal classifies data types as *simple*, *structured*, and *pointer* types. The simple types are those whose values are not made up from simpler components. The structured data types are those whose values are made up of simpler components. The pointer types are those whose values are used to locate data items in the computer's memory.

In this section we will confine ourselves to the simple data types. We will begin to study the structured data types in the next section. The simple data types are divided into *scalar types* and *subrange types*.

Scalar Data Types. Among the scalar data types we can distinguish between those that are built into the language and those that are defined by the user.

The built-in, or standard, scalar data types are INTEGER, REAL, BOOLEAN, and CHAR, all of which need no further introduction. Note that the STRING data type, which is built into UCSD Pascal, is not a simple data type since its values (strings) are made up of simpler components (characters).

Real numbers aren't suited for certain applications, such as counting. For this reason the type REAL is something of a second-class citizen among the scalar data types. You will often be told that a particular variable or value can be of "any scalar type except REAL." Values of type REAL are used only for doing real-number arithmetic. Values of other scalar types have a wide variety of applications.

The user-defined scalar types are also called *enumeration types*, since the programmer defines the type by listing, or enumerating, each of its values.

We define an enumeration type by a type definition such as the following:

```
TYPE
    DAY = (SUN, MON, TUE, WED, THURS, FRI, SAT);
```

This defines DAY as a new data type. The possible values of DAY are SUN, MON, TUE, WED, THURS, FRI, and SAT. Note that the identifiers SUN, MON, and so on now denote values in the same way as do TRUE, FALSE, 25, 3.14, and 'A'.

In a program, type definitions come immediately before variable declarations. Suppose a program contains the following type definition and variable declaration:

```
TYPE
    DAY = (SUN, MON, TUE, WED, THURS, FRI, SAT);
VAR
    D, E: DAY;
```

D and E are now variables of type DAY. Thus assignments such as

```
D : = MON;
E : = WED
```

are valid and give D the value MON and E the value WED. The assignment

```
D : = E;
```

is also valid and would assign the value of E to D.

The following are some other examples of type definitions:

```
TYPE
    COLOR = (RED, ORANGE, YELLOW, GREEN, BLUE,
            INDIGO, VIOLET);
    CHESSMAN = (PAWN, KNIGHT, BISHOP, ROOK,
            QUEEN, KING);
    MONTH = (JAN, FEB, MAR, APR, MAY, JUN, JULY,
            AUG, SEPT, OCT, NOV, DEC);
    GRADE = (F, D, C, B, A);
```

The identifiers that represent the values must be unique. The same identifier cannot appear in more than one type definition.

Operators and Functions on Scalar Data Types. Each of the scalar data types is ordered. That is, the values of each type are arranged in a particular order, so we can always say that one value precedes, is equal to, or follows another value. To the values of any scalar type we can apply the six relational operators

$$= \quad <> \quad < \quad > \quad <= \quad >=$$

For the standard data types, the order for integers and real numbers is the usual numerical order. For Boolean values, FALSE precedes TRUE, so

```
FALSE < TRUE
TRUE > FALSE
```

are both true.

For each character code, such as ASCII, there is a collating sequence that specifies the order of the characters. Although the collating sequence varies from one character code to another, invariably the letters are in alphabetical order and the digits are in numerical order. Thus

```
'3' < '5'
'C' < 'X'
'h' < 'k'
```

are true.

For enumeration types, the order of the values is the same as the order in which they were listed in the type definition. For instance, if we define the type OFFICER by

```
OFFICER = (LIEUTENANT, CAPTAIN, MAJOR, COLONEL, GENERAL);
```

then each of the following is true:

```
LIEUTENANT < COLONEL
CAPTAIN < MAJOR
MAJOR < GENERAL
```

There are two built-in functions, PRED and SUCC, that apply to all scalar types except REAL. PRED returns the value (if any) that immediately precedes the value of its argument. Thus PRED(MAJOR) equals CAPTAIN and PRED(CAPTAIN) equals LIEUTENANT. PRED(LIEUTENANT) is undefined.

SUCC returns the value (if any) that immediately follows the value of its argument. Thus, SUCC(MAJOR) equals COLONEL and SUCC(COLONEL) equals GENERAL. SUCC(GENERAL) is undefined.

We consider the values of an enumeration type to be numbered, starting with 0 for the first value. For example, the values of type DAY are numbered as follows:

```
DAY = (SUN, MON, TUE, WED, THURS, FRI, SAT);
        0    1    2    3     4     5    6
```

The numbers are called the *ordinal numbers* of the corresponding values. Pascal has a standard function, ORD, which returns the ordinal number of its actual parameter. Thus, ORD(SUN) = 0, ORD(MON) = 1, ORD(TUE) = 2; and so on.

The function ORD can be applied to Boolean and character values as well. For Boolean values, ORD(FALSE) = 0 and ORD(TRUE) = 1. For character values, the ordinal numbers vary with the collating sequence. For the ASCII code, ORD ('A') = 65, ORD('B') = 66, ORD('C') = 67, and so on.

For type CHAR only, there is a function CHR that converts an ordinal number back into the corresponding character. Thus for the ASCII code, CHR(65) = 'A', CHR(66) = 'B', CHR(67) = 'C', and so on.

An important use of ORD and CHR is to convert back and forth between the numerals '0' through '9' and the integers 0 through 9. If C is a character variable whose value is one of the numerals, then

```
ORD(C) - ORD('0')
```

yields the corresponding integer. If I is an integer variable whose value lies in the range 0 through 9, then

```
CHR(I + ORD('0'))
```

yields the corresponding numeral.

We can use any of the scalar data types except REAL for the controlled variable in a FOR statement or the selector expression in a CASE statement.

For instance, if D is a variable of type DAY, then

```
FOR D : = MON TO FRI DO
    statement
```

causes the statement to be executed five times. The first time the value of D is MON, the second time the value of D is TUE, and so on.

IF M is a variable of type CHESSMAN, then the following CASE statement causes different statements to be executed depending on the value of M:

```
CASE M OF
    PAWN: statement-1;
    BISHOP: statement-2;
    KNIGHT: statement-3;
    ROOK: statement-4;
    QUEEN: statement-5;
    KING: statement-6
END
```

If the values of M is PAWN, *statement-1* will be executed; if the value of M is BISHOP, *statement-2* will be executed, and so on.

Subrange Types. For any scalar type except REAL, we can define a new type whose values are a subrange of those of the original type. For instance,

```
WORKDAY = MON..FRI;
```

defines a subrange of type DAY. The values of type WORKDAY are MON, TUE, WED, THURS, and FRI.

The following are examples of subranges of type INTEGER:

```
NUMBERGRADE = 0..100;
DEGREE = 0..359;
MINUTE = 0..59;
```

The type used to define a subrange type is called the *associated scalar type*. For WORKDAY, the associated scalar type is DAY; for NUMBERGRADE, DEGREE, and MINUTE, the associated scalar type is INTEGER.

Any operations that can be performed on values of the associated scalar type can also be performed on values of the subrange type. The only difference is that when a value is assigned to a variable of the subrange type, the computer checks to see if the value is in the proper range. If it isn't, the program terminates with an error message.

For example, suppose we declare I and N as follows:

```
VAR
    I: INTEGER;
    N: NUMBERGRADE;
```

The assignment

```
I : = N
```

is always valid, since a value of type NUMBERGRADE is also a value of type INTEGER. But the assignment

```
N : = I
```

is valid only if the value of I lies in the range 0 through 100. Only integers in this range are also values of type NUMBERGRADE.

Now consider the two statements

```
N : = 80;
N : = N+25
```

The first statement is valid, since 80 is a value of type NUMBERGRADE as well as of type INTEGER. The second statement is invalid, however. Because of the first statement, the value of N is 80. Therefore, the value of N+25 is 105. Since 105 is outside the range 0 through 100, it cannot be assigned to N.

Note that we don't have to use type definitions to declare variables to be of enumeration or subrange types. For instance, instead of defining the types DAY and NUMBERGRADE and then declaring D and N by

```
VAR
    D: DAY;
    N: NUMBERGRADE;
```

we could just declare D and N directly by

```
VAR
    D: (SUN, MON, TUE, WED, THURS, FRI, SAT, SUN);
    N: 0..100;
```

P.16 Arrays

One-dimensional Arrays. In Pascal, arrays are values of special data types called *array types*. Array types are structured data types, since each array value is made up of simpler components, the elements of the array.

We can define an array type as follows:

```
TYPE
   LIST = ARRAY[1..5] OF INTEGER;
```

This definition refers to two other data types. The type whose description is enclosed in brackets is the *index type*. (*Index* is a synonym for *subscript*.) The subscripts used to designate particular elements of an array value must be of the index type. Index types may be any simple type except REAL or INTEGER. Subranges of type INTEGER are allowed, however, and are in fact the most commonly used index types.

The data type following the word OF is the *component type*. It is the type of the components, or elements, of the array values.

Thus the definition of LIST says that each value of type LIST is an array of five integers and that the five integers are labeled 1 through 5. Note that if we define LIST1 by

```
LIST1 = ARRAY[6..10] OF INTEGER;
```

then each value of type LIST1 is also an array of five integers, but the integers are labeled 6 through 10 instead of 1 through 5. Figure P-14 shows typical values of LIST and LIST1.

Now let's declare two variables of type LIST:

```
VAR
   A, B: LIST;
```

Suppose the value of A is the value of type LIST given in Figure P-14. We can refer to the individual components of the value using a subscript enclosed in brackets. The value of the subscript must belong to the index type. Thus, the value of A[1] is 25; the value of A[2] is −5; the value of A[3] is 11; and so on.

We can use any expression as a subscript as long as the value of the expression belongs to the index type. If I, J, and K are integer variables, then

```
A[I]    A[I+J]    A[2*I + 3*J − 4*K]
```

FIGURE P-14. Typical values of types LIST and LIST1.

	LIST			LIST1
1	25		6	30
2	−5		7	18
3	11		8	−1
4	0		9	99
5	−8		10	65

are valid, provided that in each case the value of the subscript expression
is an integer in the range 1 through 5.

We can assign the value of one array variable to another array variable
of the same type. Since A and B are both of type LIST, the assignment

```
B : = A
```

is valid. After the assignment statement is executed, the value of B is the
same as the value of A, so that B[1] = 25; B[2] = −5; B[3] = 11; and so
on.

We can also use a subscripted variable such as A[I] on the left-hand
side of an assignment statement. After the assignments

```
A[1] : = 13;
A[5] : = 29
```

A has the value:

```
A   13
    −5
    11
     0
    29
```

Arrays must be read in and printed out element by element. For example, to print the elements of the array A, we can use:

```
FOR I : = 1 TO 5 DO
   WRITE(A[I]:4)
```

If A has the value just given, the printout is

```
13   −5  11    0  29
```

To read the five elements of A, we could use the statement

```
FOR I : = 1 TO 5 DO
   READ(A[I])
```

If the input data was

```
7  9   −5  3  2
```

then A[1] would be assigned the value 7; A[2], the value 9; A[3], the value
−5; and so on.

Figure P-15 shows a Pascal program corresponding to the binary-search
algorithm DIRECTORY in Chapter 8. Note how a single FOR statement is
used to read in the values of the two parallel arrays NAME and NUMBER.

```
PROGRAM DIRECTORY;
(* DEMONSTRATE TABLE LOOKUP USING BINARY SEARCH *)
CONST
   LIMIT = 50:    (* MAXIMUM SIZE OF DIRECTORY *)
TYPE
   COLUMN = ARRAY[1..LIMIT] OF STRING;
VAR
   LOW, HIGH, MIDDLE, I, N: INTEGER;
   DESIREDNAME: STRING;
   NAME, NUMBER: COLUMN;
BEGIN
   WRITE('NUMBER OF ENTRIES IN DIRECTORY ');
   WRITE('(MAXIMUM ', LIMIT, ')? ');
   READLN(N);
   WRITELN('ENTER DIRECTORY WITH NAMES IN ALPHABETICAL ORDER');
   FOR I := 1 TO N DO
      BEGIN
         WRITELN('ENTRY NUMBER ', I, ':');
         WRITE('NAME? ');
         READLN(NAME[I]);
         WRITE('NUMBER? ');
         READLN(NUMBER[I])
      END;
   WRITELN('DIRECTORY ENTRY COMPLETE');
   WRITE('NAME TO LOOK UP? ');
   READLN(DESIREDNAME);
   WHILE DESIREDNAME <> 'STOP' DO
      BEGIN
         LOW := 1;
         HIGH := N;
         REPEAT
            MIDDLE := (LOW+HIGH) DIV 2;
            IF DESIREDNAME < NAME[MIDDLE] THEN
               HIGH := MIDDLE-1
            ELSE IF DESIREDNAME > NAME[MIDDLE] THEN
               LOW := MIDDLE+1
         UNTIL (DESIREDNAME = NAME[MIDDLE]) OR (LOW > HIGH);
         IF LOW <= HIGH THEN
            WRITELN('THE NUMBER IS ', NUMBER[MIDDLE])
         ELSE
            WRITELN('THE NAME YOU REQUESTED IS NOT LISTED');
         WRITE('NAME TO LOOK UP? ');
         READLN(DESIREDNAME)
      END
END.
```

FIGURE P-15. The program DIRECTORY.

Constant Definitions. In Figure P-15, note:

```
CONST
   LIMIT = 50;
```

This is a constant definition. It states that wherever the identifier LIMIT appears in the program, the constant 50 will be substituted. LIMIT is a constant, not a variable; we cannot assign new values to it during the execution of the program any more than we can assign new values to 50, 3.14, or 'A'.

The advantages of using a constant definition are twofold. First, if we should decide to use a limit of 75 instead of 50, we can change the one constant definition to

```
CONST
   LIMIT = 75;
```

instead of having to go through the whole program looking for 50s and changing them to 75s. Second, the word LIMIT suggests to a human reader the purpose for which the constant is used, something that 50 and 75 do not do.

Note that LIMIT is used to define the index type in the array-type definition:

```
COLUMN = ARRAY[1..LIMIT] OF STRING;
```

This is exactly equivalent to:

```
COLUMN = ARRAY[1..50] OF STRING;
```

We could not have used a variable in place of LIMIT; only constants can be used to define subrange types.

In a program, constant definitions come before type definitions. The required order is

constant definitions
type definitions
variable declarations

Two-dimensional Arrays. We define two-dimensional arrays in Pascal by listing the index types whose values will be used to label the rows and columns. Thus,

```
TYPE
   TABLE = ARRAY[1..3, 1..4] OF INTEGER;
```

defines the type TABLE whose values are tables of integers, each containing three rows and four columns. Values of type 1 .. 3 are used to label the rows of each table; values of type 1 .. 4 are used to label the columns. Figure P-16 shows a typical value of type TABLE.

Let's declare the variable T to be of type TABLE:

```
VAR
   T: TABLE;
```

Then, as in the algorithmic language, we can use subscripted variables to refer to the individual elements of T—the individual entries in the table. Thus T[2, 3] refers to the table entry in row 2 and column 3; T[3, 1] refers

FIGURE P-16. A typical value of type TABLE.

•

to the entry in row 3 and column 1. If T has the value shown in Figure P-16, then T[2, 3] has the value 12, and T[3, 1] has the value 25.

As in the algorithmic language, we frequently process two-dimensional arrays using nested FOR statements. For instance, let's see how to use nested FOR statements to read in and print out two-dimensional arrays.

To begin with, the statement

```
READ(T[I, J])
```

reads a value and assigns it to the element of T determined by the values of I and J. As a manner of speaking, we say that this statement reads a value for the element in the Ith row and the Jth column.

Now let's repeat the READ statement with J varying from 1 through 4:

```
FOR J := 1 TO 4 DO
   READ(T[I, J])
```

This statement reads values for the row determined by the value of I, for the Ith row, so to speak.

Now let's vary I from 1 through 3:

```
FOR I := 1 TO 3 DO
   FOR J := 1 TO 4 DO
      READ(T[I, J])
```

For I equal to 1, the values for the first row are read; for I equal to 2, the values for the second row are read; for I equal to 3, the values for the third row are read. Thus the value of T is read in row by row. If the input data is

```
7 80 9 −3 4 6 12 30 25 7 14 3
```

then the value read for T will be that shown in Figure P-16.

We could read in the array by columns instead of rows just by reversing the order of the two FOR statements:

```
FOR J := 1 TO 4 DO
    FOR I := 1 TO 3 DO
        READ(T[I, J])
```

We can use the same technique for printing the values of an array. For instance,

```
FOR I := 1 TO 3 DO
    FOR J := 1 TO 4 DO
        WRITE(T[I, J]:4)
```

prints out the array by rows. All the values are printed out on one line, however. We can print the array in table form by using a WRITELN statement to make the printer go to a new line after each row is printed out:

```
FOR I := 1 TO 3 DO
    BEGIN
        FOR J := 1 TO 4 DO
            WRITE(T[I, J]:4);
        WRITELN
    END
```

Figure P-17 shows a Pascal program corresponding to the algorithm AVERAGES in Chapter 8. Two points are noteworthy about the program.

First, our arrays are specified in the variable declaration part of the program rather than in separate type definitions:

```
TOTAL, COUNT: ARRAY[1..4, 1..3] OF INTEGER;
AVERAGE: ARRAY[1..4, 1..3] OF REAL;
CLASSNAME: ARRAY[1..4] OF STRING;
```

This is permissible and frequently done.

Second, note the method used to print the results in table form with row and column headings. This is an elaboration of the method just described for printing an array by rows.

P.17 Functions

A function declaration in Pascal has the same form as a program except the program heading is replaced by a function heading. For example, consider the Pascal version of the function DIAGONAL from Chapter 9:

```
PROGRAM AVERAGES;
(* COMPUTE AND DISPLAY AVERAGE GRADES BY CLASS AND MAJOR *)
VAR
   CLASS, MAJOR, GRADE: INTEGER;
   TOTAL, COUNT: ARRAY[1..4, 1..3] OF INTEGER;
   AVERAGE: ARRAY[1..4, 1..3] OF REAL;
   CLASSNAME: ARRAY[1..4] OF STRING;
BEGIN
   (* INITIALIZE COUNTS AND TOTALS TO ZERO *)
   FOR CLASS := 1 TO 4 DO
      FOR MAJOR := 1 TO 3 DO
         BEGIN
            TOTAL[CLASS, MAJOR] := 0;
            COUNT[CLASS, MAJOR] := 0;
         END;
   (* READ DATA, ACCUMULATE COUNTS AND TOTALS *)
   WRITE('CLASS, MAJOR, AND GRADE? ');
   READLN(CLASS, MAJOR, GRADE);
   WHILE CLASS <> -1 DO
      BEGIN
         TOTAL[CLASS, MAJOR] := TOTAL[CLASS, MAJOR]+GRADE;
         COUNT[CLASS, MAJOR] := COUNT[CLASS, MAJOR]+1;
         WRITE('CLASS, MAJOR, AND GRADE? ');
         READLN(CLASS, MAJOR, GRADE)
      END;
   (* COMPUTE AVERAGES *)
   FOR CLASS := 1 TO 4 DO
      FOR MAJOR := 1 TO 3 DO
         IF COUNT[CLASS, MAJOR] <> 0 THEN
            AVERAGE[CLASS, MAJOR] := TOTAL[CLASS, MAJOR]
                                     /COUNT[CLASS, MAJOR]
         ELSE
            AVERAGE[CLASS, MAJOR] := -1.0;
   (* DISPLAY RESULTS *)
   CLASSNAME[1] := 'FRESHMAN ';
   CLASSNAME[2] := 'SOPHOMORE';
   CLASSNAME[3] := 'JUNIOR   ';
   CLASSNAME[4] := 'SENIOR   ';
   WRITELN(' ':9, 'ENGLISH':13, 'HISTORY':13, 'MATHEMATICS':13);
   FOR CLASS := 1 TO 4 DO
      BEGIN
         WRITE(CLASSNAME[CLASS]:9);
         FOR MAJOR := 1 TO 3 DO
            IF AVERAGE[CLASS, MAJOR] >= 0.0 THEN
               WRITE(AVERAGE[CLASS, MAJOR]:13:1)
            ELSE
               WRITE(' ':13);
         WRITELN
      END
END.
```

FIGURE P-17. The program AVERAGES.

```
FUNCTION DIAGONAL(LENGTH: REAL; WIDTH: REAL) REAL;
BEGIN
   DIAGONAL := SQRT(SQR(LENGTH) + SQR(WIDTH))
END;
```

As in the algorithmic language, the formal parameters are listed in parentheses after the function name. The types of the formal parameters must be declared, and this is done right in the function heading. Both

LENGTH and WIDTH are declared to be parameters of type REAL; that is, only values of type REAL can be substituted for them.

Note that the first declaration ends with a semicolon but the second one does not. In general, each declaration except the final one ends with a semicolon. The final declaration is terminated by the closing parenthesis. As with variable declarations, we can combine the declarations of formal parameters that are declared to be of the same type:

```
FUNCTION DIAGONAL(LENGTH, WIDTH: REAL): REAL;
```

The colon followed by the word REAL at the end of the function heading specifies the type of the values that the function returns. Thus, the function DIAGONAL returns values of type REAL.

As in the algorithmic language, we indicate what value the function is to return by assigning that value to the name of the function.

The semicolon following the word END terminates the entire function declaration.

Local variables for a function are declared in a variable declaration part, just as for a program. For instance, the following is the Pascal version of the function FACTORIAL from Chapter 9:

```
FUNCTION FACTORIAL(N: INTEGER): INTEGER;
VAR
    F, I: INTEGER;
BEGIN
    F := 1;
    FOR I := 1 TO N DO
        F := F*I;
    FACTORIAL := F
END;
```

P.18 Variable Parameters and Procedures

Value and Variable Parameters. In the algorithmic language we use value parameters for functions and variable parameters for procedures. Pascal allows us to declare any formal parameter as either a value parameter or a variable parameter, regardless of whether it occurs in a function or a procedure. We declare a parameter to be a variable parameter by preceding its declaration with the word VAR. If a parameter isn't explicitly declared to be a variable parameter, then it is a value parameter by default.

We may sometimes wish to declare a parameter to be a variable parameter even if we don't intend to make assignments to it. In most implementations of Pascal, when a function or a procedure is invoked, the values of the value parameters are copied into special memory locations where the function or the procedure can find them. As long as the amount of data to be copied is small, no problem arises. But if a large amount of data has to be copied, say a large array, then the time required for copying can substantially slow down the execution of the program, particularly if the function or the procedure in question is invoked frequently.

With variable parameters, on the other hand, the function of the procedure is given access to the data stored under a given variable name in the calling program. No copy of the data has to be made. When large amounts of data are involved, then, it is usually more efficient to use variable parameters instead of value parameters.

For instance, consider the function SUM defined in Chapter 9. Suppose the array A is of type

```
LONGLIST = ARRAY[1..1000] OF REAL;
```

It is likely to be more efficient to use a variable parameter for A than to have the computer copy 1,000 values every time SUM is invoked. Thus we would write SUM in Pascal like this:

```
FUNCTION SUM(VAR A: LONGLIST; N: INTEGER): REAL;
VAR
   S: REAL;
   I: INTEGER;
BEGIN
   S := 0.0;
   FOR I := 1 TO N DO
      S := S + A[I];
   SUM := S
END;
```

Note that in a function or procedure heading, types may only be specified by type identifiers such as LONGLIST and REAL. For user-defined types, such as enumeration, array, and subrange types, we must include appropriate type definitions in the calling program and use the type identifiers so defined to declare formal parameters.

Procedures. Procedures have the same form as programs and functions except a procedure heading replaces the program or function heading:

```
PROCEDURE RECTANGLE(LENGTH, WIDTH: REAL;
                    VAR AREA, DIAGONAL: REAL);
BEGIN
   AREA := LENGTH*WIDTH;
   DIAGONAL := SQRT(SQR(LENGTH) + SQR(WIDTH))
END;
```

A procedure heading is similar to a function heading, except it doesn't specify the type of a value to be returned, nor does it contain an assignment to the procedure name, since procedures use the formal parameters to return values. The parameters LENGTH and WIDTH, used to supply data, are declared as value parameters; AREA and DIAGONAL, used to return results, are declared as variable parameters. AREA and DIAGONAL must be variable parameters; however, LENGTH and WIDTH could be either value or variable parameters. Declaring all parameters as variable parameters allows us to simplify the procedure heading a bit:

```
PROCEDURE RECTANGLE(VAR LENGTH, WIDTH,
                        AREA, DIAGONAL: REAL);
```

Because of the space taken up by formal parameter declarations, function and procedure headings in Pascal frequently require more than one line. When continuing a function or procedure heading to another line, the format shown in the preceding examples is recommended.

To invoke a procedure, we write the name of the procedure followed in parentheses by the list of its actual parameters. Pascal does not use a keyword such as CALL. For example, if W, X, Y, and Z are real variables, then the statements

```
W := 12.0;
X := 5.0;
RECTANGLE(W, X, Y, Z)
```

assign to Y and Z the values 60.0 and 13.0, respectively—the area and diagonal of a 12 × 5 rectangle.

The procedure call just given will work regardless of whether LENGTH and WIDTH are value or variable parameters. If LENGTH and WIDTH are value parameters, however, we could just write

```
RECTANGLE(12.0, 5.0, Y, Z)
```

eliminating the need for W and X.

Figure P-18 shows a Pascal procedure corresponding to the algorithm SORT in Chapter 9. Also included is a program, SORTER, to exercise the procedure, that is, to invoke it for testing purposes.

The first thing to notice about Figure P-18 is that the declaration of the procedure SORT is included as part of the program SORTER that invokes the procedure. In a Pascal program, function and procedure declarations are included with the other definitions and declarations at the beginning of the program. The function and procedure declarations follow the variable declarations. Thus we add another item to the growing list of definitions and declarations that can precede the statement part of a Pascal program:

constant definitions
type definitions
variable declarations
function and procedure declarations

Another thing to notice about Figure P-18 is the type VECTOR, which is used to declare the array A in the program SORTER and the formal pa-

```
        PROGRAM SORTER;
        (* "EXERCISE" THE PROCEDURE SORT *)
        TYPE
           VECTOR = ARRAY[1..50] OF INTEGER;
        VAR
           A: VECTOR;
           I, SIZE: INTEGER;

        PROCEDURE SORT(VAR LIST: VECTOR; N: INTEGER);
        (* SORT FIRST N ELEMENTS OF LIST *)
        VAR
           J, TEMP: INTEGER;
           NOEXCHANGES: BOOLEAN;
        BEGIN
           REPEAT
              NOEXCHANGES := TRUE;
              FOR J := 1 TO N-1 DO
                 IF LIST[J] > LIST[J+1] THEN
                    BEGIN
                       TEMP := LIST[J];
                       LIST[J] := LIST[J+1];
                       LIST[J+1] := TEMP;
                       NOEXCHANGES := FALSE
                    END
           UNTIL NOEXCHANGES
        END; (* SORT *)

        BEGIN (* MAIN PROGRAM *)
           WRITE('HOW MANY VALUES ARE TO BE SORTED? ');
           READLN(SIZE);
           WRITE('ENTER DATA: ');
           FOR I := 1 TO SIZE DO
              READ(A[I]);
           SORT(A, SIZE);
           WRITE('SORTED DATA: ');
           FOR I := 1 TO SIZE DO
              WRITE(A[I]:4)
        END.
```

FIGURE P-18. The program SORTER including the procedure SORT.

rameter LIST in the procedure SORT. If we wished, we could replace the declaration of A by:

```
A: ARRAY[1..50] OF INTEGER;
```

No such replacement can be made in the declaration of LIST, however. Only type identifiers such as VECTOR, not type descriptions such as

```
ARRAY[1..50] OF INTEGER
```

can be used to declare formal parameters. We must define the type VECTOR in order to declare the formal parameter LIST.

P.19 Local and Global Variables

The scope of an identifier is the part of a program in which that identifier is defined and can be referred to. In the algorithmic language we have *local variables,* each of whose scope is a single function or procedure, and *global variables,* whose scope is an algorithm together with all of the functions and procedures it invokes. In Pascal, the question of the scopes of variable-names and other identifiers is somewhat more complicated.

The complications can be traced to the possibility of nesting function and procedure declarations, a possibility that doesn't exist in the algorithmic language. A function or a procedure, except for its heading, has the same form as a program. Like a program, it can contain constant definitions, type definitions, variable declarations, and function and procedure declarations. Thus any function or procedure can contain declarations of other functions and procedures; those functions and procedures can declare still other functions and procedures; and so on.

What's more, each of these nested functions and procedures can define or declare identifiers to name constants, types, and variables. Under these conditions, we need precise rules for saying just what the scope of each identifier is. That is, in what part of the program is it defined and can be referred to. We must also face the question of when the same identifier can be defined differently and used for different purposes in different parts of a program.

We start with the idea of a block. A block consists of a set of definitions and declarations followed by a compound statement. Thus, a program consists of a program heading followed by a block; a function declaration consists of a function heading followed by a block; and a procedure declaration consists of a procedure heading followed by a block. Figure P-19 illustrates the procedure heading and block for the procedure SORT.

The scope of an identifier is simply the block in which it is declared. For the procedure SORT, then, the scope of J, TEMP, and NOEXCHANGES is the block containing their declarations.

Blocks can be nested one inside another. In Figure P-18, for instance, we have two blocks. One block extends from immediately after the program heading to the end of the program. The other extends from immediately after the procedure heading for SORT to the end of the procedure, that is, to the end of the statement part of SORT.

Each block is immediately preceded by a program, function, or procedure heading. We can use the name of the program, function, or procedure to name the following block.

In Figure P-18, for example, we have two blocks, SORTER and SORT. SORTER extends from just after the program heading to the end of the program. SORT extends from just after the procedure heading for SORT to the end of the procedure.

It's difficult to visualize blocks in complete programs. We will find it easier instead to use diagrams that illustrate blocks and the variables declared in each but leave out the rest of the details of the actual program.

Figure P-20 shows the diagram for the program SORTER. VECTOR, A, I, and SIZE can be accessed from anywhere in the outer block, SORTER.

```
Procedure heading        PROCEDURE SORT(VAR LIST: VECTOR; N: INTEGER);



Block                    VAR
                            J, TEMP: INTEGER;
                            NOEXCHANGES: BOOLEAN;
                         BEGIN
                            REPEAT
                               NOEXCHANGES := TRUE;
                               FOR J := 1 TO N-1 DO
                                  IF LIST[J] > LIST[J+1] THEN
                                     BEGIN
                                        TEMP := LIST[J];
                                        LIST[J] := LIST[J+1];
                                        LIST[J+1] := TEMP;
                                        NOEXCHANGES := FALSE
                                     END
                            UNTIL NOEXCHANGES
                         END;
```

FIGURE P-19. The procedure heading and block for the procedure SORT.

J, TEMP, and NOEXCHANGES can be accessed only from inside the inner block, SORT. It's helpful to think of the boxes representing the blocks as made of one-way glass. From inside the SORT box we can look out and see VECTOR, A, I, and SIZE. But we cannot look into a box from the outside, so J, TEMP, and NOEXCHANGES are hidden from the rest of the program.

Figure P-21 shows a more complicated example. We have a main program named P. Inside P two functions or procedures (it doesn't matter which) are declared. Finally, the function or procedure Q1 contains a declaration of another function or procedure, R.

The variables A and B are declared in the outermost block, the main program P. They can be accessed from everywhere in the block P. Specifically, they can be accessed from P, Q1, Q2, and R.

The variables C and D can be accessed from Q1 and R. They cannot be accessed from P or Q2. The variables E and F can only be accessed from R. The variables H and I can only be accessed from Q2.

We use the terms *local* and *global* in Pascal as follows. Identifiers are local to the block in which they are declared. Thus, C and D are local to Q1; E and F are local to R; H and I are local to Q2. Identifiers declared in the outermost block, which are accessible throughout the program, are said to be global. Thus A and B are global variables in the program P.

Figure P-22 illustrates the situation in which the same identifier is declared in more than one block. Thus we have an A in P and an A in Q1; a B in P and a B in Q2; an F in Q1 and an F in Q2.

Identifiers declared in different blocks have nothing to do with one another, even though they are spelled in the same way. Thus the variable A declared in P names a different memory location than the variable A

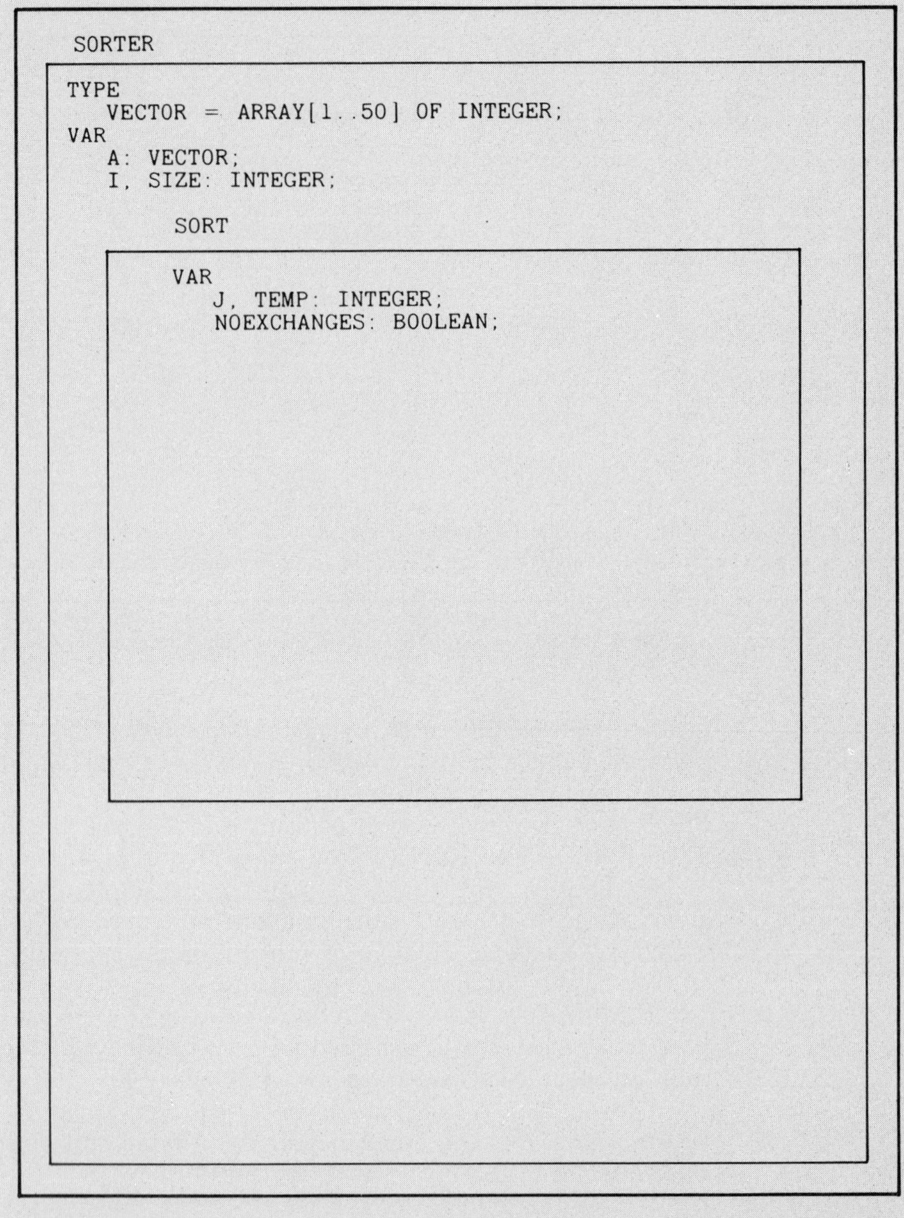

```
SORTER

TYPE
    VECTOR = ARRAY[1..50] OF INTEGER;
VAR
    A: VECTOR;
    I, SIZE: INTEGER;

        SORT

        VAR
            J, TEMP: INTEGER;
            NOEXCHANGES: BOOLEAN;
```

FIGURE P-20. This diagram illustrates the blocks and declarations in the program SORTER.

declared in Q1; the variable B declared in P names a different memory location than the variable B declared in Q2. The variable F declared in Q1 names a different memory location than the variable F declared in Q2.

A reference to F in Q1 must refer to the variable F declared in Q1, since this is the only declaration "visible" from Q1. (We can't see into Q2 from Q1; remember the one-way glass.) In the same way, a reference to F inside Q2 must refer to the variable F defined in Q2 since this is the only declaration of F visible from inside Q2.

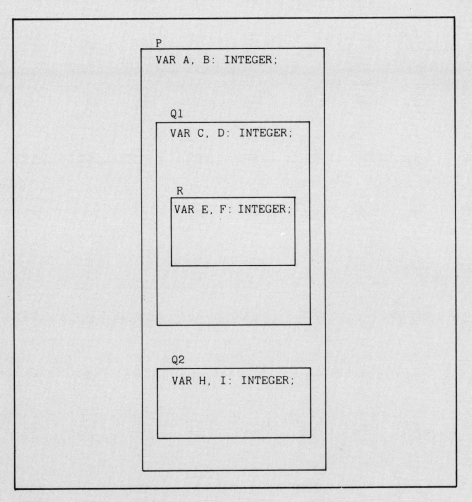

FIGURE P-21. This diagram shows a main program P that contains declarations for procedures Q1 and Q2. Q1, in turn, contains a declaration for procedure R.

But what about a reference to A in Q1 or to B in Q2? Two variables named A are visible in Q1. To which does the identifier A refer? We resolve this conflict with the rule that A refers to the variable having the smallest scope. Thus a reference to A in Q1 refers to the A declared in Q1; a reference to A in P or Q2 refers to the A declared in P. In the same way, a reference to B in Q2 refers to the B declared in Q2; a reference to B in P or Q1 refers to the B declared in P.

Another way of thinking about the matter is that the declaration of A in Q1 hides the declaration of A in P. In the same way, the declaration of B in Q2 hides the declaration of A in P. In general, a definition or declaration of an identifier in a particular block hides any definitions or declarations of the same identifier in enclosing blocks.

Note that there is no way to refer to the global variable A from inside Q1 nor to the global variable B from inside Q2. In each case the declaration

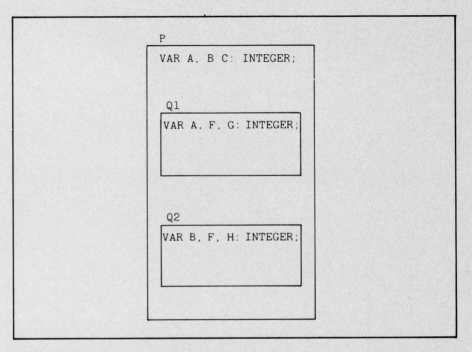

FIGURE P-22. This diagram shows a main program P that contains declarations for procedures Q1 and Q2. Variables named A are declared in P and Q1; variables named B are declared in P and Q2; and variables named F are declared in Q1 and Q2.

of the global variable is hidden by the declaration of a local variable with the same name.

So far we haven't mentioned function and procedure names or formal parameters. A function or procedure name is considered declared in the block containing the function or procedure definition. The formal parameters are considered declared in the block following the function or procedure heading, the block that defines the function or procedure.

Figure P-23 shows a Pascal program corresponding to the algorithm GAME in Chapter 9. Since SEED is declared in the outermost block of GAME, it is a global variable and can be accessed form the main program as well as from the function RANDOM.

P.20 Program Design

Figure P-24 shows a Pascal program corresponding to CRAPS, the algorithm we used as an example of top-down design in Chapter 10. The Pascal program uses a separate procedure for each module. Note that a function declaration for the pseudorandom-number generator RANDOM is also present. In the algorithmic language, we assume RANDOM to be a built-in function, but it is not built into Pascal.

Notice something peculiar about the Pascal program. Although top-down design was praised in Chapter 10, the modules of the Pascal program

```
PROGRAM GAME;
(* PLAY GUESSING GAME WITH USER *)
VAR
    SEED: REAL;
    ANSWER: CHAR;
    NUMBER, GUESS: INTEGER;

FUNCTION RANDOM(N: INTEGER): INTEGER;
(* RETURNS PSEUDORANDOM INTEGER IN RANGE 1-N
    REFERS TO AND MODIFIES GLOBAL VARIABLE SEED *)
BEGIN
    SEED:= SQR(SEED + 3.1415927);
    SEED := SEED - TRUNC(SEED);
    RANDOM := TRUNC(N*SEED) + 1
END; (* RANDOM *)

BEGIN (* MAIN PROGRAM *)
    WRITE('ENTER A NUMBER BETWEEN 0 AND 1: ');
    READLN(SEED);
    WRITELN;
    WRITELN('I AM THINKING OF A NUMBER FROM 1 THROUGH 100.');
    WRITELN('YOU ARE TO TRY TO GUESS THE NUMBER.');
    WRITELN('I WILL TELL YOU WHETHER YOUR GUESS IS RIGHT');
    WRITELN('OR WHETHER IT IS TOO LARGE OR TO SMALL.');
    REPEAT
        NUMBER := RANDOM(100);
        WRITELN;
        WRITE('I HAVE MY NUMBER. WHAT IS YOUR GUESS? ');
        REPEAT
            READLN(GUESS);
            IF GUESS > NUMBER THEN
                WRITE('TOO LARGE. TRY AGAIN: ')
            ELSE IF GUESS < NUMBER THEN
                WRITE('TOO SMALL. TRY AGAIN: ')
        UNTIL GUESS = NUMBER;
        WRITELN('YOU ARE RIGHT. CONGRATULATIONS!');
        WRITELN('WOULD YOU LIKE TO PLAY AGAIN?');
        WRITE('ANSWER Y (YES) OR N (NO): ');
        READLN(ANSWER);
    UNTIL ANSWER <> 'Y';
    WRITELN('I HAVE ENJOYED PLAYING WITH YOU.')
END.
```

FIGURE P-23. The program GAME including the function RANDOM. Note that the global variable SEED is accessible from both GAME and RANDOM.

appear in bottom-up order. The low-level modules RANDOM and ROLL-DICE come first, followed by the higher level modules, with the statement part of the main program last.

This order results from a requirement of Pascal that functions and procedures be declared before they are used. Although the requirement simplifies the design of Pascal compilers, it requires each function or procedure to be declared before the functions or procedures that call it, and all function and procedure declarations must precede the statement part of the main program. For this reason, we sometimes hear people say that Pascal isn't suitable for top-down design.

The answer to this is that nothing forces us to write the modules in the same order in which they will appear in the final program. If we work out

```
PROGRAM CRAPS;
(* PLAY CRAPS WITH THE USER *)
VAR
    AMOUNT, BET, SEED: REAL;
    WON, FINISHED: BOOLEAN;

FUNCTION RANDOM(N: INTEGER): INTEGER;
(* RETURNS PSEUDORANDOM INTEGER IN RANGE 1-N
   REFERS TO AND MODIFIES GLOBAL VARIABLE SEED *)
BEGIN
    SEED := SQR(SEED + 3.1415297);
    SEED := SEED - TRUNC(SEED);
    RANDOM := TRUNC(N*SEED) + 1
END; (* RANDOM *)

PROCEDURE ROLLDICE(VAR VALUE: INTEGER);
(* SIMULATE ROLLING OF TWO DICE *)
VAR
    DIE1, DIE2: INTEGER;
BEGIN
    DIE1 := RANDOM(6);
    DIE2 := RANDOM(6);
    VALUE := DIE1+DIE2;
    WRITELN('YOU ROLLED A ', DIE1, ' AND A ', DIE2)
END; (* ROLLDICE *)

PROCEDURE INITIALIZE(VAR SEED, AMOUNT: REAL);
(* GET SEED FOR PSEUDORANDOM NUMBER GENERATOR AND
   AMOUNT USER HAS TO PLAY WITH *)
BEGIN
    WRITE('ENTER NUMBER BETWEEN 0 AND 1: ');
    READLN(SEED);
    WRITE('HOW MUCH MONEY DO YOU HAVE TO PLAY WITH? ');
    READLN(AMOUNT);
    WHILE AMOUNT <= 0.0 DO
        BEGIN
            WRITELN('YOU CANNOT PLAY WITH A ZERO OR NEGATIVE');
            WRITELN('AMOUNT OF MONEY. PLEASE ENTER A POSITIVE');
            WRITE('AMOUNT: ');
            READLN(AMOUNT)
        END
END; (* INITIALIZE *)
```

FIGURE P-24. The program CRAPS including the function RANDOM and the procedures ROLLDICE, INITIALIZE, ACCEPTBET, PLAY, and UPDATE.

our program on paper first, we can write the modules in whatever order we please, then enter them into the computer in the order required by Pascal.

If we create our programs at the computer terminal, we can take advantage of modern text editors that allow insertions to be made at any point in the text being worked on. Thus we can start out writing the program heading, the definitions and declarations for the main program, and the statement part of the main program. Then we go back and write the function and procedure declarations, inserting each one in the position required by Pascal, but writing them in whatever order is most convenient for us.

```
PROCEDURE ACCEPTBET(VAR BET, AMOUNT: REAL);
(* FIND OUT HOW MUCH USER WANTS TO BET ON THIS GAME *)
BEGIN
    WRITE('HOW MUCH DO YOU WANT TO BET ON THIS GAME? ');
    READLN(BET);
    WHILE (BET < 0.0) OR (BET > AMOUNT) DO
        BEGIN
            IF BET < 0.0 THEN
                WRITELN('YOU CANNOT BET A NEGATIVE AMOUNT')
            ELSE IF BET > AMOUNT THEN
                WRITELN('YOU CANNOT BET MORE THAN YOU HAVE');
            WRITE('PLEASE ENTER ANOTHER BET: ');
            READLN(BET)
        END
END; (* ACCEPT BET *)

PROCEDURE PLAY(VAR WON: BOOLEAN);
(* PLAY ONE GAME *)
VAR
    VALUE, POINT: INTEGER;
BEGIN
    ROLLDICE(VALUE);
    IF (VALUE = 7) OR (VALUE = 11) THEN
        WON := TRUE
    ELSE IF (VALUE = 2) OR (VALUE = 3) OR (VALUE = 12) THEN
        WON := FALSE
    ELSE
        BEGIN
            POINT := VALUE;
            REPEAT
                ROLLDICE(VALUE)
            UNTIL (VALUE = POINT) OR (VALUE = 7);
            WON := VALUE = POINT (* BOOLEAN EXPRESSION *)
        END
END; (* PLAY *)
```

FIGURE P-24 (Cont.)

P.21 Packed Arrays and Fixed-Length Strings

We recall from Chapter 2 that a computer's memory is made up of individual memory locations, each of which can hold a fixed number of bits. It may happen that values of a particular type occupy far fewer bits than are present in any of the available sizes of memory locations. If we store only one value to a memory location, some of the bits in each location will be wasted. Clearly, it would be more economical to store more than one value in each location. This is called *packing*.

The drawback of packing is that access to the stored values is slower. To retrieve a packed value, for instance, the computer must get the contents of the memory location holding the value, then separate the desired value from the other values sharing the same location. As a rule, the second step takes much longer than the first.

Pascal allows us to declared packed arrays, which are stored with as many component values packed into each memory location as possible. We

```
PROCEDURE UPDATE(VAR BET, AMOUNT: REAL;
                VAR WON, FINISHED: BOOLEAN);
(* UPDATE PLAYER'S BANKROLL, DETERMINE WHETHER OR NOT PLAYER
   WANTS TO CONTINUE *)
VAR
   ANSWER: STRING;
BEGIN
   IF WON THEN
      BEGIN
         WRITELN('CONGRATULATIONS, YOU WIN!');
         AMOUNT := AMOUNT+BET
      END
   ELSE
      BEGIN
         WRITELN('TOO BAD, YOU LOSE!');
         AMOUNT := AMOUNT-BET
      END;
   WRITELN('YOU NOW HAVE ', AMOUNT:8:2, ' DOLLARS');
   IF AMOUNT < 0.01 THEN
      FINISHED := TRUE
   ELSE
      BEGIN
         WRITE('DO YOU WANT TO PLAY ANOTHER GAME ');
         WRITE('(YES OR NO)? ');
         READLN(ANSWER);
         FINISHED := ANSWER <> 'YES' (* BOOLEAN EXPRESSION *)
      END
END; (* UPDATE *)

BEGIN  (* MAIN PROGRAM *)
   INITIALIZE(SEED, AMOUNT);
   REPEAT
      WRITELN;
      ACCEPTBET(BET, AMOUNT);
      PLAY(WON);
      UPDATE(BET, AMOUNT, WON, FINISHED)
   UNTIL FINISHED;
   WRITELN('I ENJOYED PLAYING WITH YOU');
   WRITELN('LET''S PLAY AGAIN SOON')
END.
```

FIGURE P-24 (Cont.)

specify an array to be packed by inserting the word PACKED before the word ARRAY in the type definition:

```
NAME = PACKED ARRAY[1..20] OF CHAR;
```

Whether or not packing will save memory space depends on the component type of the array and on the particular computer system for which the program is written. Ordinarily, nothing is gained by packing integer or real values. But it may be possible to save substantial memory space by packing values of types BOOLEAN and CHAR as well as user-defined enumeration and subrange types.

We can refer to elements of packed arrays in the same way we do for ordinary arrays. Thus, if N is of type NAME and C of type CHAR, then the statements

```
N[5] := 'A';
C := N[1]
```

are valid.

There is one limitation on access to packed arrays. Subscripted variables such as N[7] that refer to elements of packed arrays cannot be substituted for variable parameters in procedure calls. Worse yet, the READ and READLN statements in Pascal are considered calls to procedures with variable parameters. Thus

```
READ(N[7])
```

is not permitted. Instead we must write something like:

```
READ(C);
N[7] := C
```

Some versions of Pascal have built-in procedures PACK and UNPACK that can pack or unpack an entire array in a single operation. Packing and unpacking an entire array at once may be less time-consuming than making repeated references to packed values. One is never required to use these procedures, however, and in fact they are not present in UCSD Pascal.

Packed array variables can appear on the left- and right-hand sides of an assignment operator, provided both variables are of the same type. Thus, if M and N are of type NAME, then

```
N := M
```

is valid and assigns the value of M to N.

Fixed-Length Strings. UCSD Pascal has a built-in data type STRING. Most other versions of Pascal do not; for these the programmer must define string data types in terms of packed arrays of characters.

For example, the type NAME defined previously consists of strings of 20 characters. If we declare

```
VAR
   M, N: NAME;
```

then the possible values of M and N are 20-character strings.

Strings constants enclosed in single quotes are allowed in all versions of Pascal and may be used to represent values of packed arrays of characters. Thus the assignments

```
M := 'JOHN JONES          ';
N := 'MARY ROBERTS        '
```

are valid. Note that the trailing blank spaces are required. Each value assigned to M or N must consist of exactly 20 characters. If a value is shorter than 20 characters, it must be padded with enough blank spaces to make up 20 characters.

We can compare packed arrays of characters of the same type using the relational operators =, <>, <, >, <=, and >=. One string precedes another if it comes first in alphabetical order (as defined by the collating sequence for the character code being used). After the assignments just given have been made

```
M < N
```

is true, since the value of M precedes the value of N in alphabetical order.

If a packed array of characters appears in a WRITE or WRITELN statement, the entire array is printed. Thus

```
WRITE(N)
```

causes 20 characters to be printed (blank spaces used for padding are printed as well as meaningful characters). A field-width parameter may be supplied if desired.

Packed arrays of characters must be read in character by character. Thus, to read a value for N, we must use

```
FOR I := 1 TO 20 DO
    BEGIN
        READ(C);
        N[I] := C
    END
```

where I is an integer variable and C is a character variable. (Why do we need C?) To enter a value for N, the user might type

```
JOHNbJONESbbbbbbbbbb
```

where the b's represent blank spaces. The trailing blank spaces are required; after typing JOHN JONES the user must hit the space bar 10 times, a procedure likely to leave the user muttering about the peculiarities of computers.

P.22 Variable-Length Strings

UCSD Pascal (and perhaps some other versions as well) provides a built-in data type STRING. Values of type STRING are variable-length strings, which are often more convenient to work with than fixed-length strings.

The following example illustrates how string variables are declared:

```
VAR
    S: STRING[10];
    T: STRING[20];
    U: STRING;
```

The number in brackets specifies the maximum length of a string that can be assigned to the variable. Thus S can hold strings from 0 to 10 characters long, and T can hold strings from 0 to 20 characters long. If a maximum length isn't specified, it is taken to be 80 characters by default. Thus U can hold strings from 0 to 80 characters long. The maximum length specified cannot exceed 255.

As we have seen in our previous programs, string values and variables can appear in READ, READLN, WRITE, WRITELN, and assignment statements. String values, like packed arrays of characters, can be compared for equality and alphabetical order with the relational operators.

String Functions and Procedures. UCSD Pascal provides four functions and two procedures for manipulating strings. Each of the four functions corresponds to a function or an operator in the algorithmic language. The two procedures do not correspond to anything in the algorithmic language. Figure P-25 shows the functions and procedures and, for each function, the corresponding function or operator in the algorithmic language.

CONCAT in Pascal corresponds to the concatenation operator, +, in the algorithmic language. CONCAT can take any number of arguments, so any number of strings can be concatenated with a single call to CONCAT. For instance, the value of

```
CONCAT('AL', 'TO', 'GET', 'HER')
```

is

```
'ALTOGETHER'
```

COPY in Pascal corresponds exactly to MID in the algorithmic language. Pascal doesn't have any functions corresponding to LEFT and RIGHT, but we can easily obtain the same results with COPY.

POS in Pascal corresponds to POS in the algorithmic language, but—WARNING—the order of the arguments in Pascal is the reverse of that in the algorithmic language. In the algorithmic language, we write

FIGURE P-25. The correspondence (such as it is) between string operators and functions in the algorithmic language and string functions and procedures in UCSD Pascal.

```
Algorithmic Language          UCSD Pascal

S + T + U + ...               CONCAT(S, T, U, ...)
MID(STRING, POSITION, LENGTH) COPY(STRING, POSITION, LENGTH)
LEFT(STRING, LENGTH)          use COPY
RIGHT(STRING, LENGTH)         use COPY
POS(STRING, SUBSTRING)        POS(SUBSTRING, STRING)
LEN(STRING)                   LENGTH(STRING)
VAL(STRING)                     —
STR(VALUE)                      —

                              INSERT(SUBSTRING, STRING, POSITION)
                              DELETE(STRING, POSITION, LENGTH)
```

```
POS(STRING, SUBSTRING)
```

where the string to be searched comes first, then the substring to be found. In Pascal, however, we must write

```
POS(SUBSTRING, STRING)
```

with the substring to be found first, then the string to be searched.

The LENGTH function in Pascal corresponds to LEN in the algorithmic language.

The Pascal procedure

```
INSERT(SUBSTRING, STRING, POSITION)
```

inserts the value of SUBSTRING into the value of STRING at the position given by the value of POSITION. The procedure

```
DELETE(STRING, POSITION, LENGTH)
```

deletes characters from the value of STRING. The value of POSITION specifies where the characters will be deleted and the value of LENGTH specifies how many.

In each procedure, STRING is a variable parameter; only a variable may be substituted for it. The other parameters are value parameters.

For instance, suppose S is a string variable. Then after executing the statements

```
S := 'ABCDEF';
INSERT('XY', S, 4);
```

the value of S is:

```
'ABCXYDEF'
```

If we now execute

```
DELETE(S, 5, 3)
```

the value of S becomes:

```
'ABCXF'
```

Figure P-26 shows a Pascal program corresponding to the algorithm FORM__LETTER. We won't discuss the entire program at this time, since it uses some elements of file processing that we haven't taken up yet. All of the string processing, however, takes place in the statements controlled by the WHILE statement, and these statements in the program correspond directly to those in the algorithm. Note the use of LENGTH for LEN, CON-

```
        PROGRAM FORMLETTER;
        (* FILL IN NAME AND CITY IN FORM LETTER *)
        VAR
            L, I, J: INTEGER;
            LINE, NAME, CITY, SOURCE, DESTINATION: STRING;
            INFILE, OUTFILE: TEXT;
        BEGIN
            WRITE('SOURCE FILE? ');
            READLN(SOURCE);
            WRITE('DESTINATION FILE? ');
            READLN(DESTINATION);
            WRITE('NAME? ');
            READLN(NAME);
            WRITE('CITY? ');
            READLN(CITY);
            RESET(INFILE, SOURCE);
            REWRITE(OUTFILE, DESTINATION);
            WHILE NOT EOF(INFILE) DO
                BEGIN
                    READLN(INFILE, LINE);
                    I := POS('#', LINE);
                    IF I <> 0 THEN
                        BEGIN
                            L := LENGTH(LINE);
                            LINE := CONCAT(COPY(LINE, 1, I-1),
                                           NAME,
                                           COPY(LINE, I+1, L-I))
                        END;
                    J := POS('%', LINE);
                    IF J <> 0 THEN
                        BEGIN
                            L := LENGTH(LINE);
                            LINE := CONCAT(COPY(LINE, 1, J-1),
                                           CITY,
                                           COPY(LINE, J+1, L-J))
                        END;
                    WRITELN(OUTFILE, LINE)
                END;
            CLOSE(OUTFILE, LOCK)
        END.
```

FIGURE P-26. The program FORMLETTER. For the moment, ignore the calls to the file-manipulating procedures RESET, REWRITE, and CLOSE.

CAT for +, and COPY for LEFT and RIGHT. Also note the reversed order of the arguments for POS.

P.23 Records

Record types, like array types, are structured types: each record value is made up of simpler components. The differences between arrays and records are as follows: (1) All of the components of an array have to be of the same type; the components of a record can be of different types. (2) We refer to the components of arrays using subscripts whose values can be computed as the program executes; we refer to the components of records using identifiers that must be specified when the program is written.

The following example illustrates how we define a record type in Pascal:

```
TYPE
    STUDENT = RECORD
                  NAME: STRING[20];
                  GPA: REAL;
                  CLASS: (FRESHMAN, SOPHOMORE,
                          JUNIOR, SENIOR)
              END;
```

NAME, GPA, and CLASS are field identifiers; they allow us to refer to the various components, or fields, of a record. For instance, suppose we declare

```
VAR
    S, T: STUDENT;
```

Then we can use S.NAME to refer to the NAME field of the value of S, S.GPA to refer to the GPA field; and S.CLASS to refer to the CLASS field. The statements

```
S.NAME  := 'MARY JONES';
S.GPA  := 3.5;
S.CLASS  := JUNIOR
```

assign values to the three fields of S.

S.NAME, S.GPA, and S.CLASS are called field designators. We can use them anywhere that we can use ordinary variables. Thus the statements

```
READLN(S.NAME)
```

and

```
WRITELN(S.GPA)
```

are valid, as is

```
G  := 10.0*S.GPA + 60.0
```

where G is a real variable.

Suppose we assign values to the fields of T as follows:

```
T.NAME  := 'JACK JONES';
T.GPA  := 2.8;
T.CLASS  := FRESHMAN
```

Then the statement

```
S := T
```

assigns the value of T to S. After the assignment, the values of S.NAME, S.GPA, and S.CLASS are 'JACK JONES', 2.8, and FRESHMAN, respectively.

Arrays of records are possible and commonplace in Pascal. Suppose we declare the variable U as follows:

```
U: ARRAY[1..2000] OF STUDENT;
```

Then if the value of I is the range 1 .. 2000, the value of U[I] is of type STUDENT. The field designators

```
U[I].NAME
U[I].GPA
U[I].CLASS
```

refer to the NAME, CPA, and CLASS fields of U[I].

The WITH Statement. We can simplify field designators by using a WITH statement. For example,

```
WITH S DO statement
```

prefixes

```
S.
```

to each field identifier in *statement*. Thus

```
WITH S DO
   BEGIN
      NAME := 'JIM BURNS';
      GPA := 3.9;
      CLASS := SENIOR
   END
```

assigns new values to S.NAME, S.GPA, and S.CLASS. In the same way,

```
WITH U[I] DO
   BEGIN
      GPA := 3.7;
      CLASS := JUNIOR
   END
```

assigns new values to U[I].GPA and U[I].CLASS. U[I].NAME remains unchanged.

More Complicated Records. Record values can be nested. That is, the components of a record value can themselves be record values, those record values can have still other record values as components, and so on.

For instance, suppose we define

```
NAMETYPE = RECORD
              FIRST: STRING[10];
              INITIAL: CHAR;
              LAST: STRING[10]
           END;
```

and

```
ADDRESSTYPE = RECORD
                 STREET: STRING[20];
                 CITY: STRING[10];
                 STATE: PACKED ARRAY[1..2] OF CHAR;
                 ZIP: PACKED ARRAY[1..5] OF CHAR
              END;
```

Now we can redefine STUDENT as

```
STUDENT = RECORD
             NAME: NAMETYPE;
             ADDRESS: ADDRESSTYPE;
             GPA: REAL;
             CLASS: (FRESHMAN, SOPHOMORE,
                     JUNIOR, SENIOR)
          END;
```

Let S be a variable of type STUDENT as before. Then S.NAME is of type NAMETYPE. To refer to the individual components of a name we must use S.NAME.FIRST, S.NAME.INITIAL, and S.NAME.LAST. Thus, the following assignments are valid:

```
S.NAME.FIRST := 'JOHN';
S.NAME.INITIAL := 'H';
S.NAME.LAST := 'DOE'
```

In the same way, to refer to the components of S.ADDRESS, we must use S.ADDRESS.STREET, S.ADDRESS.CITY, S.ADDRESS.STATE, and S.ADDRESS.ZIP.

Now consider the WITH statement

```
WITH S DO statement
```

Inside *statement* we can use NAME in place of S.NAME, ADDRESS in place of S.ADDRESS, GPA in place of S.GPA, and CLASS instead of S.CLASS.

The WITH statement

```
WITH S, NAME DO statement
```

lets us refer to the components of S.NAME as well as those of S by their field identifiers:

```
WITH S, NAME DO
   BEGIN
      WRITE('FIRST NAME? ');
      READLN(FIRST);
      WRITE('MIDDLE INITIAL? ');
      READLN(INITIAL);
      WRITE('LAST NAME? ');
      READLN(LAST)
   END
```

The WITH statement

```
WITH S, NAME, ADDRESS DO statement
```

allows all the fields of S, S.NAME, and S.ADDRESS to be referred to by their field identifiers. Thus

```
WITH S, NAME, ADDRESS DO
   BEGIN
      FIRST := 'MARY';
      STATE := 'GA';
      GPA := 2.7
   END
```

changes S.NAME.FIRST, S.ADDRESS.STATE, and S.GPA.

Record Variants. It is often convenient to allow record values of the same type to vary somewhat in structure. For instance, a company may have two kinds of employees, those who are paid a fixed salary each month and those who are paid by the hour. For a salaried employee, we need only to know the fixed-month salary. For an hourly worker, we need to know the hours worked and the hourly rate. By using a case construction in the record definition, we can define one record type that will serve for all employees:

```
EMPLOYEE = RECORD
              NAME: STRING[20];
              CASE SALARIED: BOOLEAN OF
                 TRUE: (SALARY: REAL);
                 FALSE: (HOURS,
                         RATE: REAL)
           END;
```

The fields NAME and SALARIED constitute the fixed part of the record; all values of type EMPLOYEE have these fields. The remainder of the record is the variant part. If the value of SALARIED is TRUE, the variant part of the record has just one field, SALARY. If the value of SALARIED is FALSE, the variant part has two fields, HOURS and RATE. The variant part always comes at the end of the record.

Put another way, if the value of SALARIED is TRUE, then the record has the structure

```
RECORD
    NAME: STRING[20];
    SALARIED: BOOLEAN;
    SALARY: REAL
END
```

On the other hand, if the value of SALARIED is FALSE, then the record has the structure

```
RECORD
    NAME: STRING[20];
    SALARIED: BOOLEAN;
    HOURS,
    RATE: REAL
END
```

P.24 Pointer Types and Linked Lists

In Chapter 14, we began the study of plexes, or linked structures, in which each record contains one or more pointers to other records. The approach used in Chapter 14 is to work with a one-dimensional array of records. Each possible subscript value designates a particular element of the array, a particular record, and so can be used as a pointer. This method works in any language that permits one-dimensional arrays, so it works just as well in Pascal as in the algorithmic language.

Pascal, however, offers pointer data types whose values point to variables. The variables pointed to, usually record variables, need not be elements of an array. Indeed, these variables do not have to be declared when the program is written but can be created as needed while the program is executing.

We define a pointer type by prefixing a type identifier with an upward arrow. (some systems use a circumflex (^) in place of the upward arrow.) The type identifier gives the type of the variables pointed to by the values of the pointer type. Thus values of type ↑ INTEGER point to integer variables; values of type ↑ REAL point to real variables, and so on.

The declaration

```
P:  ↑ INTEGER;
```

specifies that the value of P will point to an integer variable. The notation P↑ designates the variable pointed to by the value of P. Note that if the value of P changes, the variable designated by P↑ changes as well. (Compare with a subscripted variable such as A[I], which designates different array elements depending on the value of I.)

We can create an integer variable for P to point to by calling the standard procedure NEW. The statement

```
NEW(P)
```

creates a new integer variable and sets P to point to it. P↑, which now designates the newly created variable, can be used like any other variable. Thus

```
P↑ := 25
```

assigns 25 to the newly created variable, and

```
WRITE(P↑:4)
```

prints the current value of the newly created variable.

When we do not need the variable pointed to by P any longer, we can call the built-in procedure DISPOSE to inform the computer that the variable is no longer needed and the corresponding memory area can be used for other purposes. Thus

```
DISPOSE(P)
```

instructs the computer to dispose of the variable pointed to by P.

(UCSD Pascal does not provide the procedure DISPOSE. It provides a more restricted way of recovering no-longer-used memory areas, one that we won't go into here.)

Sometimes we need to indicate that a pointer is not currently pointing to any variable. For this purpose, Pascal provides the pointer value NIL. After the assignment

```
P := NIL
```

P doesn't point to any variable, and the expression P↑ is meaningless. NIL in Pascal serves the same purpose as the NIL we used in the algorithmic language.

Let's see how we can implement singly linked lists with pointers. We define the data types

```
PTR = ↑CELL;
CELL = RECORD
          VALUE: INTEGER;
          LINK: PTR
       END;
```

and declare

```
FIRST: PTR;
```

The value of FIRST points to a memory area that holds a value of type CELL. That memory area contains an integer value and a pointer to another memory area holding an integer value and a pointer, and so on. The situation is pictured in Figure 14-4. The link component of the last cell on the list contains the value NIL, which acts as an end-of-list sentinel.

We can easily write the list-processing algorithms of Chapter 14 in Pascal. For instance, the algorithm INSERT__AFTER becomes:

```
PROCEDURE INSERTAFTER(V: INTEGER; P: PTR);
VAR
    Q: PTR;
BEGIN
    NEW(Q);
    Q↑.LINK := P↑.LINK;
    P↑.LINK := Q;
    Q↑.VALUE := V
END;
```

The algorithm DELETE__AFTER becomes

```
PROCEDURE DELETEAFTER(P: PTR);
VAR
    Q: PTR;
BEGIN
    Q := P↑.LINK;
    IF Q <> NIL THEN
        BEGIN
            P↑.LINK := Q↑.LINK;
            DISPOSE(Q)
        END
END;
```

in UCSD Pascal, the call to DISPOSE must be omitted.

P.25 Sequential Files

A file is a sequence of values stored in auxiliary memory. All of the values belong to the same data type. The number of values stored is not fixed but may vary as the file is manipulated.

Values stored in a file must be transferrred to main memory one by one for processing. At any time, we only have access to the value that is currently in main memory. It's as if we had a window into the file through which we could see only one value. We can move the window around in the file, so at different times we can see different values through it. But at one time the only value we have access to is the one we can see through the window.

In Pascal, we can define a file type and declare a variable to be of that type as follows:

```
TYPE
   DATA = FILE OF INTEGER;
VAR
   F: DATA;
```

Each value of type DATA is a sequence of integers. The number of integers in a sequence is not fixed, but varies from one sequence to another. The empty sequence, which contains no values, is included. Some typical values of type DATA are

```
  2   4   8   6   4   -2   0   -5   25
  7   3   1   8
100
          (empty sequence)
```

F is a variable of type DATA. Therefore, the value of F is a sequence of integers. For the sake of an example, let's assume the value of F is:

```
9   5   4   7   2
```

At any one time, we have access to only one of these values, the one currently in main memory, the one that can be seen through the file window. Associated with each file variable F is another variable, $F\uparrow$, called the buffer variable, whose value is the currently accessible value of the file. We can think of $F\uparrow$ as our window into the file, through which we can see exactly one value.

For example, we can indicate the position of the window into the file as follows:

```
9   5   4   7   2
        F↑
```

The currently accessible value is 4, and 4 is the value of $F\uparrow$. Thus

```
I := F↑
```

assigns the value 4 to I, and

```
WRITE(F↑)
```

prints the value 4.

Sequential File Processing: Input. For sequential processing, we start at the beginning of the file, process values until we come to the end, then stop. To position the file window over the first component of the file, we use the built-in procedure RESET. After executing

```
RESET(F)
```

the file F looks like this

```
9    5    4    7    2
F↑
```

The value of F ↑ is 9, and this value is available for processing.

When we are ready to process the next value in the file, we move the file window forward one position using the built-in procedure GET. After executing

```
GET(F)
```

the file F looks like this

```
9    5    4    7    2
     F↑
```

The value of F ↑ is 5, and this value is available for processing.

If we execute GET(F) enough times, eventually the file window will move beyond the end of the file:

```
9    5    4    7    2
                    F↑
```

In this situation, the value of F ↑ is undefined, and the effect of any further calls to GET is unpredictable.

The program must be able to detect this situation, so it won't attempt to manipulate meaningless values or make invalid calls to GET. For this purpose, Pascal provides a Boolean function EOF(F) whose value is TRUE if the window into file F has moved beyond the end of the file and FALSE if it has not.

As an example of processing input from a sequential file, the following statements compute the sum of all the values in F:

```
SUM := 0;
RESET(F);
WHILE NOT EOF(F) DO
    BEGIN
        SUM := SUM + F↑;
        GET(F)
    END
```

Sequential File Processing: Output. To begin with, we need an empty file to hold the data we are going to output. We obtain an empty file by calling the built-in procedure REWRITE:

```
REWRITE(F)
```

F now looks like this

```
F↑
```

and is ready to receive values.

If we want to store the value 5, say, in the file, we first assign this value to F↑:

```
F↑ := 5
```

F now looks like this:

```
5
F↑
```

The value 5, however, is still in main memory. The built-in procedure PUT transfers the value to auxiliary memory and advances the file window one position. After executing

```
PUT(F)
```

F looks like this:

```
5
    F↑
```

The value 5 has been transferred to auxiliary memory and the window is now over the next unused position in the file. Executing

```
F↑ := 7;
PUT(F)
```

puts 7 in the file

```
5   7
        F↑
```

and so on.

As an example of output to a sequential file, the following statements store the integers from 1 through 100 in F:

```
REWRITE(F);
FOR I := 1 TO 100 DO
   BEGIN
      F↑ := I;
      PUT(F)
   END
```

Textfiles. Text can be stored as files of characters; however, text is normally divided into lines for convenience in printing. To recognize this division into lines in a way that is independent of the conventions of any particular computer system, Pascal has a predefined file type TEXT. We can think of TEXT as being defined by

```
TEXT = FILE OF CHAR;
```

with additional provisions for grouping the characters into lines.

Suppose we declare F by:

```
F: TEXT;
```

The value of F is a sequence of characters. The characters include not only the ordinary ones but a special line-separator character that divides the file into lines. Let's represent the line-separator character by a downward arrow, ↓. Then the value of F might look like this:

```
ABCD ↓ EFG ↓ HIJKL
```

If the contents of F were sent to a video display or a printer, the output would look like this:

```
ABCD
EFG
HIJKL
```

Pascal does not allow the user's program access to the line-separator character. The reason is that different computer systems use different characters to separate lines. A program written to recognize the line-separator character used by one system wouldn't work properly on another system that uses a different line-separator character.

To prevent programs from depending on a particular line-separator character, Pascal does two things:

1. When the file window is positioned over a line separator, the value of the buffer variable is a blank space, not the line-separator character.

2. Pascal provides a Boolean function EOLN(F) whose value is TRUE when the file window of F is positioned over a line-separator character and FALSE when it is not. The program uses EOLN to recognize the end of a line.

READ, READLN, WRITE, and WRITELN. Pascal defines some additional procedures for manipulating textfiles. We have been using these procedures all along, but with our present knowledge of files we can define them somewhat more precisely.

Let C be a character variable and F a textfile variable. Then

```
READ(F, C)
```

is equivalent to

```
C := F↑;
GET(F)
```

and

```
WRITE(F, C)
```

is equivalent to

```
F↑ := C;
PUT(C)
```

If V is a variable of type REAL, INTEGER, or CHAR, then

```
READ(F, V)
```

reads a sufficient number of characters to make up a value of the type of V and assigns to V the value so obtained.

IF E is an expression yielding a value of type REAL, INTEGER, BOOLEAN, CHAR, or packed array of character, then

```
WRITE(F, E)
```

converts the value of E into a string of characters and writes those characters to F. As we already know, field-width parameters can be supplied to specify how the values will be written.

(In UCSD Pascal, values of type STRING can be both read and written. Values of type BOOLEAN cannot be written.)

The READ and WRITE procedures can read and write more than one value in a single call. The statement

```
READ(F, V1, V2, ..., VN)
```

is defined to be equivalent to:

```
READ(F, V1); READ(F, V2); ... READ(F, VN)
```

and

```
WRITE(F, V1, V2, ..., VN)
```

is defined to be equivalent to:

```
WRITE(F, V1); WRITE(F, V2); ... WRITE(F, VN)
```

The procedure READLN moves the file window to the character following the next line separator. Thus

```
READLN(F)
```

is equivalent to:

```
WHILE NOT EOLN(F) DO
   GET(F);
GET(F)
```

The procedure WRITELN appends a line separator to the file being written. After

```
WRITELN(F)
```

the next character written to F will start a new line.

The procedures READLN and WRITELN can be combined with READ and WRITE. Thus

```
READLN(F, V1, V2, ..., VN)
```

is equivalent to:

```
READ(F, V1, V2, ..., VN);
READLN(F)
```

and

```
WRITELN(F, E1, E2, ..., EN)
```

is equivalent to:

```
WRITE(F, E1, E2, ..., EN);
WRITELN
```

The Files INPUT and OUTPUT. Pascal has two standard files, INPUT and OUTPUT, to which the following rules apply:

1. The files INPUT and OUTPUT are already declared when the program begins execution. Declarations for them must not be included in the program.

2. Before a program begins execution, the computer system in effect executes the following:

```
RESET(INPUT);
REWRITE(OUTPUT)
```

The program must not attempt to apply RESET to INPUT or REWRITE to OUTPUT.

3. If the file parameter is omitted for READ, READLN, EOF, or EOLN, then INPUT is assumed. If the file parameter is omitted for WRITE or WRITELN, OUTPUT is assumed. In the following, each statement on the left is equivalent to the corresponding one on the right:

```
READ(V1, V2, ..., VN)        READ(INPUT, V1, V2, ..., VN)
READLN(V1, V2, ..., VN)      READLN(INPUT, V1, V2, ..., VN)
EOF                          EOF(INPUT)
WRITE(E1, E2, ..., EN)       WRITE(OUTPUT, E1, E2, ..., EN)
WRITELN(E1, E2, ..., EN)     WRITELN(OUTPUT, E1, E2, ..., EN)
```

Thus the input and output statements that we have been using all along, such as

```
WRITE('AMOUNT IN YOUR ACCOUNT NOW? ');
READLN(AMOUNT)
```

read from the standard file INPUT and write to the standard file OUTPUT.

Interactive Files. We recall that for a textfile F and a character variable C, READ(F, C) is defined as equivalent to:

```
C := F↑;
GET(F)
```

This definition is unsatisfactory if the file F corresponds to a keyboard. For according to the definition, READ(F, C) assigns to C the previous character typed by the user, then gets another character from the keyboard. The program is always one character behind the user; whenever the user types a new character, the program processes the character previously typed.

Having the program one character behind the user makes any close interaction between the program and the user impossible. In particular, the common practice of letting a program accept single-letter commands, such as E for *edit*, C for *compile*, and R for *run*, isn't possible. The user would have to type the next command (or at least another character) before the command just given could be obeyed.

To avoid these problems, UCSD Pascal has a file type INTERACTIVE, which is the same as type TEXT except:

1. READ(F, C) is defined to be equivalent to:

```
GET(F);
C := F↑
```

Thus a character is delivered to the program as soon as GET(F) obtains it from the keyborad.

2. Executing RESET for an interactive file does not get the first character from the file. The first character is not obtained until GET or READ is executed.

3. A special key is designated that, when pressed, causes EOF(F) to become true. This key must be pressed immediately after typing the last character of input. (Special keys sometimes confuse users and lead to mistakes, so there is much to be said for using a sentinel to indicate the end of keyboard input, rather than relying on EOF.)

In USCD Pascal, the standard file INPUT is an interactive file corresponding to the user's keyboard.

External Files. If we declare a file F by a declaration such as

```
F: FILE OF INTEGER;
```

but do nothing else to establish any connection between F and some existing file, then F represents a *local* or *internal* file. A local file exists during the execution of the program in which it is declared, but vanishes when the program terminates. Local files are suitable only for temporary storage during the execution of a program.

Ordinarily, however, we want to input data from an existing disk file, say, or create a new file for storing output, a file that will continue to exist on disk after the execution of the program terminates. Or we may want a file to correspond to some input or output device, such as a printer. We need some way to establish a connection between files declared in Pascal and actual disk files, input devices, and output devices.

In many versions of Pascal this is achieved by listing external files as parameters in the program heading. For instance, if a program uses the file F in addition to the standard files INPUT and OUTPUT, then the program heading looks like this:

```
PROGRAM PROCESSFILES(INPUT, OUTPUT, F);
```

When we request the computer's operating system to execute this program, we inform it what actual disk files, input devices, or output devices correspond to the file parameters listed in the program heading.

This approach is not convenient for interactive programs. We would like for the program itself to be able to get the necessary file names from the user, rather than having to rely on the operating system for this task. The program can prompt for the file names in such a way as to make sure that even an untrained user knows what responses are required.

For this reason, UCSD Pascal uses the procedures RESET and REWRITE to associate file names in PASCAL programs with the names under which the files are stored externally. UCSD Pascal ignores any file parameters listed in the program heading.

Thus,

```
RESET(F, 'TESTDATA')
```

resets F and establishes a correspondence between it and the existing disk file TESTDATA. The statement

```
REWRITE(F, 'RESULTS')
```

makes F correspond to an empty, newly created disk file named RESULTS.

Better yet, we can obtain the necessary file names from the user, instead of writing them into the program. If S is a string variable, then we can obtain the name of an already existing file as follows:

```
WRITE('NAME OF INPUT FILE? ');
READLN(S);
RESET(F, S)
```

To obtain the name of a file to be used for output, we can write

```
WRITE('NAME OF OUTPUT FILE? ');
READLN(S);
REWRITE(F, S)
```

In UCSD Pascal, any file to which output has been sent must be closed after use. Closing a file assures that all data has been transferred from main memory to the file and that all necessary information about the file has been entered in the directory for the disk on which it is stored. In UCSD Pascal,

```
CLOSE(F, LOCK)
```

causes the file corresponding to F to be stored permanently on disk, while

```
CLOSE(F, PURGE)
```

causes the file to be deleted from the disk.

Example Programs. Now let's look at some examples of sequential file processing. Bear in mind that these programs are written in UCSD Pascal and would have to be modified somewhat to run under other versions of Pascal.

Our first example is the program FORMLETTER in Figure P-26, which we have already looked at in connection with strings. The form letter is read line by line from the textfile INFILE. After the insertions have been made in each line, the line is written to the textfile OUTFILE (OUTFILE could be a printer). Note how the names of the source and destination files are obtained and then used in the RESET and REWRITE statements. Note also the use of EOF in the WHILE statement, the file names in the READLN and WRITELN statements, and the CLOSE statement.

Our final example, Figure P-30, is a program for updating a sequential file. To support it, we first write programs for creating a master file and a transaction file and for listing (displaying the contents of) the master file after it has been updated.

CREATEMASTER, Figure P-27, creates a master file with records of the form

```
RECORD
    KEY: INTEGER;
    BALANCE: REAL
END
```

The user is asked to enter the key and balance for each record. The user presses the EOF key immediately after typing the balance for the last record to be entered. The program then writes a final sentinel record with key 9999. (The file update program is simplified when the master and transaction files have a sentinel record). Note the call to PUT and the use of MASTERFILE↑.KEY and MASTERFILE↑.BALANCE to refer to the fields of MASTERFILE↑.

CREATETRANS, Figure P-28, creates a transaction file with records of the form

```
RECORD
    KEY: INTEGER;
    KIND: TRANSTYPE;
    AMOUNT: REAL
END
```

FIGURE P-27. The program CREATEMASTER.

```
PROGRAM CREATEMASTER;
(* CREATE A MASTER FILE *)
CONST
    SENTINEL = 9999;
TYPE
    MASTER = RECORD
                 KEY: INTEGER;
                 BALANCE: REAL
             END;
VAR
    MASTERFILE: FILE OF MASTER;
    FILENAME: STRING;
BEGIN
    WRITE('FILE NAME? ');
    READLN(FILENAME);
    REWRITE(MASTERFILE, FILENAME);
    WHILE NOT EOF(INPUT) DO
        BEGIN
            WRITE('KEY AND BALANCE? ');
            READLN(MASTERFILE↑.KEY, MASTERFILE↑.BALANCE);
            PUT(MASTERFILE)
        END;
    MASTERFILE↑.KEY := SENTINEL;
    PUT(MASTERFILE);
    CLOSE(MASTERFILE, LOCK)
END.
```

```
PROGRAM CREATETRANS;
(* CREATE TRANSACTION FILE *)
CONST
   SENTINEL = 9999;
TYPE
   TRANSTYPE = (ADD, UPDATE, DELETE);
   TRANSACTION = RECORD
                    KEY: INTEGER;
                    KIND: TRANSTYPE;
                    AMOUNT: REAL
                 END;
VAR
   TRANSFILE: FILE OF TRANSACTION;
   FILENAME: STRING;
   TYPECODE: 1..3;
BEGIN
   WRITE('FILE NAME? ');
   READLN(FILENAME);
   REWRITE(TRANSFILE, FILENAME);
   WHILE NOT EOF(INPUT) DO
      BEGIN
         WRITE('KEY, TYPE CODE, AMOUNT? ');
         READLN(TRANSFILE↑.KEY, TYPECODE, TRANSFILE↑.AMOUNT);
         CASE TYPECODE OF
            1: TRANSFILE↑.KIND := ADD;
            2: TRANSFILE↑.KIND := UPDATE;
            3: TRANSFILE↑.KIND := DELETE
         END;
         PUT(TRANSFILE)
      END;
   TRANSFILE↑.KEY := SENTINEL;
   PUT(TRANSFILE);
   CLOSE(TRANSFILE, LOCK)
END.
```

FIGURE P-28. The program CREATETRANS.

where TRANSTYPE is the enumeration type defined by

```
TRANSTYPE = (ADD, UPDATE, DELETE);
```

The KIND field indicates which of three kinds of transactions is to be done for a particular transaction record. Note that values of enumeration type cannot be entered directly, so the user must enter a code of 1 for ADD, 2 for UPDATE, and 3 for DELETE. A CASE statement converts the code entered by the user into the corresponding value of type TRANSTYPE.

LISTMASTER, Figure P-29, displays the contents of a master file. Note the use of the GET statement. Since a master file has a sentinel record, LISTMASTER uses the sentinel, rather than EOF(MASTERFILE), to determine when the end of the file has been reached.

FILEUPDATE, Figure P-30, corresponds to the algorithm FILE__UP-DATE in Chapter 17. The program follows the algorithm closely, so little further explanation is needed here. The procedure OPENFILES obtains the names of the files to be used and performs the necessary resets and rewrite. Resetting OLDFILE and TRANSFILE makes available the first record of each, so we do not need initial input statements for these files as was

```
PROGRAM LISTMASTER;
(* PRINT LISTING OF MASTER FILE *)
CONST
   SENTINEL = 9999;
TYPE
   MASTER = RECORD
                 KEY: INTEGER;
                 BALANCE: REAL
             END;
VAR
   MASTERFILE: FILE OF MASTER;
   FILENAME: STRING;
BEGIN
   WRITE('FILE NAME? ');
   READLN(FILENAME);
   RESET(MASTERFILE, FILENAME);
   WRITELN('KEY':10, 'BALANCE':10);
   WHILE MASTERFILE↑.KEY <> SENTINEL DO
      BEGIN
        WRITELN(MASTERFILE↑.KEY:10, MASTERFILE↑.BALANCE:10:2);
        GET(MASTERFILE)
      END
END
```

FIGURE P-29. The program LISTMASTER.

required in the algorithm. The enumeration type TRANSTYPE is used to represent the kind of transaction, rather than an integer transaction code as in the algorithm.

Where might some of these programs be simplified by the use of WITH statements?

P.26 Random Files

Most versions of Pascal provide for sequential-access files only. UCSD Pascal also allows random access to files. The randon-access facilities of UCSD Pascal will be described quite briefly here ánd left for further exploration by those who have access to UCSD Pascal systems.

To begin with, UCSD Pascal assumes the records of a file to be numbered, starting with 0. Thus, the first record of a file is record 0; the next record is record 1, the next is record 2, and so on.

The build-in procedure

```
SEEK(FILE, RECORDNUMBER)
```

positions the file window of FILE to the record specified by RECORDNUMBER. Thus

```
SEEK(F, 5)
```

positions the file window of file F to record 5.

```
      PROGRAM FILEUPDATE;
      (* UPDATE MASTER FILE FROM TRANSACTION FILE *)
      CONST
         SENTINEL = 9999;
      TYPE
         TRANSTYPE = (ADD, UPDATE, DELETE);
         MASTER = RECORD
                     KEY: INTEGER;
                     BALANCE: REAL;
                 END;
         TRANSACTION = RECORD
                         KEY: INTEGER;
                         KIND: TRANSTYPE;
                         AMOUNT: REAL
                       END;

      VAR
         CURRENTKEY: INTEGER;
         OLDFILE, NEWFILE: FILE OF MASTER;
         TRANSFILE: FILE OF TRANSACTION;
         INUSE: BOOLEAN;

      PROCEDURE OPENFILES;
      (* GET FILE NAMES, RESET OLDFILE AND TRANSFILE,
         REWRITE NEWFILE. RESETTING OLDFILE AND NEWFILE
         GETS THE FIRST RECORD OF EACH FILE *)
      VAR
         OLDMASTER, NEWMASTER, TRANS: STRING;
      BEGIN
         WRITE('OLD MASTER FILE? ');
         READLN(OLDMASTER);
         WRITE('TRANSACTION FILE? ');
         READLN(TRANS);
         WRITE('NEW MASTER FILE? ');
         READLN(NEWMASTER);
         RESET(OLDFILE, OLDMASTER);
         RESET(TRANSFILE, TRANS);
         REWRITE(NEWFILE, NEWMASTER)
      END; (* OPENFILES *)
```

FIGURE P-30. The program FILEUPDATE including the procedures OPENFILES, GET-NEXTKEY, ADDRECORD, UPDATERECORD, DELETERECORD, and PROCESSTRANSAC-TIONS.

Although SEEK positions the file window, it does not transfer any data between the buffer variable F↑ and the file. SEEK must be followed by GET to transfer a record from the file to the buffer variable or by PUT to transfer a record from the buffer variable to the file.

Thus

```
SEEK(F, 5);
GET(F)
```

locates record 5 of file F and transfers that record to the buffer variable F↑. On the other hand,

```
PROCEDURE GETNEXTKEY;
(* SET CURRENTKEY TO NEXT KEY TO BE PROCESSED. IF CURRENTKEY IS
   THE KEY OF A RECORD IN THE MASTER FILE, THEN PLACE THAT
   RECORD IN NEWFILE↑, SET INUSE TO TRUE, AND READ ANOTHER
   RECORD FROM OLDFILE. OTHERWISE, SET INUSE TO FALSE *)
BEGIN
   IF OLDFILE↑.KEY <= TRANSFILE↑.KEY THEN
       BEGIN
           CURRENTKEY := OLDFILE↑.KEY;
           NEWFILE↑ := OLDFILE↑;
           INUSE := TRUE;
           GET(OLDFILE)
       END
   ELSE
       BEGIN
           CURRENTKEY := TRANSFILE↑.KEY;
           INUSE := FALSE
       END
END; (* GETNEXTKEY *)

PROCEDURE ADDRECORD;
(* ADD ONE RECORD *)
BEGIN
   IF INUSE THEN
       BEGIN
           WRITE('CANNOT ADD RECORD ', CURRENTKEY);
           WRITELN('--RECORD ALREADY IN MASTER FILE')
       END
   ELSE
       BEGIN
           NEWFILE↑.KEY := TRANSFILE↑.KEY;
           NEWFILE↑.BALANCE := TRANSFILE↑.AMOUNT;
           INUSE := TRUE
       END
END; (* ADDRECORD *)

PROCEDURE UPDATERECORD;
(* UPDATE ONE RECORD *)
BEGIN
   IF INUSE THEN
       NEWFILE↑.BALANCE := NEWFILE↑.BALANCE + TRANSFILE↑.AMOUNT
   ELSE
       BEGIN
           WRITE('CANNOT UPDATE RECORD ', CURRENTKEY);
           WRITELN('--RECORD NOT IN MASTER FILE')
       END
END; (* UPDATERECORD *)
```

FIGURE P-30 (Cont.)

```
SEEK(F, 25);
PUT(F)
```

writes the contents of F ↑ in record 25 of F.

P.27 Sets

Sets in Pascal do not correspond to anything in the algorithmic language. For this reason, they have been saved until last and are covered fairly briefly.

```
          PROCEDURE DELETERECORD;
          (* DELETE ONE RECORD *)
          BEGIN
              IF INUSE THEN
                  INUSE := FALSE
              ELSE
                  BEGIN
                      WRITE('CANNOT DELETE RECORD ', CURRENTKEY);
                  WRITELN('--RECORD NOT IN MASTER FILE')
                  END
          END; (* DELETE RECORD *)

          PROCEDURE PROCESSTRANSACTIONS;
          (* PROCESS ALL TRANSACTIONS WHOSE KEYS ARE EQUAL TO
              CURRENTKEY *)
          BEGIN
              WHILE TRANSFILE↑.KEY = CURRENTKEY DO
                  BEGIN
                      CASE TRANSFILE↑.KIND OF
                          ADD: ADDRECORD;
                          UPDATE: UPDATERECORD;
                          DELETE: DELETERECORD
                      END;
                      GET(TRANSFILE);
                  END
          END; (* PROCESSTRANSACTIONS *)

          BEGIN (* MAIN PROGRAM *)
              OPENFILES;
              WHILE    (OLDFILE↑.KEY <> SENTINEL)
                  OR (TRANSFILE↑.KEY <> SENTINEL) DO
                  BEGIN
                      GETNEXTKEY;
                      PROCESSTRANSACTIONS;
                      IF INUSE THEN
                          PUT(NEWFILE)
                  END;
              NEWFILE↑.KEY := SENTINEL;
              PUT(NEWFILE);
              CLOSE(NEWFILE, LOCK)
          END.
```

FIGURE P-30 (Cont.)

A set is a collection of values. We display a set by listing the values it contains between square brackets. Thus the set

```
[1, 3, 11, 25]
```

contains the values 1, 3, 11, and 25. Note that Pascal uses the square brackets [and] in place of the braces { and } used in mathematics.

We can describe sets that contain ranges of values. Thus the set

```
[1..5, 7, 9..11]
```

contains the values 1, 2, 3, 4, 5, 7, 9, 10, and 11.

The set

```
[ ]
```

is the empty set, which contains no values.

We can use variables and expressions as well as constants to describe sets. If I and J are integer variables with the values 3 and 5, respectively, then the set

```
[I, J, I+J, I*J]
```

contains the values 3, 5, 8, and 15.

The relational operator IN tests whether a given value belongs to a set. Thus the condition

```
3 IN [1, 3, 9, 20]
```

is true, while

```
4 IN [1, 3, 9, 20]
```

is false.

The main application of sets is to simplify conditions. Thus, it is much easier to write

```
IF I IN [1..5, 10, 23..38] THEN
    statement
```

than the equivalent

```
IF    (I >= 1) AND (I <=5)
   OR (I = 10)
   OR (I >= 23) AND (I <= 38) THEN
   statement
```

Set Types. The following examples show how set types are defined:

```
LETTERSET = SET OF 'A'..'Z';
RANGESET = SET OF 1..500;
COLORSET = SET OF COLOR;
```

COLOR is the enumeration type we have used as an example previously.

The type following the work OF is called the *base type*. All of the elements of a set of a given type must belong to the base type. If we declare

```
VAR
   S: LETTERSET;
   T: COLORSET;
```

then

```
['A', 'B', 'C']    ['C', 'L'..'R', 'W']
```

are possible values of S and

```
[RED, YELLOW, VIOLET]    [RED..GREEN]    []
```

are possible values of T.

The maximum number of elements a set can have varies from on version of Pascal to another, and, consequently, so do the permissible base types. In UCSD Pascal, a set can contain up to 4,080 elements (for many versions of Pascal this number is far smaller). Therefore, the following types, or subranges of them, can be used as base types in UCSD Pascal:

```
BOOLEAN
CHAR
0..4079
Any enumeration type with 4080 or fewer values
```

Operations on Sets. Three operations that can be applied to sets and yield sets as results are union, intersection, and difference.

The union of two sets contains those elements belonging to either of the two sets or to both. In Pascal, union is represented by the + sign;

```
[1, 2] + [5, 6] = [1, 2, 5, 6]
[1, 2, 3, 4] + [3, 4, 5, 6] = [1, 2, 3, 4, 5, 6]
```

The intersection of two sets contains those elements belonging to both sets. In Pascal, intersection is represented by a * sign:

```
[1, 2] * [5, 6] = []    (*EMPTY SET*)
[1, 2, 3, 4] * [3, 4, 5, 6] = [3, 4]
```

The difference of two sets contains those elements of the first set that do not belong to the second. In Pascal, set difference is represented by a − sign:

```
[1, 2, 3, 4, 5, 6] − [3, 4, 5] = [1, 2, 6]
[1, 2, 3, 4] − [7, 8] = [1, 2, 3, 4]
```

Sets can be compared for equality and for one set being a subset or a superset of another.

Two sets are equal if they contain the same elements and are unequal otherwise. As usual in Pascal, we represent the relational operator for equality by = and for inequality by <>. Each of the following conditions is true:

```
[1, 5, 8, 9] = [1, 5, 8, 9]
```

```
[ ] = [ ]
[1, 4, 5] <> [1, 4, 6]
[1, 4, 5] <> [1, 4, 5, 8]
```

If all of the elements of one set also belong to a second set, we say that the first set is a subset of the second and the second set is a superset of the first. In Pascal, the relational operator for subset is < = and for superset is > =. Each of the following conditions is true:

```
[1, 3, 9] <= [0, 1, 2, 3, 7, 9]
[1, 2, 3] >= [1, 3]
[5, 8, 9] <= [5, 8, 9]
```

and each of the following is false:

```
[1, 3, 7] <= [1, 3, 9]
[1, 3, 7] >= [1, 3, 9]
```

In Pascal, operator symbols have the same priorities regardless of the operations they represent. Thus, + has the same priority whether it represents addition or set union; < = has the same priority whether it represents "is less than or equal to" or "is a subset of." The relational operator IN has the same priority as the other relational operators.

Appendix:
Pascal Reserved Words

AND	END	NIL	SET
ARRAY	FILE	NOT	THEN
BEGIN	FOR	OF	TO
CASE	FUNCTION	OR	TYPE
CONST	GOTO	PACKED	UNTIL
DIV	IF	PROCEDURE	VAR
DO	IN	PROGRAM	WHILE
DOWNTO	LABEL	RECORD	WITH
ELSE	MOD	REPEAT	

Index

†